WHITELASH

If postmortems of the 2016 U.S. presidential election tell us anything, it's that many voters discriminate on the basis of race, which raises an important question: In a society that outlaws racial discrimination in employment, housing, and jury selections, should voters be permitted to racially discriminate in selecting a candidate for public office? In *Whitelash*, Terry Smith argues that such racialized decision-making is unlawful and that remedies exist to deter this reactionary behavior. Using evidence of race-based voting in the 2016 presidential election, Smith deploys legal analogies to demonstrate how courts can both decipher when groups of voters have been impermissibly influenced by race, and impose appropriate remedies. This groundbreaking work should be read by anyone interested in how the legal system can re-direct American democracy away from the ongoing electoral scourge that many fear 2016 portended.

Terry Smith has spent more than 25 years teaching at national law schools, most recently as a Distinguished Research Professor. His legal scholarship has been cited by federal courts, and he is the author of the book *Barack Obama, Post-Racialism, and the New Politics of Triangulation* (2012).

Whitelash

UNMASKING WHITE GRIEVANCE AT THE BALLOT BOX

TERRY SMITH

CAMBRIDGE
UNIVERSITY PRESS

University Printing House, Cambridge CB2 8BS, United Kingdom

One Liberty Plaza, 20th Floor, New York, NY 10006, USA

477 Williamstown Road, Port Melbourne, VIC 3207, Australia

314–321, 3rd Floor, Plot 3, Splendor Forum, Jasola District Centre, New Delhi – 110025, India

79 Anson Road, #06–04/06, Singapore 079906

Cambridge University Press is part of the University of Cambridge.

It furthers the University's mission by disseminating knowledge in the pursuit of education, learning, and research at the highest international levels of excellence.

www.cambridge.org
Information on this title: www.cambridge.org/9781108426725
DOI: 10.1017/9781108698412

© Terry Smith 2020

First published 2020

A catalogue record for this publication is available from the British Library.

ISBN 978-1-108-42672-5 Hardback
ISBN 978-1-108-44546-7 Paperback

Cambridge University Press has no responsibility for the persistence or accuracy of URLs for external or third-party internet websites referred to in this publication and does not guarantee that any content on such websites is, or will remain, accurate or appropriate.

Lincoln Pettaway is a lifelong mentor who taught me the most important lesson of my life: no one can control your destiny unless you allow them. Thanks for being the consummate teacher, Mr. Pettaway.

Contents

Tables

Preface

Even as a lawyer and legal scholar, I have written this book for non-lawyers because its concerns are far too important to be limited to a boutique audience. We all have a role in rooting out racial discrimination in the democratic process, and that role begins by being cognizant of how and why we vote the way we do. When I began this project in 2017, my ambitions were admittedly more constrained than they ultimately turned out to be. Yet the more I witnessed American democracy being buffeted by foreign influence, a petulant and incurious president, a compromised Supreme Court, and the sheer inability of the nation's ossifying institutions to instill trust, the more driven I became to reach for a solution to what undergirds most of the ongoing tumult: voters' distrust of each other. More specifically, the 2016 presidential contest demonstrated that a significant segment of American voters harbors racial stereotypes of their fellow Americans and carries these preconceptions into the ballot box. When a candidate such as Donald Trump legitimates these stereotypes with jeremiads against Latino immigrants and Muslims, a political process already characterized by racially polarized voting becomes even more tainted. But Trump's 2016 campaign and his continuation of its provocative themes during his presidency are simply part of a historical continuum of whitelash, albeit one on which Trump excels for the sheer blatancy of his demagogy. The question, though, is how much more of this cycle of whitelash can American democracy bear without unhinging?

Although I am a political progressive, even conservatives who embrace "colorblindness"—the idea of race neutrality in all situations—should also embrace the central premise of this book: voters have no right to vote for or against a candidate based on their racial stereotypes of the candidate's supporters or their racial stereotypes of the beneficiaries of the candidate's policies. Yet it is not enough to simply declare such decision-making improper. It is, in fact, illegal. Americans may conceive of the act of voting for one candidate versus another as a personal choice; the law, however, views it as an action of the state. Voters' choices are thus subject to legal limitations, the most important of which is the prohibition against racial discrimination embodied in the Equal Protection Clause of the Fourteenth Amendment. The remedies that courts may impose upon finding an equal protection violation are broad in scope and possess the potential to deter voter whitelash or, at the very least, to blunt its effects. The containment of voter whitelash, in turn, offers transformative potential to American democracy at a time when it is ailing and when its participants are becoming increasingly heterogeneous.

Indeed, it is perhaps more accurate to say that American democracy is ailing because of the threat of its increasing heterogeneity. The prospect of more nonwhite voters—or simply greater numbers of all voters—exercising more power in the political process has not been greeted with uniform enthusiasm. Consider, for instance, Senate Majority Leader Mitch McConnell's reaction to a proposal to make election day a federal holiday, which would likely increase voter turnout. McConnell deemed the proposal a Democratic "power grab,"[1] reflecting the basic premise of Republicans that when it comes to voter participation, less is more.

Consider also the response of former Maine governor Paul LePage to a proposal to bypass the Electoral College, which concentrates disproportionate power in smaller, rural states and has twice in this young century deprived a plurality of voters of their preferred candidate for president. LePage was shockingly impolitic in his assessment of a plan in which states would allocate their electoral votes based on the national popular vote: "Actually what would happen if they do what they say they're gonna do is white people will not have anything to say. It's only going to be the minorities that would elect. It would be California, Texas, Florida."[2]

McConnell's and LePage's views lay bare an uncomfortable truth that animates this book: antiquated and often contrived electoral structures like Tuesday voting and the Electoral College are the conduits by which voters who violate their legal obligation not to discriminate on the basis of race at the ballot box gain control of American democracy. The 2016 presidential contest starkly illustrates this convergence of malevolent intent and antidemocratic structures. The judicial remedies I propose in this book, however, would make the ballot box a far less welcoming terrain for racial discrimination.

My goals for readers of this book are simple. If I succeed in provoking readers to think about the obligations that attend the right to vote, then this book has accomplished a central mission. Beyond this, I expect that readers will come away with an accessible vocabulary for discussing race in our democracy—one that steers the conversation to evidence and facts rather than polemics. Most importantly, though, I hope the reader will enjoy what follows.

Acknowledgments

A project of this magnitude is never accomplished singlehandedly. Matt Gallaway of Cambridge University Press was an unfailing champion for the project. Some very able law students aided me as research assistants: Terrie Sullivan, Candace Watkins, Brittany Whitfield, Stephanie Gibbons, and Bryanna Jenkins. Some very smart colleagues provided critical readings and suggestions: Charlton Copeland, Gregory Parks, Sumi Cho, Darren Hutchinson, Jason Nance, Valerie Johnson, Patrick Bradford, Hosea Harvey, Audrey McFarlane, Matthew Shaw, Atiba Ellis, Henry Chambers, and Iyiola Solanke. Karin Horler provided outstanding editorial support. Friends suffered my obsession to complete this project, including Gemma Solimene, Leah Hill, Tanya Hernandez, Nitza Escalera, and John Banks. None, however, bore as much of the brunt as Renilson Carmo, for whom I am immensely grateful. Finally, Valparaiso University Law Review graciously allowed me to draw on my article *White Backlash in a Brown Country*, 50 Val. U. L. Rev. 89 (2015), in writing this book.

Introduction

The Long Night of Déjà Vu

Election night, Tuesday, November 8, 2016, seemed interminable for many Americans. It certainly was for me. I was scheduled to teach an election law class the following day, during which my students and I would discuss the legal implications of the presidential and congressional elections. But before that, I had to fulfill a commitment to speak to a high school audience about the election. I was to address students at Chicago's Legal Prep Charter Academy first thing Wednesday morning—a daunting task because I had been up all night puzzling over election returns that had elevated a reality television show host, Donald Trump, to the most powerful position in the world.

In the wee hours of the morning on election night, when it became clear that Trump would clinch a victory in the Electoral College, I penned an op-ed for the *Huffington Post* titled "Will White Voters Never Learn?"[1] White voters had delivered mightily for Trump, who bested Hillary Clinton by a 21-point margin among this demographic. Black voters had hewed to their overwhelmingly Democratic bent: Clinton beat Trump 10 to 1 among them. Surprisingly, although Latinos preferred Clinton by better than 2 to 1, they nonetheless gave Trump nearly 30 percent of their vote, a curious tally for an ethnic group that had borne the brunt of Trump's racial ridicule. Still, white Americans constituted 71 percent of the electorate, and they delivered the White House to Trump, particularly in three key states: Michigan, Pennsylvania, and Wisconsin. Why?

In my *Huffington Post* opinion piece, I argued that white voters had yet again succumbed to a classic American con job. A candidate pitched himself as an elixir to the nation's supposed equalitarian excesses, and white voters— eager to assert control over "their" nation—drank it readily, oblivious to the tonic that would follow. Richard Nixon campaigned in 1968 on "law and order," only to be driven from the White House by the lawlessness of Watergate. Ronald Reagan's crusades against "welfare queens" and "reverse discrimination" against whites did nothing to halt globalization's and technology's indiscriminate appetite for the jobs of the working- and middle-class whites who propelled Reagan to victory in 1980. George H. W. Bush's 1988 campaign used the racial boogeyman of convicted felon Willie Horton to notch a victory over Massachusetts governor Michael Dukakis, only to be booted out of office after one term in the throes of a recession. George W. Bush was effectively installed to the presidency by Reagan's and the elder Bush's conservative Supreme Court majority in *Bush v. Gore.*[2] Two wars and a Great Recession later, the world was still paying the price when Trump came along.

As an objective historical matter, when white voters have moved right in the post-Civil Rights era, the shifts have usually been accompanied by race as a national issue or divide, and the outcomes have come at a handsome cost to white voters and the nation generally. What made white voters think 2016 would be different? More to the point of this book, what made white voters think they were at liberty to keep making the same calculation, prodded at least in part by their disapproval of racial liberality, whether defined by their perception of a welfare state that had become too generous, a government that protected minorities at their expense, or an out-of-control immigration policy? Voting, after all, is not some impressionistic exercise unbounded by norms. It is, instead, an occasion when citizens directly assume the levers of democratic government in order to select their representatives. If we do not allow the government to discriminate based on race, we cannot allow voters to do so in choosing the government's elected personnel.

The hard part about this proposition, of course, is proving that a voter or a group of voters has voted with discriminatory animus toward another group. At the Legal Prep Charter Academy where I spoke the morning after the election, Trump's racial animus was taken as a given among the overwhelmingly black student body, as it had been among many black voters. One student blurted, "He hates us." As a law professor, I would never allow such a raw, unsubstantiated statement to stand in one of my classes, so I tried to engage the students about the bases for their suspicions that Trump would be the president only of white America. Their data points were at least as good as those of many of the talking heads I heard on television throughout the campaign and on election night.

One commentator in particular, CNN's Van Jones, had labored memorably to make sense of Trump's victory on election night. Clearly shaken by the impending result, Jones opined on national television:

> This was many things. This was a rebellion against the elites, true. It was a complete reinvention of politics and polls, it's true. But it was also something else. We've talked about … everything but race tonight. We've talked

about income. We've talked about class. We've talked about region. We haven't talked about race. This was a white-lash against a changing country. It was a white-lash against a black president, in part.[3]

Whitelash is a portmanteau derived from the term "white backlash." Consciously or not, Jones had revived the term from debates during the 1960s. In 1964, after Republican presidential candidate Senator Barry Goldwater unsuccessfully opposed passage of the Civil Rights Act of 1964, Senator Allen J. Ellender, a Louisiana Democrat, predicted a "whitelash" among voters against the act's enforcement.[4] Similarly, segregationist Alabama governor George Wallace's highly successful third-party presidential run in 1968, in which he won five southern states, was dubbed "The Wallace Whitelash." In short, whitelash describes the reactionary impulse of many white voters toward racial equality movements and societal shifts they perceive as excessive. Of necessity, then, the phenomenon is based on the erroneous, racist view that racial inequality is a natural order and that whites should control the pace at which it is dismantled.

It is one thing to coin or revive a pithy term but quite another to supply a clear framework for its use. Claiming or even explaining whitelash is easy; proving its existence among millions of voters is the difficult task. As I later reflected on my discussion with the students at Legal Prep and continued to read the voluminous postmortems of the 2016 election, it struck me that popular discourse on the question of whether racism had driven Trump's election was divorced from the way lawyers and legal scholars talk about whether race has influenced a decision. I've taught election law and employment law for a quarter-century, and I have litigated employment discrimination cases. Bringing together these two areas of focus, I realized that we could apply the frameworks of antidiscrimination law to the collective decision-making of voters to ascertain whether their support for or opposition to a candidate was based on racial animus.

I do not necessarily or even primarily mean racial animus against a specific candidate, but rather animus toward racially identifiable groups of the candidate's supporters, who in turn engender biases against the candidate. For instance, while credible evidence suggests that misogyny hobbled Hillary Clinton's chances in the general election,[5] no one claims that *her* race did. Instead, her identification with racial progressivity, and Trump's identification with the opposite, acted as racial proxies in the 2016 election, as such ideological positioning has in many elections past.

Antidiscrimination law's frameworks for ascertaining racial bias are not superior to other ways of thinking about and discussing race and the 2016 election. They are, however, a different lens, and they are surprisingly intui-tive. Indeed, because antidiscrimination law governs important facets of every American's life—from workplace discrimination to our ability to buy and sell property as we choose—it must, at its core, be comprehensible by the public. I argue in these pages that the same legal precepts that prevent us from refusing to hire a Latino based on his national origin or prevent a legislature from passing a law that makes it more difficult for blacks to vote also prohibit voters from casting a ballot based on racial animus—even if racial animus is one motivation among several.

Moreover, the tools that courts have historically used to ascertain racist motivations on the part of decision-makers like legislators and employers can and should be applied to voters in candidate elections. Where a breach of the antidiscrimination norm is found, legal remedies exist. These remedies may not change the mind or vote of the discriminatory voter, but they can mitigate the effects of the voter's discrimination on the body politic.

There is a certain irony, however, to advancing antidiscrimination law as a corrective to voters' racial misconduct: under conservative jurisprudence, antidiscrimination law is just as likely to perpetuate discrimination as it is to inhibit it. This conundrum requires understanding whitelash not just as an electoral phenomenon but rather as a social one that connects the political branches of government, the judiciary, and organic reactionary movements like white nationalism. Through voter ID laws and the dismantling of voting protections for minorities, a racially regressive judiciary makes voter whitelash easier to express. Once an electoral victory is achieved, the racially regressive bent of the judiciary gets reinforced by the appointment of additional "con-servative" judges—a term that, as we shall see, now correlates rather well with the denial of civil rights to minorities and women. Meanwhile, as politicians like Donald Trump shred the veneer of respectability politics, white nation-alists percolate just outside mainstream conservatism—close enough to have a decided effect. The convergence of these ostensibly disparate parts is the sum of whitelash—the sustained push to retard or retreat from racial equality.

Using the 2016 presidential election as a focal point, this book unpacks contemporary whitelash by applying antidiscrimination law. Rather than plunge into the niceties of legal doctrine, I use a series of legal analogies to help orient the reader. Reflecting my years as an employment law scholar, my analogies often ask you to equate the voter with an employer who is making a hiring decision. At other times, you are an employee who stands to be adversely impacted by an employer's arbitrary decision-making, in much the same way as a voter is negatively affected by a politician's refusal to rely on facts when making decisions. Sometimes, you are placed in the shoes of a juror, who, like a voter, must adjudicate the merits of a case that has two sides. In still other instances, you are asked to place yourself in the position of a legislator voting on a proposed statute, something that voters are asked to do in a referendum or citizens' initiative. What is the commonality among these heuristics? In each, racial discrimination is forbidden. Why, then, should we allow it in candidate elections?

Chapters 1 through 3 set forth the architecture of what I refer to throughout this book as the "antidiscrimination norm." Chapter 1 focuses largely on how the 2016 presidential contest violated modern understandings of this norm by reverting to primitive forms of racial appeals. Using abundant social science data, Chapter 2, "The Exoneration of White Voters," discusses and then debunks the plausibility of white voters' denial that race played a role in their 2016 decision. Chapter 3, "White Voters and the Law of Alternative Facts," argues that voting, like law, requires a respect for facts, and that racial stereotypes are necessarily at odds with a fidelity to facts.

Chapters 4 and 5 place whitelash in its broader framing beyond the ballot box—a reach that nevertheless fortifies its potency at the ballot box. Chapter 4, "The Sirens of White Nationalism," demonstrates the impact of heretofore fringe political philosophies and groups on mainstream conservatism and the electoral viability of the Republican Party. Chapter 5, "Law as Pretext," explains how conservative jurisprudence reinforces voter whitelash and racial inequality more generally.

In everyday parlance, when someone practices one thing and does the opposite, we call it hypocrisy. In law, this type of behavior is evidence of pretext—an untruth proffered to cover up the real illicit or discriminatory reason for one's actions. In Chapter 6, "Voting While White," I survey the myriad contradictions that undergird white voters' support for conservative candidates, contradictions that reveal many white voters professing a belief in small or limited government while feeding at the government's trough. If they are not really supporting conservative candidates because of a belief in the core tenet of conservativism—limited government—why are whites supporting these candidates? In light of white voters' racial predispositions in the 2016 election, racial animus is a distinctly credible possibility, as I argue in Chapters 1 and 2. Ironically, however, because progressives stand ready to rescue the social safety net that many white voters spurn hypocritically, voter whitelash goes unchecked.

So how should our democracy respond to whitelash if the two-party system itself encourages it? In Chapters 7 and 8, I propose legal remedies to curtail the impact of whitelash on our body politic. Constitutional guarantees of free speech and free association necessarily limit the government's ability to prevent citizens from casting votes based on racial animus. Still, the citizen who votes is participating in a state-sponsored exercise, the outcome of which constitutes "state action" for the purpose of determining whether, under the Constitution's requirement of equal protection, an election's process or result impermissibly discriminates against an identifiable group of citizens. The remedies I propose fit within established legal doctrine that I introduce to readers through the legal analogies used early on.

Viewed as a vector of white racial resentment, whitelash is not a uniquely American problem, yet America has a unique role in its spread and deterrence. A nation that boasts of its ability to encourage democracy throughout the world must be mindful of its similar ability to foster racist ideology. The conclusion of this book discusses this cautionary truth.

*****

I arrived at my election law class the evening after the 2016 presidential election still shocked by the results and with the words "He hates us" seared in my memory. In a democracy, no citizen, let alone a child, should sense this of the nation's leader. Yet a July 2018 Quinnipiac University poll found that 49 percent of Americans believed President Trump was a "racist."[6] Forty-seven percent of respondents believed he was not. That a nation can hear the same words, view the same actions, and reach opposite conclusions demonstrates the need for a shared lexicon about racial discrimination. In the pages that follow, largely by analogy, I have adapted the vocabulary of our justice system—the place where every citizen can go to right a wrong, and a central feature of any democracy—to look at the 2016 election through a new lens.

The right to vote should never be used to spite one's fellow citizens. When it has been misused in this fashion, white voters have "cut off their noses to spite their faces," and democracy itself has repeatedly suffered. How long will we allow this recurring harm before it strikes a final, fatal blow?

1

Electing Trump and Breaching Norms

Politicians often extoll the common sense of running government like a business. Indeed, business acumen was arguably the principal qualification of then-candidate Donald Trump to become president of the United States. Likening government to a business, however, invites another analogy: voters as employers. Employers are constrained by practical and legal considerations in choosing employees. For example, it's almost impossible to imagine a board of directors selecting Donald Trump as its CEO after the revelation of the *Access Hollywood* tape on which he boasted of grabbing women by their genitalia without their consent. The reputational and legal exposure for the business would be too great. Yet American voters elected Trump as the nation's CEO.

Imagine as an employer you hired Trump, a businessman who had declared bankruptcy six times, over a woman who had served as secretary of state, U.S. senator, and first lady. Our nation's laws prohibiting gender discrimination would not take at face value your explanation for such a suspect hiring decision.[1] Even if the *Access Hollywood* tape had not surfaced, Hillary Clinton was the more qualified candidate by any objective measure. Indeed, a September 2016 *Washington Post* poll mirrored other pre-election polling in finding by 62 percent to 36 percent that Trump was not qualified to serve as president.[2]

Yet there is ample evidence that it was not gender discrimination alone—or even primarily—that shaped the election results. Although misogyny infected the 2016 presidential election, Trump's behavior during the 2016 election was foregrounded by an eight-year campaign to racialize and delegitimize the first African American president. That orchestration was, in turn, part of the decades-long tradition of GOP race-baiting in American politics.

If you believe that antidiscrimination norms apply to voting decisions, then you should also believe that people have no right to base their votes on discriminatory animus. It makes little sense that Donald Trump, for instance, could not legally refuse to rent property to African Americans because of their race—for which he was sued by the federal government—but that race can be allowed to infiltrate white voters' decision to support Trump. It makes even less sense that a candidate for public office, let alone the presidency, can traffic in racial stereotyping that we would never allow in other public deliberative settings such as juries or legislative debates.

In this chapter, after sketching the racialized milieu in which the 2016 campaign transpired, I demonstrate how in various legal contexts, this conduct would constitute evidence of illicit discrimination. I then address—and debunk—the notion that voting in candidate elections is different than the other areas in which we as a society prohibit racial discrimination. Left unanswered in this chapter, but addressed going forward, is the question of how we can ascertain whether voters have based their decision at least in part on race—that is, whether they have engaged in whitelash.

WHITELASH AND FEAR

Whitelash is the reaction of many white Americans when they believe that strides toward racial equality have run amuck, to the point of threatening their own material well-being, even as they remain far better-off economically than people of color. The phenomenon is anchored in a fear and resentment of cultural change, change that will eventually render the white majority a racial minority. This fear manifests itself through individual and collective efforts to retain the benefits of a structure of racial inequality, efforts that erroneously cast equality for people of color as discrimination against whites. Thus, the default position—the social baseline—from which too many whites define the normalcy of race relations is racial inequality. When viewed as the privilege-hoarding tactic that it is, whitelash is a contempt of citizenship, a violation of societal norms, and even a violation of law.

A salient feature of whitelash is the construction of equality as zero-sum: the advancement of racial minorities must necessarily come at the expense of whites.[3] Or, as Senator Jeff Sessions put it before his elevation to Attorney General of the United States, "Empathy for one party is always prejudice against another."[4] Forty-five percent of Trump voters believed that whites face greater discrimination than blacks, Latinos, or Muslims.[5] A majority of white Americans now believe that discrimination against whites is at least as big a problem as discrimination against blacks and other minorities.[6] Yet, few white Americans report being the victims of discrimination. In a poll conducted by NPR and Harvard University in 2017, only 19 percent of whites reported being discriminated against because they are white when applying for a job, and 11 percent when applying for college admission.[7] In contrast, 56 percent of African Americans surveyed reported personally experiencing racial discrimination when applying for a job.[8] For white Americans, and certainly for Trump voters, race discrimination against whites is more a meme than a personal reality. Whitelash thus requires an alternative reality of its perpetrators because the facts on the ground do not generally support their grievances.

NO DOG WHISTLES NEEDED

Somewhat ironically, it has become common practice to avoid using the term "racism" to describe words and actions that convey racial prejudice. Progressives have been as complicit in this counterintuition as anyone, coining terms like "subtle discrimination," "unconscious discrimination," and "implicit bias" that elide the harsh, accusatory tone of racism. The problem is not just one of nomenclature. As Professor Michael Selmi has argued, allowing this distinction in language means also ceding conceptual territory to the dangerous notion that discrimination which requires indirect or inferential proof is different in kind from overt prejudice.[9] From judicial opinions to everyday discourse, there is an assumption that if an action or statement does not look like historical racism (think Jim Crow laws), then we should label and treat it differently.

Yet even historical racism was denied as being racist in its day. In *Plessy v. Ferguson*, the U.S. Supreme Court rationalized the segregation of blacks and whites in railway passenger cars by noting, "We consider the underlying fallacy of the plaintiff's argument to consist in the assumption that the enforced separation of the two races stamps the colored race with a badge of inferiority. If this be so, it is not by reason of anything found in the act, but solely because the colored race chooses to put that construction upon it."[10] Thus, benchmarking the definition of racism to historical racial practices may constitute little more than the ongoing practice of denying racism's existence in its present-day form.

In electoral politics, the term *dog-whistle politics* is often a stand-in for the more pungent term *racism*. Dog-whistle politics are racial appeals targeted at whites primed to hear such messages but masked in code so as not to offend the median white voter.[11] Lee Atwater, the infamous Republican strategist, provided the textbook explanation of this brand of politics in 1981:

> You start out in 1954 by saying, "Nigger, nigger, nigger." By 1968 you can't say "nigger"—that hurts you, backfires. So you say stuff like, uh, forced busing,

states' rights, and all that stuff, and you're getting so abstract. Now, you're talking about cutting taxes, and all these things you're talking about are totally economic things and a byproduct of them is, blacks get hurt worse than whites ... "We want to cut this," is much more abstract than even the busing thing, uh, and a hell of a lot more abstract than "Nigger, nigger."[12]

In the age of Trump, Atwater's understanding of the impermissibility of direct racial appeals may be outdated.

Trump's campaign was the first of its kind in the post-Civil Rights era. Gone was the adroit racial symbolism of Ronald Reagan, who used the backdrop of Philadelphia, Mississippi, a destination fraught with antagonism to black civil rights, to convey to white voters that they were free to disregard the interests of African Americans.[13] Where Reagan railed against welfare queens to cue white stereotypes of blacks as wards of the government, Trump openly advocated a ban on admitting Muslims to the United States.[14] Where Reagan indirectly stoked white resentment by opposing affirmative action, Trump crudely called for a wall along the southern border to keep out Mexicans, whom he had characterized as rapists and drug traffickers.[15] In short, Trump's campaign left little to the imagination; it was festooned with unadulterated racism.

Thus, when Donald Trump announced his candidacy for president on June 16, 2015, his stereotyping of Mexican immigrants was hardly off-the-cuff:

> When Mexico sends its people, they're not sending their best. They're not sending you. They're not sending you. They're sending people that have lots of problems, and they're bringing those problems with us. They're bringing drugs. They're bringing crime. They're rapists. And some, I assume, are good people.[16]

Trump was playing to a partisan base in which the majority of Republicans (53 percent) believed that immigrants make America worse off in the long run, while less than a third (31 percent) said immigrants made the nation better-off.[17] And his reference to Mexicans as drug dealers and "rapists" was even more finely tailored to the Republican base. Seventy-one percent of Republicans believed that immigrants to the United States make crime worse.[18] Yet immigrants are one-half to one-fifth as likely to be incarcerated for a crime as a native-born American.[19]

But Trump had no monopoly on racial tropes during the Republican primaries or the 2016 general election. Nor was 2016 a departure from recent history. Table 1–1 culls some of the more glaring racial infelicities from major Republican candidates who sought the presidency in 2012 or 2016. (There's simply nothing comparable among Democratic contenders.) The comments range from the portrayal of the first African American president as

TABLE 1-1 *Racial Rhetoric—Presidential Candidates*

Subject	Speaker	Comment and Date
Nativism	Senator Marco Rubio	"We sometimes feel like strangers in our own land." January 2016
Barack Obama	Senator Marco Rubio	"It's now abundantly clear: Barack Obama has deliberately weakened America." January 4, 2016
Responding to a question about increasing the number of African Americans in the GOP	Former Gov. Jeb Bush	"Our message is one of hope and aspiration ... It [is not] one of division and get in line and we'll take care of you with free stuff. Our message is one that is uplifting—that says you can achieve earned success." September 24, 2015
Whether Barack Obama is a Christian	Governor Scott Walker	"I don't know." February 21, 2015
Barack Obama	Former Mayor Rudy Giuliani	"I do not believe, and I know this is a horrible thing to say, but I do not believe that the president loves America ... He doesn't love you. And he doesn't love me. He wasn't brought up the way you were brought up and I was brought up through love of this country." February 18, 2015
Explaining Republicans' loss of the 2012 presidential election	Mitt Romney	Romney talked about "big issues for the whole country" while Obama targeted "gifts" to specific groups, "especially the African-American community, the Hispanic community and young people." November 14, 2012

TABLE 1–1 (*continued*)

Subject	Speaker	Comment and Date
Responding to a question about government entitlement programs	Rick Santorum, runner-up in 2012 GOP primaries	"I don't want to make black people's lives better by giving them somebody else's money. I want to give them the opportunity to go out and earn the money." January 1, 2012
Barack Obama	Former House Speaker Newt Gingrich	"We are going to have the candidate of food stamps, the finest food stamp president in American history, in Barack Obama, and we are going to have a candidate of paychecks." December 6, 2011
Barack Obama	Former House Speaker Newt Gingrich	"What if [Obama] is so outside our comprehension that only if you understand Kenyan, anti-colonial behavior, can you begin to piece together [his actions]? That is the most accurate, predictive model for his behavior." September 11, 2010

a Manchurian agent out to destroy the country, to the depiction of blacks and Latinos as freeloaders. Each lines up with salient views among the Republican base. For instance, at the start of the presidential primary season in 2015, 43 percent of Republicans believed President Obama was a Muslim.[20] To appreciate the potency of this falsehood, it helps to understand that in 2015, fully 55 percent of all Americans had a negative view of the religion of Muslims, Islam.[21] Candidates' comments portraying racial minorities as inveterate freeloaders likewise dovetailed with popular Republican misconceptions. A 2016 General Social Survey found that 55 percent of white Republicans believed that blacks "just don't have the motivation or willpower to pull themselves up out of poverty[.]"[22]

These quotations merely glide the surface of the racial stereotyping which Republican politicians engaged in during the Obama era and continue to traffic in today. There have been even more tawdry insults, such as a congressman's reference to Obama as a "tar baby," a slur repeated in reference to Obama's policies by former Mississippi governor and GOP national chairman Haley Barbour.[23] One Republican congressman referred to Obama as "uppity," while another referred to him as a "boy."[24] Training on Obama's middle name, Hussein, Representative Steve King of Iowa forewarned that if Obama were elected, "Then the radical Islamists, the al Qaeda, the radical Islamists and their supporters, will be dancing in the streets in greater numbers than they did on Sept. 11 because they will declare victory in this War on Terror."[25] Although President Trump's press secretary deemed it a "fireable offense" when a black ESPN sports commentator called him a "white supremacist" in 2017, in 2012 Trump, then television host of *The Apprentice*, labeled Obama a "racist" for favorably referencing Obama's former pastor, Rev. Jeremiah Wright, in a 2007 speech.[26] The list goes on and on. The era of Obama ushered in a racial promiscuity among Republican politicians and officials that gave them license to utter miasma that would get the average employee terminated from a job.

Even before he became a candidate, Donald Trump stirred this pot of racial contempt. In Trump's fertile imagination, the first African American president could not have been born a citizen of the United States and therefore, under the Constitution, was not entitled to be President. Trump taunted President Obama over the made-up issue of his birthplace for years. "Why doesn't he show his birth certificate? There's something on that birth certificate that he doesn't like," Trump mused in 2011 on the program *The View*.[27] Trump even fabricated statements by Obama's family: "His grandmother in Kenya said, 'Oh, no, he was born in Kenya and I was there and I witnessed the birth.' She's on tape. I think that tape's going to be produced fairly soon. Somebody is coming out with a book in two weeks, it will be very interesting."[28] No such tape was ever produced. What was produced, by Obama, was his long-form birth certificate verifying that he was born in Hawaii. This, however, did not ground Trump's flight of fantasy. Trump tweeted more than a year after Obama supplied his birth certificate, "An 'extremely credible source' has called my office and told me that @BarackObama's birth certificate is a fraud."[29]

Although Trump tried to put the birther controversy behind him when he became the Republican nominee by admitting Obama was born in the United States, the issue figured dramatically in his first debate with Hillary Clinton. Clinton portrayed Trump as being outside acceptable norms for an American president, essentially calling him a racist. Noting that Trump had been sued by the federal government in the 1970s for refusing to rent apartments to African Americans, Clinton inveighed: "He has a long record of engaging in racist behavior. And the birther lie was a very hurtful one."[30] It marked the first time in the history of televised presidential debates where one major-party candidate so pointedly insinuated that the other was a racist.

Trump left so little to the imagination that by the conclusion of his campaign, most Americans (52 percent) believed he was a racist.[31] Race was in the air. In the run-up to the 2016 election, a series of high-profile killings of unarmed black males by white police officers had given rise to the Black Lives Matter movement and nationwide protests against police brutality. Republicans trained on the protests and the protesters rather than the police killings. Trump described Black Lives Matter as "divisive."[32]

During the first debate with Clinton, Trump exploited the unrest caused by the police killings to channel a mantra from Richard Nixon's 1972 reelection campaign. Trump insisted that the nation needed "law and order" and "stop and frisk," even though he was responding to a question about how to *heal* the nation's racial divide.[33] More than four decades after this Nixonian speak had been decoded as racist, this was no dog whistle; it was an explicit disregard of African Americans.

If more law and order was needed, it would be imposed on their backs and those of Latinos. After all, a supermajority of blacks (61 percent) believed that police are more likely to use excessive force on an African American than a similarly situated white person.[34] These views align with the statistics. A 2015 *Washington Post* analysis concluded that unarmed black men were seven times more likely to die from police gunfire than whites.[35] A separate analysis by *The Guardian* concluded that in 2015, while racial minorities made up 37.4 percent of the U.S. general population, they constituted 62.7 percent of unarmed people killed by the police.[36] In his book *Chokehold*, Georgetown University law professor Paul Butler presents a staggering array of use-of-force statistics demonstrating that blacks are far more likely than whites to be on the receiving end of coercive police tactics.[37] Indeed, as Butler writes, "Police brutality is so widespread, and so predictable, that many small and medium-size cities actually purchase insurance policies to pay money to people who have been subject to police abuse."[38] No rational listener could conclude that Trump was appealing to blacks and Latinos for their votes with his rhetoric on crime. His audience was white voters in whom he could stoke fear.

Doused in Trump's racial rhetoric, the Clinton–Trump contest unfolded not merely in the backdrop of an eight-year campaign to racialize and delegitimate President Obama, and national discord over police mistreatment of minorities, but also alongside a convergence of white nationalist ideology with mainstream political and judicial thought. The latter had been in the making years before Trump's political ascent, but its enabling of his rise and its contributions to whitelash are greatly underappreciated. I will return to the subject of white nationalism in Chapter 4, but a brief explanation is in order here. White nationalism is white identity politics.[39] It summons whites to coalesce around their interests as a racial group in the same way minorities have had to do to combat their historical racial disadvantage. The Ku Klux Klan is the most violent and antiquated representation of white nationalism.

Yet, the problem with assuming that white voters will no longer tolerate classical forms of racism in politics is that there is no daylight between their beliefs about the discrimination to which whites are subjected and those of white supremacist leader David Duke. A basic premise of white supremacist ideology is that whites are being discriminated against in favor of less qualified, less deserving people of color. According to Duke, "The fact is that in the United States of America, Canada, the UK and in many other areas of Europe Whites face a powerful state-sanctioned, and often mandated, racial discrimination against White people who are better-qualified than their non-White counterparts."[40] In a political environment in which this kind of convergence of thought could occur between everyday white Americans and racial extremists, Reagan-era political strategist Lee Atwater's preoccupation with maintaining a veneer of racial respectability seems quaint.

Events in Charlottesville, Virginia, in the summer of 2017 clearly demonstrated the direct links between the new white nationalism and its ancestry. Throngs of neo-Nazis marched through the college town of Charlottesville with lit torches, chanting anti-Semitic slogans in protest of the removal of Confederate monuments. Two days of confrontations culminated in the death of Heather Heyer when a member of the neo-Nazi protestors drove his car into a counterdemonstration. Instead of instantly condemning the neo-Nazis, President Trump contended that there were "some very fine people" marching among them.[41] America had lurched back in time.

I argue that white voters could reasonably have anticipated this reversion when they voted overwhelmingly for Trump. Trump's campaign slogan was "Make America Great Again," a phrase whose ambiguity was greatly reduced coming from a candidate who proposed to deport millions of illegal immigrants, to ban Muslims from entering the country, and to limit legal immigration to those with a "likelihood of success" in the United States.[42] White voters either did not care about the racial overtones of Trump's campaign or were drawn to Trump because of them. Either sentiment violated their duty of citizenship.

THE ANTIDISCRIMINATION NORM

It is not an exceptional or even debatable proposition that racial prejudice has no place in the American legal system. In *Peña-Rodriguez v. Colorado*, a juror in the sexual assault trial of a Latino defendant infused the deliberations with harmful stereotypes such as "I think he did it because he's Mexican and Mexican men take whatever they want."[43] The Supreme Court held that in instances of overt bigotry, the Sixth Amendment right to an impartial jury trumps the rule against use of a juror's testimony to invalidate a verdict.[44]

If *Peña-Rodriguez* applied to candidate elections, the case might render illegitimate the victory of Donald Trump, who, like the juror in *Peña-Rodriguez*, stereotyped Mexican-Americans and blacks in ways that were indisputably racist. When Trump claimed that a federal judge could not be impartial in a fraud case brought against "Trump University" because of the judge's Mexican heritage, House of Representatives Speaker Paul Ryan, a fellow Republican, called Trump's comments "the textbook definition of a racist comment."[45] In a democracy in which elections are as rudimentary an institution as jury trials, why should we tolerate racism from a major-party candidate for president of the United States, but not from a juror in a criminal trial? Certainly in the past, courts have intervened in elections where the court has concluded that voters' choices were guided by racial discrimination or other impermissible animus.

In *Romer v. Evans*, the Court held that state voters could not adopt by referendum a law that prohibited the Colorado state legislature or localities from passing legislation barring discrimination on the grounds of sexual orientation. To do so, according to the Court, "withdraws from homosexuals, but no others, specific legal protection from the injuries caused by discrimination . . ."[46] The Court concluded that Colorado voters had acted with irrational "animus" toward their fellow citizens; thus, the law violated the federal Constitution's guarantee of equal protection under the law.[47]

The Court took a similar stand against majoritarian malice in *Reitman v. Mulkey*, in which California voters ratified an initiative that prohibited state or local governments from passing legislation regulating the sale or rental of housing.[48] The initiative, Proposition 14, was designed to overturn state fair housing laws and to enable private discrimination that would be prohibited by the Fourteenth Amendment if it were engaged in by a government. Yet, because Proposition 14, with its allowance and encouragement of private discrimination, was now California policy, the Court found that voters' passage of this initiative violated the Equal Protection Clause of the Fourteenth Amendment.[49]

Similarly, when voters in the city of Akron, Ohio, approved an amendment to the city charter that abolished the city's fair housing law and required approval by a majority of voters to enact similar legislation, the Court in *Hunter v. Erickson* struck the charter amendment.[50] It did so because the charter modification made seeking relief against racial discrimination in housing more difficult than seeking relief against other kinds of discrimination: "[T]he State may no more disadvantage any particular group by making it more difficult to enact legislation in its behalf than it may dilute any person's vote or give any group a smaller representation than another of comparable size."[51]

The Court later applied *Hunter* in *Washington v. Seattle School District No. 1.*[52] There, voters in Washington state passed an initiative aimed at ending Seattle's desegregative busing program by requiring students to attend their nearest or next nearest school. In so doing, state voters deployed their power to deprive Seattle of decision-making authority ordinarily undertaken at the local level. Yet Initiative 350 allowed student reassignment for reasons other than racial desegregation. The Court declined to allow Washington to differentiate among types of student reassignments because Initiative 350 "uses the racial nature of an issue to define the governmental decisionmaking structure, and thus imposes substantial and unique burdens on racial minorities."[53]

The common thread across these cases is that, contrary to political cliché, the voter is not always right. In fact, when voters engage in harmful discrimination at the polls, in the Constitution's eyes, they're dead wrong. To be sure, referenda and initiatives, in which voters enact laws through "direct democracy," are different from candidate elections. This distinction, however, has not generally led the Court to treat the two kinds of elections differently as a constitutional matter. Indeed, where the Court has drawn distinctions, it has actually afforded states *greater* latitude to regulate candidate elections.[54]

Some scholars have argued that referenda and citizen initiatives, particularly when focused on race-laden issues such as affirmative action, provide more of an opportunity for animus-motivated voting.[55] Yet because the same voters participate in candidate elections as in referenda and initiatives, there is no reason to suspect racial animus cannot be as effectively stoked in one type of election versus the other. There is thus simply no reason to exempt candidate elections from the constitutional bar against invidious discrimination in direct democracy.

Here, we need to acknowledge a feature of the American legal system that frustrates every first-year law student and will undoubtedly frustrate some readers. American jurisprudence can sometimes seem contradictory; Supreme Court cases that stand for opposite propositions can coexist as "good law." Thus, while the Supreme Court has intervened in elections on multiple occasions where the results reflect impermissible voter animus, the Court has also assumed that "a democracy has the capacity—and the duty—to learn from its past mistakes; to discover and confront persisting biases; and by respectful, rationale [sic] deliberation to rise above those flaws and injustices."[56] The Court made this statement when rejecting a challenge to a Michigan voter initiative that banned race-based affirmative action in the state's constitution. Yet the excising of affirmative action by Michigan voters in *Schuette v. Coalition to Defend Affirmative Action* hardly resembled an attempt to "confront persisting biases."[57] To the contrary, the Michigan referendum uniquely harmed racial minorities by allowing public universities in Michigan to continue admitting whites based on criteria like familial legacy—often a proxy for white racial advantage—but insisting that racial disadvantage could only be taken into account in admissions if approved by Michigan voters.

The Supreme Court's evisceration of a key portion of the Voting Rights Act of 1965 (VRA) in *Shelby County, Ala. v. Holder* also casts doubt on the principle that democracy is self-correcting.[58] Section 5 of the VRA had been a historically successful means of preventing voting discrimination in jurisdictions with long track records of such discrimination by requiring them to seek the federal government's permission before modifying their election laws. A conservative majority of the Court, led by Chief Justice John Roberts, found that Congress's attempt to correct the democratic flaw of racial discrimination in voting was itself flawed because Congress had not accounted for the progress the nation had made. According to the majority, "things have changed dramatically" since enactment of Section 5, and Congress's failure to account for the changes in the jurisdictions covered by Section 5 violated those states' right to "equal sovereignty."[59]

Ironically, then, the Court rested its insistence that Congress respond to modern circumstances on the decidedly dated legal construct of states' rights. Moreover, the very premise of *Holder*—that "things have changed dramatically"—counseled the *opposite* outcome in the case. If it is true that things have changed significantly, this very fact may lead whites to react adversely—the essence of whitelash. Whites now believe that people of color advance only at their expense.[60] This helps to explain the election of 2016, in which classical forms of racism appeared to galvanize white voters and, in any case, did not disqualify Trump, the purveyor of unmistakable prejudice.

So which strand of the Court's ballot-box jurisprudence should we follow— the interventionist model or the self-correcting model? I argue we should follow the better-reasoned approach, and, as you may have gathered, I believe the interventionist model is more compelling. I build on this point in Chapters 2 and 8. If we apply the Court's earlier, interventionist jurisprudence to Donald Trump's election, certainly his racial appeals — and his stated intent to harm certain racial groups — would be analogous to the racial animus underlying these referenda and initiatives that the Court held violated the Constitution. In addition to proposing a ban on Muslims entering the United States, for example, Trump also proposed surveilling mosques and compiling a database of Muslims living in the United States.[61] We may lack direct evidence that voters supported Trump because of these proposals; unlike a referendum or initiative, a candidate election involves multiple issues, not to mention candidates' personalities. A candidate's admixture of racist proposals with nonracist proposals, however, does not mitigate the role of race in his election. Indeed, the fact that Trump's racial rhetoric *was not disqualifying* in the eyes of tens of millions of white Americans is itself evidence of at least a healthy tolerance for racism. In any case, despite the difficulties in ascertaining voter intent in a candidate election as opposed to a referendum or initiative, these difficulties do not prevent application of the antidiscrimination principle; they merely warrant an adaptation of it.

ADAPTING ANTIDISCRIMINATION LAW TO CANDIDATE ELECTIONS

Antidiscrimination law's approach to ascertaining discriminatory intent in legislative statutes suggests how we might adapt our antidiscrimination norms to candidate elections. In *Hunter v. Underwood*, plaintiffs challenged Alabama's felony disenfranchisement law on grounds that it was enacted to keep African Americans from voting. Recognizing that states may pass statutes with multiple and divergent intentions, and that a statute may have both constitutional and unconstitutional purposes, the Court applied the following test:

> To establish a violation of the fourteenth amendment in the face of mixed motives, plaintiffs must prove by a preponderance of the evidence that racial discrimination was a substantial or motivating factor in the adoption of [the felony disenfranchisement statute]. They shall then prevail unless [Alabama] prove[s] by a preponderance of the evidence that the same decision would have resulted had the impermissible purpose not been considered.[62]

To put it simply, this test required those challenging a law to prove that discrimination was a major factor in the decision, *and* it required those defending the law to prove that the same decision would have been made in the absence of discrimination. *Underwood's* approach to discerning intent, and its allocation of the burdens of proof, should inform how we interpret voter conduct in candidate elections. First, we need not show that all voters who supported Trump were motivated by racial animus, or even that most were. It is enough if racial animus was a "motivating factor" in Trump's election, in the sense that it played a role in a significant number of individuals' decisions to support Trump. Second, while popular discourse has placed the burden of proving racial motive on the accuser, the law assigns the burden of proof—technically an affirmative defense—to the accused. That is, given the likelihood that race was at least a motivating factor in Trump's election, it is not enough for Trump supporters to simply deny the charge, insist on direct proof, or disclaim individual culpability. Instead, at least in legal terms, the burden shifts to them to demonstrate that Trump would have prevailed even if racist appeals had not been a prominent part of his campaign.

Apart from its helpful proof regimen, *Hunter v. Underwood* is yet another case that sets forth the antidiscrimination norm in the context of public deliberations—in this instance, legislative deliberations. Legislators deliberate on bills. Voters deliberate on whom to elect to pass those bills. If the Constitution does not permit legislators to enact racist laws, its antidiscrimination norms also counsel against the election of racist candidates. Candidate Trump's proposed "Muslim ban" exemplifies this point in a very practical way. As president, Trump changed his proposed ban on Muslims entering the country to one that instead banned citizens from six predominantly Muslim countries seeking entry into the United States.[63] The countries identified in President Trump's executive order were said to present a high risk of terrorism.

The state of Hawaii, among others, challenged the ban as a violation of the Establishment Clause of the First Amendment, claiming that it imposed a religious test for entry into the country. Despite the lack of any reference to religion in its text, a federal district court ruled against Trump's executive order, relying in large part on statements Trump made during the campaign in which he touted his position as a "total and complete shutdown of Muslims entering the United States."[64] Although the Supreme Court would ultimately reverse the district court on the narrow basis that presidents have unique authority over national security matters, Trump's divisive words as a candidate shadowed his actions as an elected official. If the candidate cannot disown his positions, how can his supporters? We do not vote for candidates a la carte; we must elect the whole person, in much the same way a court examining the constitutionality of a statute must examine both the permissible and impermissible reasons for its enactment. When a candidate has proffered anti-egalitarian reasons for his election, and voters nevertheless support him, their decision is as suspect as that of a legislature enacting an arguably unconstitutional statute or Trump's enacting his Muslim ban.

If candidate Trump, a businessman who had dealt with unions, had made these or any of his other racially inflammatory statements as an employer waging a successful fight against a union organizing campaign, the results would likely be invalidated. That is because the National Labor Relations Board (NLRB) bars the use of "racial propaganda in an irrelevant and inflammatory manner."[65] If he had deployed racial prejudice to win a union election, Trump would be required to prove that his racialized statements were true and relevant to the campaign. Imagine Trump attempting to demonstrate the truth or relevance of his ridiculous fib that President Obama was not born in the U.S. The NLRB prohibits racial appeals in union elections because of their insidious potential *in all types of elections*: "[I]t is self-evident that racial appeals, whether in union campaigns or in broader contexts, pollute the atmosphere necessary for a free and rational election because, when unrelated to an election campaign issue, they can only have the effect of inflaming passions and distorting the sober, informed exercise of the franchise."[66] A great irony of the 2016 presidential election is that Donald Trump could inject racially prejudiced statements into a national election that he would be prohibited from spewing to his own employees.

Consider again Trump's conduct in a candidate election in the political sphere. In a hypothetical VRA case under Section 2—a section left intact after *Shelby County, Ala. v. Holder*—Trump's racial propaganda and white voters' tolerance of it would constitute evidence of a violation.[67] Section 2 codifies the antidiscrimination norm articulated in the Fifteenth Amendment, which provides that "[t]he right of citizens of the United States to vote shall not be denied or abridged by the United States or by any State on account of race, color, or previous condition of servitude." Section 2 of the VRA, which applies nationwide, protects voters of all races from having their votes diluted because of their race. Dilution can occur in myriad ways, from outright denial of the right to vote, to gerrymandering that spreads voters of a specific race across so many districts that they are unable to constitute a majority in any district. Although Section 2 has been applied primarily to protect the rights of black and Latino voters, it has also been invoked in jurisdictions where whites are a minority.[68]

A court faced with determining liability under Section 2 must initially determine whether voting occurs along racial lines, a concept known as racially polarized voting. That is, a court must find that the plaintiffs' racial group, as a rule, prefers different candidates than the majority racial group and that, as a result, the plaintiffs' preferred candidates tend to lose elections. This inquiry into voter choice under Section 2 demonstrates yet again that the voter is not always right; our laws do not always defer to the will of the majority where racial minorities would be harmed. Section 2 therefore requires scrutiny of white voter choice in candidate elections. It also involves an examination of racial appeals made during campaigns, and the responsiveness of white elected officials to the needs of racial minorities.[69] Although Section 2 of the VRA does not require proof that the majority is motivated by racial animus, racially polarized voting can be a manifestation of majoritarian animus, just as its antithesis—in which members of majority and minority racial groups form winning coalitions—tends to demonstrate the absence of such animus. In this regard, Justice Clarence Thomas's bald assertion that "racially polarized voting is not evidence of unconstitutional discrimination" is counterintuitive, at best.[70] Section 2 is evidence of an antidiscrimination norm in candidate elections, even if the statute itself does not purport to regulate individual voters' choices.

The antidiscrimination norm extends further still. We cannot refuse to rent or sell housing on the basis of race.[71] Nor under federal law is racial discrimination allowed in any other type of transaction.[72] Title VII proscribes racial discrimination in the terms and conditions of Americans' employment.[73] Under Title VII, an employer's stated reasons for its decision to hire, fire, promote, or demote an employee are not taken at face value. Instead, plaintiffs are allowed to demonstrate that the employer's stated reasons for its actions are pretextual.[74] A pretext is a dishonest explanation or one that is unworthy of credence.[75] It is a common precept in antidiscrimination law that "[p]roof that the defendant's explanation is unworthy of credence is simply one form of circumstantial evidence that is probative of intentional discrimination, and it may be quite persuasive."[76]

Returning to the analogy of voters as employers, applying the antidiscrimination norm to candidate elections means probing, and at times rejecting as pretextual, voters' reasons for supporting a candidate. This is true even when, for example, a voter purportedly casts a ballot out of religious conviction, which is often thought to be an incontestable assertion. Yet courts have long probed the sincerity of religious beliefs to guard against circumstances in which such beliefs may be asserted fraudulently for self-interested purposes, as by a prison inmate seeking to avoid a condition of his confinement.[77]

None of the cases and laws surveyed thus far command a voter not to vote based on racial prejudice. They do, however, at least establish an ethos against doing so. I contend that millions of white voters departed from this ethos in supporting Donald Trump's candidacy and that many white voters routinely do the same when supporting racially divisive candidates up and down the ballot. Questions regarding the enforceability of a norm against voting based on racial prejudice are addressed in Chapters 7 and 8. For now, I turn to two preemptive arguments against the norm.

"BUT VOTERS ARE NOT RATIONAL"

An initial objection to antidiscrimination norms in voting is that voting, by its very nature, is an irrational process. Stated differently, if people have no obligation to vote rationally, it is irrational to expect them to abide by a nondiscrimination ethos and impractical to attempt to enforce one. The short answer to this critique is that legal norms often require us to behave in a better way than we would if they did not exist.

In *The Myth of the Rational Voter*, George Mason University economist Bryan Caplan analogizes irrationality to a commodity. Like most commodities, a voter's demand for irrationality depends on its costs to the voter. According to Caplan, voter irrationality, in the form of systematic biases on economic matters, is pervasive because the social costs of bad decision-making are spread across society. The economic costs of a bad decision for the individual voter pale in comparison to the mental cost of having to relinquish one's worldview. Caplan refers to this phenomenon as "rational irrationality."[78]

Other disciplines corroborate Caplan's economic theory. In 2004, Emory University political psychologist Drew Westen conducted neuroimaging of the brains of partisan men presented with evidence that both Democratic presidential candidate Senator John Kerry and Republican incumbent George W. Bush had made contradictory statements. Democrats were more critical of Bush's statements, and Republicans were more critical of Kerry's. The neuroimaging revealed that the portion of the brain associated with reasoning—the dorsolateral prefrontal cortex—played no role in eliciting the partisans' responses to the candidates' statements. Instead, the emotion circuits of the brain lit up when the subjects responded.[79]

To further illustrate irrationality's creeping influence on political discourse and choice, consider again candidate Trump's portrayal of President Obama as a foreigner. Trump's harassment of the first black president over his place of birth was as studied as his violent caricature of Mexican immigrants. It played to a base that was inclined to believe him no matter the evidence to the contrary. By the summer of 2016, five years after Obama had made his birth certificate public, 72 percent of registered Republicans still doubted his place of birth, compared with 20 percent of registered Democrats.[80] Moreover, Republican voters who were more informed about politics were just as likely to doubt the president's birthplace as less knowledgeable Republicans.[81] This is the archetype of motivated reasoning, in which the desired result determines the validity of the evidence rather than the other way around.[82]

In the face of this evidence of voters' irrationality, it is certainly fair to question the feasibility of an antidiscrimination norm in voting. Antidiscrimination law, however, does not accept irrationality as a defense. Indeed, under pretext theory, an employer's irrational explanation for preferring a white job applicant to a black one can be evidence of an intent to discriminate; a legislature's inability to articulate a rational basis for laws that draw distinctions between classes of citizens can invalidate its actions; and when a jury's verdict is inconsistent with the evidence, it is subject to being overturned. There is no good reason for affording greater latitude for irrationality at the ballot box. Moreover, according to the U.S. Supreme Court, the constitutional premise of most state regulation of elections is to facilitate "rational voter choices."[83]

Thus, regardless of the debates about whether voters are rational, our democratic framework rightly seeks to avoid or nullify the effects of irrationality rather than accommodate them. A system that acquiesced to voter irrationality would not aspire to the ideal articulated by the Supreme Court "to learn from its past mistakes; to discover and confront persisting biases; and ... to rise above those flaws and injustice."[84]

"WHAT ABOUT BLACK VOTERS' PREFERENCE FOR OBAMA?"

This book focuses on racist appeals and whether white voters, reacting adversely to the progress and population growth of racial minorities, embrace those appeals at the polls. Yet some would argue that racial appeals are not limited to figures on the right like Trump. Moreover, people of color, not just whites, might also embrace racial appeals. Finally, in some instances, such as the election of the first African American president, voting on the basis of race may actually be positive.

In the post-racial age, the mere mention of race is often dubbed racist.[85] This creates a conundrum whereby efforts to eradicate racism—presumed to be unnecessary in a post-racial society—are met with resistance under the guise of opposing racism. Thus, racism persists. It is easy to see how the rhetorical move to label all things pertaining to race as racist can be a self-serving dodge on the part of those seeking to enshrine racial inequality. Simply put, however, not all racial appeals are racist.

In seeking to become the first black mayor of Chicago in 1982, for instance, Harold Washington declared, "Chicago is a city divided where citizens are treated unequally and unfairly."[86] There was no mistaking whose unfair treatment Washington was referring to—blacks and Latinos. Indeed, as a condition of running, Washington, then a congressman from Chicago's South Side, insisted that his supporters register at least 50,000 new black voters.[87] Washington's campaign was undeniably predicated in part on a racial appeal to Chicagoans of color who believed that they had been mistreated under decades of machine politics run by and largely for whites. But contrast Washington's engagement of racial issues with that of his general election opponent, Republican Bernard Epton. Epton's campaign slogan was "Epton for Mayor … Before it's too late." Too late for what, though? The racial overtones of Epton's slogan were widely understood—support him, or the blacks will take over city hall.[88] To paraphrase Justice John Paul Stevens's defense of race-based affirmative action, the difference between Washington's seeking to include African Americans in city government versus Epton's "Before it's too late" slogan is the difference between "a welcome mat" and a "no trespassing" sign.[89]

Still, since African Americans tend to vote as a bloc in most elections—at least at the general election stage—this will tempt a false equivalence between them and white voters who bloc voted for Trump in the 2016 presidential election. Why, in other words, aren't black voters and other racial minorities who display political cohesion at the polls guilty of violating the antidiscrimination norm?

First, it's odd to level such a charge against black voters when black voters primarily support white candidates for most major elective offices, given the small numbers of minority candidates on major-party tickets. Despite blacks' constituting 13 percent of the nation's population, they account for less than 7 percent of its elected officials.[90] Black people have been voting primarily for white candidates since they obtained the unfettered right to vote. Although this does not preclude the possibility that their choices violate the antidiscrimination norm, the shortage of minority elected officials makes proof of a violation far more difficult.

Even when presented with the opportunity to elect an African American, blacks often choose white candidates over black candidates whose views on issues differ from their own. Former Congressman Artur Davis, who had voted against Obamacare, learned the hard way that ideology matters more than race to blacks. In 2010, Davis lost his bid to become the first black Democratic gubernatorial nominee in Alabama to a white candidate who secured most of the black vote.[91] Though isolated exceptions exist, the clear pattern is that black voters reject black candidates when an opposing white candidate is more liberal.[92]

Thus, black voters' rational consistency in voting in line with their economic and racial equality interests differentiates their bloc voting from white bloc voting. In other words, white voters' frequent mismatch of their economic interests with their preferred candidates' positions, often coupled with those candidates' racist appeals, casts credible suspicion that they are violating the antidiscrimination norm. It is reasonable, therefore, to probe whether many white voters' stated concerns are pretexts to cover up their racial animus.

None of the foregoing addresses a more nuanced issue: the election of Barack Obama as the first African American president. Race undoubtedly played a role, but it cut both ways. In *Obama's Race*, political scientists Michael Tesler and David Sears explain that while Obama faced significant racially resentful opposition—a clear breach of the antidiscrimination norm—he also benefited from a historic wave of racially liberal support.[93] Racial liberals, particularly white racial liberals, made a conscious decision to embrace Obama's candidacy in part because they would be electing the first African American president.[94]

A continuing debate in American constitutional law is when, if ever, the government may take race into account when making a decision. Despite the heat engendered by discussions of affirmative action and other racial remedies, the government is allowed to consider race when a compelling reason exists and when the use of race is narrowly tailored to advance that purpose.[95] In a candidate election, no less than in a referendum or initiative, voters become state actors—that is, they are the government. Thus, the question concerning racial liberals in 2008 is not whether they violated the antidiscrimination norm because they voted for Obama in part based on his race. The question, instead, is whether there was a compelling reason to do so. Here again, Justice Stevens's analogy of the welcome mat versus the "no trespassing" sign is apt. If Obama's election represented racial progress, what did Trump's election—fueled, as we shall see further in the next chapter, by racially resentful whites—represent? And which of these outcomes can reasonably be equated with advancing a compelling national interest?

2

The Exoneration of White Voters

"They're all the people I grew up with. They're their kids. And they're not racist. They're not sexist. But we didn't talk to them."

— Vice President Joe Biden, discussing the white working-class vote
in the aftermath of Trump's 2016 victory[1]

"Some people think that the people who voted for Trump are racists and sexists and homophobes and deplorable folks. I don't agree, because I've been there."

— Senator Bernie Sanders, 2016 runner-up for the Democratic presidential
nomination[2]

Donald Trump won 58 percent of the white vote to Hillary Clinton's 37 percent, a record-shattering 21 points, surpassing Ronald Reagan's 20-point margin in 1984.[3] These exit polling numbers nearly mirror a poll taken almost two months before the election. When asked whether they thought Trump was a "racist," 54 percent of whites responded no, while 37 percent said yes.[4] With contortionist logic, while 54 percent of whites believed that Trump was not a racist, 54 percent also believed that Trump "appeals to bigotry." It is implausible that there was no overlap among these 54-percenters, and it is equally implausible that both statements could be true at the same time. As sociologist Eduardo Bonilla-Silva has paradoxically observed, how can there be racism—here, appeals to bigotry—without racists?[5]

Under antidiscrimination law, "Direct evidence [of discrimination] typically consists of clearly sexist, racist, or similarly discriminatory statements or actions by the employer."[6] In November 2015, candidate Trump tweeted that 81 percent of white homicides are perpetrated by blacks.[7] According to the Federal Bureau of Investigations, the actual figure for that year is 15 percent. In June 2016, Trump misrepresented the black youth unemployment rate as 59 percent; the Bureau of Labor Statistics put the official number at

27.1 percent.[8] Ignoring slavery and Jim Crow, in September 2016, Trump proclaimed that "[o]ur African-American communities are in the worst shape they've ever been in before. Ever. Ever. Ever."[9] The reader should notice a pattern of racial stereotyping here.[10] Trump displayed this propensity time and again: contending that a judge of Mexican descent could not objectively evaluate fraud claims brought against him; berating illegal Mexican immigrants as rapists and criminals; and propagating the demeaning lie that President Obama was born in Kenya.

If Trump were an employer, his statements would constitute direct evidence of racial discrimination. Indeed, if he uttered these statements to his minority employees as regularly as he made them on the campaign trial, he'd be guilty of creating a racially hostile work environment.[11] In *Fulmore v. M&M Transport Services, Inc.*, the trial court treated a worker's statements "referring to it being cold on President Obama's inauguration day because it was a cold day in hell when he became President and saying it was a day when pigs flew" as evidence of racial harassment.[12] Similarly, in *Tribble-Toney v. Palmetto Health Baptist Hospital*, a black plaintiff whose supervisor made statements and sent emails referencing black stereotypes ("watermelon" and "fried chicken"), referring to the White House as the "Black House" under Obama, and calling Obama a "monkey" successfully stated a triable claim for a racially hostile work environment.[13] Trump's stereotypes of minorities' criminality and slothfulness, and his portrayal of Obama as a foreigner, carry racial connotations at least as plausible as those demonstrated in these cases. Our understanding of discriminatory conduct should not change merely because Trump's statements were uttered during a political campaign instead of in an employment context.

That a white voter could understand that Trump was appealing to bigotry but still not consider him a racist is a disturbing denial of reality. More insidious still is the mental block by a majority of Republicans—who are overwhelmingly white[14]—who believed that Trump neither appealed to bigotry nor was himself a bigot.[15] Ignorance would be an easy explanation, but as the author Ibram Kendi writes, "Ignorance is the byproduct of the racist coverup, not the source."[16] What would these same voters have concluded if candidate Barack Obama had made similar misstatements about *white* Americans?

These rationalizations by white voters propelled Trump to his record-setting margin among this cohort. Their conduct in 2016 disproved the Supreme Court's 2013 assertion in *Shelby County, Ala. v. Holder* that things had indeed "changed dramatically" enough to relax efforts to protect minorities in the election process.[17] If whites believe racial progress has come at their expense, then whitelash comes into play, and progress will be short-lived. It turns out, however, that it was not just the conservatives on the Supreme Court who were in denial about whitelash. Progressives like Vice President Joe Biden, Senator Bernie Sanders, and even filmmaker Michael Moore were also complicit.[18] So, too, were members of the learned class.

THE INNOCENT WHITE WORKING CLASS

Making excuses for white voters—working-class whites especially—is an incessant theme of post-2016 election analysis. Yet this objectification long preceded 2016's unexpected outcome. In academic circles, the white working class—which is difficult to define, as I address below—is said to enjoy only "marginal whiteness."[19] This concept purports to recognize the unequal distribution of white privilege and thereby contribute to a more nuanced consideration of working-class whites' views on racial issues.[20] More specifically, "[C]ontemporary discussions of white privilege may unwittingly fuel and even ignite hostility in marginal whites who might otherwise be allies in disrupting the effects of white privilege."[21]

Perhaps unwittingly as well, the theory of marginal whiteness is based on the concession that racial backlash is likely if whites (i) perceive racial equality concerns to conflict with their material interests, or (ii) are perceived as beneficiaries of racial privilege that they in fact cannot access. Rather than critiquing marginal whites' misdirection of their ire as inherently racialized, adherents to this theory often fault people of color for a lack of empathy. A case in point is Professor Lisa Pruitt, who has written: "Critical race theory has typically presented whiteness as monolithic. The existence of poor and working-class whites is sometimes acknowledged, their plight then quickly dismissed as nevertheless paling (no pun intended) in comparison to the plight of (low-income) blacks."[22]

Pruitt even attempts to explain working-class whites' voting against their economic interests as that group's attempt to separate themselves from poor whites who do not work. According to Pruitt, "Racial animus toward nonwhites is not necessarily implicated by these political choices. In some cases, the desire to differentiate oneself is greater among whites than between whites and other races."[23]

Absent in Pruitt's account is an explanation of the relationship of the black working class to nonworking poor blacks. Blacks, like whites, differentiate among themselves on the basis of class.[24] Yet unlike the white working class, the black working class does not oppose policies that might benefit the nonworking poor.[25] Indeed, unlike the white working class, blacks overwhelmingly believe that those who receive welfare have a genuine need for it.[26] Given these differences, a solely economic motivation for whites' political choices is unlikely.

Echoes of marginal whiteness theory could be heard loudly in analyses of the 2016 presidential contest. According to former MSNBC talk show host Krystal Ball, Democrats got their comeuppance because they "lectured a struggling people watching their kids die of drug overdoses about their white privilege. Can you blame them for calling bullshit?"[27] The runner-up for the Democratic nomination, Senator Bernie Sanders, likewise blamed Hillary Clinton's loss on too great a focus on "identity politics" rather than class-based economics:

> It is not good enough for somebody to say, "I'm a woman, vote for me." No, that's not good enough. What we need is a woman who has the guts to stand up to Wall Street, to the insurance companies, to the drug companies, to the fossil fuel industry.[28]

There is, however, one problem with this narrative: it does not take whites' racial identification into account. The assumption of white "racelessness" has long undergirded constitutional doctrine in ways that yield lessons for our understanding of voter behavior. In 1993, Professor Barbara Flagg argued that "the white person has an everyday option not to think of herself in racial terms at all. In fact, whites appear to pursue that option so habitually that it may be a defining characteristic of whiteness: to be white is not to think about it."[29] Thus, she argued, the discriminatory intent requirement of *Washington v. Davis* for finding violations of the Equal Protection Clause of the Fourteenth Amendment was flawed because race infiltrates whites' decision-making in unconscious ways. As a result, whites' self-conception of themselves as raceless lends an aura of equality to official decision-making by whites when in fact the decisions may be rooted in their unawareness of white racial privilege.[30]

At the time, Flagg's insight was celebrated in legal academic circles as a critical advancement toward the demolition of structural barriers to racial equality. In the years since, however, white race consciousness has evolved in ways other than the sort that Flagg advocated as a means of addressing racial privilege. Instead, a dangerously self-focused white race consciousness now coexists with unconsciousness of the ways in which white norms are equated with race neutrality.

A 2012 American National Election Studies (ANES) analysis asked white respondents, "How important is being white to your identity?" Thirty-four percent of whites indicated that their racial identity was either "extremely important" or "very important."[31] The study was repeated in 2013, at which point fully 40 percent of white respondents indicated that their racial identity was either extremely important or very important.[32] Fifty-two percent of white respondents indicated it was extremely important or very important that "whites work together to change laws that are unfair to whites."[33] The study concluded that these and other markers of white race consciousness were highly predictive of "negative affect toward Obama, endorsement that Republicans better represent whites compared to Democrats, and positive affect toward the Tea Party movement, even after controlling for racial resentment."[34]

A 2016 ANES study measured the effect of white race consciousness on candidate choice. Those respondents who felt their white identity was "extremely important" were 30 percentage points more likely to support Trump than those who ascribed no importance to their whiteness.[35] White Americans who concluded that whites face "a great deal" of discrimination were nearly 40 percentage points more likely to support Trump than those who believed that whites face no discrimination. Those whites who attributed white job loss to minority hiring were 50 percentage points more likely to support Trump than those who did not blame minorities. And whites who considered it extremely important for whites to work together to change laws that are unfair to whites were nearly 40 points more likely to support Trump.[36]

White race consciousness correlates significantly with measures of racial stereotyping and racial resentment.[37] Racial resentment is difficult to quantify. Typically, it is measured using questions that probe beyond what the respondent would say if bluntly asked, "Do you resent people of color?" Across varied measures of racial resentment, those ranking highest in this sentiment were more likely to support Trump. To begin with, a Gallup study demonstrated that the partisan divide on racial resentment between white Republicans, on the one hand, and white Democrats and independents, on the other, widened during the Obama presidency. The study used a "sympathy" index to measure white racial resentment. For instance, one of the eight questions asked was: "In general, do you think that blacks have as good a chance as whites in your community to get any kind of job for which they are qualified, or don't you think they have as good a chance?"[38] Whites' response that blacks have an equal chance is not supported by the objective data. Results of a 2017 study published in the *Harvard Business Review* revealed that hiring discrimination against blacks has not receded in the past quarter-century.[39] Thus, whites harboring the "equal chance" sentiment were deemed "unsympathetic" and high on the resentment scale for that question. When these sentiments were measured in the pre-Obama years of 2004 and 2007, white Republicans had a high overall racial resentment score of 0.87, on a scale of 0 to 1, with 1 being the most resentful.[40] During the same years, white Democrats had a lower resentment score of 0.73, a statistically significant difference.[41]

The Gallup study found that as the Obama presidency progressed, Republicans' racial resentment score remained unchanged while Democrats' racial resentment score decreased to 0.62 in 2015 and 2016, a statistically significant reduction.[42] What explains Republican stasis and Democratic progress? White flight. As political scientist Michael Tesler explains, "Racially prejudiced whites ... have increasingly left the Democratic Party during Obama's presidency—especially racially prejudiced whites without a college degree."[43] This transformation manifested itself during the 2016 presidential contest. According to Tesler's analysis, whites who believed that discrimination against whites is as big a problem as discrimination against minorities—again, a view without factual basis—were more likely to vote for Trump than they were to support the 2012 Republican nominee, Mitt Romney.[44] Similarly, whites who ranked high in ethnocentrism—the belief that whites are superior to racial minorities—were considerably more likely to support Trump than Romney.[45]

Tesler's findings were corroborated by another political scientist, Professor Thomas Wood, who analyzed ANES data from 1988 to 2016 to determine the correlation between racial animosity and voter choice. Using a different measure of white racial resentment toward minorities, the "symbolic racism scale," Wood concluded in reference to the 2016 presidential race that "[s]ince 1988, we've never seen such a clear correspondence between vote choice and racial perceptions. The biggest movement was among those who voted for the Democrat, who were far less likely to agree with attitudes coded as more racially biased."[46]

The transformation of racial attitudes among Democrats during the Obama era explains a puzzling phenomenon from the 2016 election: white voters who supported Trump after supporting Obama in 2008 or 2012. Progressive filmmaker Michael Moore insisted after the election, "They're not racist ... They twice voted for a man whose middle name is Hussein."[47] As evidenced by the appreciable decrease in Democrats' racial resentment score, however, more racially regressive Democrats existed at the start of Obama's presidency than toward the end. These Democrats voted for Obama because they were Democrats, not because they were racially progressive.[48] Indeed, 20 to 25 percent of whites *who opposed interracial dating* nevertheless supported Obama in 2008.[49]

In any case, voting for a black president can no more immunize a white individual from the charge of racial animus than a white employer's hiring, then firing, a black employee can. In employment discrimination law, a factfinder may deduce the lack of discrimination from the fact that the "same actor" hired and then, shortly thereafter, fired the minority plaintiff.[50] Yet such an inference is not mandatory, and, in any case, its evidentiary value is diluted by other circumstantial evidence of discrimination.[51] To be sure, President Obama was reelected in 2012—but with 10 percent fewer white voters than in 2008. Hillary Clinton's share of the white vote receded 14 percent from the Democrats' 2008 share. In assessing the Obama-to-Trump voters' racial motivations, we must examine not only the overtly racist appeals of Trump to which these voters may have responded, and the evidence of their racial resentment, but also Clinton's appeals to racial minorities, which likely stoked further resentment among this group.[52]

The racial resentment of Trump voters, taken together with evidence of heightened race consciousness, satisfies the Equal Protection Clause's intent-based standard that these voters made their decision at least in part "because of" race and not merely "in spite of" the harmful effects their support of Trump might have on racial minorities.[53] But is the same showing of discriminatory intent required in the context of a candidate election as in, for example, a legislature's enactment of a statute? As seen in Chapter 1, when the Supreme Court has treated the electorate as the lawmaker in cases involving referenda and initiatives, it has generally discerned the racial intent of the voters from the racial nature of the measure being voted upon and its adverse impact on minorities. *Schuette v. Coalition to Defend Affirmative Action*, the case involving an initiative on Michigan's public university admissions practices, is less a departure from this approach than it is a case in which the Court saw a factual distinction between state action that affirmatively injures people of color versus state action, namely affirmative action, that confers a "grant of favored status to persons in some racial categories and not others."[54]

Whatever the dubious merits of the Supreme Court's factual distinction in *Schuette*, Donald Trump racialized the 2016 election to the point where the discriminatory intent of many of his voters was as discernible as that of the voters who overturned California's fair housing law in *Reitman v. Mulkey*,[55] or the voters who overturned Akron's fair housing law in *Hunter v. Erickson*,[56] or those who overturned Seattle's desegregation program in *Washington v. Seattle School District No. 1*.[57]

In fact, Trump's racialization of the 2016 presidential contest was so successful that other Republican campaigns immediately copied it. In the 2017 Virginia gubernatorial race, Ed Gillespie—a lobbyist, former chairman of the Republican National Committee, and mainstream Republican—predicated his campaign on support for confederate monuments, opposition to sanctuary cities for illegal immigrants, and opposition to restoration of voting rights for ex-felons. Gillespie's race-baiting campaign ads, which included equating illegal immigrants with the violent MS-13 street gang allegedly rooted in Central America, shocked many Republicans, even leading some of his allies to lament, "[H]is TV ad campaign is gross."[58] Political scientist Norman Ornstein denounced Gillespie's ads as demonstrating "a level of amorality that even in rough-and-tumble politics is encouraging the worst instincts in people."[59] The overt racism of Gillespie's television ads dislodged few voters from the overwhelmingly white base of Virginia's Republican Party: Trump took 59 percent of the white vote in 2016, while Gillespie took 57 percent in 2017.[60]

As was the case with the Trump campaign nationally and in Virginia, Gillespie performed exceedingly well among whites without a college degree, winning this demographic by a staggering 46 points.[61] In 2016, Trump out-performed Hillary Clinton nationally among this group 67 percent to 28 per-cent, a 14-point decline from the group's support for Barack Obama in 2012.[62] Although these data may initially seem to support narratives of white working-class disaffection, a closer look reveals the larger underlying phenomenon of whitelash.

First, the intense focus on the white working class risks exculpating the much larger portion of Trump's coalition who were white and middle-class or white and well-off. An analysis of the 2016 ANES by professors Nicholas Carnes and Noam Lupus revealed that only 35 percent of white Trump voters made below the median household income of $50,000 annually.[63] Nearly two-thirds of Trump's support in the general election came from voters in the top half of the income distribution.[64] Although exit polls accounted for race and education, education level among whites is a poor proxy for class or income.[65] Twenty percent of white Trump voters without a college degree had household incomes in excess of $100,000.[66] A similar coalition of better-off white voters propelled Trump to the Republican nomination in the first place. Whitelash is a white problem, not just a problem of the white working class.

Second, the frequently assumed relationship between higher education levels and decreasing levels of prejudice is qualified significantly by partisan-ship. College-educated Republicans are 40 percentage points less likely than college-educated Democrats to believe that racism against blacks is prevalent, and they are 24 percentage points more likely to believe that racism against whites is widespread.[67] Indeed, according to a 2017 Gallup analysis for *The New York Times*, college-educated Republicans were *less likely* than non-college-educated whites to believe that racism against blacks was widespread (though they were also less likely than non-college-educated whites to believe that racism against whites was widespread).[68] In sum, in addition to conflating issues of education and class, popular post-election narratives fail to recognize that substantial resentment against minorities exists even at higher education levels.

Third, even using lack of a four-year degree as an imperfect stand-in for white working-class status, the lock that the New Deal coalition enjoyed on this demographic began to fray with the equality demands of various minority groups—especially blacks—during the 1960s.[69] Race was the principal force behind the exodus of the white working class from the Democratic coalition.[70] Democratic presidential candidates' vote share of the white working class declined 20 points, to 35 percent, between 1960 and 1972.[71] The subsequent economic turmoil of the 1970s and early 1980s—"stagflation" and declining wages and living standards—intensified racial resentment.[72] Yet flight from the Democratic Party was not limited to the white working class; middle-class whites' identification with the Democratic Party dropped substantially from 1962 to 2004.[73] The overall effect was a narrowing of partisan differences between the white upper class and the white working and middle classes.[74]

In effect, then, the white working and middle classes have been advancing the economic interests of the white upper class. If this sounds reminiscent of Thomas Frank's thesis in *What's the Matter with Kansas*, that is because it is. Frank, however, consciously eschews the role of race in his exposé on how the conservative movement and Republican Party duped the middle class into turning on itself. According to Frank, Kansas, representing middle America in general, "may shriek for concealed carry and gasp at imagined liberal conspiracies; but one thing it doesn't do is racism."[75] This is a curious claim to make about the very state out of which *Brown v. Board of Education*[76] arose and whose recent secretary of state, Kris Kobach, was the leading figure in national efforts to restrict access to the ballot under the false guises of preventing illegal immigrants from voting and stopping unproven voter fraud.[77] Whether the focus is on Frank's American "heartland," or elsewhere, the post-Civil Rights era history of white voter behavior is simply too entangled with race to minimize its role.

This history underscores the significant limitations of marginal whiteness theory and Senator Bernie Sanders's call for a focus on class rather than identity politics. From the very beginning of their exodus from the Democratic Party in the 1960s, white voters have been responding to something more pernicious than their class interests. In 2016, a Gallup study of 87,000 participants cast doubt on many of the assumed motivations of Trump supporters. Voters who expressed support for Trump were not worse off economically than those who expressed opposition, and they were more likely to be employed full-time than to be unemployed or employed part-time.[78] Although Trump railed against the vagaries of globalization and U.S. trade agreements, the study revealed that Trump supporters were only "slightly" more likely to work in industries facing stiff competition from global trade and immigration; indeed, many of Trump's supporters were business owners and managers who benefit from global competition.[79]

Finally, although Trump made illegal immigration—and, at times, legal immigration—the centerpiece of his campaign, the study showed that those who favored Trump typically lived in zip codes without substantial racial or cultural diversity. With other factors held constant, the study demonstrated higher support for Trump in "white, segregated enclaves, with little exposure to blacks, Asians, and Hispanics."[80] The authors cited contact theory as a possible explanation, noting that this degree of social homogeneity may breed cultural alienation and mistrust among Trump supporters.[81]

WHAT GOES AROUND COMES AROUND

Exploring the racialized motivations of Trump supporters, or white voters generally, is not intended to diminish the economic hardship that many whites face. Whitelash, however, is an invidious reaction by white Americans to their perception of diminished economic opportunity and to cultural change. The secrecy of the ballot box, together with the widespread notion that voters are free to be irrational, leads us to ignore that whitelash is also a negation of our nation's social and legal norms of equality.

Because it so often calls upon whites to undercut their own economic self-interests, whitelash makes them complicit in maintaining the economic unfairness that supposedly creates their angst in the first place. At a minimum, this diminishes their moral standing and political credibility. As I have written elsewhere,

> [W]hen a controlling majority in a liberal democracy experiences hardship at the hands of its own *chosen* government, the inequality it suffers is different in kind than that imposed on a racial minority whose electoral choices are often different. In short . . . white Americans have often gotten what they voted for even when it has not been good for them.[82]

Still, the economic vagaries and social ills being visited upon segments of white Americans are poignant. In June 2016, the Obama White House issued a report documenting the continued decline in the share of American men of prime working age (25–64 years) participating in the workforce—that is, either employed or looking for employment. In 1964, there was virtually no difference in the labor force participation rates (LFPRs) of men with a college education and those with a high school diploma or less. By 2015, however, the LFPR for men with only a high school diploma or less had dropped by 14 points to 83 percent, while the rate for college-educated men declined only modestly.[83] The United States now has the second lowest male LFPR among industrialized countries.

The decline in the male LFPR is symptomatic of what economists call labor force polarization—the disappearance of jobs requiring moderate skills and providing a middle-class standard of living, and the concomitant growth of low-skill and high-skill occupations.[84] Although the causes of polarization are the subject of academic debate, the hollowing of America's manufacturing sector is a significant contributor,[85] with more than forty thousand manufacturing facilities in the U.S. closed or idled since 1989.[86] The effects of this deindustrialization on different demographic groups have been asymmetrical. The LFPR for black men of prime working age has historically been lower than that of whites or Latinos, and that gap has grown even wider.[87] The LFPR among prime-age white males has fallen to the point where it converges with that of Latinos, which has been stable for the past two decades.[88]

Although millions of prime-age men of all races who hold only high school diplomas or less are being idled by a deindustrializing economy, race played a role in how this condition came to be and in how the decline in American manufacturing was used as a wedge issue in 2016. Blacks and Latinos—both less educated on average than whites—have historically constituted a disproportionate share of the manufacturing sector. This imbalance has contributed to a demeaning view of manual labor in the U.S.[89] Moreover, Trump's rhetoric about the offshoring of manufacturing jobs, which he deployed to rally whites in the upper Midwest and elsewhere, has a whiff of déjà vu. Those same jobs had migrated from the inner cities of St. Louis, Detroit, and Cleveland, wreaking havoc on the lives of the black working class.[90] Empathy for the fed-up white working class did not extend to these broken black and brown city dwellers. As the author Louis Uchitelle writes, "[W]e blame working-age people themselves for the departure of manufacturing from urban neighborhoods. The blame falls particularly on African Americans: if only they would get themselves educated, this line of reasoning goes, jobs would materialize."[91]

But what goes around, comes around. Whites in the bottom quintile of the income distribution now face living conditions comparable to those that poor blacks have long suffered.[92] Historically, to be white and working-class has never meant the same as to be black and working-class, either materially or with respect to basic freedoms: working-class whites, after all, could still access public goods and spaces denied to African Americans.[93] But now to be white and working-class means having to compete with minorities and women, who previously faced many more discriminatory barriers, for a shrinking number of "good jobs." The "psychological wage" of whiteness—that is, the intangible sense of being better-off simply because one is nonblack—simply is not what it used to be.[94] Neither is the real wage. The real median hourly wage for white men with only a high school diploma declined from $19.79 in 1979 to $17.50 in 2014.[95]

These changes have wrought despair among the white working class. Even though blacks and Latinos on average are less well-off and more vulnerable to economic downturns, members of the working class among these groups are more optimistic for their children's future and report greater faith in the power of education to improve their lots than their white working-class compatriots.[96] This despair has been attributed to a rise in the number of suicides, drug overdoses, and alcoholism-related deaths among less educated, middle-aged whites.[97]

Amid this climate of decline, Trump's margin of victory among non-college-educated whites was the largest of any Republican nominee since 1980.[98] More striking, though, is that Hillary Clinton lost non-college-educated white men by more than three to one (71 percent to 23 percent).[99] Among nonwhites with no college degree—the closest analog the exit polls permit—Clinton prevailed 76 percent to 20 percent. Meanwhile, among all black men, Clinton bested Trump 82 percent to 13 percent. Given the common ravages of postindustrialism that cast a low ceiling on the life chances of non-college-educated men whether black, brown, or white, what explains their divergent political preferences in the 2016 election? Is the white working class offloading blame for its declining standard of living on people of color?

Probably. And so are other whites who find themselves in greater precarity than they are accustomed to. Ask a Trump voter whether "average Americans have gotten less than they deserve," and a whopping 64 percent agree.[100] Substitute "blacks" for "average American," and the number falls to 12 per-cent.[101] Consider, also, that only 19 percent of whites believe that they have been denied a job because of their race.[102] Yet, more than twice this number (40 percent) agree that "many whites are unable to find a job because employ-ers are hiring minorities instead."[103] More curious still, as of 2015, a majority of whites (52 percent) agreed with the view that "[t]oday discrimination against whites has become as big a problem as discrimination against blacks and other minorities."[104]

Why does a group whose members have experienced so little discrimination so readily blame discrimination? It would surely require uncommon compartmentalization for white voters harboring these kinds of ill-founded beliefs to have gone to the polls in the racialized atmospherics of 2016 and not to have been influenced by their own predispositions.

UNREALISTIC (AND "TRANSPARENTLY WHITE") EXPECTATIONS

We should not be surprised by any of this. Yet our polity (and our jurisprudence) assumes that even during perceived scarcity of opportunity, white Americans can preternaturally abide by equality norms, not turn inward, and not blame the "other." Even the political left embraces such magical thinking, as in former vice president Joe Biden's characterization of Trump's white supporters as "not racist" and "not sexist." A failure to reckon with race, however, is itself a symptom of race's continuing salience. Biden, Sanders, and other progressives resist seeing average white Americans as perpetrators of racial caste divisions because, to them, white decision-making is presumed to be, as Professor Flagg noted, transparent or raceless. If we view racism as deviant and whiteness as a norm largely immune to its influences, even the election of Donald Trump can be rationalized as simply a failure to talk the right way to white voters.

A less superhuman image of white Americans in the age of globalization, economic precarity, and cultural change would acknowledge their frailty. In a striking—yet entirely coincidental—parallel to the opioid epidemic dispro-portionately pummeling white Americans, clinical psychologists have begun to explore the addictive properties of white privilege. Reference to "privilege" can be misleading. In the current context, it's best understood as a set of perquisites to which one has become accustomed, whether consciously or unconsciously. Psychologists James E. Dobbins and Judith H. Skillings describe the interplay of addiction and racial privilege in this fashion:

> Racism takes many forms, some of which are readily identified as being grounded in white supremacist values; most, however, are far more subtle and easier to overlook within ourselves. Habitual access to power ... can create an insidious reliance on the source of that power; in seeking to sustain their sense of wellbeing, individuals in the dominant culture become addicted to the perquisites of power. Thus, while it would be simpler to think of racism as an ingroup/outgroup phenomenon that will fade with cross-group contact, the proper framing of this problem requires that we probe more deeply into the addictive properties of racism.[105]

If a white man is not used to competing against people of color and women for a job, the lack of competition can become a condition to which he grows accustomed. What happens when this advantage is curtailed, as it has been by civil rights laws and the increased educational attainment of minorities and women?

Equating whiteness with race neutrality—Flagg's "white transparency"— would lead us to predict neutral decision-making by employers, and no racial resentment by whites adversely affected by the new rules. But not even whites themselves believe this. Many have told pollsters bluntly that they resent the changed racial landscape in our country. Even in the face of continuing minority inequality, 40 percent of Trump supporters believed that people of color have "too much influence."[106] Indeed, a June 2016 Gallup poll revealed that 59 percent of Republicans, and 41 percent of all white respondents, believed that "too much attention is paid to race and racial issues in the U.S. today."[107] Many whites, Republicans in particular, are fleeing the issue of race—except when they choose to blame it for their plight.

Dobbins's and Skillings's addiction taxonomy would describe white voters' behavior as exhibiting a number of defense mechanisms. The frustration–aggression–displacement mechanism describes whites' attempts to scapegoat members of the non-dominant group for problems for which they are not at fault or that have nothing to do with them.[108] Relatedly, ego defense targets members of the non-dominant group for blame to avoid confronting personal deficiencies that threaten one's ego.[109] White voters who blame minorities and illegal immigrants—who do not and cannot control the levers of political power—for the country's ills exhibit such defense mechanisms.

White Americans additionally rationalize their racial privilege in various ways.[110] Even as growing numbers of whites complain about discrimination against whites, a 2015 *New York Times* survey found that most whites (55 percent) believe blacks and whites have an equal chance of advancing in today's society.[111] The same survey, however, revealed that a supermajority of white respondents (68 percent) reported having regular contact with only "a few" blacks or none at all.[112] Thus, when white people opine that equal opportunity exists among the races, they do so from a position of relative racial isolation. Yet, researchers have found that white Americans' underestimation of race-based economic disparity is not primarily a function of lack of information, but is instead shaped by motivational forces that encourage their denial of racial inequality.[113] From this vantage point, whites speak of equal opportunity even as they rely on racially homogenous social networks for job opportunities that remain unavailable to people of color who are separated from whites' social spheres.[114] White people tell themselves a story about meritocracy that could just as easily be about racial exclusivity.[115]

Similar rationalizations prevent many whites from acknowledging either their own racial prejudice or that of a candidate they support. We see the latter exculpatory move by those whites who refused to even acknowledge that Donald Trump appealed to bigotry during his 2016 campaign. Dobbins's and Skillings's work suggests an explanation for these voters' denial: selective comparison. Like the alcoholic who applauds himself for drinking only after work while other addicts imbibe continuously, white Americans compare themselves favorably to a benchmark of overt racism.[116] If Jim Crow isn't as bad as slavery, how can Jim Crow be bad? And if Trump isn't as bad as George Wallace in 1968 or segregationist presidential candidate Strom Thurmond in 1948, how can Trump be bad? Thus, claiming that the nation's first black president was in fact not eligible to be president is not as bad as calling him a "nigger." And so on. Selective comparison uses the nation's vile history of inhumanity against people of color to justify modern mutations of that inhumanity that are "not as bad."

Dobbins and Skillings's addiction framework is a useful analogy even if one might argue with the underlying science. Think about any habit you have, particularly one that is especially personal in nature. What are the chances of kicking it cold-turkey? What are the chances of never relapsing? And if someone else forced you to drop the habit, might you feel resentment toward those imposing the change on you or toward third parties who may benefit from the change? Finally, might you resist the change? Until America can see itself as recovering from an addiction to racial caste—a recovery that entails relapses such as whitelash—it will never fully understand how Donald Trump ascended to the presidency or why more figures like Trump may be yet to come.

THE ANTIDISCRIMINATION NORM REVISITED

Think back to Ed Gillespie's 2017 gubernatorial campaign in Virginia. It's unusual for a major campaign to run television ads opposing the restoration of voting rights for ex-felons. Gillespie was appealing to the view that in a democracy, voting is a privilege afforded only to those who abide by the social contract.[117] But what happens when voters themselves breach the social contract by voting out of animus against their fellow citizens? The social contract consists of more than positive (i.e., statutory) law. In fact, it consists of norms that sometimes may be the antithesis of positive law. Consider Martin Luther King Jr.'s letter from a Birmingham jail, in which he wrote:

> An unjust law is a human law that is not rooted in eternal law and natural law. Any law that uplifts human personality is just. Any law that degrades human

personality is unjust. All segregation statutes are unjust because segregation distorts the soul and damages the personality. It gives the segregator a false sense of superiority and the segregated a false sense of inferiority."[118]

Where King relied on the force of "eternal law" or "natural law" to establish the norms on which the social contract rests, I rely on the laws that were passed or newly enforced in the wake of the Civil Rights Movement to establish an antidiscrimination norm that forbids invidious discrimination in every citizen's voting decision. Although I expand on this reasoning in later chapters, the following illustration gives context to what the reader has consumed so far. Quite apart from the social contract, U.S. antidiscrimination law forbids racial discrimination in private contracts:

> All persons within the jurisdiction of the United States shall have the same right in every State and Territory to make and enforce contracts ... as is enjoyed by white citizens, and shall be subject to like punishment, pains, penalties, taxes, licenses, and exactions of every kind, and to no other."[119]

Imagine that a white Trump voter declined to give a person of color a job because, to use language from one of the surveys cited in this chapter, "many whites are unable to find a job because employers are hiring minorities instead." This would be a race-based refusal to enter into a contract and hence would be illegal. To be sure, extracting such a confession from a white employer would ordinarily be difficult. Yet we have direct evidence (i.e., confessions) that a substantial number of white voters hold these views. In other words, whites are permitted to behave in the voting booth in a discriminatory manner that we do not tolerate in private spheres such as employment.

This cannot be the way American democracy is intended to function.

3

White Voters and the Law of Alternative Facts

"Same untruths from an utterly untruthful president."

> —Republican Senator Bob Corker, responding to a tweet by President Trump, October 24, 2017[1]

"We did not become great by calling true things fake."

> —Republican Senator Jeff Flake, criticizing Trump during a speech announcing his retirement from the U.S. Senate, October 24, 2017[2]

"If our leaders seek to conceal the truth and we as people become accepting of alternative realities that are no longer grounded in facts, then as an American people we are on a pathway to relinquishing our freedom."

> —Former Trump Secretary of State Rex Tillerson, May 16, 2018[3]

It's highly unusual for a sitting president's truthfulness to be questioned as pointedly by members of his own party as President Trump's has. Then again, perhaps no president has expressed as conflicted a relationship with the truth as Trump. In an unintended spoof of George Washington's fabled "I cannot tell a lie," Trump has explained, "I always want to tell the truth. When I can, I tell the truth. And sometimes it turns out to be where something happens that's different or there's a change, but I always like to be truthful."[4]

Even more remarkable still is the degree to which Republicans have become accustomed to the transparent falsehoods of the leader of the free world. According to *The Washington Post*'s Fact Checker, Trump made 8,158 false or misleading statements during his first two years in office.[5] The president averaged 5.9 false or misleading statements a day in his first year in office and tripled that number during his second. Commenting on Trump's dishonesty, presidential historian Robert Dallek observed: "Politicians lie, but this is different."[6]

Despite his obvious tendency toward mendacity, Trump's approval rating among Republicans after two years in office was 87 percent, according to a January 2019 Gallup poll.[7] During the first eleven months of his term, it ranged from a high of 89 percent to a low of 78 percent.[8] Clearly, then, Trump supporters either have a high threshold for untruths uttered by the president or, as embracers of "alternative facts" themselves, do not distinguish truth from falsity. Either characteristic is misplaced in a democracy, particularly one that aspires to be free of racial bias.

Imagine yourself as the defendant in a criminal trial for felony assault. The jury rejects your defense that you were acting in self-defense. Later, after the verdict against you, your attorney discovers that two jurors said they were voting to convict you because you reminded them of "one of those black gangbangers, the type who have been making our streets unsafe." Your attorney seeks a new trial because the verdict was contaminated by bigotry.

If such an off-color utterance during jury deliberations seems unlikely, consider *Peña-Rodriguez v. Colorado*. In that case, a defendant of Mexican descent was charged with sexual assault.[9] During deliberations, one juror opined that he "believed the defendant was guilty because, in [his] experience as an ex-law enforcement officer, Mexican men had a bravado that caused them to believe they can do whatever they wanted to with women." The U.S. Supreme Court held that the Sixth Amendment right to an impartial jury trial meant that the juror's statements could be used to impeach (discredit) the verdict.[10]

Decided less than a month before 2016's racialized election elevated Donald Trump to the presidency, Justice Kennedy's opinion for the Court in *Peña-Rodriguez*, though referring only to the Sixth Amendment, seemed to hold true for democracy generally. Kennedy observed that the jury system was "central to democracy," that it was "a tangible implementation of the principle that the law comes from the people," and that the use of racial stereotypes in the deliberative process would cause "systemic loss of confidence" in the jury system.[11] By extension, the Court concluded, racial stereotypes and democracy are incompatible given "the promise of equal treatment under the law that is so central to a functioning democracy."[12]

This decision, coming as it did at the height of a racially fraught election, raises a constitutional question: What happens when an election—which, like the jury system, is "central to democracy" and "a tangible implementation of the principle that the law comes from the people"—is infected by racial bias?

And if unchecked racial bias would cause "systemic loss of confidence" in the jury system, what effect might it have on deliberative democracy?

Peña-Rodriguez illustrates that our legal system and our democracy both depend on fidelity to facts and a commitment to nondiscrimination, the former facilitating the latter. Without fidelity to truth and nondiscrimination, democracy cannot fulfill its duty—again in the words of Justice Kennedy—"to learn from its past mistakes; to discover and confront persisting biases; and by respectful, rationale [sic] deliberation to rise above those flaws and injustices."[3] Democracy, in short, cannot function.

In this chapter, I explore a proposition that has been hidden in plain view about Donald Trump and those who helped elect him: people who have an attenuated relationship with facts of all types are more likely to have a conflicted relationship with facts about people of different racial backgrounds. When a voter's perception of the "other" influences his vote, "alternative facts" about that voter's social position vis-à-vis people of color are as concerning as the white juror's stereotypes about Mexican men in *Peña-Rodriguez*. A disdain for—or, put more gently, a selective appreciation of—facts is simply the historical modus operandi for achieving discriminatory objectives, as documented by Ibram Kendi in *Stamped from the Beginning*.[14] Yet law is the pursuit of truth. And a democracy predicated on the rule of law must likewise have truth as an overriding value, even if the conclusions that flow from uniform facts might be divergent. A principal way in which law pursues truth, but where our democracy has allowed laxity, is to view with skepticism explanations that do not add up. Antidiscrimination law in particular denudes untruths on which racial stereotypes rest by piercing the rationalizations that mask them. On this understanding, it is not plausible to view Trump or his supporters as merely unenlightened; instead, they had and have active agency in the cultivation of a racialized national political milieu.

Here, we return to the concept of pretext, a tool widely used in employment discrimination litigation to detect status-based bias. Analogizing voters' embrace of alternative facts to an employer's use of pretext to hide or rationalize discrimination permits us to test individual voters' rationale for their candidate choice in a similar fashion as the law would test an employer's explanation for not hiring a particular employee. Pretext need not be an outright lie: an employer's explanation that elicits incredulity might qualify as pretextual. In the same way, a voter's explanation might initially seem rational but become suspect when viewed in the context of other factors suggesting racial resentment, such as those discussed in Chapter 2. How does the law determine whether an explanation is valid or a pretext? I explore this question—and how we can use it to explain voters' choices—after discussing more fully the idea of "alternative facts" as a prism through which voters view racial issues. What happens if race is mixed with legitimate factors? And in some situations, can facts be justifiably disregarded in reaching a decision? These questions are common to both law and voting, and I explain in this chapter how legal precepts can help us to understand voters' candidate choices that, strictly speaking, may not be the result of pretext but that nonetheless suggest that voters were motivated by racial considerations.

WHO'S AFRAID OF FACTS?

Trump presidential counselor Kellyanne Conway famously defended press secretary Sean Spicer's inflated estimates of the crowd size for President Trump's 2017 inauguration by deeming Spicer's numbers "alternative facts."[5] The interviewer immediately reminded her that alternative facts are simply falsehoods. Yet the 2016 presidential campaign involved parallel universes in which diametrically opposed contentions could, depending on the eye of the beholder, both be true. The depth of this reality divide is illustrated by the national dissonance on issues about which there simply can be no disagreement.

For instance, during Barack Obama's two terms as president, the stock market rose by 150 percent, the third-largest rise during any presidency since World War II.[16] Yet 39 percent of Trump voters believed that the stock market had decreased, while 57 percent of all Republicans believed the same.[17] Just 9 percent of Democrats concurred.[18] A staggering 67 percent of Republicans believed that unemployment went up during Obama's presidency even though the unemployment rate was at a nine-year low of 4.7 percent when Obama left office.[19] Twenty-six percent of Democrats believed unemployment increased.[20] And despite Obama's signature achievement of enacting the Affordable Care Act ("Obamacare"), which decreased the number of Americans without health insurance coverage to historic lows, 40 percent of Republicans believed that the uninsured rate increased, compared with 24 percent of Democrats.[21]

The aversion to facts among Republican voters extends beyond economic issues. Forty percent of Republicans believe that Trump won the presidential popular vote, nearly six times the percentage of Democrats who think so. Clinton outpaced Trump by nearly 3 million votes.[22] Republicans are also significantly more likely to believe that millions of illegal votes were cast in the 2016 presidential election, a claim propagated by Trump to explain his popular vote loss, but for which there is no evidence.[23]

It is not only Republicans who permit their partisan lenses to skew reality. During Donald Trump's first 15 months as president, the stock market rose, but not in the eyes of most Democrats: while two-thirds of Trump supporters correctly noted the stock market's acceleration, only 35 percent of Clinton voters did.[24] The same polarity exists in perceptions of the economy. Prior to Trump's election, 61 percent of Democrats believed that the economy was improving; only 16 percent of Republicans agreed.[25] Merely days after the election, 49 percent of Republicans believed the economy was improving, while the proportion of Democrats who agreed declined to 46 percent.[26]

That partisanship affects both Republicans' and Democrats' perceptions of the state of the nation should not, however, misguide us to a facile equivalence between groups of voters. It is important to understand the difference between misinformed and uninformed voters. Political scientists have long lamented the uninformed voter who is oblivious to basic facts about our democracy and functionally illiterate about policy.[27] More pernicious, however, is the misinformed voter: a person confidently armed with wrong "facts."[28] Misinformed voters actively resist correction to their wrongly held facts. Why? Their preferences, or worldviews, influence their processing of facts.[29] These preferences guide the inferences these voters make when facts are unknown. The problem is that these inferences will not be objective but will be biased toward the misinformed voter's worldview. Once committed to memory, these biased inferences are treated like facts by the misinformed voter.[30]

Although the misinformed voter is not impervious to correction of wrongly held facts, the extent to which such attempts will be successful is a matter of scholarly debate.[31] Indeed, evidence suggests that efforts to correct misperceptions can intensify the misinformed voter's wrongheadedness, creating a "back-fire effect."[32] This is a shade beyond the concept of motivated reasoning, which posits that individuals are biased toward and seek to gather evidence and facts that further their desired outcome.[33] Motivated reasoning has a veneer of objectivity because there is at least some concern with appearing reasonable. Not so with the back-fire effect: nonfacts are clung to regardless of whether a disinterested party would find them persuasive.

A candidate with as casual a relationship to the truth as Donald Trump would obviously benefit from misinformed voters, and focus groups of Trump's supporters indicated that many of them fit this mode.[34] Yet partisan differences in respect for facts and expert knowledge predate Trump's ascendency. The polarization that marks contemporary American politics has been long in the making and developed asymmetrically—that is, Republicans have moved further to the right from the political center than Democrats have moved to the left. Thus, political scientists Thomas E. Mann and Norman

J. Ornstein conclude in their bestseller *It's Even Worse Than It Looks* that Republicans have become "an insurgent outlier—ideologically extreme; contemptuous of the inherited social and economic policy regime; scornful of compromise; *unpersuaded by conventional understanding of facts, evidence, and science*; and dismissive of the legitimacy of its political opposition."[35]

Political psychology research reveals that conservatives exhibit a greater propensity to believe information concerning threats than information concerning benefits.[36] The opposite is true of progressives. This propensity helps to explain the embrace of implausible conspiracy theories among conservatives, such as the 2015 canard that a military exercise during the Obama administration was intended to occupy and impose martial law on Texas. In response to reports in the right-wing blogosphere, the governor of Texas ordered the state's National Guard to track the military exercise.[37]

Perceived threats, of course, come in different forms. A proliferating body of scholarship on the 2016 election rejects the economic explanation for Trump's margin of victory among white voters and instead points to "status threat" as pivotal. University of Pennsylvania political scientist Diana Mutz, for instance, conducted a panel study consisting of the same voters from the 2012 and 2016 presidential elections. While finding little correlation between voters' individual economic circumstances and their likelihood of voting for Trump, Mutz found a significant relationship between voters' social dominance orientation (SDO) and support for Trump.[38] SDO is measured through questions intended to ascertain animus toward outgroups—that is, minorities—and a preference for hierarchy over equality. SDO increases within a dominant group when its members feel threatened.[39] SDO increased significantly from 2012, and, ironically, the presidency of Barack Obama partially accounts for this increase. That is because black success breeds white insecurity, which in turn accelerates SDO.[40]

Other post-election studies have identified this apprehension among white voters as a fear of "cultural displacement." A 2017 Public Religion Research Institute (PRRI) survey of nearly 3,000 participants concluded that in addition to partisanship, the strongest predictors of support for Trump among the white working class, who constitute a plurality of the adult public (33 percent), were fears concerning immigration and cultural displacement.[41] Cultural displacement was measured in three ways: (1) 65 percent of white working-class respondents believed that the American way of life had deteriorated since the 1950s (even though de jure segregation existed in much of the country then); (2) 68 percent of this demographic believed that the American way of life must be protected from foreign influence; and (3) nearly half of the white working class said that the pace of cultural change made them feel like strangers in their own country. Those respondents exhibiting fear of cultural displacement were three and a half times more likely to vote for Trump than those who did not.[42] Heightened SDO and fear of cultural displacement do not necessarily correlate with economic insecurity. Despite their preference for Trump, a CNN/Kaiser poll taken prior to the 2016 election found that almost 63 percent of the white working class were actually satisfied with their own personal financial circumstances.[43] Moreover, the PRRI study concluded that working-class whites in worse economic conditions were, in fact, somewhat more likely to support Hillary Clinton than Donald Trump.[44]

Trump's campaign brilliantly played to white voters' fears. One day the boogeyman was Mexicans, the next Muslims. Blacks had their turn when Trump fabricated FBI statistics about black-on-white murders and villainized the Black Lives Matter movement. There was China and its theft of American jobs. There was Barack Obama, the "foreign-born" president who was so incompetent that when he left office he handed Trump a rebounding economy with the lowest unemployment rate in nine years. Notice a pattern here? So much of Trump's fearmongering was done on the backs of people of color—too much to be coincidental. Trump's ability to exploit misinformed voters was matched by his penchant for stoking their worst racial instincts.

A LOVING ELECTORATE?

In America, we take for granted that the government cannot punish citizens for associating with others as they choose. Our second-nature comprehension of this First Amendment right is rooted in a long line of Supreme Court precedents. Thus, voters have a right to associate with the party of their choice.[45] They cannot generally be deprived of government employment on the basis of their political affiliation.[46] They have a right to associate with and vote for the candidate of their choice, subject only to reasonable and evenly applied electoral regulations.[47] And they have a right to contribute money to their preferred candidate and an even broader right to make independent expenditures on behalf of that candidate.[48]

But what happens when it is not government itself that is discriminating against citizens on the basis of their associations with other citizens, but rather citizens as citizens carrying out this associational chauvinism? To appreciate how this can happen—and, in the 2016 election, did happen—and the role that racialized alternative facts played, it helps to step back from politics for a moment.

In 1967 the U.S. Supreme Court, in *Loving v. Virginia*,[49] struck down antimiscegenation laws forbidding interracial marriages. This case was not

technically a freedom of association case, though the right of intimate association was restricted by anti-miscegenation laws. The associational discrimination in *Loving* was based on crude racial stereotyping: Virginia sought "to
preserve the racial integrity of its citizens," "to prevent the corruption of
blood," and to avoid the "obliteration of racial pride."[50]

Fifty years removed from *Loving*, it seems shocking that Virginia's law was
defended on such unabashed grounds of white supremacy. Yet what is the
difference between seeking to preserve "racial integrity" in *Loving* and seeking
to preserve the "American way of life," untainted by "foreign influence," in the
2016 election?[51] And if we should rightly be embarrassed by the America
portrayed in *Loving* 50 years ago, what explains the supermajority of working-
class whites (65 percent) who appear to pine for the 1950s today?[52] Indeed, in
a literal sense, the underlying racial animus that *Loving* attacked remains with
us today and manifests itself in a clear partisan divide: in 2018, 28 percent of
Republicans versus 12 percent of Democrats found interracial marriage to be
"morally wrong."[53]

The difference between segregation under *Loving* and segregation at
the voting booth is simply this: where Virginia sought to enforce the
separation of the races, white voters in 2016 who feared cultural displacement were far more likely to *voluntarily* disassociate themselves from the
multiracial coalition of voters led by Hillary Clinton. Given the dissonance between the voting choices of the white working class and the
actual policy benefits afforded them by Republicans, the more accurate
description of what occurred in 2016 (and has occurred in American
electoral politics since passage of the Voting Rights Act of 1965) is not
"realignment," but rather simple "white flight." Although this term is
primarily understood as a spatial concept describing white residential self-
segregation, Harvard University professor of government Ryan Enos has
documented a "social geography" that encompasses the political and
psychological dimensions of racial segregation. According to Enos:

> You might assume that demographic change, and the proximity of different
> groups, would by itself breed familiarity. It turns out that's true only in the
> rare cases in which those groups are integrated. When spatial patterns other
> than integration develop, diversity can drive us apart . . . Even when holding
> the size of the black population constant, in 2008 and 2012, white voters who
> lived in areas where the black population was segregated, such as urban
> Hamilton County, Ohio—home of Cincinnati—or rural Hot Springs
> County, Arkansas, were far less likely to vote for Obama than white voters
> living in areas where the black population was integrated, such as Santa Clara
> County California.[54]

Given the motivational and subliminal biases at work in social geography, Republicans have not had to offer much at all in exchange for the support of the white working class. Why not? That group's flight (along with the white middle class) from the Democratic to the Republican Party is about spurning association with voters of color and the politicians who speak to their interests, rather than a rational move based on self-interest. There is little wonder, then, that it has been more than a half century since a majority of whites voted for the same presidential candidate as a majority of African Americans.[55] The durability of this pattern is one of the most remarkable features of politics in the United States.

In the American South in particular, this pattern is unexplainable without reference to race. Recall from Chapters 1 and 2 that in 2013 the U.S. Supreme Court, declaring that "things have changed dramatically," gutted a provision of the Voting Rights Act of 1965 (Section 5) that required most states of the old Confederacy to preclear any changes in their election laws with the federal government.[56] But how dramatically had things really changed? At the time of the Court's decision, 37 percent of whites in jurisdictions covered by Section 5 believed that "Blacks have too much influence in American politics today," compared with 21 percent of whites in noncovered jurisdictions who believe the same.[57] Could we realistically expect the more than one-third of whites in the covered jurisdictions who held this belief to vote in a way that would give blacks more influence? A 2010 Cooperative Congressional Election Study interviewed 50,000 white voters to measure their degree of racial animosity toward African Americans. Significantly higher levels of racial resentment were found among whites in covered jurisdictions than in noncovered jurisdictions (66 percent versus 53 percent).[58] Among all states, Mississippi and three covered southern jurisdictions (Alabama, Georgia, and Louisiana) reported the highest levels of racial animosity among whites.[59]

White southerners, as well as white conservatives generally, have consistently sought refuge in partisanship to mask the racial underpinnings of their voting behavior. And the Supreme Court has enabled them by declining to police voting discrimination based on partisanship.[60] At the same time, however, the Court has insisted that race is distinct from partisanship.[61] Functionally, though, they are similar—especially in the South. From 2000 to President Obama's election in 2008, support for the Democratic presidential candidate among whites in covered jurisdictions decreased to a mere 26 percent, while support among whites in noncovered jurisdictions increased to 48 percent.[62] It may be that whites in noncovered jurisdictions are simply more Democratic-leaning. But if partisanship alone explained the polarization among whites in formerly covered jurisdictions, we should see similar patterns in other conservative, Republican states outside of the South. In 2012, white Mississippians gave only 11 percent of their votes to President Obama. At the same time, Utah—a reliably conservative bastion, the home state of the Republican nominee Mitt Romney, and a state that is 90.9 percent white[63]— delivered 25 percent of its vote to Obama.[64] Idaho, a resolutely conservative, Republican stronghold that is 93.2 percent white,[65] managed to reward Obama with 33 percent of its vote in 2012.[66] These examples, as well as comparisons with other robustly conservative Republican states like Wyoming (28 percent support for Obama in 2012[67] in a state that is 92.8 percent white[68]), are indicative of heightened racial animosity in the South toward the first African American president.[69] As I argue in Chapter 5, it is also evidence that the Supreme Court engages in pretextual reasoning to justify outcomes that are foreseeably harmful to people of color.

We also know that partisanship is often a stand-in for race because attitudes about race diverge substantially between white Democrats and white Republicans. A 2012 Associated Press poll employed a battery of questions to measure explicit racism among members of the Democratic and Republican parties. Republicans were more likely to express explicit racism in response to these questions, by a remarkable margin of 79 percent to 32 percent.[70] Although both Republicans and Democrats demonstrated similar levels of implicit racism in a separate battery of questions (55 percent of Democrats and 64 percent of Republicans), the explicit racism survey tested some of the oldest and most virulent racial tropes associated with African Americans.[71] The respondents were asked, for instance, whether they agreed with statements describing blacks and Latinos as "lazy" and "violent."[72] The Associated Press survey revealed that traditional racism remains hidebound within the GOP.[73] It's naïve to think that a white voter's invective toward racial minorities does not affect voting behavior, given that these same racial minorities tend to vote opposite the prejudiced white voter.[74] The survey estimated that racial prejudice would cost Obama an approximately 2 percent decrease in his share of the popular vote in his 2012 reelection contest against Republican Mitt Romney.[75] That is more than two and half million votes.

More recent survey data corroborates the Associated Press survey. In 2015, for instance, nearly half of white respondents attributed black inequality to their belief that "most blacks just don't have the motivation or willpower to pull themselves out of poverty."[76] Less than 30 percent of whites attributed black inequality to racial discrimination. Data from the 2016 General Social Survey (GSS) highlights the partisan differences in white Americans' perceptions of black inequality. The survey asked: "On average, blacks have worse jobs, income and housing than white people. Do you think those differences are because most blacks don't have the motivation or will power to pull themselves up out of poverty?"[77] Fifty-five percent of Republicans attributed black inequality to a lack of motivation or willpower, compared with 26 percent of Democrats.[78]

The GSS also asked respondents whether they believed blacks were lazier than whites. Forty-two percent of Republicans said that they were, while 24 percent of Democrats agreed.[79] Finally, the GSS asked white respondents if they believed blacks were less intelligent than whites. Twenty-six percent of Republicans believed this to be the case, while 18 percent of Democrats agreed.[80] Furthering the GSS's findings, a 2017 Pew Research survey highlighted the partisan divide on reasons for racial inequality. Three-quarters of all Republicans believed that "blacks who can't get ahead in this country are mostly responsible for their own condition."[81] Just 28 percent of Democrats agreed.

Given partisan differences like these, it is no wonder that tens of millions of white voters were able to stomach a presidential candidate who had explicitly claimed that the performance of *one* African American (Barack Obama) could be imputed to *all* African Americans. Said Trump in a tweet in 2014: "Sadly, because president Obama has done such a poor job as president, you won't see another black president for generations!"[82] Imagine a black presidential candidate making the same remark about President Trump's performance in office: "Sadly, because President Trump has done such a poor job as president, you won't see another *white* president for generations!" The remark would be instantly disqualifying. When called upon to explain his tweet, Trump dug himself further into a racial ditch: "I think that he has set a very poor standard. I think that he has set a very low bar and I think it's a shame for the African American people."[83] Trump would later eliminate any reasonable doubt about whether he harbored stereotypes of blacks when he blanketly referred to African nations as "shithole" or "shithouse" countries.[84]

The racial (mis)perceptions of Trump and large numbers of Republican voters are the product of motivated reasoning or alternative facts. A 2017 study by Yale University researchers published by the National Academy of Sciences concluded that "[h]igher-status individuals are especially motivated to perceive society as fair and, thus, their elevated societal status as justified and merit-based rather than due, at least in part, to luck and/or macro level structures or discriminatory systems."[85] White Americans had a significantly greater tendency to underestimate the stark inequality that still exists between blacks and whites, as exemplified by the fact that African American families earn only $57.30 for every $100 in income earned by whites.[86] Even college-educated blacks earn 20 percent less than their white counterparts.[87]

But, as economist Robert H. Frank explains in *Success and Luck*, "[T]hose who are oblivious to their own advantages are often similarly oblivious to other people's disadvantages."[88] Frank traces the motivations for this disregard in part to the same explanation as the Yale University researchers: the need to downplay the role of chance in one's success "may owe in part to the fact that by emphasizing talent and hard work to the exclusion of other factors, success-ful people reinforce their claim to the money they've earned."[89] Racial discrimination is among the "other factors" that get diminished in the fable of meritocracy. And armed with stereotypes about black motivation, work ethics, and intellect, white partisans can churn racist alternative facts into "hindsight bias" in which racial disparity is explained after the fact as the inevitable consequence of traits known or suspected all along.[90] Partisanship is easily conflated with race in this exercise, supplying a constitutional veneer for long-standing prejudices. If, as Professor Kendi teaches in *Stamped from the Beginning*, discriminatory objectives precede and produce racial stereotypes, then Republican partisanship in the American South and elsewhere is often a Trojan horse serving to marginalize voters of color.[91]

My aim is not to discount all the other issues—whether guns, abortion, or taxes—that might influence white voter choice. Instead, this book is about how to ferret out the impermissible consideration of race in that choice—a consideration that may coexist and interrelate with other influences on a voter's candidate preferences. When it does, the voter's decision is tainted because it violates the antidiscrimination norm. The next section explains why.

PRETEXTUAL VOTING?

Whitelash against cultural transition is a recurring phenomenon, yet assessing its role in individual voter decisions or election outcomes has too often been relegated to punditry. Courts have escaped inquiry into white voter motivation even under the Voting Rights Act of 1965, since a violation for vote dilution under that act's primary provision (Section 2) requires no showing of discriminatory intent by voters.[92] Attempts to show white voter animus purely through statistical analyses have been deemed "junk science" by judges.[93] Some social science experiments have persua-sively shown the effects of the race of the candidate on white voter choice,[94] but focusing on the race of the candidate tells us only so much about voter motivation. As the election of Donald Trump after eight years of the first black president demonstrates, black electoral suc-cess does not negate, and may well encourage, whitelash.

Antidiscrimination law, however, conceives of racial bias in practical terms that may be useful in our analysis of discrimination in politics. The fundamental lesson to be adopted from antidiscrimination law is that, as the Supreme Court has noted repeatedly, "[t]he law makes no distinction between the weight or value to be given to either direct or circumstantial evidence."[95] A couple of examples are helpful to illustrate the distinction between these two types of proof. If you are called as a witness in a murder trial, and you testify that you saw X fire the gun that killed Y, you are providing direct evidence of the crime. If, on the other hand, you testify only that you saw X in the vicinity before Y was killed, you are providing circumstantial evidence. We sentence people to prison, and sometimes to death, based on circumstantial evidence; surely we are allowed to conclude that they have voted with a discriminatory intent based on this same type of evidence.[96] Even conservative justices, who are most skeptical of discrimination claims, acknowledge the value of circumstantial evidence in proving discrimination. Notably, Justice Clarence Thomas has written: "The reason for treating circumstantial and direct evidence alike is both clear and deep rooted: Circumstantial evidence is not only sufficient, but may also be more certain, satisfying and persuasive than direct evidence."[97]

The Title VII model of inferring discriminatory intent using circumstantial evidence sidesteps the loaded inquiries about whether Trump or his supporters are "racist" and avoids the need for mindreading, as the relevant question becomes not what's in the heart or head of the actors, but rather what reasonable minds can conclude. I acknowledge here, and discuss further in Chapter 5, that courts are often unfaithful to their own precedents, particularly when those precedents would tend to lean the decision toward litigants of color or other marginalized groups. But this is hardly a reason not to press for the application of relevant law to discrimination by white voters. The only alternative would be to acquiesce to a visible injustice. So, for now, it's important to appreciate—if only as a thought experiment—how antidiscrimination principles might deter whitelash at the voting booth. In Chapter 8 of this book, I will make more definitive claims: that white voters can be held liable for whitelash in the voting booth.

PRETEXT AND MIXED MOTIVES

When voters elect politicians, they are in effect making a hiring decision. For this reason, the proof structures of Title VII of the Civil Rights Act of 1964, which apply to both private and government employment, offer a sound method for probing voter intent. One initial objection to the use of Title VII either as an analogy or as a direct legal precedent, however, is that the 2016 election involved the rejection by white voters of a white candidate—Hillary Clinton. Like Clinton, white Democratic candidates are consistently rejected by a majority of white voters in all kinds of elections across the country. Because Title VII protects job applicants and employees from discrimination "because of such individual's race,"[98] how can a *white* candidate be the victim of racial discrimination at the hands of *white* voters? The answer is that, like *Loving v. Virginia*, Title VII protects individuals from discrimination based on the people with whom they choose to associate.[99] Indeed, Title VII has been held to apply to a claim by an employee that he was treated disparately by his employer because his marriage was interracial.[100] White Democrats such as Hillary Clinton often lose the white vote because of their real or perceived association with people of color and interests linked to voters of color. Thus, Title VII is a logical basis for exploring discriminatory intent in voting.

Two overlapping methods for proof of racial discrimination are available under Title VII. Chapter 1 introduced the concept of pretext, which can be shown by "such weaknesses, implausibilities, inconsistencies, incoherencies, or contradictions in the employer's proffered legitimate reasons for its action that a reasonable factfinder could rationally find them unworthy of credence and hence infer that the employer did not act for the asserted non-discriminatory reasons."[101] To contextualize pretext in the employment setting, consider the following example: You read about a job opening for a cashier's position at a grocery store. You have several years' experience as a cashier, so you are certainly qualified for the position. The employer, however, selects a less qualified white employee over you, a person of Hispanic descent. Under Title VII, you have made out what is called a "prima facie" (apparent) case of discrimination: there was a job opening for which you were qualified, but an individual from outside your racial group was selected instead. Under the pretext method of proof, the employer is now required to come forward with a legitimate, nondiscriminatory reason for not hiring you. You, in turn, can challenge those reasons as pretextual—that is, as unworthy of being believed. If you succeed, "the trier of fact can reasonably infer from the falsity of the explanation that the employer is dissembling to cover up a discriminatory purpose."[102]

And just so with discrimination in voting. Under Title VII, a prima facie case need not take a particular form; instead, it is a flexible concept.[103] The prima facie case that white voters rejected Hillary Clinton because of her association with voters of color is amply demonstrated by the survey data and studies discussed earlier in this chapter and in Chapters 1 and 2. What about the economic anxiety theory offered as a legitimate, nondiscriminatory reason for the votes of the white working class? This theory qualifies as pretext because, among other things, far more than half of these voters acknowledged that they were satisfied with their personal financial circumstances prior to the 2016 election.[104] Establishing pretext shows that race "made a difference."[105] This finding is sufficient for liability under Title VII.

One criticism of this analogy to employment discrimination is that voting involves a greater variety of factors than a hiring decision. The accuracy of this criticism is debatable: employment decisions are based on many variables, some objective and others not. But even assuming that voting is more complex than hiring, mixed-motive analysis answers this concern. Under Title VII, if race is a "motivating" factor in an employment decision, the employer is liable for discrimination even if nondiscriminatory reasons for the decision are also present.[106] "Motivating" in this context does not mean exclusive, nor does it mean that a plaintiff must demonstrate that the employer's decision would have been different if it were not for the impermissible factor—the "but for" test of causation. To avoid having to pay compensatory damages, the employer may demonstrate that it would have reached the same decision even if it had not acted in part with a discriminatory motivation. Avoidance of such damages, however, does not exculpate the employer: when race is a motivating ingredient, the employer has violated the law.[107] Here again, the analogy to voting is apt: many voters undoubtedly vote for discriminatory and nondiscriminatory reasons at the same time. The fact that multiple factors may inform a voter's decision does not displace race as a factor when we have evidence—circumstantial or direct—of its impact.

The motivating-factor standard under Title VII is much like that used throughout constitutional law. Race need not be the sole factor or even the primary factor in most instances. Instead, we may treat the decision of a voter or a class of voters in the same way the Supreme Court treats the decision of a legislative body in attempting to ferret out discrimination:

> Rarely can it be said that a legislature or administrative body operating under a broad mandate made a decision motivated solely by a single concern, or even that a particular purpose was the "dominant" or "primary" one. In fact, it is because legislators and administrators are properly concerned with balancing numerous competing considerations that courts refrain from reviewing the merits of their decisions, absent a showing of arbitrariness or irrationality. But racial discrimination is not just another competing consideration. When there is a proof that a discriminatory purpose has been a motivating factor in the decision, this judicial deference is no longer justified.[108]

So, even in the realm of voting, where multiple impulses might steer a voter, antidiscrimination law provides a template for determining whether the voter's decision is infected by race. Chapters 7 and 8 present specific legal remedies for white voter discrimination. But from the analogies to antidiscrimination law considered so far, this much should be clear: the law looks unkindly on alternative facts. Indeed, when a person embraces alternative facts, the law infers an intent to hide an ulterior motive, such as discrimination. Law is the search for truth, and in a democracy based on the rule of law, there is no space for alternative facts. This is not to suggest that facts are never in dispute. Where the truth is unclear, however, some arguments are usually more persuasive than others, and some inferences more plausible. The alternative to this guidepost is the statement made by former New York City mayor Rudolph Giuliani, as Trump's attorney, in reference to Robert Mueller's investigation of collusion between the 2016 Trump campaign and Russia, that "truth is relative … They may have a different version of the truth than we do."[109] Such a conclusion would make democracy unsustainable.

WHEN FACTS DON'T MATTER: VOTING AS NULLIFICATION

Why would some voters show such an evident disregard for truth? Might voters ever have a valid reason to look beyond the facts? Earlier in this chapter, we used a criminal case about juror racial bias, *Peña-Rodriguez v. Colorado*, as a lens through which to view the relationship of race, democracy, and facts in the 2016 election. Here we must revisit the criminal jury context, for sometimes facts do not matter there, just as sometimes they should not matter in an election.

Jury nullification occurs when a jury votes to acquit a defendant, despite the evidence and the law, because it wants to send some larger social message to the system. Many people think of *California v. O.J. Simpson* as the modern iconic example of jury nullification. For our purposes, we might think of the 2016 election as the trial of two candidates, Hillary Clinton and Donald Trump, one of which—Trump—was acquitted contrary to the overwhelming weight of evidence and the country's accepted political norms.

Jury nullification sometimes makes sense. For instance, Professor Paul Butler has argued that jurors might sometimes rationally decide that the costs of sending another black male to prison outweigh the benefits of convicting him.[110] But Butler emphasizes that such nullification should be an option for black jurors only in cases involving nonviolent crimes. That's because a jury's choice to acquit violent criminals would easily make the black community much worse off by allowing gangbangers and rapists to return to their communities and continue to commit crimes. The point of nullification is to leave society better-off, not worse.

A classic example of jury nullification involves the Fugitive Slave Act. In *United States v. Morris*, three defendants were charged with aiding slaves to escape to Canada.[111] The defense urged jurors to assess the constitutionality of the Fugitive Slave Act and, by implication, the morality of the institution of slavery itself. The defendants were acquitted. As it did in this case, nullification of laws or institutions or systems must have some higher, moral purpose.

Here's where the analogy falls apart. The white working-class voters who voted for Trump to send a message to the so-called establishment or express their frustration may have thought they were engaged in an act of resistance similar to jury nullification. But acts of resistance that have the foreseeable effect of leaving the participant and society as a whole worse off are simply irrational, not to mention abdications of the social contract. A case in point is the number of working-class white Americans who would be harmed by repeal of the Affordable Care Act. According to the Urban Institute, in the five Rust Belt states that flipped from Obama to Trump, more *non-college-educated whites* gained insurance coverage under the law than college-educated whites and minorities combined.[112] Yet exit polls indicated that blue-collar whites who opposed Obamacare supported Trump by a margin of 13 to 1. This isn't juror nullification; it isn't a repudiation of the establishment—it's simple nihilism.

Did Donald Trump appeal to an overarching sense of justice, or did he simply articulate many of the complaints that have become endemic to an American culture of white grievance? In the 2016 election, Trump portrayed illegal immigrants and workers in emerging economies as windfall beneficiaries of globalization, although they were not nearly as well-off as Americans. Add to these provocations the ongoing angst of whites about a menu of other issues ranging from abortion to guns, where other questionable pretexts may come into play, and you have a highly susceptible electorate. But there's a difference between whipped-up anxiety and the righteous indignation that justifies nullification of existing orders and social norms.

Is white economic anxiety real? Probably, but so too is black and brown economic anxiety, yet these groups overall chose a very different course than electing a man who is unqualified to sit in the Oval Office. This isn't merely a matter of a difference of opinion among voters. White Americans elected a racist, and many understood they were doing as much. As Trump's campaign manager Kellyanne Conway said, "There's a difference for voters between what offends you and what affects you."[113] In other words, Trump's overt racism did not matter to millions of white voters; their perceived self-interests came first. What Conway's theory ignores, however, is that a majority of white Americans have a pretty lousy track record of selecting presidents who advance their interests—a point I take up in Chapter 6. Her theory also elides the difficult question of whether Trump's appeals to white voter self-interests were appeals to white identity that infused his basic economic message with an inseparable racial one.

In the final analysis, nullification cannot justify white voter conduct in the 2016 presidential election. Alternative facts prevailed. The question is, can the law hold white voters accountable for their embrace of alternative facts in the same fashion as it holds other actors liable for pretextual conduct? To answer this question in context, the reader must appreciate that white voters in 2016 were not acting alone. Whitelash does not exist as a product of a disorganized mob; it is supported by institutional actors—politicians, the media, and courts. And it is fostered by the absence of true accountability in the American two-party structure, where the limited choice (i.e., Democrat versus Republican) essentially ensures that each party will eventually return to power, even if it has a history of irresponsible and bigoted conduct. I elaborate on these contextual matters in the next three chapters.

4

The Sirens of White Nationalism

"Make America Great Again."

—Trump campaign slogan, 2016

"You know what I am? I'm a nationalist, O.K.? I'm a nationalist. Nationalist! Use that word! Use that word!"

—President Trump, October 23, 2018[1]

In *Aman v. Cort Furniture Rental Corp.*, a federal court of appeals found the following remarks directed at black employees to reveal discriminatory intent: "another one," "one of them," "that one in there," and "all of you."[2] None of these terms even mention race, but, as the court explained, "while discriminatory conduct persists, violators have learned not to leave the proverbial 'smoking gun' behind. As one court has recognized, [d]efendants of even minimal sophistication will neither admit discriminatory animus [n]or leave a paper trail demonstrating it."[3] Thus, in the court's view, we don't need to hear openly racist statements to know that racism exists.

Political discourse is not different from antidiscrimination law in this regard. Racial discrimination is often hidden behind code words. But as these racial code words get decoded as pretexts, they should cease to enjoy the presumption of innocence once attached to them. Instead, once identified, they should logically be treated as part of the telltale lexicon of racial animus. Yet the game of codes persists in American political discourse. Time and again, politicians' rhetoric forces us to revisit the meanings of terms (and actions) that suggest racism. Even when these meanings are not entirely settled as a matter of social consensus, the use of such codes should place the burden of proof on the speaker who knowingly treads so closely to the line of racism.

Consider the following wink-and-nod exercise by President Trump. Knowing full well the racial freight of the term *nationalist*, President Trump proudly labeled himself as one during a rally in the fall of 2018. Afterward, Trump professed ignorance of any racial meaning behind the term—even though he told the crowd during the rally, "Really, we're not supposed to use that word."[4] And why not? On the association between racist movements and the nationalist moniker, Trump demurred, "I never heard that theory about being a nationalist."[5] Here, the president's self-incrimination and implausible claim of cultural ignorance belied his attempt to deny intentional racial incitement.

At the more subtle end of the linguistic spectrum are then-Congressman Paul Ryan's 2014 comments about the work ethic of inner-city men: "We have got this tailspin of culture, in our inner cities in particular, of men not working and just generations of men not even thinking about working or learning the value and the culture of work."[6] Ryan, the 2012 Republican vice presidential nominee, later apologized for his comments, calling them "inarticulate" and maintaining that they had nothing to do with race. Pretext analysis says otherwise, however. "Inner-city" is commonly understood as a proxy for "black," and not necessarily a flattering one.[7] Couple this with the picture of indolence created by Ryan's statement, and you have a classic racial stereotype.

Ironically, it was House Speaker Ryan who recognized as a "textbook example of a racist comment" candidate Donald Trump's remark that a federal judge of Mexican descent could not objectively hear a fraud claim against "Trump University" because of the judge's Latino heritage.[8] However, Ryan rationalized that Trump was still fit to serve as president of a country whose population is among the most racially diverse in the world.[9] To psychologists who study racial privilege as a clinical addiction akin to, say, alcoholism, Ryan's rationalization is evidence of the "schema of irrelevance" through which whites mediate egalitarian ideals and the unequal treatment of their fellow citizens of color.[10] That is, for Ryan, it was more important to push a "conservative" political agenda than to disavow a candidate spouting "textbook" racism. Stopping racism was only worthy of lip service; conservatism was a higher ideal. But this prioritization simply made Ryan and other Trump backers complicit in undermining the antidiscrimination principle that is a central ideal of democracy.

Ryan's rationalization of Trump's comments was not a one-off. The very mantra of Trump's campaign was "textbook" racist. "Make America great again," we are told, is too ambiguous or innocuous to offend the antidiscrimination norm. The slogan, however, is rife with racial connotations because what made America great for some made it a plantation for others. America was great for many generations of whites precisely because they benefited from the country's color caste system. Thus, Trump's campaign slogan was no more "coded" than his reference to himself as a nationalist or his comments about the Mexican-American federal judge. Instead, it openly appealed to white Americans' protean resistance to racial change dating back at least to Reconstruction.

That the conduct of Trump's presidential campaign could so blatantly hark back to classical bigotry is disturbing, yet unsurprising. Because white-lash is a reaction to social progress, it often reaches back in history for its playbook. In so doing, whitelash forgoes the subtlety of dog-whistle racism and instead reverts to more primitive forms — sirens rather than dog whistles. These sirens become louder not only as the sense of cultural loss among whites increases, but also as the continuous process of decoding racist fare bears fruit.

This chapter examines how institutional actors urge voters toward whitelash by embracing white nationalist ideas, both wittingly and unwittingly. The contours of contemporary white nationalism, explored in this chapter, are elastic, but I invoke the term as an umbrella phrase for a white identity politics incompatible with racial egalitarianism. By institutional actors, I mean participants in government, in the judiciary, and in media, entertainment, and public intellectual life whose words and actions both shape and reflect public opinion. Voters do not vote in a vacuum; rather, they absorb and help sculpt the zeitgeist of a period. To understand contemporary whitelash, then, I probe the cultural and political cues that invariably affect the conduct of many whites at the ballot box.

EVERYTHING OLD IS NEW AGAIN: CONTEMPORARY WHITE NATIONALISM

In her study of the mainstreaming of white supremacist ideology, political scientist Carol Swain warns that white supremacist groups have pivoted from racial hatred to white nationalism.[11] In *The New White Nationalism in America*, Swain describes this nationalism in terms that ring familiar in current American political discourse and even jurisprudence:

> Calls for white identity are occurring at a time when many Americans are uncertain about the future, and some have come to see the government as more geared toward advancing the rights of racial and political minorities than those of the undifferentiated mass of white people. Using frames associated with the black civil rights movement and multiculturalism, some ordinary white Americans are making a case for increased white solidarity and white consciousness by employing the same brand of identity politics that

minorities have successfully used in the past to further their own group interests and group identities.[12]

Through interviews with a variety of white supremacist groups, Swain documents the mainstream pitch and appearance they are now assuming—a dissembling that Swain contends allows them "to pass themselves off as mainstream conservatives."[13] Largely ignored by Swain, who in 2018 ran as a conservative Republican candidate for mayor of Nashville, Tennessee, is the dialogic relationship between white nationalists and conservatives. That is, white nationalists may well try to conflate their ideology with conservatism; conservatism, however, is hardly a passive victim of identity theft. On the contrary, race—or more precisely, racial antagonism—has clearly played a significant role in the rise of the modern conservative movement.[14]

Professor Ronald W. Walters takes up this point in *White Nationalism, Black Interests*. For Walters, because white nationalism and conservatism both involve alienation from the government by whites who believe their needs have been neglected and displaced by the demands of others (minorities), nationalism is a radical extension of conservatism.[15] To be sure, not all white conservatives are white nationalists, but "the overlap between them is such that the effects of Conservatism may often yield the same outcome as those of White Nationalism," Walters writes.[16] For instance, the conservative effort to starve government social safety net programs of resources abets white nationalists' efforts to harm disfavored racial groups.[17]

Both Swain and Walters were writing before the advent of the "alt-right," a term that rebrands white nationalism but does not fundamentally alter its preoccupation with race, its grievances about perceived preferences for minorities that disadvantage whites, or its desire for racial separation. As investigative reporter Mike Wendling concludes from a deep dive into the alt-right movement, white racial solidarity is the animating, and perhaps most cohesive, idea of the alt-right.[18] Wendling does not address the debate about the line between white nationalism and conservatism,[19] yet there are striking similarities between the alt-right and the Republicans who propelled Trump to his party's nomination. Fully 40 percent of Trump supporters during the Republican primary believed that their white racial identity was extremely important to them.[20] Fifty-one percent of Republican primary voters, but 61 percent of Trump supporters, believed that the government favored blacks over whites.[21]

The familiar white nationalist vision of racial domination may differ from white conservatives' nostalgia to "make America great again," but the anger that riled white Trump supporters during the Republican primary grew from the same place: the perceived loss of the advantages of being white in America. When, according to Pew Research, an astonishing 81 percent of Trump supporters (compared with only 19 percent of Clinton supporters) believe that life is worse for people like them than it was 50 years ago,[22] they are not reminiscing about *I Love Lucy*. The most marked societal difference between now and 50 years ago is the browning of America and its progress toward economic, political, and social equality for racial minorities, women, and members of the LGBTQ community. While deindustrialization looms large in this picture, the Civil Rights Movement magnified its effect for whites by bringing increased competition for educational attainment and employment. A "power theory" of intergroup relations predicts greater hostility from a dominant group as the threat to its power increases.[23]

After winning the Republican nomination, Trump fanned the flames of racial grievance by appointing Stephen K. Bannon as his campaign's chief executive—and later as his chief White House political strategist. Bannon had been the executive chairman of *Breitbart*, an online tabloid that he once described as "the platform for the alt-right."[24] In reporting on Trump's selection of Bannon as his campaign's chief executive, *The New York Times* described *Breitbart* as "focused primarily on pushing Republicans away from what it calls a globalist agenda and toward a hard-line and often overtly racial one, railing against what it sees as the threats of free trade, Hispanic migration and Islamist terrorism."[25] Bannon would later corroborate *The Times*'s description of his politics as "overtly racial." In 2018, Bannon, speaking overseas to the far-right French National Front party, inveighed: "Let them call you racists. Let them call you xenophobes. Let them call you nativists. Wear it as a badge of honor."[26] Here, Bannon exhibits a key tactic of the alt-right: deflecting charges of racism by dismissing the label as overwrought or converting it into a badge of white victimhood.[27]

Prior to Trump's election, 48 years had passed since the last overtly racist presidential campaign, when avowed segregationist George Wallace ran as a third-party candidate in 1968 under the American Independent Party banner.[28] Not unlike Trump, Wallace also ran as the "angry man's candidate."[29] The similarities between Trump's and Wallace's rhetoric are striking:

> Although Wallace's rhetoric was often crude and his reasoning and proof often absurd, his twisted syntax and his use of common language served a purpose. His target audiences were primarily white, middle- or lower-income citizens. He based his bid in 1968 on a broad appeal to the "white backlash" voter who consistently opposed the values of the "New Politics,"

gave the highest priority to law and order, opposed political protest, and was unequivocally hostile to counter-culture. One of his major goals was to create a sense of unity and identity with his audiences.[30]

Trump is no segregationist. Yet even on the fraught issue of racial segregation, it is not unfair to compare Wallace and Trump. No serious presidential candidate since 1968 has so deliberately flirted with segregationist ideas as Trump, who called for a ban on Muslims entering the United States, the surveillance of mosques, and mass deportation of illegal (read, Latino) immigrants.

In retrospect, perhaps no one should have been surprised by the potency of Trump's campaign, even in the face of its open alignment with the likes of Bannon and the alt-right. After all, Wallace carried five southern states in 1968, winning 46 electoral votes and 13 percent of the popular vote.[31] Four years later, running strongly against forced busing to desegregate public schools, he racked up Democratic primary victories in North Carolina, Michigan, Maryland, Florida, and Tennessee.[32] While it is true that 2016 is not 1968 or 1972, it is also true that whitelash is like cancer in a body's cells, posing an ongoing threat of recurrence. Although pronounced "post-racial" by opponents of racial equality, the country, reeling from numerous deaths of black men at the hands of white police, was hardly cured of its racial woes by 2016. George Wallace had come and gone, but white Americans had not yet buried the anger and backlash that his politics represented.

UNDERNEATH THE REPUBLICAN TENT

Instead, whitelash reincarnated itself during the presidency of Barack Obama. To understand the rise of Trump and the ascendency of contemporary white nationalism, we must look beyond Trump. Whitelash is built in part on an interactive relationship between white nationalist sentiment and political (and even judicial) conservatism.[33] There is no better illustration of this than Representative Steve Scalise, who was the majority whip of the U.S. House of Representatives before the Democrats regained control in 2018.[34] In 2002, Scalise, then a member of the Louisiana House of Representatives, spoke before a white nationalist group called the European-American Unity and Rights Organization, a white supremacist group founded by former Ku Klux Klan Grand Wizard David Duke.[35] Despite the group's alarming name, Scalise claimed ignorance of its purpose.[36] The racial etiquette in 2002 dictated that Republican Senator Trent Lott resign his post as Senate majority leader when he lionized Senator Strom Thurmond for his 1948 run for the presidency as a segregationist.[37] Twelve years later, when Scalise's even more racially insensitive conduct was revealed, no such etiquette remained: Scalise was not forced to resign his position as majority whip.[38]

According to one reporter in Scalise's home state of Louisiana, Scalise had once told her during an interview that "he was like David Duke without the baggage."[39] The reporter explained: "I think he meant he supported the same policy ideas as David Duke, but he wasn't David Duke, that he didn't have the same feelings about certain people as David Duke did."[40] Yet separating the racial invective of white nationalist groups from their political common ground with conservatives is difficult to do when a candidate, or party, courts the votes of organized and unorganized white nationalists. Scalise's political survival in the face of revelations about his appearance before a white supremacist group is emblematic of the increasing tolerance in American politics of an alliance, albeit unspoken, between white nationalists and mainstream Republicans.

Scalise hails from the Tea Party wing of the modern Republican Party, a wing that emerged during the Obama presidency and in many respects now defines the party.[41] Although the Tea Party was ostensibly concerned with the nation's ballooning long-term national debt, a look at its overwhelmingly white demographics and the racial beliefs of its adherents belies its good-government rhetoric. In 2010, 60 percent of Tea Party adherents believed that the country had gone too far to guarantee equal rights.[42] A majority of Tea Party adherents believed that the government should be allowed to racially profile its citizens, a view rejected by most white Americans.[43] Tea Party members were far more likely than the average white American to reject historical discrimination as contributing to the economic plight of blacks and to believe that blacks simply do not try hard enough.[44] They were twice as likely to believe that the Obama administration favored blacks over whites.[45]

I do not mean to suggest that the racial beliefs of Tea Party adherents are identical to those of white nationalists, which more clearly veer to the crudest forms of white supremacy. But if, as Carol Swain contends, the racial views of conservatives and white supremacists have drawn together, any conflation of them is made possible only because there is some degree of kinship. And because the American political structure, for better or worse, remains a two-party system, a logical question is, why have the most racially extreme elements of our polity migrated to the Republican Party?

Rather than repelling these elements, modern political conservativism has relied in part on groups that push the boundaries of the right flanks of the American political spectrum, including anti-immigrant and "patriot" groups.[46] The polarization of the American electorate, and the consequent closeness of many elections, make the two parties hesitant to disavow any supporters. Conservative political leaders, even those who do not make direct appeals to such groups, show a reluctance to alienate them.[47] The reticence of mainstream conservative leaders to reject extremism within their ranks illustrates what clinical psychologists call "social effect": racist conduct goes unchecked because challenging it would risk alienating dominant group members whose support is needed.[48]

Thus, when Republican presidential candidate Dr. Ben Carson declared that a Muslim should not become president of the United States, he had substantial leeway and even upside potential to make such an intolerant statement because, as reported at the time by *The Washington Post*, "the chief dynamic that has driven the fight for the [2016] nomination is a current of anger in the GOP base, aimed at what many see as unsettling cultural and political changes and a party establishment that they believe has failed them."[49] Matthew Dowd, a GOP strategist for George W. Bush in 2004, said during the 2016 nomination contest, "Many in the GOP have gotten more and more angry during the Obama years, and the conservative media environment has gotten more shrill and less reasonable . . . In addition, conservatives have seen more of their traditional institutions under attack, and their version of America going away."[50]

So, we should not be surprised to find white nationalists in the same coalition as white conservatives, being responsive to similar appeals, particularly when those appeals are as unvarnished as Trump's were during the 2016 campaign. Nor should conservatives or the Republican Party be angered by or dismissive of comparisons between white nationalists and themselves. Conservatives and Republicans could move beyond regressive appeals to white identity—whether Trumpian or coded—as the Democratic Party decided to do from 1964 forward, when the New Deal coalition that had linked southern segregationists with northern labor unions and racial progressives split over the push for civil rights. Such a stance, however, would mean rejection of an electoral orthodoxy that has been the lifeblood of the Republican Party since Richard Nixon's "southern strategy" in 1968. All decisions have a cost, though: Donald Trump's 2016 campaign is the metastasis of the party's 40-year refusal to renounce less conspicuous appeals to white identity.

POLITICAL DISCOURSE

White nationalist rhetoric is now deployed in mainstream political discourse with an ease not seen since George Wallace's third-party bid for the presidency as a segregationist in 1968.[51] Table 4–1 shows some of the more astonishingly racialized public statements made by politicians in recent years. (Table 1–1 previously listed such statements from presidential candidates.)

The list is not exhaustive, for any such endeavor would be its own book. What the reader should immediately appreciate, though, is the flirtation of these remarks with overt racism. When a U.S. congressman proclaims that black protesters against police brutality "hate white people because white people are successful and they're not," how far removed are we from the eugenics arguments that justified the enslavement of Africans and "separate but equal"? And when a Republican nominee for a House seat contends that because of diversity efforts, "if somebody is lesser qualified, they will get a job anyway or they'll get into college anyway because of the tribe that they're with, what group, what box they fit into,"[52] it is instructive to compare his language to that of white nationalist David Duke: "[t]he fact is that in the United States of America, Canada, the UK and in many other areas of Europe Whites face a powerful state-sanctioned, and often mandated, racial discrimination against White people who are better-qualified than their non-White counterparts."[53]

Politicians have been guilty of even more explicitly racist statements and actions. In 2018, a Florida Republican state senator, Frank Artiles, who is Cuban-American, used the slang "niggas" in a conversation with two black senate colleagues.[54] Also in 2018, Virginia Republicans nominated Corey Stewart, a stalwart defender of Confederate monuments, as their candidate for the U.S. Senate. In 2017, Stewart attended an "Old South Ball" in Danville, Virginia, where he gave a speech proclaiming that the Confederate flag "is our heritage, it's what makes us Virginia, and if you take that away, we lose our identity."[55]

The "identity" that Stewart was referring to was clearly white identity: a 2017 survey found that white southerners held a view of the Confederate flag that was three times more favorable than that of black southerners.[56] Stewart likened politicians who supported the removal of Confederate monuments to the terrorist organization ISIS. He tweeted in April 2017, "Nothing is worse than a Yankee telling a Southerner that his monuments don't matter."[57] In keeping with his defense of white nationalist culture, Stewart backed a 2016 primary challenge to House Speaker Paul Ryan by Paul Nehlen, a self-described "pro-White Christian American candidate,"[58] who publicly questioned why Muslims exist in the United States.[59] Stewart's main primary opponent for the Republican nomination in the 2018 Virginia Senate race urged voters to "reject Corey Stewart's dog-whistling of white supremacists, anti-Semites and racists."[60] None of this, however, dissuaded President Trump from endorsing him.[61]

TABLE 4–1 *White Nationalist Rhetoric from Politicians*

Speaker and Date	Comment
Republican U.S. Senator Cindy Hyde-Smith, campaigning against Mike Espy, the first African American U.S. Secretary of Agriculture, for a Senate seat in Mississippi, November 2, 2018	"If he [referring to a Hyde-Smith supporter] invited me to a public hanging, I'd be on the front row." (Approximately one-eighth of the 4,743 lynchings that occurred in the U.S. between 1882 and 1968 took place in Mississippi.)
Republican U.S. Senator Lindsey Graham, discussing the possible outcomes if he took a DNA test, as Democratic U.S. Senator Elizabeth Warren did to demonstrate her Native American heritage, October 2018	"I'll probably be Iranian. That would be, like, terrible."
Republican Arizona State Representative David Stringer, discussing the threat of immigration, June 2018	"Immigration today represents an existential threat to the United States … If we don't do something about immigration very, very soon, the demographics of our country will be irrevocably changed and we will be a very different country. It will not be the country you were born into."
Republican Congressional candidate Seth Grossman, of New Jersey, attacking diversity, April 2018	"The whole idea of diversity is a bunch of crap and un-American. [Diversity is] an excuse by Democrats, communists and socialists, basically, to say that we're not all created equal, that some people, if somebody is lesser qualified, they will get a job anyway or they'll get into college anyway because of the tribe that they're with, what group, what box they fit into."
Republican Kansas State Representative Steve Alford, suggesting that all African Americans are drug users, January 2018	"What you really need to do is go back in the '30s, when they outlawed all types of drugs in Kansas [and] across the United States. What was the reason why they did that? One of the reasons why, I hate to say it, was that the African Americans, they were basically users and they basically responded the worst off to those drugs just because of their character makeup, their genetics and that."

TABLE 4–1 *(continued)*

Speaker and Date	Comment
Republican Senate candidate and former Alabama Supreme Court Chief Justice Roy Moore, explaining the meaning of Donald Trump's mantra, "Make America great again," September 2017	"I think it was great at the time when families were united—even though we had slavery. They cared for one another. People were strong in the families. Our families were strong. Our country had a direction."
Republican Congressman Mo Brooks, explaining Democratic opposition to the nomination of Jeff Sessions to become U.S. Attorney General, January 10, 2017	"It's really about political power and racial division and what I've referred to on occasion as the 'war on whites.'"
U.S. Representative Robert Pettinger Jr., commenting on black protesters in Charlotte, North Carolina, after the police shooting death of a black man, Keith Lamont Scott, September 22, 2016	"They hate white people because white people are successful and they're not. I mean, yes, it is, it is a welfare state. We have spent trillions of dollars on welfare, and we've put people in bondage so they can't be all that they are capable of being."
U.S. Representative Steve King, who maintains a miniature Confederate flag on his desk, discussing different races' contributions to society, July 2016	"This whole 'white people' business, though, does get a little tired, Charlie. I mean, I'd ask you to go back through history and figure out where are these contributions that have been made by these other categories of people that you're talking about. Where did any other subgroup of people contribute more to civilization?"
U.S. Representative Steve King, defending his proposal to block a black abolitionist from being featured on the twenty-dollar bill, June 21, 2016	"It's not about Harriet Tubman, it's about keeping the picture [of former President Andrew Jackson, a white supremacist by twenty-first century standards] on the $20. Y'know? Why would you want to change that? I am a conservative, I like to keep what we have."
Republican Georgia State Senator Fran Millar, in an email, objecting to early voting by black Democrats, September 2014	"Now we are to have Sunday voting at South DeKalb Mall just prior to the election. Per Jim Galloway of the [*Atlanta Journal-Constitution*], this location is dominated by African American shoppers and it is near several large African American mega churches

TABLE 4–1 *(continued)*

Speaker and Date	Comment
	such as New Birth Missionary Baptist . . . I have spoken with Representative Jacobs and we will try to eliminate this election law loophole in January."
Republican Congressman Trent Franks, of Arizona, tying African Americans to abortion, February 26, 2010	"And yet today, half of all black children are aborted . . . Far more of the African-American community is being devastated by the policies of today than were being devastated by the policies of slavery."
Republican Congressman Lynn Westmoreland, of Georgia, attacking the first African American first lady, September 2008	"Just from what little I've seen of her [Michelle Obama] and Mr. Obama, Sen. Obama, they're a member of an elitist-class individual that thinks that they're uppity."

Although national Republicans other than Trump immediately sought to distance the Republican Party from Stewart after he became its nominee, what they did not do—in fact, what Republicans almost never do—is to renounce the *voters* who support racist candidates like Stewart. That is because Republicans depend on these same voters in other elections. Stewart took more than 136,000 votes (44.87 percent) in winning the 2018 Senate primary; a year before that, he took more than 155,000 votes (42.5 percent) in nearly toppling the Republican establishment pick for the gubernatorial nomination.[62] Clearly, Stewart's supporters knew what they were voting for. Were Republicans willing to forgo these votes by saying, "Not only don't we welcome racist candidates, we also do not want their voters in our party"? Of course not. Instead, Republicans engaged in a ritualistic dance with white nationalism, one where they attempted to reject the leader (Stewart) without also rejecting his followers. Consider, for instance, Virginia Congressman Scott Taylor's tortured attempt to share Stewart's base of voters while nominally distancing himself from Stewart. Accused by his Democratic opponent of supporting Stewart, Taylor responded,

> I don't give a shit about Corey Stewart . . . No one else does either except for Democrats who are trying to target me . . . What are they trying to say? That

Scott Taylor likes Corey Stewart so therefore he's a racist? Do you think that's going to play here? My son is named after a black guy.[63]

It was the same two-step Republicans did in 1990, when David Duke became the Republican U.S. Senate nominee in Louisiana. Republicans condemned Duke, who called affirmative action discrimination against whites and campaigned against "the rising welfare underclass."[64] Duke captured 43 percent of the vote against a sitting Democratic incumbent, J. Bennett Johnston.[65] In that race, too, Republicans were willing to condemn hate, but only one of the haters (Duke) rather than all of them (Duke and his voters). The 2016 presidential contest marked an even more regressive stance: with Trump, Republicans were willing to condemn hate without renouncing the candidacy of the hater, let alone renouncing Trump's millions of like-minded supporters.

To some readers, this account of the infiltration of white nationalism into mainstream conservative politics may appear too anecdotal. But taken together with empirical data from the myriad studies and polling on racial attitudes and partisanship presented in the previous three chapters, and viewed against the backdrop of Trump's 2016 campaign, these contemporary spectacles of racism—an elected official using the term "nigga" in a conversation with black colleagues, a major-party nominee for the U.S. Senate defending the Confederate flag and Confederate monuments, and a sitting congressman openly doubting the contributions of nonwhites to civilization—portray, in a way that statistics alone cannot, a new era of overtly racialized politics. Politicians are now, as they did during Jim Crow and throughout the 1960s, providing voters with overt encouragement to vote their prejudices, thereby normalizing racist discourse once again.

I have intentionally used examples with which the reader is less likely to be familiar to demonstrate the breadth of the infiltration of white nationalist thought. No one should be misled to think, however, that the white-identitarian ideology exhibited in those remarks is limited to (or even primarily the domain of) fringe political figures. Well-known politicians are doing the same. Republican presidential candidate Mike Huckabee chastised the Black Lives Matter movement, which originated in protest of police shootings of unarmed black men, because, according to Huckabee, the movement "elevat[es] some lives above others."[66] Although Huckabee did not specify which lives were being subordinated by the movement, his incantation that "all lives matter" is poorly disguised self-referentialism and emblematic of white privilege's "schema of irrelevance" toward the needs and interests of people of color.[67] If systemic shootings of *white* citizens by *black* police officers happened, one couldn't imagine Huckabee not noting the race of the victims.

Speaking to an all-white audience about government entitlement programs during his 2012 presidential campaign, former Senator Rick Santorum, a conservative, stated: "I don't want to make black people's lives better by giving them somebody else's money. I want to give them the opportunity to go out and earn the money."[68] Santorum's singling out of African Americans in the context of a discussion on government entitlements—which both blacks and whites receive—is classic stereotyping. Audience members, however, immediately began to applaud his racialized comments.[69] Santorum won eleven primaries during the 2012 campaign and was the runner-up to Mitt Romney for the Republican nomination.[70]

Romney, himself, after losing the general election, lamented that Obama had won because he offered "gifts" to targeted groups "especially the African American community, the Hispanic community, and young people."[71] In 2016, Republican candidate Jeb Bush continued the trope of minorities seeking handouts when he responded to a question about how to attract African American voters by saying in part: "Our message is one of hope and aspiration ... It [is not] one of division and get in line and we'll take care of you with free stuff. Our message is one that is uplifting—that says you can achieve earned success."[72] Whether expressed in explicitly racial terms—as Santorum, Bush, and Romney chose—or more indirectly, the government dependency trope is racially loaded. White Americans' attitudes toward government programs to help the poor—"welfare"—are closely correlated with perceptions that antipoverty programs disproportionately benefit racial minorities, and also with the degree of white prejudice against racial minorities.[73] Thus, even though welfare programs had become less generous, and even as a severe recession set in, white opposition to welfare programs increased in 2008 with the election of Barack Obama, whom former House Speaker Newt Gingrich has called the nation's "greatest food stamp president."[74] In contrast, black support for welfare spending increased during the Great Recession.

What explains this divergence? Rachel Wetts of the University of California at Berkeley and Rob Willer of Stanford University conducted an experiment in which some white participants were exposed to data portraying the loss of majority status by whites—a condition projected for the middle of the current century—while others were presented with data showing a stable white majority, a condition projected through 2020. The group informed of loss of majority status expressed greater opposition to welfare spending than its cohort, suggesting that status threat influences opposition to welfare.[75] What is more, those informed of the loss of white majority status displayed significantly greater racial resentment than those informed of a stable white majority, suggesting that racial resentment contributes to opposition to welfare.[76]

To some, Santorum's, Romney's, and Bush's use of a government depen-dency trope vis-à-vis people of color is removed from the realm of classic racism, because these politicians are not associated with white nationalists. But Wetts's and Willer's study showed that "principled conservatism" could not explain the greater opposition to welfare spending by those who perceived their majority status as threatened. This group did not express more conserva-tive positions on *nonracial* issues than the other cohort in the experiment.[77] Furthermore, if the Santorum-Romney-Bush comments—blacks want "free stuff" and are unaccustomed to "earned success"—are not racism, what would constitute racism short of a message of unadulterated hatred of people of color, which only the most marginal of politicians would propagate? As discussed in Chapter 1, the stereotyping represented by these comments avoids the racist label, if at all, only by using historical racism as a benchmark. In this compar-ison, the brute candor of Jim Crow-style racism (falsely) excuses its modern mutations because they are "not as bad." But because our society has long since decoded comments like these, and politicians are aware of how they may reasonably be construed, they are not entitled to a presumption of innocence. This type of racism is as bad as its progenitors.

If voters are given the option to hedge on matters of race by voting for candidates who, while perhaps bigoted, are not as bigoted as they could be, then we should not be surprised that a white supremacist, a white nation-alist, or a member of the alt-right would prefer the rhetoric of Santorum, Romney, Bush, or Trump to that of a prototypical Democratic candidate. The attempt to parse "acceptable" bigotry from "fringe" bigotry calls to mind a quip by Florida Democratic gubernatorial candidate Andrew Gillum, who during the 2018 midterms criticized his Republican opponent, Congressman Ron DeSantis, for speaking at conferences held by white nationalists. "I'm not calling Mr. DeSantis a racist," said Gillum. "I'm simply saying the racists believe he's a racist."[78] In other words, it is almost never a coincidence when a candidate or a party draws the support of bigots.

No party, of course, is free of bigotry. Thus, for example, Democratic U.S. Senate candidate Loretta Sanchez's remark that President Obama endorsed her African American opponent, Kamala Harris, in the primary because both Harris and Obama are black, is a racial epithet.[79] (Sanchez went on to lose to Harris by more than 20 percentage points.[80]) And, though the action was committed decades before he entered public life, Virginia Governor Ralph Northam's dressing in blackface during medical school is certainly racist.[81] On this score, however, the modern Democratic and Republican parties are far from equivalent. For one thing, Democrats have not nominated a candidate as ostensibly racist as Donald Trump in nearly 90 years. For another, if the parties were equivalently racist, we would see alt-right support for Democratic candidates. Most of all, though, to argue that the mere presence of some bigotry in both parties means that they are equally guilty is to miss the larger point. It is not merely the display of racial animus by individual politicians, or even white nationalists' open support of Republicans, that should most concern us. Rather, the concern is the convergence of one party's policies with the worst aims and instincts of white nationalists.

Immigration is a case in point. Richard Spencer, who heads a white nationalist think tank called National Policy Institute, is perhaps the most identifiable public face of the alt-right. Spencer's (and the alt-right's) position on U.S. immigration policy is pithily summed up by a statement Spencer made in 2014: "Immigration is a kind a proxy war—and maybe a last stand—for White Americans, who are undergoing a painful recognition that, unless dramatic action is taken, their grandchildren will live in a country that is alien and hostile."[82] Spencer's time as a history PhD student at Duke University overlapped with Trump White House senior policy advisor Stephen Miller's. Although Miller has disavowed Spencer, Spencer claims to have mentored Miller at Duke.[83] Whatever their actual past relationship, their views on immigration are of a piece. Miller has a long history of criticizing Muslims and Latino immigrants,[84] but his right-wing extremism on immigration is dressed up in precisely the way Carol Swain warns us about in *The New White Nationalism in America*. So, instead of Spencer's dire warning that white people are about to lose their country to immigration, Miller offers this blandishment: "We can have an immigration system that 10, 20, 30, 50 years from now produces more assimilation, higher wages, more economic opportunity, and better prospects for immigrants and U.S.-born alike."[85]

How exactly does an immigration system produce "more assimilation"? Consider the modifications supported by President Trump. In 2017, Senators Tom Cotton of Arkansas and David Perdue of Georgia introduced the Reforming American Immigration for a Strong Economy (RAISE) Act.[86] The legislation would "establish a skills-based immigration points system" and "eliminate the Diversity Visa Program."[87] The latter program awards approximately 50,000 visas annually to applicants from countries with comparatively low immigration rates to the United States. Although it accounts for just 5 percent of the one million legal immigrants to the United States each year, in recent years half of the lottery winners, who are screened prior to entry into the country as other legal immigrants are, have come from Africa.[88]

The other part of the RAISE Act—a skills-based immigration points system that emphasizes educational attainment and work skills and experience—would also favor applicants from more highly developed countries, such as European nations, where the opportunity for educational attainment is greater.[89] By itself, the introduction of immigration legislation that would lower the number of African and Central and Latin American immigrants is perhaps not suspect; in antidiscrimination law, however, disparate impact is a factor to be considered in determining discriminatory intent.[90] When the foreseeable disparate impact of Trump's proposal is placed in the broader context of his campaign pledge to ban Muslims from entering the country, his vow to deport illegal immigrants en masse, and his references to African nations as "shithole" or "shithouse" countries and to illegal immigrants as "murderers and thieves" and "animals,"[91] any claim that Trump, unlike Spencer, does not desire a whiter country fares poorly under pretext analysis.

Trump all but flags his own pretext by falsely equating illegal immigration with increased crime. In seeking to justify his administration's "zero tolerance" of illegal crossings at the nation's southern border—a policy that caused a humanitarian crisis by separating thousands of children from their parents—Trump insisted that his draconian actions were necessary to prevent crime: "Democrats are the problem. They don't care about crime and want illegal immigrants, no matter how bad they may be, to pour into and infest our Country, like MS-13."[92] In antidiscrimination law, some courts recognize that even when an employer proffers an incredible explanation for its action, the explanation is not pretextual if the employer honestly believed it. An important check on the honest belief defense, however, is that "the employer must be able to establish its reasonable reliance on the particularized facts that were before it at the time the decision was made."[93] In other words, the employer's belief and subsequent decision have to appear reasonable in light of the facts at hand; alternative facts and motivated reasoning are not defenses to pretext. At the time of Trump's zero tolerance policy, the facts were not in dispute. In 2018, the libertarian Cato Institute examined the criminal conviction rates in Texas, a border crossing state, for 2015. It found that there were *56 percent fewer* convictions of illegal immigrants than of native-born persons.[94] What was President Trump's response to these statistics? "It's not true," Trump said when confronted with studies contradicting his claims that illegal immigration leads to increased crime.[95]

Perhaps a more truthful response by President Trump would have been, "I don't care, do you?"—the words adorning the back of a jacket worn by Trump's wife Melania (without apparent irony) as she boarded a plane to visit detention centers holding children separated from their parents.[96] Facts do not matter if politicians and their followers are seeking to thrive on racial hysteria. And this disregard for facts means that Trump's America fails to follow the self-correcting model of democracy envisioned by Justice Anthony Kennedy in *Schuette v. Coalition to Save Affirmative Action*. As will be seen in Chapter 8, the era of Trump puts a lie to any notion that democracy can heal itself of its racial woes in the absence of anti-whitelash jurisprudence.

THE MEDIA

Responding to a question from a reporter about whether President Trump's characterization of African nations as "shithole" or "shithouse" countries indicated racism, White House press secretary Sarah Huckabee Sanders said: "I think that is an outrageous claim, and frankly I think if the critics of the president were who he [sic] said he was, why did NBC give him a show for a decade on TV?"[97] This defense was puzzling, even by the standards of a president who traffics in alternative facts. Far from being a bigotry-free zone, television and talk radio are indispensable to fomenting whitelash. Conservative media borrows liberally from the discourse of white nationalism, and this assault is fortified by commentary on blogs, Twitter, and Facebook and in the reader comments section of online publications. Table 4–2 is a sampling of what white Americans hear and read about race and racial minorities every day across the airwaves and on the internet.

The hosts and guests of Fox News are disproportionately represented, reflecting that network's outsized influence in electoral politics. Gregory J. Martin and Ali Yurukoglu of Stanford University found in a 2017 study that Fox News has the highest "persuasion rate" among cable news channels — that is, it is the most successful at converting viewers from one party (Democrat) to the other (Republican).[98] Martin and Yurukoglu estimate that Fox News viewing accounts for increases in the Republican vote share in presidential elections ranging from .46 percentage points in 2000 to 6.34 percentage points in 2008.[99] In 2016, Fox News was the primary source of news for 40 percent of Trump voters.[100] Fox News, however, is far from race-neutral.[101]

The preference of African Americans for MSNBC and whites for Fox News cannot be chalked up to a taste for, say, *Everybody Hates Chris* versus *Seinfeld*. Rather, African Americans rationally abstain from watching Fox News to avoid being offended by its shockingly intolerant content. The "conservatism" represented by Fox News is one that even erstwhile members of the right-wing media concede is laced with bigotry. Center-right *Washington Post* columnist Jennifer Rubin wrote in seeming exasperation during the 2016 election that "[t]he degree to which Fox fake-news programming (e.g. Sean Hannity, Bill O'Reilly,

TABLE 4–2 *White Nationalism from Media and Entertainment Figures*

Speaker and Date	Comment
NBC *Today Show* host **Megyn Kelly**, in an on-air discussion with an all-white panel, October 23, 2018 (NBC soon thereafter canceled her show)	"What is racist? You truly do get in trouble if you are a white person who puts on blackface at Halloween or a black person who puts on whiteface for Halloween. Back when I was a kid, that was OK, as long as you were dressing up as like a character."
Roseanne Barr, comedienne, tweeting about Barack Obama advisor Valerie Jarrett, an African American, May 29, 2018	"Muslim brotherhood & planet of the apes had a baby=vj"
Kanye West, rap artist and Trump supporter on MLK and Malcolm X, April 18, 2018	"Man, I know this is going to cause an uproar, but certain icons are just too far in the past and not relatable and that's what makes them safe."
Jesse Watters, co-host of Fox News' *The Five*, defending President Trump's reference to African nations as "shithole countries," January 11, 2018	"I think it's either fake news or if it's true, this is how the forgotten men and women in America talk at the bar. This is how Trump relates to people . . . I'm trying to put it in perspective here and an off the cuff comment from the president isn't a big deal."
Robert Massi, Fox News legal analyst and host of *The Property Man*, commenting on the plans of some Democratic lawmakers to boycott President Trump's State of the Union address, January 2018	"The other thing is, Ainsley, and I say this very carefully, when is it—does racism come the other way? In other words, is this a political statement or are these people also, as they call the president a racist, are they potentially racist against him [Trump]?"
Bill O'Reilly, former Fox News TV host, rejecting calls to abolish the Electoral College after Donald Trump won the presidency while losing the popular vote, December 2016	"This is all about race. The left sees white privilege in America as an oppressive force that must be done away with. Therefore white working class voters must be marginalized . . . [W]hite men have set up a system of oppression and that system must be destroyed . . . The left wants power taken away from the white establishment and they want a profound change in the way America is run."
Andrea Tantoros, Fox News co-host of *The Five*, who later sued Fox for sexual harassment, May 2015	"The last acceptable form of discrimination in this country now is two groups—one, Christians and, two,

TABLE 4–2 *(continued)*

Speaker and Date	Comment
	white men … Where [is] the organization in defense of white men? Where are the marches? Where are the editorials penned?"
Ann Coulter, commentator and conservative author, on Fox's *Hannity*, May 2015	"Yes, America does owe black America for slavery, for the Democratic policies of Jim Crow. I think we've—we're making it up now. When, you know, you're getting admitted to Princeton when you can't read, is that enough yet?"
Franklin Graham, Christian evangelist and son of Rev. Billy Graham, tweeting about President Obama and his administration, February 28, 2015	"Why is Israeli Prime Minister Benjamin Netanyahu being shunned by the liberal media, congress, and President Barack Obama? I believe it's because this administration has been heavily influenced by Muslims speaking into and giving advice in various areas of the White House. They are anti-Israel and anti-Semitic—and they are influencing the president who as we all know was raised with a strong Muslim influence in his life."
Dinesh D'Souza, conservative commentator and convicted felon, later pardoned by President Trump, tweeting about President Obama, February 18, 2015	"You can take the boy out of the ghetto … Watch this vulgar man show his stuff, while America cowers in embarrassment."
Rush Limbaugh, radio talk show host January 19, 2007	"Look, let me put it to you this way: the NFL all too often looks like a game between the Bloods and the Crips without any weapons. There, I said it."

'Fox and Friends') has mainstreamed and defended blatant racism is shocking."[102] The object of Rubin's ire at the time was Fox News celebrity Sean Hannity, who during his prime-time program directed this missive at President Obama:

> You want to go to Canada? I'll pay for you to go to Canada. You want to go to Kenya? I'll pay for you to go to Kenya. Jakarta, where you went to school back in the day, you can go back there. Anywhere you want to go. I'll put the finest

food—caviar, champagne, you name it. I have one stipulation: You can't come back.[103]

Hannity was perpetuating the "otherization" of the nation's first black president, continuing the "birther" movement—the lie that Obama was not born in the United States and therefore was not qualified under the Constitution to be president.[104] Although birtherism met with limited success—by 2015, *only* 20 percent of Americans said Obama was born outside the United States—the fact that it was not an immediate disqualification to Trump's candidacy portrays a tolerance within conservative circles of race-baiting.[105] As former radio talk show host Charlie Sykes noted, "At one time, racist language was a ticket to exile, but that had changed in the new media environment."[106] Catering to its conservative viewership, Fox News acted as a primary transom for birtherism and thereby played an indispensable role in this racial slander.

Probe the racial dispositions of Fox News's monochromatic viewership (blacks account for only 1 to 1.5 percent of its viewers[107]), and you begin to see the synergy between content and audience. Demos Action policy analyst Sean McElwee used responses by whites self-identifying as conservative in the 2012 American National Election Studies to determine whether regular viewers of Fox News and its then most popular program, *The O'Reilly Factor*, harbored heightened racial animus.[108] White conservatives who regularly watched Fox News and *O'Reilly* were twice as likely as nonregular viewers to believe that blacks have too much political power; indeed, nearly 40 percent of routine viewers believed this.[109] Nearly 50 percent of regular viewers believed that blacks were lazy, compared with 40 percent of nonregular viewers who held this belief—still a disturbing level.[110] Supermajorities of both groups also believed black inequality was due to blacks not trying hard enough; indeed, half of *O'Reilly* viewers believed there was little to no discrimination against blacks.[111] Overall, McElwee's findings suggest that while there may be daylight between white nationalists and Fox News-loving conservatives, they both dwell philosophically in dark places.

THE JUDICIARY

On Fox's *Hannity*, conservative commentator Ann Coulter made this reference in a discussion of first lady Michelle Obama, who graduated from Princeton University: "Yes, America does owe black America for slavery, for the Democratic policies of Jim Crow. I think we've—we're making it up now. When, you know, you're getting admitted to Princeton when you can't read, is that enough yet?"[112] Compare Coulter's jab with a statement made by Justice Antonin Scalia during oral arguments in *Fisher v. University of Texas*, a case about the constitutionality of race-based affirmative action at the University of Texas:

> There are … those who contend that it does not benefit African Americans to—to get them into the University of Texas where they do not do well, as opposed to having them go to a less-advanced school, … a slower-track school where they do well. One of—one the briefs pointed out that most of the black scientists in this country don't come from schools like the University of Texas … They come from lesser schools where they do not feel that they're—that they're being pushed ahead in—in classes that are too—too fast for them … I'm just not impressed by the fact that—that the University of Texas may have fewer [blacks]. Maybe it ought to have fewer. And maybe some—you know, when you take more, the number of blacks, really competent blacks admitted to lesser schools, turns out to be less.[113]

What is the difference between these two statements? Both suggest—nay, assert—that blacks are getting into colleges for which they are unqualified. Let's add to the mix David Duke's contention that affirmative action is state-sanctioned discrimination against better-qualified whites, a view shared by Richard Spencer. Neither Duke nor Spencer is likely to disagree with Justice Clarence Thomas's condemnation of affirmative action in *Grutter v. Bollinger*, which echoes Scalia's: "[O]vermatched students … find that they cannot succeed in the cauldron of competition. And this mismatch crisis is not restricted to elite institutions."[114] And since white nationalists equate remedial actions to correct the effects of past racial discrimination with "reverse discrimination" against whites, what alt-right adherent would disagree with Chief Justice Roberts's simplistic condemnation of Seattle's efforts to ensure some racial integration of its public schools: "The way to stop discrimination on the basis of race is to stop discriminating on the basis of race"?[115]

As with political conservatism, there is a disturbing, even if coincidental, convergence between judicial conservatism and white nationalist views. This alignment aids and abets whitelash, regardless of the purported intentions of conservative jurists. Yet those intentions cannot be presumed innocent when, for example, Justice Antonin Scalia calls the Voting Rights Act of 1965, which conferred the unfettered franchise on millions of blacks and Latinos in the South and Southwest, a "perpetuation of racial entitlement."[116] Scalia would later join four other conservative justices in striking down a key provision of the act because it "differentiates between the States, despite our historic tradition that all the States enjoy equal sovereignty."[117] This "differentia[tion] between the States" on which the Supreme Court's decision rested sounded eerily like the whitelash rhetoric of Ronald Reagan, who invoked states' rights four decades earlier in opposing the Voting Rights Act, calling the act "humiliating to the South."[118]

No less susceptible to a white nationalist construction is Justice Samuel Alito's concurrence in *Ricci v. DeStefano*, a case involving the use of a standardized test to determine promotion opportunities for firefighters in New Haven, Connecticut. Setting aside any possibility that the test might be biased, as black firefighters claimed, Justice Alito suggested that the black firefighters were simply less industrious than the white (and one Hispanic) firefighters who performed well on the exam:

> Petitioners are firefighters who seek only a fair chance to move up the ranks in their chosen profession. In order to qualify for promotion, they made personal sacrifices. Petitioner Frank Ricci, who is dyslexic, found it necessary to "hir[e] someone, at considerable expense, to read onto audiotape the content of the books and study material[s]." He "studied an average of eight to thirteen hours a day ..., even listening to audio tapes while driving his car." Petitioner Benjamin Vargas, who is Hispanic, had to "give up a part-time job," and his wife had to "take leave from her own job in order to take care of their three young children while Vargas studied." "Vargas devoted countless hours to study ..., missed two of his children's birthdays and over two weeks of vacation time," and "incurred significant financial expense" during the [three]-month study period.[119]

In this way, Alito portrays the largely white firefighters who excelled on the written exam as model candidates, disregarding the concerns of the black applicants who had questioned the exam's relevance and evenhandedness. In other words, if blacks would just try harder, they too would succeed. There is little daylight between Alito's concurrence and the prevailing view among Republicans and Trump voters that "It's really a matter of some people not trying hard enough; if blacks would only try harder they could be just as well off as whites."[120] The portraits that emerge from the conservative political arena and the judiciary morph into one: blacks are not smart enough to attend the same colleges as whites, and they are indolent. For conservative justices who purport to oppose racial remedies like affirmative action because of their supposed tendency to stereotype, these justices themselves do a superb job of stereotyping blacks.

Of course, it is not stereotyping of blacks about which conservative jurists are really concerned. It's the stereotyping of whites as "racist." Indeed, the preoccupation of the conservative majority on the Court with the protection of whites against supposed discrimination mirrors the current unwarranted belief by a majority of white Americans that "discrimination against whites has become as big a problem as discrimination against blacks and other minorities."[121] The reality is quite different: most of the racial discrimination claims handled by the United States Equal Employment Opportunity Commission annually are filed by blacks.[122] But, as discussed in the next chapter, conservative jurists, like misinformed voters, do not allow facts to get in the way of the outcomes they seek.

Under President Trump, the convergence of white nationalist thought with the judiciary threatens to get worse. One Trump nominee for a federal district court in Louisiana declined to state whether *Brown v. Board of Education*, which ended the "separate but equal" doctrine, was correctly decided.[123] A Trump nominee for the U.S. Court of Appeals for the Sixth Circuit blogged under an alias about President Obama's Kenyan heritage, favorably citing white nationalist websites that peddled the false claim that Obama was born in Kenya.[124] Yet another Trump pick, Ryan Bounds, nominated to the Ninth Circuit Court of Appeals, had a prolific history of racist statements, including some that are indistinguishable from those of white nationalists like Richard Spencer, such as comparing racial minority affinity groups to white Aryan supremacist groups.[125] Still, this nomination was unanimously supported by Republicans on the Senate Judiciary Committee—all white men. It was ultimately withdrawn when the lone black Republican in the Senate, Tim Scott, intimated that he would not support Bounds because of his racially insensitive past writings.[126]

How is it possible that in the United States in the twenty-first century, any president would dare to nominate judicial candidates with openly racist pasts? Perhaps because Trump is an unabashed racist. But to embrace only this explanation is to miss a historical continuum among conservatives. In 1986, President Ronald Reagan, far more linguistically adept in his use of racial code than Trump, nominated Supreme Court associate justice William Rehnquist to become chief justice. Although allegations of voter intimidation and suppression of blacks and Latinos by Rehnquist in his days as a Republican Party activist in Arizona swirled around his nomination, many defended Rehnquist's actions as those of a committed conservative, rejecting charges of bigotry.[127] In appointing federal court nominees whose backgrounds on race should disqualify them in a society that takes seriously its antidiscrimination norms, Trump is simply picking up where Reagan, "the Great Communicator," left off. And the message remains the same: the "conservative" label is a Trojan horse, allowing into our democracy racist actions and outcomes to which no white nationalist or supremacist would ever object.

THE INDIGNANT DENIAL

The routine reaction of conservatives when they are compared to white nationalists is not different from the stock reaction of most whites when they are confronted with their own racism. They display what author Robin DiAngelo calls "white fragility," a set of defensive behaviors intended to cut off any discussion of race that might cause a white person discomfort.[128] DiAngelo explains that a cardinal rule of white fragility is that whites must never be *publicly* confronted about their racist behavior; indeed, the tacit agreement—certainly among whites themselves—is that racist behavior is not to be critiqued at all.[129]

Bill Kristol of the now-defunct conservative *Weekly Standard* breached these rules when he called out Fox News host Tucker Carlson, a former mentee of Kristol's. Reflecting on Carlson's performance on his nightly program, *The Tucker Carlson Show*, Kristol remarked, "I mean, it is close now to racism, white—I mean, I don't know if it's racism exactly—but ethno-nationalism of some kind, let's call it."[130] Carlson responded with white fragility: "I'm not even sure what he's accusing me of. He offers no evidence or examples, just slurs, and then suggests that I'm the demagogue."[131]

No evidence or examples? In one segment of his show, Carlson noted the change in demographics in a Pennsylvania town from 2 percent Latino in 2000 to majority Latino in 2018. He then asked his three million viewers, "How would you feel if that happened in your neighborhood?"[132] In another segment, Carlson responded to a guest's lament about Latino immigration by calling the growth in the Latino population "bewildering" and stating, "I don't think you have to be motivated by hate to say maybe I should have some say in how my country evolves."[133] In still another segment of his show, Carlson attacked the proposition that the nation's demographic diversity is a strength: "How, precisely, is diversity our strength ... Can you think, for example, of other institutions such as, I don't know, marriage or military units in which the less people have in common, the more cohesive they are?"[134]

Statements like these could easily be transported in time back to the 1940s or 1950s. That is why conservatives of conscience are now denouncing the Republicans' explicit turn to white identity politics. Some are even leaving the Republican Party. Steve Schmidt, a chief political strategist for Senator John McCain's 2008 presidential bid and for George W. Bush's reelection in

2004, publicly renounced his affiliation with the Republican Party in 2018, singling out President Trump's policy of separating families who illegally cross the southern border. Schmidt tweeted, "This child separation policy is connected to the worst abuses of humanity in our history. It is connected by the same evil that separated families during slavery and dislocated tribes and broke up Native American families. It is immoral and must be repudiated."[135]

None of this may matter to President Trump's base, which is also the base of the Republican Party. During his second year in office, Trump averaged 87 percent support among Republicans and even saw an uptick in his support among the party during the controversy over his zero-tolerance illegal immigration policy. Other than George W. Bush after the attacks of 9/11, no modern president has been as popular with his party in his second year.[136] We have seen that the process of attempting to persuade misinformed voters, those who willfully ignore facts, can backfire, leading them to dig in. The willingness to brush off charges of racism and the aversion to facts on the part of Trump supporters paint a grim prognosis for our democracy. Starting in the middle of the last century, American courts could be relied on to intervene and check the worst vices in our democracy, including the racial tyranny of whitelash. By the mid-1970s, however, the Supreme Court was actively participating in whitelash. The machinations by which this occurred bore a striking resemblance to the conduct of misinformed voters—rejecting facts and relying on intuition reasoned from incomplete or mistaken facts, all with seemingly pretextual reasoning. The same Court that defined and interpreted the anti-discrimination norm was thus itself guilty of breaching it. To this matter we now turn.

5

Law as Pretext

"[T]he white 'majority' itself is composed of various minority groups, most of which can lay claim to a history of prior discrimination at the hands of the State and private individuals. Not all of these groups can receive preferential treatment and corresponding judicial tolerance of distinctions drawn in terms of race and nationality, for then the only 'majority' left would be a new minority of white Anglo-Saxon Protestants."

—Justice Louis Powell, *Regents of the Univ. of Cal. v. Bakke* (1978)[1]

It is difficult to pinpoint when the latest round of judicial whitelash began, but the 1978 decision in *Regents of the University of California v. Bakke* is perhaps as good a starting place as any. In *Bakke*, Justice Powell, announcing the U.S. Supreme Court's judgment, ignored the history of how various European immigrant groups—whether Jews, Irish, or Italians—have been absorbed into the white race regardless of their previous categorization.[2] Justice Powell equated their history with that of African Americans and used this ahistorical comparison to invalidate an affirmative action program at the University of California School of Medicine at Davis. Save for the judicial trappings, there is little difference between Justice Powell's views and the sentiment of a supermajority of Trump supporters in 2018 that "if blacks would only try harder they could be just as well off as whites."[3] Justice Powell's equating of European immigrants with slaves' descendants lives on as a judicial ceiling under which not just affirmative action but racial equality itself has consistently been smothered.

Justice Powell's opinion illustrates what Professor Darren Hutchinson has called "factless jurisprudence" and "pervasive and comprehensive ... decontextualized juridical analysis."[4] Indeed, before Trump advisor Kellyanne Conway's coining of the laughingstock "alternative facts," courts were engaged in factless jurisprudence as their own form of factual dissonance. At times resembling the selective factual arguments of motivated reasoning, but often resembling the misinformed voter's disregard of established facts, factless jurisprudence presaged and now abets Trumpian whitelash in ways that may not always be apparent, but which deserve attention in any deconstruction of modern white backlash.

With a judiciary not immune to whitelash, we need to critique judicial opinions regarding race. The following two sections explore judicial whitelash and the psychological mechanisms underlying it in more detail. In the remainder of the chapter, antidiscrimination law is used to critique judicial opinions regarding race. The discussion illuminates the pretextual guises of judicial decision-making in three areas of the law: voting rights, employment discrimination, and campaign finance. Although the third category is not explicitly racial, the Supreme Court's campaign finance jurisprudence is an illustration of how nonracial cases, decided using pretextual, motivated reasoning, can stoke whitelash against people of color. *Richardson v. Ramirez*, discussed in the next section, also exemplifies this type of case. The illustrations reveal how the judiciary has been indispensable in contemporary whitelash, for it is impossible for racial inequality to continue to flourish as it has without the complicity of the courts.

JUDGING JUDGES: THE PARABLE OF *RICHARDSON V. RAMIREZ*

Suppose you were the victim of sexual harassment on the job. How would you feel if the judge in your case had previously criticized the #MeToo movement in a tweet like the following?

> How Appealing: "[All female] Law Clerks for Workplace Accountability launches a web site, a Twitter account, and issues its 'Response to the Federal Judiciary Workplace Conduct Working Group's Report.'" New Spanish Inquisition by SJWs [social justice warriors]? Thank goodness for Article III.[5]

Federal district court judge Richard G. Kopf wrote these actual words on July 20, 2018. You would not want Judge Kopf to adjudicate your sexual harassment claim. You would rightly suspect a predisposition against sexual harassment claims, and even if your suspicions were not ultimately borne out, Judge Kopf's adjudication of such cases would have a fox-guarding-the-henhouse quality to it.

Voting rights have faced similar threats from the judiciary charged with guarding it. Justice William Rehnquist, the author of the 1974 *Richardson v. Ramirez* decision, which empowered states to permanently disenfranchise ex-felons who have completed their sentences, was a Republican Party operative before his appointment to the Supreme Court. He participated in "voter integrity" operations that challenged the credentials of voters in Arizona — voters who were overwhelmingly Democrats and people of color. Earlier in his career, as a Supreme Court clerk, he advised Justice Robert H. Jackson to rule against school desegregation in *Brown v. Board of Education*. Rehnquist wrote to Jackson, "I realize it is an unpopular and unhumanitarian position, for which I have been excoriated by 'liberal' colleagues, but I think Plessy v. Ferguson was right and should be reaffirmed."[6]

If you are a black or Latino litigant before the Supreme Court in a case involving racial equality, you would not want a supporter of the "separate but equal" doctrine that *Brown* overturned hearing your case any more than a sexual harassment victim would want Judge Kopf hearing her case. Yet in *Richardson*, Justice Rehnquist authored a decision that to this day has limited the political voice of black and Latino voters without a clear constitutional justification. According to the Brennan Center for Justice at New York University, in 2017, one in every thirteen African Americans of voting age were barred from voting by felony disenfranchisement laws.[7] We know that Justice Rehnquist's decision in *Richardson* lacked a clear constitutional basis because he said so: "The legislative history bearing on the meaning of the relevant language of § 2 is scant indeed . . ."[8]

Section 2 of the Fourteenth Amendment, at issue in *Richardson*, punishes states that deprive their citizens of the right to vote by reducing the population basis on which their congressional representation is calculated. The population-reduction penalty, however, does not apply where a person is deprived of the franchise "for participation in rebellion, or other crime."[9] The question for the Court was whether the exception "for participation in rebellion, or other crime" gave states unfettered authority to permanently disenfranchise ex-felons even if there was no compelling (or even rational) reason to do so. Whatever one may think of the Court's historical analysis in *Richardson*, Justice Rehnquist's participation in the case and his authorship of the decision bore hallmarks of discriminatory intent. Should citizens forget Justice Rehnquist's support of "separate but equal" when he authors an opinion that legalizes the disenfranchisement of millions of blacks and Latinos? Should they disregard his background as a Republican political operative who challenged the credentials of black and Latino voters? Wouldn't a reasonable juror in any antidiscrimination case take these facts into account? Of course. And there is no reason to treat a judicial decision bearing on racial equality any differently. The Supreme Court established in 1948 that the judiciary cannot constitutionally enforce private discrimination;[10] certainly, then, the courts must not themselves engage in discrimination. And if a juror's racial bias is known to threaten a defendant's constitutional due process rights,[11] judges' racial biases pose no less of a constitutional menace. In short, because the judiciary is not above the law it makes, judicial decisions should be evaluated using the same antidiscrimination principles, including pretext analysis, that apply to any other person's behavior.

Rehnquist's acknowledgment that the Court didn't have much legislative history to base its decision on was in effect a concession that the Court had the latitude to rule either way. Rehnquist chose the outcome most consistent with his own racial background. More often than not, however, judges deny even the possibility that their rulings might reflect political or racial biases. Such denials overlook the significant number of decisions, like *Richardson v. Ramirez*, that invite the exercise of judicial discretion.

Racial discrimination by judges is most likely to come into play where discretion is called for—that is, where the legal rule is unclear—because a court's violation of well-established rules would make its discrimination glaring. In the same vein, an employer is most likely to discriminate where the credentials separating a white applicant from an applicant of color are close rather than starkly different. As Professor Melissa Hart has explained, "[D]iscrimination is most likely to occur in contexts where it can be justified as something other than discrimination."[12] Thus, whitelash in the judiciary is unlikely to take the crude forms that President Trump favors, though in Chapter 4 we have seen barely disguised white nationalism by some Supreme Court justices.

Rather, modern judicial whitelash is clothed in pretextual reasoning whose results work a disparate impact on people of color. Therefore, deconstructing whitelash in its totality requires that judges be treated no differently than an electorate, a legislature, or a jury in attempting to ascertain whether a decision violates the antidiscrimination norm. Indeed, the judiciary is not immune from the racial animus that permeates the decision-making of many white voters. Comparing judges appointed by Democratic and Republican presidents, Professors Alma Cohen and Crystal Yang of Harvard Law School found in a 2018 study that Republican-appointed federal district court judges gave substantially longer sentences to black defendants than to similarly situated nonblack offenders.[13] The disparity persisted even after controlling for other judge characteristics, and the greater the amount of discretion in sentencing, the greater the disparity.[14] Moreover, the study found larger disparities among judges serving in states with higher indicators of racial bias, primarily in the South.[15]

Although they did not purport to show causation, Cohen and Yang concluded that their results "are consistent with some judges holding discriminatory attitudes given that we find larger disparities among judges who serve in courts from states with higher racial bias, which are disproportionately located in the South."[16] But considering the evidence that Republicans as a group have higher racial resentment than Democrats,[17] perhaps we should not be surprised that Republican-appointed judges engage in disparate sentencing of black and nonblack defendants. Cohen's and Yang's findings are simply a variation of what we already know about Republican voters. Why would Republican judges be different?

Professors Pat Chew and Robert Kelley analyzed racial harassment decisions under Title VII to determine what variables contributed to case outcomes. Title VII is the principal federal protection against employment discrimination based on race, gender, or national origin. Examining racial harassment cases from 1981 to 2003 from six federal circuits, Chew and Kelley found that judges appointed by a Democratic president ruled for plaintiffs in 29.3 percent of the cases, while those appointed by Republican judges found for plaintiffs in only 17 percent of the cases, a difference not attributable to chance.[18]

Similarly, Professors Cass Sunstein and David Schkade, along with law student Lisa Ellman, examined a sample of 320 cases filed by African American Title VII plaintiffs and appealed in the federal courts between 1985 and 2002.[19] In addition, the authors examined 155 cases involving affirmative action from 1978 through 2002. Looking at published appellate decisions, Sunstein et al. found that in Title VII cases, judges appointed by a Democratic president voted for the plaintiff 41 percent of the time, while Republican-appointed judges sided with plaintiffs 35 percent of the time. This evidence of ideological voting was "small but nearly statistically significant."[20] In contrast, in the affirmative action cases, where questions of past discrimination and generational benefit are brought into sharpest relief, the authors found that Democratic appointees voted to uphold affirmative action plans 74 percent of the time versus 48 percent of the time for Republican ones—a disparity the authors characterized as "striking evidence of ideological voting."[21] Yet judges continue to insist that their decisions are not politically motivated. Judge Neil Gorsuch, in his Supreme Court confirmation quest, offered the blandishment that "[t]here is no such thing as a Republican judge or Democratic judge."[22] Similarly, controversial Supreme Court nominee Judge Brett Kavanaugh insisted that "[t]he Supreme Court must never be viewed as a partisan institution"—even after Kavanaugh himself had delivered unprecedented partisan attacks against Senate Judiciary Committee Democrats.[23]

The findings by Chew and Kelley and by Sunstein et al. are consistent with polling data on partisan differences in the perceptions of the prevalence of discrimination. A 2017 Pew Research survey found that most Republicans (59 percent) believe the country has already made the changes needed to give blacks equality with whites; only 36 percent believe that more needs to be done.[24] In contrast, a staggering 81 percent of Democrats believe that more needs to be done.[25] Similarly, 64 percent of Democrats believe racial discrimination is the primary reason blacks cannot get ahead, whereas 75 percent of Republicans reject that idea. The share of Republicans that embrace racial discrimination as a primary barrier to black progress was lower in 2017 (14 percent) than in 1994 (26 percent).[26] Republicans likewise were far more likely to believe that affirmative action unfairly discriminates against whites, with 61 percent of Republicans taking this position in a 2018 NPR poll, compared with 37 percent of all respondents.[27]

What lurks behind these partisan differences is an unstated but unmistakable view by many Republicans of black inferiority and slothfulness. As Ibram Kendi crystalizes in *Stamped from the Beginning*, "When you truly believe that racial groups are equal, then you also believe that racial disparities must be the result of racial discrimination."[28] Absent statistical anomalies across myriad black–white disparities, if racial discrimination is not to blame, then racial inferiority must be the cause. This is the *reductio ad absurdum* of Republicans' (and hence conservatives') denials of the existence of meaningful discrimination against African Americans and other people of color. That this attitude infiltrates conservative jurisprudence—and that conservatives have been a majority on the U.S. Supreme Court for at least the past 40 years—explains the complicity of the judiciary in whitelash.

A CLOSER LOOK AT JUDICIAL WHITELASH

The implicit claim at the heart of discrimination denials—that is, the assumption that those who are unequal are unequal because they are inferior—is typically couched in euphemisms to elide social opprobrium. Social dominance theory refers to such euphemisms as "hierarchy-legitimizing myths."[29] This theory posits that societies characterized by inequality maintain stability by propagating ideologies that assign superiority to one group over others, thus rationalizing inequality.[30] In the United States, hierarchy-legitimating myths such as "meritocracy" are essential to normalizing inequality.

Persons with a high social dominance orientation (SDO, introduced in Chapter 3) tend to favor ideologies and public policy that perpetuate hierarchical societal arrangements and thus inequality itself.[31] SDO is highly correlated with political–economic conservatism.[32] That is, the more conservative a person's political ideology, the greater the person's SDO tends to be. The correlation between conservatism and SDO, in turn, may explain why conservatism is correlated with racism: persons with high SDO also tend to harbor anti-black predispositions.[33]

Professor David Simson has deployed SDO to explain the overall pro-defendant bent of employment discrimination jurisprudence. According to Simson, the largely negative outcomes for employment discrimination plaintiffs aren't surprising given law's centrality in spawning hierarchy-legitimizing myths and the dominant-group (i.e., white male) composition of the judiciary.[34] A study by Chew and Kelley lends support to this thesis. This time looking at reported racial harassment cases in six federal circuits from 2002 to 2008, Chew and Kelley found that plaintiffs were successful in 42.2 percent of cases where the trial judge was African American versus only 20.6 percent of cases where the trial judge was white.[35] The difference was statistically significant—that is, it is not a chance occurrence. Chew and Kelley's explanation of their findings points to different understandings of the cases among white versus African American judges. Although Chew and Kelley do not specifically discuss SDO, their explanation suggests its presence:

> It could be that White judges as a whole are less likely to connect the dots. Or, they discount some of the dots, explaining them away as typical workplace behavior or an insensitive form of humor that is not race-related or serious. In contrast, African American judges may be more inclined to connect the dots ... They are also more likely to give credence to subtle stereotyping of minority groups, such as "coded" statements linked to stereotyping of racial minorities ... [I]n American society, African American judges have more probably been targets of race-related behavior during their lives (whether it be taxi drivers refusing to pick them up, strangers insulting them with racial slurs, or supervisors crediting their achievements to affirmative action rather than their merits). Simply stated, African American judges could be much further up the learning curve of what constitutes racial harassment than their White counterparts.[36]

Chew and Kelley also observed a comparatively lower success rate for black plaintiffs, who constituted the majority of plaintiffs in racial harassment cases.[37] This finding is consistent with those in the criminal sentencing context, where Cohen and Yang found that blacks received harsher sentences than nonblacks.[38] In addition to disparities in sentencing, blacks are more likely to be searched for contraband than similarly situated whites and are more likely to be convicted, more likely to be incarcerated, and more likely to be assigned higher monetary bail amounts than comparable white defendants.[39] Thus, it is little wonder that Judge Theodore McKee, a black federal court of appeals judge with an intimate knowledge of the American judicial system, commented that "[r]acism is . . . very deeply ingrained in our society and in our justice system."[40] Similarly, George Crockett Jr., a former U.S. congressman and former chief judge of Detroit's criminal court, opined:

> I think it was Benjamin Cardozo, in his *Judicial Process*, who emphasized how the judge is the product of his own experiences and his own background. That's why it's important to make sure that judges on the trial court level are not just shot through and through with prejudice based on race, creed, or color. And that's why it becomes important for Black people and other minorities to get judges who have somehow shared their experiences and their backgrounds: those experiences will influence the judicial discretion that the law authorizes a judge to use in certain cases.[41]

Crockett spoke those words in the latter part of the twentieth century. In 2017, the National Center for State Courts conducted its annual survey about the public's perceptions of state courts. The survey asked respondents whether they agreed with this statement: "[J]udges in (STATE) courts reflect the values of our communities and understand the challenges facing the people who appear in their courtrooms."[42] Whites were twice as likely to agree than blacks (38 percent versus 19 percent). The survey also asked respondents whether they agreed with the statement "Too many judges in (STATE) courts don't understand the challenges facing people who appear in their courtrooms and need to do a better job of getting out into the community and listening to people." Black respondents were 20 percentage points more likely to agree with that statement (78 percent versus 58 percent).[43] In other words, Crockett's assessment is as applicable today as it was in the last century.

Judges McKee and Crockett were among more than a dozen black jurists who gave candid appraisals of the American justice system in Linn Washington's *Black Judges on Justice*. In the same volume, Judge Damon Keith of the U.S. Court of Appeals makes the connection, as argued in this chapter, that judicial whitelash often serves societal whitelash. Noting that Presidents Reagan and George H. W. Bush had appointed no African American judges to the Sixth Circuit Court of Appeals over the course of twelve years, Keith observed,

When a president reflects that myopic point of view, it trickles down. People on the courts—I'm speaking of judges, personnel, and staff—CEOs of corporations, and other leaders tend to follow the president's lead. If the president has the attitude that excluding Blacks is acceptable, then it becomes more acceptable to everyone else.[44]

One might think the racial composition of the judiciary is not important so long as the judges do not demonstrate overt racial bias. Indeed, given the professional norms to which judges are held, racism in its classical form is even less likely to be manifested among judges than among the general population. Yet a 2009 study of implicit bias among federal judges published in the *Notre Dame Law Review* confirmed that the same kinds of bias that infiltrate decision-making outside the judiciary affect judges. Implicit biases are unconscious stereotypes that affect our perception of others and our behavior toward them.[45]

The Notre Dame study recruited 133 judges from multiple jurisdictions and regions of the country.[46] The researchers had these judges take the Implicit Association Test (IAT), a widely recognized tool for assessing implicit bias that tests participants' inclination to associate white images with positive words and black images with negative words.[47] Although the implications of the test's results continue to be debated, its most consistent finding is a strong "white preference" among white Americans.[48] That is, white Americans more readily associate images of white people with positive adjectives and images of black people with negative adjectives, rather than the reverse.[49]

Consistent with the outcomes among white laypeople, white judges in the Notre Dame study revealed a strong white preference.[50] In fact, the white judges exhibited an even greater white preference than whites in the general population did.[51] Black judges, on the other hand, "demonstrated no clear preference overall," just as black laypersons "do not exhibit the same white preference that whites express, but neither do they show a mirror-image black preference."[52]

The IAT, however, only tells us the degree to which implicit bias may exist in the judiciary; the test does not reveal how such bias affects the administration of justice, if at all. To make this assessment, the researchers in the Notre Dame study gave the 133 judges hypothetical vignettes in which they manipulated the race of a criminal defendant.[53] In the two vignettes in which the race of the defendant was not explicit, judges with a white preference on the IAT did indeed sentence the defendant to more jail time when they were primed to think the defendant was black than when they were not.[54] The difference, however, was only "marginally significant."[55] In a third vignette, where the race of the defendant and the race of the victim were made explicit, the researchers did not find that IAT scores played a role in the decision-making of white judges, but they did find that black judges whose scores indicated a preference for blacks were more willing to acquit the black defendant.[56] The researchers concluded that while judges who harbor implicit biases are not necessarily influenced by them, implicit bias can affect judicial decision-making under some circumstances, and the risk of this occurring is "sizable."[57]

There is, however, no way to know when those circumstances occur unless we subject judicial decisions to the same scrutiny for pretext and other indicia of discrimination to which we subject a range of other decisions, including employer decisions, jury verdicts, and legislative actions. Consider again the statement of then-Judge Neil Gorsuch, nominated by President Trump to the Supreme Court, that "[t]here is no such thing as a Republican judge or Democratic judge." Yet the studies just examined show that justice clearly is not blind, and judges are often dangerously oblivious to their potential biases. As the authors of the Notre Dame study concluded, "Control of implicit bias requires active, conscious control."[58] If a judge operates from the premise that there's no "bigot in the brain," then the risk of unconscious biases infecting her decision are greater than if she acts with consciousness of the potential for her own racial bias.[59] Contrast Gorsuch's statement with that of Justice Harry Blackmun, who observed, "[J]udges are never free from the feelings of the times or those emerging from their own personal lives."[60] Whitelash in the judiciary is much more likely to stem from judges who hold false beliefs about their partisan and race blindness than from those who engage in conscious reckoning with the influence of partisan and racial ideology on judicial decisions.

VOTING RIGHTS, RACE, AND DEMOCRACY

It's helpful to look at how the potential biases discussed earlier in this chapter manifest themselves in actual judicial opinions. These biases emerge in unobvious ways, often dissembled as law or fact when they are at best a justice's or a judge's gut inference—one that may be infected by bias. When these inferences harm people of color, they should be probed for pretext in the same way we would probe an employer's explanation for not hiring a person of color.

Prior to its partial demise at the hands of the Supreme Court in 2013 (*Shelby County, Ala. v. Holder*), the Voting Rights Act (VRA) required states of the old Confederacy (and a few others) to seek the permission of the federal government or federal courts before changing their voting laws. These states and localities, called "covered jurisdictions," were sub-jected to this process—called "preclearance"—because of their unique history of voting discrimination against blacks and Latinos. Notwithstanding Justice Antonin Scalia's pugilist view that Congress reauthorized the VRA only to avoid being called "racist,"[61] even in the new millennium there was good reason to continue preclearance. In 2000, for instance, 37 percent of whites in covered jurisdictions believed that "Blacks have too much influence in American politics today," compared with 21 percent of whites in noncovered jurisdictions who believed the same.[62] Significantly more whites in covered jurisdictions harbored high levels of racial resentment towards blacks than whites in noncovered jurisdictions.[63] And whites in covered jurisdictions were 14 percentage points more likely than whites in noncovered jurisdictions to disagree with the following sentiment: "Generations of slavery and discrimination have created conditions that make it difficult for Blacks to work their way up."[64] None of these differences, however, mattered to the United States Supreme Court when it invalidated the VRA's preclearance regime in *Shelby County, Ala. v. Holder*.[65]

The decision to free southern states from the federal check on their histor-ical propensity to discriminate in voting rested on states' rights rhetoric resembling that of the antebellum era: "Not only do States retain sovereignty under the Constitution, there is also a fundamental principle of *equal* sover-eignty among the States."[66] In fact, there is no constitutional principle of equal sovereignty among the states once a state is admitted to the union. In uphold-ing the constitutionality of the very same preclearance provision of the VRA in *South Carolina v. Katzenbach*, the Supreme Court specifically held that "[t]he doctrine of the equality of States ... applies only to the terms upon which States are admitted to the Union, and not to the remedies for local evils which have subsequently appeared."[67]

So what should we make of Chief Justice Roberts's flat-out misstatement of the law? Perhaps it was a simple error. Or perhaps it was earnest intellectual disagreement about the meaning of *Katzenbach*. But if Chief Justice Roberts and his conservative colleagues were defendants in a Title VII employment discrimination suit, a juror would be free to treat Roberts's misstatement as a lie. As such, it would be evidence of pretext to hide the real reason for the decision in *Shelby County*—the majority's intent to allow discrimination against black voters. As the Supreme Court has held in Title VII employment discrimination cases, "the factfinder is entitled to consider a party's dishonesty about a material fact as affirmative evidence of guilt."[68] Whatever deference Chief Justice Roberts's opinion might be entitled to in our constitutional democracy, it is not entitled to moral or intellectual deference if it violates the antidiscrimination norm. Because judges are susceptible to partisan and racial biases, we should never assume that a judicial decision is free of these biases if the logic of the decision, combined with its impact on discrete racial groups, provides reasonable grounds for suspicion.

Even if states were entitled to equal sovereignty, the selective application of this principle would raise questions of discrimination if a court applied it to the detriment of people of color but not in other cases. This selective application indeed happened a mere two years after *Shelby County* was decided. In *Arizona State Legislature v. Arizona Independent Redistricting Commission*,[69] Arizona's Republican-controlled legislature, frustrated by its inability to gerrymander the state's congressional districts in favor of Republicans, sought to strip the state's Independent Redistricting Commission of its authority to draw congressional lines. Even though the commission had been created by a citizens' initiative duly authorized by Arizona's constitution, the legislature argued that under the U.S. Constitution, only it, and not a commission, could draw congressional lines.[70] The Court rejected the legislature's position, refusing to accept a twisted reading of the term "legislature" in the Elections Clause of the Constitution that would, in effect, elevate the will of a state legislature over that of the people who elected it in the first place.[71] In his dissent, Chief Justice Roberts showed none of the concern with states' rights that animated his majority opinion in *Shelby County*. Instead, Roberts and the Court's most devout conservatives were willing to displace the voice of the people of Arizona in this case, contrary to the most fundamental precept of sovereignty that the Court had set forth two decades earlier in *New York v. United States*: "The Constitution does not protect the sovereignty of States for the benefit of the States or state governments as abstract political entities, or even for the benefit of the public officials governing the States. To the contrary, the Constitution divides authority between federal and state governments for the protection of individuals."[72]

A second major fallacy in *Shelby County* may not qualify as an outright lie, but it still rings of pretext because the majority ignored important facts in the record of the case. Chief Justice Roberts predicated the majority's decision on an inexplicably narrow view of discrimination: "Regardless of how to look at the record ... no one can fairly say that it shows anything approaching the 'pervasive,' 'flagrant,' 'widespread,' and 'rampant' discrimination that faced Congress in 1965, and that clearly distinguished the covered jurisdictions from the rest of the Nation at that time."[73] In other words, using the rationalizing device of selective comparison, Chief Justice Roberts and the Court's conservatives found that things are not "as bad"; therefore congressional intervention is no longer necessary. The possibility of white voter backlash against increased black and Latino empowerment was completely ignored. Yet that is precisely what was occurring in the South at the time of the Court's decision as well as long before it, and even now.

Racially polarized voting in the South is extreme and has deepened in recent years. Whites vote overwhelmingly for Republicans, while almost all blacks vote for Democrats. In the 2006 congressional elections, Republicans won the white southern vote by 16 percentage points. By 2014, one year after *Shelby County*, that margin had increased to 40 percentage points.[74] Democrats lost the white vote in the Deep South (Alabama, Georgia, Louisiana, Mississippi, and South Carolina) in 2014 by 81 percent to 17 percent, making white southerners in those states substantially more Republican than the country as a whole.[75] When one party is almost all-white and the other is disproportionately black, partisanship may act as a pretext for racial discrimination by the nearly all-white party against its browner competitor.[76]

Recall from Chapter 1 that the renowned Republican political strategist Lee Atwater, who managed George H. W. Bush's 1988 Willie Horton-themed campaign, intended for race to permeate nonracial issues in order to give Jim Crow politics a more respectable appearance: "'We want to cut this' is much more abstract than even the busing thing, uh, and a hell of a lot more abstract than 'Nigger, nigger.'"[77] Atwater's vision of a more opaque racial politics was taking root well before he came to prominence. Since at least Richard Nixon's "southern strategy" in 1968, racial resentment has correlated with facially race-neutral political issues and with party preference.[78]

Political scientist Adam Ender and researcher Jamil Scott documented that this correlation has been increasing over the past 28 years. Using the standard battery of questions from the American National Election Studies to measure racial resentment among whites, Ender and Scott found that racial resentment has held relatively steady at approximately 0.6 on a scale of 0 (no racial resentment) to 1 (most racially resentful) from 1988 to 2016, dipping slightly in the last presidential election.[79] The correlation of racial attitudes with nonracial political issues and partisan dispositions, however, has increased over time.[80] Given this connection, the extreme racially polarized voting of the South cannot be dismissed as a partisan coincidence: race infuses even nonracial matters.

How does Chief Justice Roberts address racially polarized voting in *Shelby County*? He doesn't. The majority opinion literally does not mention the term, even though Justice Ginsburg's dissent challenged Chief Justice Roberts to engage the issue. Justice Ginsburg's dissent reflects legal (and political) realism rather than alternative facts: "[A] governing political coalition has an incentive to prevent changes in the existing balance of voting power. When voting is racially polarized, efforts by the ruling party to pursue that incentive will inevitably discriminate against a racial group."[81] Consistent with Justice Ginsburg's understanding, when the Court struck down a minority subcontracting set-aside program that purportedly disadvantaged *whites* in *City of Richmond v. J.A. Croson Co.*, it noted that Richmond was 50 percent black and that blacks controlled the city council. It then applied the highest level of constitutional scrutiny to Richmond's set-aside program, declaring that "a political majority will more easily act to the disadvantage of a minority based on unwarranted assumptions or incomplete facts . . ."[82]

But where was this concern for the vulnerability of nonwhite racial minorities in *Shelby County*? Under antidiscrimination law, the unequal treatment of similarly situated parties is evidence that the proffered justification for an outcome is actually a pretext for discrimination.[83] When we compare *Shelby County* to *Croson*, the Court's greater solicitude for a white minority than for a racial minority is evidence of racial discrimination by the Court. Moreover, the *Shelby County* majority's complete failure to address Justice Ginsburg's argument about racially polarized voting is tantamount to a defendant's refusal in a discrimination suit to supply a reason for its adverse job action: we are rightly suspicious that the employer's silence is meant to hide something nefarious.[84]

In *Shelby County*, Roberts's opinion remained silent in the face of potent evidence that (1) racially polarized voting was extreme in the South, (2) it rendered blacks and Latinos vulnerable, and (3) Congress predicated its renewal of the VRA on these facts. This silence suggests that he and the majority prized an outcome that was harmful to voters of color over intellectual honesty (or even intellectual engagement). Quite apart from this, because courts themselves treat a party's failure to respond to a material argument as a concession of the argument's validity,[85] there is no reason not to treat Chief Justice Roberts's nonresponse the same. *Shelby County* is thus a model of motivated, pretextual reasoning and judicial reliance on "alternative facts." The judiciary cannot protect minorities against whitelash when it participates in whitelash itself.

In the aftermath of *Shelby County*, the formerly covered jurisdictions predictably enacted new barriers to voting that preclearance would likely have prevented. For instance, Alabama quickly implemented a restrictive voter photo identification law that had been blocked by preclearance. It then proposed closing 31 driver's license offices located primarily in black and rural areas of the state, thus making the needed photo identification harder to obtain.[86] In 2016, three years after *Shelby County*, a survey of 381 of 800 counties previously covered by VRA preclearance requirements found that 43 percent of them had reduced the number of voting locations, a step that would have required federal approval before *Shelby County*.[87] All told, heading into the 2016 election, these counties had 868 fewer places to vote than they had before the Supreme Court's decision in *Shelby County*. Among the most egregious rollbacks, Phoenix's Maricopa County reduced polling places by 70 percent from 2012 to 2016, resulting in 21,000 registered voters per polling place and five-hour waits to vote during the 2016 Democratic primary.[88] There is perhaps no more effective way to disenfranchise a voter than to reduce the places available to cast a ballot.

Emboldened by Donald Trump's victory and his intention to move the judiciary further to the right, formerly covered jurisdictions—particularly those located in the South—will likely hasten the pace of their voter disenfranchisement. A 2017 poll found that 46 percent of white southerners believe white people in the United States are under attack today[89]—presumably by people of color. Under these circumstances, how can we expect the formerly covered jurisdictions to protect (or even respect) the voting rights of racial minorities?

We can't. In fact, well before *Shelby County*, the Supreme Court had signaled to resentful whites in the South that it was more concerned with their perceptions of being under attack than it was with minority voting rights. In *Shaw v. Reno* (1993), the state of North Carolina, then acting under supervision of VRA preclearance, created two majority-black congressional districts. These districts sent African Americans to Congress for the first time since Reconstruction. Despite this milestone, the districts were invalidated. Conservatives on the Court compared North Carolina's redistricting plan to "political apartheid."[90] Political apartheid, as understood from the South African experience with which the term is usually associated, is the subjugation of a group to a state of relative political impotence because of some characteristic of its members. North Carolina's redistricting plan, however, empowered a previously disenfranchised group (blacks) and still left whites with a disproportionate share of congressional representation from the state.[91]

Imagine an employer reducing the pay of a black employee purportedly to equalize the black employee's pay with that of similarly situated coworkers—except that the coworkers, who are white, already made more than the black employee. You would instantly suspect that the employer is up to something nefarious and that the stated rationale is pretextual. Essentially, this was the state of play in *Shaw*. The increase in black political power was the subject of heightened scrutiny in the name of equal protection under the Constitution even though whites remained in a superior position politically. Why single out black districts that do no more than give blacks rough equality, not an advantage over whites? According to Justice O'Connor's majority opinion, the creation of North Carolina's two black-majority districts "reinforces the perception that members of the same racial group—regardless of their age, education, economic status, or the community in which they live—think alike, share the same political interests, and will prefer the same candidates at the polls. We have rejected such perceptions elsewhere as impermissible racial stereotypes."[92] Here, the Court makes a very poor analogy to impermissible stereotyping. The plaintiffs in *Shaw* were white Republicans; thus they lacked legal standing to complain that a congressional district unfairly stereotyped black people, most of whom voted for Democrats. Instead, their complaint was that they, as white people, were in some unspecified manner harmed by North Carolina's creation of two majority-black districts. They were, in the words of the 2017 poll taken of white southerners, "under attack."[93]

Shaw picks up where *Regents of the University of California v. Bakke* left off, instantiating in the political realm the culture of white grievance legitimated by *Bakke*. White victimology is a theme of whitelash. Although a 2016 American National Election Studies pilot survey found that 74 percent of white Democrats said whites face little or no discrimination, only 51 percent of Republicans agreed.[94] Nearly 60 percent of white Republicans believe that the government favors blacks; only slightly more than 10 percent of Democrats agree.[95]

But if the government favors African Americans, it has a strange way of showing it. In 2017, the median white family wealth was 10 times that of the median black family; blacks were 2.5 times more likely to be in poverty than whites; blacks earned 82.5 cents for every dollar made by a white; the rate of black homeownership was 30 percentage points less than whites'; and the rate of black incarceration was six times that of whites, marking a tripling of the share of blacks in prison from 1968 to 2016.[96]

Facts like these do not matter to regressive white voters. Nor do they matter to the judicial conservatives who indulge whitelash by committing baseline errors in their consideration of discrimination cases. A baseline error is one that incorrectly assumes the legitimacy of the status quo.[97] An example of an appropriate baseline is the presumption of defendants' innocence; there is no alternative presumption that would offer the defendant due process or fairness. On the other hand, there is no sound reason for presuming the legitimacy of social and political inequality or the innocence of its beneficiaries; such an assumption needlessly ratifies the effects of past discrimination. In *Shaw*, for instance, we should not presuppose that it is normal for North Carolina, with its heavily black population, to fail to send any black representatives to Congress for nearly 100 years. Calling efforts to rectify this situation "political apartheid" distorts history and pretextually elevates formal symmetrical treatment above substantive political equality.[98]

WORKPLACE DISCRIMINATION

Many of the analogies made in this book are to employment discrimination law. An important companion to the right to be free of workplace discrimination based on race, gender, or national origin is the right not to be retaliated against for complaining about such discrimination. Dr. Naiel Nassar, a person of Middle Eastern descent, invoked this right, secured by Title VII, when he sued his employer, the University of Southwestern Texas Medical Center.[99] After Nassar penned a letter to his employer explaining that he was resigning his teaching post because of racial harassment by his supervisor, the chair of Nassar's department vowed that since Nassar had "publicly humiliated" his supervisor by writing the letter, it was "very important that [Nassar's supervisor] be publicly exonerated."[100] To this end, the department chair contacted the hospital at which Nassar had secured new employment to dissuade it from employing Nassar. The ostensible reason for this action was that the hospital that offered Nassar his new position could only fill vacant staff positions with faculty from the University of Southwestern Texas, a status that Nassar no longer enjoyed after his resignation.[101]

Nassar's claim of retaliation was a mixed-motive claim—that is, the department chair had legal and illegal reasons for urging the hospital not to employ him. In discrimination cases based on race, for example, if an employer acts against an employee for both racially discriminatory reasons and legal reasons, the employer loses the case. The employer, however, may limit its damages by showing that it would have reached the same decision even in the absence of the impermissible reason. The question in *University of Southwestern Texas Medical Center v. Nassar* was whether this same regime applied to companion claims of retaliation, or whether a retaliation plaintiff is required to meet a higher standard than a discrimination plaintiff must meet.

A conservative five-justice majority decided, counterintuitively, that the standards should be discordant. Writing for the majority, Justice Kennedy, although attempting to justify the outcome on the basis of what he saw as the plain language of the statute, ultimately revealed his and the majority's real motive. Noting the rise in the number of retaliation cases,

Kennedy expressed concern that affording retaliation claims the same treatment as discrimination claims would encourage *false* discrimination claims:

> [L]essening the causation standard could contribute to the filing of frivolous claims, which would siphon resources from efforts by employer, administrative agencies, and courts to combat workplace harassment. Consider in this regard the case of an employee who knows that he or she is about to be fired for poor performance, given a lower pay grade, or even just transferred to a different assignment or location. To forestall that lawful action, he or she might be tempted to make an unfounded charge of racial, sexual, or religious discrimination; then, when the unrelated employment action comes, the employee could allege that it is retaliation. If respondent [Nassar] were to prevail in his argument here, that claim could be established by a lessened causation standard, all in order to prevent the undesired change in employment circumstances.[102]

Justice Kennedy's argument shares a feature of white Americans' views on racial discrimination: the unfounded belief that most claims of discrimination are a product of the accuser's imagination, manipulation, or dishonesty. A 2017 Pew Research survey asked respondents which was the bigger problem: people seeing discrimination where there is none, or people failing to see discrimination where it exists. Among whites, 46 percent said that the bigger problem was people seeing discrimination where there is none.[103] This compares with 84 percent of blacks and 66 percent of Latinos who said that the bigger problem in society is the failure to recognize discrimination where it exists.[104] Among conservative Republicans—from which the Supreme Court majority is currently drawn and with which President Trump is currently stacking the federal courts—a striking 68 percent believe that the bigger problem is people seeing discrimination where it doesn't exist.[105] What are the chances that conservative judges, as a class, are immune to a racial predisposition held by nearly seven in ten conservative Republicans? To be sure, professional norms may alter behavior, but psychology research reveals that one's baseline belief about the prevalence or rarity of discrimination influences the individual's willingness to attribute specific events or actions to discrimination.[106]

The willingness of conservative Republicans to dismiss discrimination claims as slackers' malingering runs counter to reality and to the well-documented challenges of fighting discrimination in the workplace and in the courts. Although more than half of African Americans say they have personally experienced discrimination in applying for a job or promotion or seeking equal pay,[107] they have not flooded the courts. Between 1997 and 2017, the number of racial discrimination charges filed with the Equal Employment Opportunity Commission—a first step for most employment discrimination lawsuits—has never exceeded 36,000, or a tiny fraction of the millions of black workers who report experiencing job-related discrimination.[108]

Workers do not make charges of discrimination lightly. First, most workers hesitate to complain about discrimination because they fear retaliation.[109] After *Nassar*, they must fear it even more. Second, individuals simply aren't inclined to fabricate claims of discrimination—least of all discrimination directed at them personally. The reason is that when one perceives discrimination against oneself, that perception carries with it harmful psychological and health ramifications.[110] Victimhood (particularly in the context of employment discrimination) entails feeling powerless over one's own fate— hardly a feeling that most people would readily embrace. Third, although people of color believe that racial discrimination is more prevalent than do whites, this belief has not displaced their meritocratic ideals—that is, their desire to get ahead by working hard.[111]

Justice Kennedy addresses none of these realities. He instead reverts to stereotype, insisting that retaliation claims must be made more difficult to bring because the people who bring them are likely to abuse them. Such "factless jurisprudence"—judicial decision-making based on alternative facts—makes Kennedy and the Court's conservatives no better, morally or intellectually, than the masses of Trump supporters who believe that "if blacks would only try harder they could be just as well off as whites."[112]

Although conservative judicial hostility to employment discrimination claims is usually shrouded in factless jurisprudence like Kennedy's, occasionally a judge dispenses with pretense. Judge Edith Jones of the U.S. Court of Appeals for the Fifth Circuit, an appointee of President Ronald Reagan, certainly did in a speech at Harvard Law School:

> Seldom are employment discrimination suits in our court supported by direct evidence of race or sex-based animosity. Instead, the courts are asked to revisit petty interoffice disputes and to infer invidious motives from trivial comments or work-performance criticism. Recrimination, second-guessing and suspicion plague the workplace when tenuous discrimination suits are filed creating an atmosphere in which many corporate defendants are forced into costly settlements because they simply cannot afford to vindicate their position.[113]

You would not want Judge Edith Jones to hear your case as an employment discrimination plaintiff any more than you would want Chief Justice Rehnquist to. Her comments drip with contempt for the plight of people of color (and women), who constitute the overwhelming number of employment discrimination plaintiffs. And while Jones's denial of discrimination is extreme and overt, she is hardly in a class by herself. In *Ash v. Tyson Foods, Inc.*,[114] two black male employees, who were referred to as "boys" by their white supervisor, were not selected by that supervisor for a promotion to the position of shift manager. Among other irregularities, the plaintiffs claimed that they had superior qualifications to the two white males who were selected for the position, that the white supervisor used criteria that were not required by company policy, and that the supervisor had offered the job to one of the white employees before even interviewing both plaintiffs.[115] A jury found for both plaintiffs, but the trial judge overturned one verdict and entered a judgment in favor of the employer, and ordered a new trial with respect to the other plaintiff on the grounds that the damages awarded were excessive.

The judge's actions here were highly unusual: In the American system of civil adjudication, it's quite difficult for a judge to sidestep the jury's judgment of the facts in this way. To do so—that is, to enter a "judgment as a matter of law"—requires the party not favored in the jury's verdict to demonstrate that the facts were so one-sided that reasonable minds could not disagree on the outcome. It's a heavy lift. Nevertheless, on appeal in *Ash*, a panel of federal judges, consisting of three white male Republican appointees, went out of its way to diminish the jury's verdict in favor of the black plaintiffs. For instance, racial epithets are often viewed as direct evidence of discrimination. Nevertheless, the court of appeals found that referring to a black man as a "boy" was not evidence of discriminatory intent unless the term was modified by a racial adjective like "black" or "white."[116] Just as absurd, the appeals court gave no weight to the plaintiffs' evidence that they were more qualified than the whites selected for the shift manager positions. This comparative evidence could establish pretext, the court held, "only when the disparity in qualifications is so apparent as virtually to jump off the page and slap you in the face."[117]

The appeals court's transparent resistance to recognizing discrimination proved too much even for the conservative-dominated U.S. Supreme Court, which reversed and remanded the decision in a terse, unsigned opinion.[118] But cases rarely reach the Supreme Court, and as illustrated by *Nassar*, in cases less obvious than *Ash*, the Court is disinclined to find for an employment discrimination plaintiff. Thus, the fate of the black plaintiffs in *Ash* in the district court and in the court of appeals typifies plaintiffs' difficult task in most employment discrimination cases. Employment discrimination plaintiffs have "shockingly bad" results in court.[119] An examination of federal employment discrimination cases from 1988 to 2003 reveals that plaintiffs win relief in only 4 percent of the cases that are not settled or voluntarily dismissed by plaintiffs.[120] The other 96 percent of cases result in trial wins for defendants or pretrial dispositions in their favor.[121]

When employment discrimination plaintiffs do advance to trial, they prevail in only 28 percent of the cases, compared with a win rate of 45 percent in other categories of federal cases.[122] And, as illustrated by *Ash*, these trial victories are far from secure. Employment discrimination judgments for plaintiffs are reversed on appeal 41 percent of the time, compared with a reversal rate for prevailing defendants in employment discrimination cases of 9 percent, and a reversal rate for other categories of federal plaintiffs of 28 percent.[123]

Although disparate impact by itself does not constitute a constitutional violation, it is often a sign of intentional discrimination. These figures suggest that courts have an aversion to employment discrimination plaintiffs—that they are discriminating against victims of discrimination. Factless jurisprudence like the *Nassar* ruling and lower court decisions in *Ash*, and admissions of bias like that of Judge Edith Jones, are convincing evidence that these statistics are not random. Rather, they are a function of whitelash in the American judiciary, distinguishable from political whitelash only by the authority that judges wield in the form of their decisions.

CAMPAIGN FINANCE

Money talks. It speaks loudly to angry white voters, but it does not speak for them. Campaign donors to both major parties are wealthier and whiter than nondonors.[124] Yet the political views of wealthy donors to the Democratic Party are more closely aligned to the views of Democratic nondonors than are the views of wealthy Republican donors to Republican nondonors.[125] A report by Demos, a progressive think tank, examined five issues ranging from increasing the minimum wage to reducing greenhouse gas. It concluded: "The average percentage point difference (preference gap) between GOP donors and Republican non-donors on the five core questions was 20 points, compared with 9 points among Democrats. Among independents the average preference gap was even larger: 23 points."

In other words, wealthy GOP donors are further to the right of GOP nondonors than wealthy Democratic donors are to Democratic nondonors. The net effect of donor versus nondonor asymmetry "pulls American politics in a rightward direction" because, according to a growing body of evidence, politicians tend to be more responsive to donors' interests than to constituents.[126] An important collateral consequence of this asymmetry is that it feeds whitelash because, by pulling already racially stratified parties further apart, money in politics exacerbates racial divisions and inequality.

Do conservative billionaires like the Koch brothers spend political dollars to promote the interests of the white working class? Yes, if the white working class benefits from opposing an increase in the federal minimum wage.[127] Yes, if the white working class benefits from stripping public unions of bargaining rights.[128] And yes, again, if the white working class benefits from the 2017 corporate tax cuts promoted by the Koch brothers, which will reportedly enrich them by more than $1 billion annually.[129] Wealthy white donors to the Republican Party are not filling the party's coffers to promote the interests of the white working class or even the white middle class. Instead, they are spreading their largesse to encourage white voters to turn against themselves.

Whitelash is part and parcel of this self-immolation. In *Dark Money*, Jane Mayer traces the tentacles of deep-pocketed white political donors to forces such as the Tea Party movement and initiatives to suppress the minority vote through voter ID laws.[130] In the case of the Tea Party movement, what appeared to be a spontaneous uprising of common folk was in large part a Trojan horse for elite interests.[131] Those elites were willing to tolerate and even stoke racism in the Tea Party movement in order to achieve their economic goals—goals that did not benefit the foot soldiers of the movement. Billionaire David Koch, for instance, joined in the otherization of President Obama, noting that Obama's father was a "hard core economic socialist in Kenya" and that "Obama didn't really interact with his father face-to-face very much, but was apparently from what I read a great admirer of his father's points of view."[132]

People of color wind up not just bearing the scars of whitelash but also suffering disproportionately from the skewed policy outcomes that result from a system of political money dominated by wealthy white men. If conservative white donors do not represent the interests of the white masses, they certainly do not represent the interests of people of color. But because people of color are more economically vulnerable than whites, they are disproportionately harmed by a political process that caters to the wealthy.[133]

You will not hear a discussion of any of money's distorting effects on democracy in the majority opinion in *Citizens United v. Federal Election Commission*.[134] Although the case itself, unlike most discussed earlier, does not involve race, it does involve political money, which is deployed to foment racial division. Moreover, how the Supreme Court reached its result mimics the pretextual, motivated reasoning it often deploys in its race cases.

In *Citizens United*, the Court grappled with the question of whether a federal ban on corporations' (and unions') use of their general treasuries to influence federal elections violated the First Amendment rights of these entities.[135] Yet the Court had already answered this question twenty years earlier in *Austin v. Michigan Chamber of Commerce*.[136] In this case, the Chamber of Commerce, a nonprofit organization composed of dues-paying businesses, sought to place an ad in a local newspaper in support of a political candidate. Because the ad was not coordinated with the candidate's campaign, it was considered an "independent expenditure." Although Michigan law, like federal law, allowed a corporation to create a separate fund for independent expenditures on behalf of candidates, corporations could not use their general treasuries — composed of profits from customer sales and funds from investors' purchases of equity in the business — for such expenditures.[137]

The Supreme Court in *Austin* upheld the Michigan law against the Chamber's complaint that the law violated the First Amendment. Noting the special benefits that states confer on corporations, the Court held that Michigan had a compelling interest in preventing "the corrosive and distorting effects of immense aggregations of wealth that are accumulated with the help of the corporate form and that have little or no correlation to the public's support for the corporation's political ideas."[138] In the Court's view, the fact that the Michigan law involved something other than direct contributions to candidates did not matter for the outcome of the case.[139] Because the Chamber's general treasury was composed of dues paid from the general treasuries of its member businesses, which included for-profit corporations, the Court found that the Chamber could still be used as a "conduit" for these businesses to distort the electoral process;[140] therefore, it was reasonable for the state to limit the Chamber's independent expenditures.

In *Citizens United*, the court overruled this precedent. What were Justice Anthony Kennedy's reasons for overturning *Austin*? Normally, *stare decisis* is the cornerstone of American law. When the facts of cases are materially the same, this doctrine requires courts to follow their past decisions unless there is a good reason for jettisoning them. Think of an employer who has had a consistent policy of docking pay when an employee is more than 15 minutes late to work. The employer docks the pay for the first 99 tardy employees but then fails to do so for the 100th employee. Absent some good explanation, you'd suspect that the employer has acted arbitrarily. *Stare decisis*, then, safeguards the institutional integrity of our courts: overturning precedents too often or without a compelling reason signals arbitrariness and would diminish the courts' stature.

In *Citizens United*, Kennedy, writing for a conservative, five-justice majority, first found that although federal law allows a corporation to engage in election-related speech by setting up a fund — known as a political action committee (PAC) — separate from its general treasury, the requirements for doing so were simply too onerous. How did the majority know this? In three short paragraphs, with no citation to a factual record developed in the trial court, Justice Kennedy deduced that the federal regulations for creating PACs must be burdensome because otherwise more than a mere 2,000-odd corporate PACs would exist.[141] But as *Austin* illustrates, corporations often speak through trade associations like chambers of commerce; this obviates the need for individual corporations to create their own PACs. Furthermore, it's simply not the role of an appellate court, which hears no expert witness testimony, to make the kind of factual finding on which Kennedy's opinion rests.

More concerning still, the Court in *Citizens United* rejected the possibility that an independent expenditure to benefit a candidate could have a corrupting influence on the candidate. According to Kennedy, "The absence of prearrangement and coordination of an expenditure with the candidate or his agent not only undermines the value of the expenditure to the candidate, but also alleviates the danger that expenditures will be given as a *quid pro quo* for improper commitments from the candidate."[142] This was judicial fiction. Contributions to "super PACs," a vehicle of choice for independent expenditures because they can accept unlimited donations from corporations and wealthy individuals, now eclipse direct contributions to candidates in many elections. As *The New York Times* reported in 2015 after super PACs were unleashed by *Citizens United*, these conduits had left most Republican presidential hopefuls "deeply reliant on a handful of ultra-wealthy donors."[143]

Do politicians, as the Demos report indicates, advocate for policies favored by wealthy donors over the public interest? Not according to Justice Kennedy, who concluded that politicians' own views arise naturally, and the money follows: "It is in the nature of an elected representative to favor certain policies, and, by necessary corollary, to favor the voters and contributors who support those policies."[144] How does Justice Kennedy know this? He does not rely on testimony from politicians to sort out the roles of conviction versus money — and which comes first — in legislative decision-making. Instead, Justice Kennedy rests his judgment solely on his own intuition; he cites for support not even a past ruling of the Court but rather his own concurring (i.e., nonmajority) opinion from a past case.[145] Essentially, it's like the employer explaining the differential treatment of tardy employee number 100 by saying, "Because I said so!" In his self-referentialism, Kennedy ignored a developed factual record from prior case law that would have undercut his naïve conception that campaign donations and independent expenditures are purely ideological rather than transactional.[146]

Yet, perhaps the most farfetched fiction endorsed by *Citizens United* is this assertion by Justice Kennedy: "The appearance of influence or access ... will not cause the electorate to lose faith in our democracy."[147] He was wrong:

perceptions of Congress as "corrupt" increased after *Citizens United*.[148] And surveys of the American public taken since *Citizens United* have consistently shown that Republicans and Democrats alike believe that the rich have too much influence on the political process and that the role of money should be curtailed.[149]

Thus, *Citizens United*'s departure from *stare decisis* is not, for example, the same kind of overruling as *Brown v. Board of Education* was of *Plessy v. Ferguson*'s ignominious "separate but equal" doctrine. Among other distinguishing attributes, *Brown* was informed by expert opinion—psychological studies demonstrating the deleterious effects of segregation on schoolchildren of color.[150] *Citizens United*, on the other hand, is a paradigm of alternative facts and an example of the solicitude that judicial conservatives extend to powerful interests. Specifically, in *Citizens United*, Justice Kennedy held himself to a much lower standard of factual rigor than he imposed on the city of New Haven in *Ricci v. DeStefano* when the city wanted to disregard test results that disproportionately disqualified black firefighters from promotion opportunities.[151] In that case, the Court's conservative majority found that New Haven could not present "a strong basis in evidence" that race-conscious action was necessary to avoid a disparate impact on minority candidates.[152] Courts, especially the Supreme Court, should bear the same burden of proof in justifying their opinions that is required of a party presenting its case to the court. Justice Kennedy's majority opinion in *Citizens United* lacked a "strong basis in evidence."

In contrast to *Brown v. Board of Education* and other precedents that rightly corrected historical injustices, *Citizens United* follows a disturbing pattern in the Roberts Court. Between 2005 and 2015, in all cases in which a business faced off against a nonbusiness litigant, the Roberts Court decided in favor of the business 61 percent of the time. That pro-business bias is 17 percentage points greater than that of the Court under Roberts's immediate predecessor as chief justice, William Rehnquist, and 16 percentage points greater than that of the Court helmed by Chief Justice Warren Burger, Rehnquist's predecessor.[153] Using the U.S. Chamber of Commerce as a proxy for business interests, the Constitutional Accountability Center concluded that between 2006 and the end of its 2017–2018 term, the Supreme Court supported the Chamber's position, as expressed in briefs submitted to the Court, a striking 70 percent of the time.[154] Again, that rate towers above that of the Rehnquist Court (56 percent) and the Burger Court (43 percent).

Imagine what the landscape of the American workplace would look like if employment discrimination plaintiffs enjoyed a 70 percent success rate. And imagine the relative impotency of whitelash if the judiciary acted as a champion of the marginalized rather than an accomplice to the powerful. Yet over the last four decades, during which a conservative revolution has occurred in the federal judiciary, plaintiffs in civil rights cases (both employment discrimination and constitutional tort litigation) have enjoyed considerably less success than other categories of federal litigation.[155]

If a plaintiff in an employment discrimination suit presented evidence of bias in favor of one race and against another, the court would treat such evidence as relevant to the claim of intentional discrimination. We should do no less when the judiciary manifests such biases against classes of litigants. We should, in other words, acknowledge that racial inequality and whitelash could not have flourished without the complicity of the judiciary.

6

Voting While White

"I am the poor white, fooled and pushed apart,
   I am the Negro bearing slavery's scars."

                    —Langston Hughes, *Let America Be America Again*[1]

A common adage in politics is that "elections have consequences." It's a catchy aphorism, but it masks the relationship between a voter's candidate choices and the *personal* fallout for that voter. What if you could rail against "big government" and still feed at its trough? What if you could complain about the federal debt and then drive it up with gigantic tax cuts? What if you could be a single-issue voter on guns or abortion, but then, when the economy sours under the party you supported, you still reap the benefits of the social safety net that the party opposes?

All these questions implicate modern conservatism, or what might aptly be termed "freeloading conservatism." Freeloading conservatism allows whites to vote their whims but then cry their economic woes. The costs of their decisions spread to their fellow Americans. And as the 2016 presidential contest robustly illustrates, among the distracting whims on which millions of white voters feed are their stereotypes of Americans of color. This process of externalizing the consequences of voter choices allows whitelash to continue undeterred.

Consider this example: Whitley County, Kentucky, gave 82 percent of its votes to Donald Trump.[2] Under Obamacare, the uninsured rate for the county had declined by *60 percent*. After Trump's victory, when the reality of a possible repeal of Obamacare set in, many Trump-supporting Obamacare enrollees in Whitley County began to panic. One of them, Debbie Mills, explained: "I guess I thought that, you know, he would not do this, he would not take health insurance away knowing it would affect so many peoples [sic] lives. I mean, what are you to do then if you cannot pay for insurance?"[3]

Social Security offers another example of whites voting against their own economic interests. A 2007 analysis by the federal government's Social Security Office of Policy provided a demographic breakdown of recipients of Social Security retirement benefits for individuals reaching retirement age between 1993 and 2007. Whites accounted for 79 to 81 percent of the near-retirement recipients.[4] This means that whites, who are disproportionately represented among the nation's elderly, benefit disproportionately from Social Security retirement benefits. The longer life span of whites than African Americans also yields more Social Security benefits for whites.[5] A study by the Urban Institute concluded, "When considered across many decades—historically, currently, and in the near future—Social Security redistributes from Hispanics, blacks, and other people of color to whites."[6] And while elderly whites are on the whole wealthier than elderly nonwhites, they nevertheless depend on Social Security to replace about one-third of their earnings on average, compared with 38 to 41 percent for blacks and Latinos.[7]

Despite their dependency on Social Security—to say nothing of the program's overall skew in their favor—older white voters, regardless of education, favor Republicans over Democrats.[8] Yet, when President George W. Bush attempted to privatize Social Security, he was blocked by uniform *Democratic* resistance.[9] Although as a candidate Donald Trump promised to keep Social Security intact, after Trump signed into law a $1.5 trillion tax cut, his fellow Republicans moved with alacrity to pay for it through so-called entitlement reform, which includes curtailing the cost of Social Security.[10] Not even Republicans agree with this approach. A 2017 Pew Research survey revealed that only 10 percent of Republicans support cuts to Social Security benefits.[11] Why, then, do white voters, including elderly white voters, support Republicans?

The typical response to these observations is that those supporting Republicans obviously "vote on other issues." That may be true, but it underscores a democratic paradox: the American two-party system allows some partisans to neglect basic needs—like how to feed themselves and their families—and vote on "other issues" that are often tinged with race. It's a lot easier to be carefree with your vote if you know that, in the final analysis, someone else will attend to the matters that you have neglected.

Our polarized two-party system has licensed racial free-riders: white voters can act out their prejudices at the polls—even when it is against their material interests to do so—secure in the knowledge that proponents of the social safety net (Democrats) will later attempt to correct the harm these voters have visited on themselves and society. In short, white voters have been able to have their prejudices and vote them, too. In this chapter, I explore this democratic paradox with the specific objective of foregrounding Chapters 7 and 8, in which I advocate legal remedies for voter whitelash. Such remedies are essential to combat a structural deficiency of a democracy that encourages irresponsible, race-based voting.

On this score, in light of the trove of data demonstrating anti-immigrant and anti-black sentiments among many whites who vote Republican, readers should keep one major theme in mind: White conservatives believe that when people of color fall behind whites, it's because of a moral shortcoming—that is, a lack of motivation. If moral shortcomings rather than discrimination explain racial inequality, however, then moral shortcomings must also explain the white working class's inability to live at the same or better economic standards as their parents. They must explain white workers' vulnerability to globalization. Such moral deficiencies must explain the opioid epidemic ravaging rural white America. And so on. Yet white Americans routinely blame Americans of color not only for their own life circumstances, but also for the travails suffered by whites.

Of course, political narratives almost never blame whites for their adverse life circumstances. The blame gets externalized as effectively as do the consequences of economically precarious whites' votes that make their own and others' lives even more economically precarious. In short, the political process rarely if ever points the finger at white voters for their misjudgments.

Because a democracy must allow the political participation of everyone—ignorant or well informed, beneficent or malevolent—it is easy to conflate the right to vote with the right to vote wrongly. Georgetown University philosopher Jason Brennan persuasively argues in *The Ethics of Voting* that "[n]ot all voters are equal. They have equal voting power, but their contributions are not of equal quality. Some people tend to make government better; some tend to make it worse."[12]

White voters don't just get it wrong; they often get it wrong because their attention is trained directly or indirectly on race. Because our political structure allows them to avoid the consequences of their decisions, our legal structure must kick in to hold them minimally accountable. I take up legal accountability in the next two chapters. For now, I invite the reader to marvel at the internal contradictions that mark much white voter behavior, contradictions that suggest pretext—and worse—on the part of millions. Such political incoherence and irresponsibility is, I argue, a luxury of voting while white.

WHO BENEFITS FROM THE SOCIAL SAFETY NET?

Approximately 70 percent of all Americans rely on a means-tested government program at some point during their lives.[13] A 2017 report by the Center on

Budget Priorities and Policy focused specifically on the role of government antipoverty programs (e.g., food stamps, Earned Income Tax Credit, Child Tax Credit) in reducing the poverty rate among various demographic groups. Using census data from 2014, and focusing on adults aged 18 to 64 without a college degree—a common proxy for "working-class"—the report concluded that federal antipoverty programs lift a greater percentage of white working-class adults above the poverty line than any other racial group.[14] Of the 14.1 million white adults in poverty before government assistance, 44 percent were lifted above the poverty line after government assistance, compared with 43 percent of blacks, 28 percent of Latinos, and 37 percent of other races.[15]

The share of working-class whites lifted out of poverty by federal antipoverty programs is even greater in the Rust Belt and middle America states that tipped the presidency to Donald Trump. Among all adults elevated from poverty by these programs, working-class whites constituted 77 percent in Iowa, 64 percent in Ohio, 61 percent in Pennsylvania, 59 percent in Michigan, and 51 percent in Wisconsin.[16] Nearly half of Donald Trump's votes in 2016 came from whites without a college degree.[17] Similarly, following the 2018 midterms, 85 percent of Republican House districts are more white than the national average of 62 percent, and more than 75 percent of these districts have fewer four-year college graduates than the national average of 30.3 percent.[18] In short, non-college-educated whites form the base of the Republican Party even as that group benefits the most from the federal safety net that Republicans routinely seek to shred.

Apart from the antipoverty effects of federal transfer payments, Social Security and Medicare are two federal programs that increase the personal incomes of voters in Trump states. According to a 2014 study by George Washington University's Milken Institute School of Public Health, from 1972 to 2012, "The Southeast region has consistently had the highest level of Social Security payments as a share of personal incomes . . ."[19] The picture for Medicare is the same—southern states benefit disproportionately. In 2012, the states with the highest share of personal income provided by Medicare benefits were West Virginia (6.3 percent), Mississippi (6.1 percent), Florida (5.8 percent), Kentucky (5.5 percent), Alabama (5.5 percent), Arkansas and South Carolina (each 5.3 percent), and Louisiana and Tennessee (each 5.0 percent).[20] In 2016, Hillary Clinton carried no states in the South except Virginia, whose massive DC suburbs partly disqualify it as a member of the region.

Government transfer programs are not the only way in which white Americans rely on the federal government that many of them love to hate. Cornell University professor Suzanne Mettler supplies a broader view of the social safety net by including so-called submerged benefits, delivered through the tax code.[21] These benefits include tax-exempt employer-supplied healthcare and retirement benefits, and the federal tax deduction for mortgage interest. Looking at benefits this way, Mettler's survey indicates that the average American has used 4.5 government policies that subsidize their cost of living.[22] The submerged benefits that disproportionately benefit upper-income Americans—and thus disproportionately benefit whites—cost the government approximately $1.5 trillion annually.[23]

Compounding this paradox, compared with Clinton voters, Trump supporters had a greater tendency to overestimate the share of African Americans receiving government aid of various types.[24] Indeed, although the proportion of blacks and whites receiving the prototypical welfare benefit—Temporary Assistance to Needy Families—is roughly equal, psychology research reveals that most Americans perceive the average welfare recipient as an undeserving African American.[25] Yet majorities of Republicans and conservatives report having benefited from one of the six major federal entitlement programs—including Social Security, Medicare, and Medicaid. Although a greater percentage of blacks reported having received assistance, a significant majority of both blacks and whites were beneficiaries (64 percent versus 56 percent).[26] The idea that racial minorities are the face of the American social safety net also ignores the reality that white Americans collect a disproportionate share of federal aid. In 2012, while African Americans made up 22 percent of the poor, they received only 14 percent of government entitlement spending, nearly proportionate to their 12 percent share of the U.S. population.[27] In contrast, non-Hispanic whites constituted 42 percent of the poor but received 69 percent of all government entitlement spending.[28]

White Americans' reliance on the social safety net apparently came as a surprise to President Trump. During a spring 2017 meeting with the Congressional Black Caucus (CBC), a CBC member informed Trump that his proposal to "reform" welfare would hurt that member's constituents, "[n]ot all of whom are black."[29] This prompted Trump to query skeptically, "Really? Then what are they?" The answer is, in large part, working-class whites. As the Center on Budget and Policy Priorities concluded in 2017, "[T]he percentage of people who would otherwise be poor that safety net programs lift out of poverty is greater for white working-age adults without a college degree than for other adults without a college degree."[30] In other words, at least by one measure, the white working class benefits disproportionately from federal poverty prevention programs. This cohort nevertheless supported a presidential candidate whose policies—including tax cuts slanted toward corporations and the rich—have weakened the social safety net.[31]

TABLE 6–1 *Support for Progressive Initiatives/Referenda in Trump States*

State	Trump Percentage	Ballot Measure
Arkansas	60%	Increase minimum wage from $8.50 to $11 by 2021 (68.46% Yes)
Idaho	59%	Medicaid expansion (61.58% Yes)
Missouri	56%	Raise minimum wage from $7.85 to $12 by 2023 (62.34% Yes)
Montana	56%	Increase taxes on tobacco to pay for Medicaid expansion (47.3% Yes)
Nebraska	59%	Medicaid expansion (53.55% Yes)
South Dakota	62%	Decrease minimum wage for workers under age 18 (71.13% No)
Utah	45%[a]	Medicaid expansion (53.32% Yes)

[a] Independent candidate received 21.54% of the vote.

What's more, while the Republican Party platform generally opposes government spending and regulations, many of the voters in red states carried by Donald Trump actually embrace Democratic policies like increasing the minimum wage and expanding Medicaid coverage, as illustrated in Table 6–1. The percentage of voters supporting these left-leaning policies in state initiatives and referenda is far higher than the percentage that voted for Democratic presidential candidates, suggesting that economic conservatism and opposition to "big government" are not the primary drivers of their votes.

WELFARE, ALASKA-STYLE

The ritualistic broadsides by Republicans against "big government" generally and "federal interference" specifically do not match Republican practices and lifestyles in some of the reddest states in America. Exhibit A is Alaska, a state Donald Trump carried by 15 percentage points. Indeed, since it was admitted to the union in 1959, Alaska has voted for the Republican presidential nominee in every election except one. Yet, Alaskans live a very un-Republican lifestyle. Each year, every adult and child living in the state receives a payment from the Alaska Permanent Fund, composed of a percentage of the state's oil revenues.[32] Since 1982, the payments have ranged from $1,000 to $3,000 per resident. These payments, which are effectively a guaranteed minimum income and require nothing but residence in the state, have helped Alaska achieve the least income inequality of any state in America.[33] None of this sounds very Republican; it instead is a group of people collecting a government check because they happen to live in an oil-rich state.

Surely a state wealthy enough to distribute no-strings annual payments to its residents can afford to pay for unforeseen contingencies like natural disasters. Yet when a 7.0 magnitude earthquake struck Anchorage in November 2018, President Trump's immediate response was, "Federal Government will spare no expense."[34] Why the feds? Like other red states struck by disaster, Alaska sets aside its disdain of federal interference when it seeks funding for disaster recovery, which costs the nation tens of billions of dollars annually. Indeed, seven of the top ten states receiving the most federal disaster aid from 2013 through 2018 have been reliably Republican either at the state level or in presidential elections, or in both: Louisiana, Texas, Florida, North Carolina, South Carolina, Mississippi, and Missouri.[35]

Another measure of the federal safety net is the amount of federal aid contributed to a state's general revenues. Federal aid takes many forms, from Medicaid to transportation grants. Here, we look not at what the federal government gives individuals but rather at what it contributes to a state's bottom line in its annual budget. By this metric, reliably red states look like hypocrites. According to the Tax Foundation, for fiscal year 2014, seven of the top ten federal aid recipients were reliably red states, with Mississippi ranked number one.[36] In 2012, federal aid accounted for 45.8 percent of Mississippi's revenue, and for every dollar the state paid in federal taxes, it received $3.07 in federal monies.[37] Either white Mississippians believe that having nearly half their state's revenues come from the federal government does not benefit them, or there is something else besides partisan orthodoxy that influences their vote—with race being one of the more obvious possibilities.[38] Red states further down the list, though less dependent on federal aid than Mississippi, still rely substantially on Washington. For instance, Texas, which ranked twenty-eighth, nevertheless received 31.8 percent of its general revenues from the federal government.[39]

Comparing aggregate tax dollars sent to Washington by each state's taxpayers with the amount of aid received by a state produces a similar paradox: red states—those whose Republican politicians argue for a "limited federal government"—get more. A 2018 study sought to determine the states most dependent on federal dollars by examining (1) the amount of tax dollars sent to Washington, DC; (2) the amount of federal funding received by each state both in the form of payments made to the state and payments such as Social Security benefits made directly to its citizens; and (3) the percentage of a state's budget comprised of federal dollars. For all their railing against the intrusiveness of the federal government, and for all their canonization of states' rights,

16 of the top 20 most dependent states were "red" states carried by both Mitt Romney in 2012 and Donald Trump in 2016.[40] The study, by wallethub.com, ranked the traditionally blue state of New Mexico as the most dependent, followed by nine Republican states: Kentucky, Mississippi, Alabama, West Virginia, South Carolina, Arizona, Alaska, Montana, and Louisiana.[41] The eleven states that receive more than $2 from the federal government for every dollar their residents send to Washington are likewise primarily red states — South Carolina, North Dakota, Louisiana, Alabama, Mississippi, Kentucky, West Virginia, and Indiana — with Florida, Hawaii, and New Mexico as blue or purple outliers.[42] South Carolina, which has not voted for a Democratic presidential candidate since 1976, receives nearly $8 in federal funds for each tax dollar its residents send to Washington.[43] Yet South Carolina has one of the lowest state tax burdens in the country, a feat made possible by the outsized returns its residents receive on the federal taxes they pay.[44]

Adding insult to the injury of this hypocrisy, many of the states that receive the most federal disaster aid have sent the largest number of climate change deniers to Congress.[45] And as a final measure of insincerity, many of the same Republican senators and congressmen who opposed relief for New York and New Jersey, hit by Hurricane Sandy in 2012, supported billions in federal disaster relief for Texas when Hurricane Harvey wrecked it in 2017.[46] To be sure, these Republicans attempted to distinguish the relief legislation on grounds that the Hurricane Sandy package contained "excessive pork" while Hurricane Harvey aid was pure. Even if this criticism were true, the question remains why conservative Republicans, who criticize the scope of the federal government at every turn, would vote to send federal disaster aid to *any* state.

What whitelash voters who extend their hands to the federal government after a natural disaster fail to understand is that their fellow Americans of color experience the same needs as they do, in circumstances that are equally beyond their control.[47] Where is the empathy when these white voters go to the polls? What these whitelashers are never told, or perhaps simply choose to ignore, is that federal largesse for natural disasters is an invention of the Great Society — the liberal, activist government that these voters pretend to disdain even as they reap the benefits of its vision.[48] Voting while white means not having to reconcile this cognitive dissonance, because their political opponents will gladly supply what they vote against. While freeloading conservatism is performed on the backs of all progressive voters, as will be shown momentarily, it ultimately disproportionately relies on the political sacrifices of African Americans.

Conservative politicians do not try to hide their guile. In 2009, in the dead of the Great Recession, all but three Republicans in Congress voted against

President Barack Obama's economic stimulus package, known as the American Recovery and Reinvestment Act (ARRA).[49] With unemployment at 8 percent and rising, and state and local governments severely curtailing their spending, the nation was at a crossroads: the federal government could step into the breach, or the economy would contract into depression. Congressional Republicans were unmoved by this existential threat despite the harm it would cause their constituents: According to the Congressional Budget Office and the Brookings Institute, it was precisely the less-well-off for whom the ARRA provided the greatest benefit. Between 2009 and 2014, through its combination of tax cuts and increased government transfers, the ARRA "offset virtually all the market [salary] income losses" for lower-income Americans.[50] For middle-income Americans, the stimulus package offset nearly 90 percent of wage losses. For these reasons, the Brookings Institute concluded that "[b]y almost any measure the policy was a resounding success."[51]

Tacitly, Republican naysayers understood and acknowledged—through deed, though not word—the necessity of Obama's stimulus plan. While virtually all Republican congressmen and senators voted against the plan, many nonetheless petitioned federal agencies for stimulus money for their constituents.[52] But why hold Republican lawmakers to a standard of consistency if their own constituents do not?

NARRATIVES OF WHITE DISAFFECTION

To vote while white is to reward this kind of hypocrisy, to say nothing of the illogical policymaking it begets. To vote while white is to ignore the inconsistencies between what you get from government and what you insist others do not deserve. So what if this (mis)behavior at the polls harms society and leads to self-inflicted wounds? There will always be another Obama with another stimulus package to fix what went wrong at the hands of the candidate you supported. Then again, why did you support that candidate to begin with?

In a 2015 study, the Pew Research Center interviewed approximately 25,000 Americans to determine their partisan leanings. Each of the ten most loyal groups of Democratic voters were some subgroup of African Americans.[53] Although this book has focused on the voting behavior of whites, political scientists have devoted considerable scholarship attempting to explain the near unanimous support of African Americans for the Democratic Party.[54] Yet the question of why blacks vote Democratic is hardly the mirror image of the question why whites vote largely Republican. Even at the level of mass media and popular discourse, it is hardly a stretch of the imagination that an economically less-well-off group would support a party whose policies tend to benefit poorer Americans.

Given that government has helped black and white Americans, and has the potential to transform the lives of both black and white Americans—and when it has failed them, it has arguably failed blacks more—why is there a racial divergence in voting behavior among economically vulnerable blacks and whites?

In antidiscrimination law, courts look to comparators to determine whether a plaintiff has received the same treatment as similarly situated employees, or to determine whether government has accorded equal protection of the law to citizens. Although it may not be possible to make a precise comparison to the voting context, we can still make inferences from the misaligned voting conduct of blacks and whites in similar economic conditions, particularly in light of the fact that the United States voted for the racial antithesis of its first African American president immediately after Barack Obama's term ended. Comparing white voters' tolerance of or support for Trump's conduct and policies to their much less forgiving treatment of Obama allows for a classic inference of racial discrimination.

A less direct but still important application of the concept of comparators involves comparing white voters' behavior with that of voters of color. For instance, almost anyone who was not rich faced economic troubles during the Great Recession, yet whites in 2010 forcefully turned their backs on the attempted recovery helmed by the first African American president. African Americans, far from the primary beneficiaries of economic recovery, stuck with Democrats. Are we to believe that race played no role in these divergent decisions? A jury in a Title VII case would certainly be free to infer that an impermissible reason accounted for an employer's differential treatment of similarly situated employees. The flipside of this protection for a plaintiff is that, barring special circumstances, an employer is entitled to expect similar performance from comparably situated employees. So, when looking at groups of voters who are similar in ways other than race but who vote differently, race emerges as a likely fault line, much as it does in employment discrimination cases.

Looking at the situation somewhat differently, we might once again analogize voters to employers, and treat political candidates as applicants for high-level positions. If an employer opts for the applicant with a long history of racial discrimination and misogyny, that decision would figure significantly in an employment discrimination case brought against the employer. Moreover, where an employer offers vague or inconsistent justifications for an adverse job action against a plaintiff, courts treat these explanations as evidence of pretext.[55] Imagine an employer explaining to a jury that a female applicant was turned down for a male-dominated position because she didn't fit into the "culture" of the firm or wasn't the right "fit." Vague, difficult-to-disprove reasons like these invite a juror to infer discriminatory intent.[56] Yet such nebulous (and often counterintuitive) reasoning is the hallmark of many white voters' explanations for their supposed "anger" and dissatisfaction with the Democratic Party.

In *What's the Matter with White People*, political analyst and *Nation* magazine editor Joan Walsh partly attributes the white working and middle classes' disaffection with Democrats to the party's failure to offer bold alternatives to a corporatized Republican agenda.[57] Walsh repeatedly acknowledges race's diversionary role in whites' voting calculus, yet she says liberals should not "dismiss the white working class as hopelessly Republican and racist . . ."[58] Why not? Walsh finds "interesting" the fact that in 2008, Barack Obama carried 46 percent of whites without a college degree who earned between $30,000 and $75,000—a modern highwater mark for a Democratic presidential candidate.[59] Noting that many of these same voters returned to the Republican column in 2010, inflicting historic midterm losses on the Democrats, Walsh ponders, "What if their reaction derived from frustration with Democratic leaders who hadn't pursued an economic turnaround agenda aggressively enough at a time when unemployment stood at more than 10 percent—and almost 15 percent for whites without a college degree?"[60]

In 2010, however, the unemployment rate for black men was 18.4 percent; for white men, 9.6 percent.[61] The unemployment rate for black women was 13.8 percent; for white women, 7.7 percent. Hispanics also had higher unemployment rates than whites. Yet in the 2010 congressional midterms, the white vote shifted a net 16 percentage points to the Republicans, compared to a 6-percentage-point shift for blacks and an 8-point shift for Hispanics.[62] Why would the white reaction be so much greater?

Although Walsh finds promise in Obama's 2008 share of the working-class white vote, it is just as reasonable to despair. The country was careening toward an economic depression in 2008, and, causation debates aside, it is customary to hold the incumbent party—in this instance, Republicans—responsible for the performance of the economy. The 2008 Republican presidential nominee, Senator John McCain of Arizona, had in 2007 made this startling admission: "I'm going to be honest. I know a lot less about economics than I do about military and foreign-policy issues. I still need to be educated."[63] Yet a majority of working-class white voters earning between $30,000 to $75,000 a year supported McCain. What did they see in him that blacks and Latinos did not?

If the answer is that they were voting on "other issues" — even *at the outset of the steepest recession in modern history* — then these voters should not be surprised that their fellow Americans suspect that race was at least part of their motivation. As citizens in a common democratic enterprise, we are entitled to expect that our neighbors will act with reason, yet this voting behavior defies logic. What issue could possibly be more pressing than the economy when the nation is on the brink of a second great depression? If your house is on fire, you must prioritize what you save from the flames. Voting is not different. When you cannot get everything you want, you must decide what you really need.

If, as Joan Walsh speculates, white voters sought a bolder economic program in 2010 than Obama offered, wouldn't it make more sense to vote out the Republicans who almost unanimously opposed any stimulus spending? Some might answer that "voters aren't rational," but it is no answer to indulge a voter's subjective thought processes instead of measuring them against a community standard of competence and decency. Although it often works indirectly, voting decides matters of war and peace, life and death, health and sickness, and justice and injustice. Philosophy professor Jason Brennan provides this helpful analogy: if you would not want your surgeon to operate on you without being learned about medicine, why would we want voters to vote without being informed on the issues and candidates?[64] Just as we hold surgeons to an established standard of care, so too should a voter's conduct have to meet a standard of communal responsibility. Voting from a place of ignorance or stereotype is morally wrong and, more to the point of this book, legally suspect.

Millions of voters who supported and continue to support Donald Trump lack a logical, fact-based justification; rather, their mindset is one of self-cultivated ignorance, cloaked in indignant defensiveness. Consider how these voters behave when they are insulted and lied to by the president and his party. Walsh believes that because Republicans have started to denigrate the white working class in the same terms as they have historically denigrated people of color, this provides an opportunity for a multiracial coalition of blacks and working-class whites.[65] It is true that Republicans often express disdain for their own base. After he won the Nevada caucuses in 2016 candidate Donald Trump patronizingly proclaimed, "I love the poorly educated!"[66] His statement was largely forgiven as Trumpian misspeak. In contrast, in 2008, candidate Barack Obama was deemed "elitist" for making an observation about whites in the decaying towns of the industrial Midwest that much social science research has come to bear out: "They get bitter, they cling to guns or religion or antipathy to people who aren't like them or anti-immigrant sentiment or anti-trade sentiment as a way to explain their frustrations."[67]

If white voters are going to be offended, they should be offended by what Republicans think they can get away with at the expense of their working- and middle-class white voter base. During the 2016 primaries, Donald Trump boasted, "I could stand in the middle of 5th Avenue and shoot somebody and I wouldn't lose voters."[68] Trump, in short, believed his voters were a cult. Once elected, he treated them as such. Republicans, for instance, convinced their base that Trump's $1.5 trillion tax cut favored the middle class over the rich: by the time Trump signed the Jobs and Tax Cut Act of 2017 into law, six in ten Republicans believed this.[69] When he signed the bill, however, Trump admitted that the 14-point tax rate reduction for corporations was "probably the biggest factor in our plan."[70]

If that did not discredit Republicans' rhetoric about their tax cut favoring the middle class, Trump's subsequent actions indubitably did. As the 2018 midterms approached, Trump promised "a middle-income tax reduction of about 10 percent—we're doing it now for middle-income people. This is not for business."[71] But Republicans had already played that card: in defending the 2017 tax cuts, House Speaker Paul Ryan insisted that "[t]he entire purpose of this is to lower middle class taxes."[72] In short, Republicans were scamming the American people, including their own base. Still, non-college-educated white women supplied 56 percent of their votes to Republican congressional candidates in 2018, and non-college-educated white men delivered 66 percent of their votes to Republicans.[73]

If outright duplicity does not offend these economically precarious voters, it is hard to see what would. Indeed, this duplicity is one of many glaring flaws of Trump and the party that he has remade in his image—the Republican Party—that are so deleterious to these voters that their candidate decisions simply cannot be understood apart from race (or whatever euphemism one might use for it, such as "culture"). Stated in the language of antidiscrimination law, the alternative explanations for white voter behavior are so lacking in plausibility that a reasonable factfinder could conclude that these voters were basing their candidate decision at least in part on race.

Rather than voting with reasonable justification, Trump's supporters rationalize his lies and harmful policies. During the 2018 midterm elections, Trump converted his 2016 tall tale that Mexico would pay for a wall along the southern border of the United States into a new fabrication that Congress had already appropriated $5 billion for the wall. There was no such appropriation.[74] Still, President Trump repeated the fabrication that "[w]e've started building our wall" 86 times in the seven months prior to the midterm elections, causing *The Washington Post* to create a new category of inaccurate information—"the bottomless Pinocchio."[75] Confronted with this inconsistency, a Trump supporter convinced herself that "it doesn't bother me, because he's going to make everything balance out in the end."[76]

White rural America exhibited a similar forgiveness of Trump during the 2018 midterms, even as his trade war, and the retaliatory tariffs on American agriculture it incited, contributed to a level of farm bankruptcies in the upper Midwest that surpassed the Great Recession of 2008.[77] A $12 billion government bailout fund intended to compensate farmers for their lost income—the sort of fund many conservatives would call "welfare" if people of color received it—was not even remotely sufficient to offset the effects of the retaliatory tariffs.[78] Yet, even as commodity prices fell by 20 percent after Trump began a trade war with China and other countries, farmers continued to steadfastly support him.[79] One southern Illinois farmer seemed to express the prevailing sentiment: "It's still pain, now, here, for us. But it will get better."[80]

It may well. But if white voters like these had displayed the same patience in 2010, when the economy needed breathing room to recover, as they have granted to Trump's shifting promises concerning his border wall and his trade war, the nation's trajectory from the Great Recession would have been much different. If they had displayed the same patience with the Affordable Care Act, Republicans would not have been emboldened to vote dozens of times to repeal it, and President Trump would not continually seek to destabilize the very insurance markets that affect millions of his supporters.[81]

And if they displayed the same *impatience* with Trump over soaring budget deficits and a rising national debt that they expressed with President Obama,[82] they surely would not tolerate a $1.5 trillion unfunded tax cut. The same Tea Partiers who insisted that the first African American president demonstrate unrealistic fiscal restraint during an unprecedented recession supported Trump, who described himself during the 2016 election as "the king of debt."[83] These same white voters continue to support a president whose response to the growing federal deficit and debt is reportedly "Just run the presses—print money."[84] Indeed, the federal budget deficit grew by 17 percent to a six-year high during Trump's first fiscal year as president.[85] White Trump supporters, however, do not appear to be unsettled by their internal contradictions, nor bothered by Trump's falsehoods.

We never quite learn from Joan Walsh what's the matter with white voters, but what we find is that voting while white means something different than voting as any other race. It means addressing your own needs, but not those of citizens you deem undeserving. Like Walsh, sociologist Arlie Russell

Hochschild, in *Strangers in Their Own Land*, attempts to understand white working- and middle-class America beyond mere political difference. Hochschild examines what she refers to as "the deep story"—the tale of how white Americans on the right see themselves and their station in life.[86] According to Hochschild, "We, on both sides, wrongly imagine that empathy with the 'other' side brings an end to clearheaded analysis when, in truth, it's on the other side of that bridge that the most important analysis can begin."[87]

And what does Hochschild see on the other side, when she looks closely at white Louisianans who have not voted for a Democratic presidential candidate since Bill Clinton in 1996? Anger. Moral superiority. Denial. Their anger is directed at the federal government because, according to Hochschild's subjects, it has aided and abetted "line cutters" in the queue to the American Dream. The line cutters, in their view, are not genuinely worthy individuals, because many of them lack a work ethic and are simply looking for government handouts. Among the line cutters are blacks and women, but immigrants tend to get the most mention.[88] In this narrative, welfare and disability fraud are pervasive, though, as with voting fraud, the proponents of this view offer no hard numbers, just anecdotes.

Hochschild's subjects often attach their faith, religion, or morality to their conservative views on politics. We should, however, view "values" and religiosity with due suspicion in explaining white voters' embrace of the right. First, 10 percent of Americans believe it is okay to racially discriminate based on religious beliefs.[89] Religion, then, can be used to rationalize prejudice.

Moreover, as measured by certainty of belief in God, frequency of church attendance, the importance of religion in one's life, and frequency of prayer, African Americans are more religious than whites or Latinos. According to a 2018 Pew Research study, 70 percent of black men and 83 percent of black women are highly religious, according to these four metrics,[90] compared with 58 percent of white women, 67 percent of Hispanic women, 44 percent of white men, and 50 percent of Hispanic men.[91] Yet blacks are not flocking to the political right.

In 2016, white evangelicals voted for Donald Trump, a thrice-married man accused by multiple women of unwanted sexual groping, by the largest margin of any Republican presidential candidate in history.[92] Thereafter, black evangelicals began leaving predominantly white evangelical congregations, distraught by Trump's anti-Mexican-immigrant rhetoric and his criticism of black NFL players kneeling in protest of police brutality.[93] Black evangelicals identify overwhelmingly as Democrats (69 percent); most white evangelicals identify as Republicans (49 percent) or independents (31 percent).[94] On the issue that Trump staked his 2016 campaign, immigration, the divide between black and white evangelicals is stark. Fifty-three percent of black evangelicals believe that immigration strengthens American society, compared with 32 percent of white evangelicals. In contrast, 53 percent of white evangelicals believe that immigration threatens American values.[95]

Indeed, a 2018 survey found that 52 percent of white evangelical Protestants viewed the prospect of a majority nonwhite nation, projected to occur in 2045, as a negative development.[96] The irony of this statistic is that white evangelicals, without support, perceive *themselves* as victims of discrimination. University of Maryland professor Janelle Wong has found that "white evangelical conservatism correlates strongly with their perceptions [of] anti-white discrimination, even after taking into account economic status, party, age and region. Fully 50 percent of white evangelical respondents to our 2016 survey reported feeling they face discrimination that's comparable to, or even higher than, the discrimination they believe Muslim Americans face."[97] Hochschild's subjects may invoke their faith in justifying their politics, but when we probe deeper, religiosity or morality appear at least in part to be pretexts for racial prejudice.[98]

Yet, the white conservatives Hochschild interviews do not consider themselves racist and indeed believe that the label is part of a piling-on by the North.[99] Of course, virtually all racism is built on denials of being racist; hence the moral justifications for slavery. To be fair, though, Hochschild brings intellectual clarity to the recitation of her interviewees' perceptions of themselves as nonracist. She notes that "racism refers to the belief in a natural hierarchy that places blacks at the bottom, and the tendency of whites to judge their own worth by distance from that bottom. By that definition, many Americans, north and south, are racist."[100] Yet Hochschild's ultimate aim, like Walsh's, is to steer the reader to a more empathetic view of white working- and middle-class voters on the right, and away from the explanatory power of race.[101]

White voters' self-perceptions undoubtedly influence how they vote; in this regard, Hochschild's contribution is notable. These self-perceptions, however, cannot support the reasonableness or legality of their vote. Anyone who believes that no baseline exists for determining reasonableness should consider the following analogy. Suppose your local tax assessor had overvalued your home, causing you to pay hundreds or thousands of dollars more in property taxes each year. You appeal the ruling, arguing that the assessor failed to accurately account for "comps"—that is, houses of similar quality in your neighborhood. If the assessor's office responds that it based your home's value on its "gut" or its own "high levels of intelligence"—two sources of President

Trump's decision-making on the economy and climate change[102]—you'd be appalled. Why? Because you're entitled as a homeowner to a fact-based assessment of your property's value. Put in constitutional terms, government owes its citizens, at minimum, a "rational basis" for its actions—that is, a rational relationship between the action and a legitimate objective of government.[103]

It would be odd and insupportable to require government to act rationally toward its citizens, but to allow citizens to behave irrationally in electing the government on which we impose a duty of rationality. It likewise defies reason to accord credence or respect to voters' (or politicians') decisions that rest on "gut" or self-confidence in their own "high levels of intelligence" when objective facts belie their instincts. So, while Professor Hochschild's sociological exploration of how white voters in Louisiana feel about their treatment at the hands of the government is important, its main utility from the standpoint of whitelash is its documentation of the stream of racially tinged grievances that lie at the heart of much white voting behavior. Voters who cannot give a consistent, rational explanation for their conduct at the polls and who show signs of racial prejudice are voters whom we should suspect of violating the antidiscrimination norm. The victims of that violation are not merely voters of color but rather society itself, which must absorb and then try to correct the harms inflicted on our government by whitelash.

VOTING WHILE BLACK: AN EXAMPLE IN MISSISSIPPI

Most white conservatives are not conservative—at least not fiscally. They are, however, racially conservative. These distinctions matter for a variety of reasons, not least of which is the burden placed on voters of color in the political process to, quite literally, save white voters from themselves. Sometimes, voters of color are even forced to abet their own subjugation. A case in point is Mississippi.

Partisan debates about the size of government and the degree to which it should aid states and their citizens are not unusual. That debate most often happens between Democrats and Republicans, reflecting ideological divides between the two major parties. In Mississippi, however, the 2014 U.S. Senate primary was an intramural battle between the establishment and Tea Party factions of the Republican Party. Yet the contest between longtime incumbent Thad Cochran and a voluble state senator, Chris McDaniel, may also be the moment when Mississippi discovered that its emperors have no clothes. For decades, white conservative Mississippians had sent a succession of very conservative senators such as Cochran to Washington to accomplish a very liberal end: to obtain federal dollars for the state.[104] McDaniel challenged that tradition, running as a limited-government conservative who would eschew "pork barrel spending."[105]

Mississippi's senators had been so adept at defying conservative fiscal orthodoxy that at the time of the Cochran–McDaniel contest, Mississippi was tied with New Mexico as the states most dependent on the federal government.[106] Both Mississippi and New Mexico are poor states that rely heavily on federal largesse, but their congressional profiles could not be more different: New Mexico is represented by two relatively liberal Democratic senators, while Mississippi has not sent a Democratic senator to Washington in nearly 30 years. As discussed earlier in this chapter, white conservative Mississippians' belief in a limited federal government stops where their state budget begins: the state's Republican governor voiced no objection to having federal dollars constitute more than 45 percent of its state budget.[107] For a state that disdains the long arm of federal justice, Mississippi is curiously willing to extend its hands for federal funds.

Given the propensity of white Americans to view poor blacks as emblematic of American welfare, it is important to understand that the federal largesse to Mississippi cannot somehow be passed off as state beneficence to help the state's black poor. Few states treat the poor as harshly as Mississippi. Ranked last in the nation for life expectancy,[108] Mississippi refused to expand its Medicaid program under the Affordable Care Act, becoming the only state in the union in which the number of uninsured actually increased in the first year of the act's implementation.[109] The decision left 138,000 uninsured Mississippians, most of them black, with no ability to afford health insurance.[110] Nor does the state fare better in other provisions for its poor. More than 24 percent of the state's citizens live below the poverty line, the highest rate in the country.[111] In a 2013 survey, more than a quarter of Mississippi respondents reported not having funds for food at some point during the preceding twelve months.[112] To be sure, Mississippi is a welfare state, but not the kind portrayed by whites' stereotype of black welfare recipients.

Despite these facts, the political reality is that if Cochran had boasted to Republican primary voters that he had brought home federal dollars to help Mississippi's black poor—or even its white poor, for that matter—he would likely have lost decisively in the first round of voting. Mississippi's antipathy toward the federal government is far too deeply rooted to make such an argument palatable, particularly in the Tea Party era.[113] Instead, Cochran and his emissaries highlighted his role in securing agricultural support for

Mississippi farmers, for securing post-Katrina disaster relief for the Gulf region, and for bringing naval installations and other federal spending projects to Mississippi.[114]

For nearly half of the Republican primary electorate, however, Cochran's accomplishments did not merit his reelection. His Tea Party opponent, McDaniel, bested him in the first round of voting but fell just short of an outright majority. This necessitated a runoff that would reveal the strategic choices that black voters are forced to make while whites indulge the luxury of being "conservative." Mississippi law allowed Democratic voters to vote in the Republican runoff as long as they had not voted in the Democratic Senate primary.[115] Mississippi is politically segregated: most Democrats in Mississippi are black; almost all Republicans are white. Turnout in the Democratic Senate primary was low, as the contest was uncompetitive. This meant that thousands of blacks were eligible to participate in the Republican runoff between Cochran and McDaniel.

The runoff was a contest between a southern racial conservative—Cochran— and a de facto white nationalist, McDaniel. Throughout the campaign, McDaniel was forced to defend his appearance before a neo-Confederate conference sponsored by a local chapter of the Sons of Confederate Veterans.[116] McDaniel also attempted to walk back past racially tinged comments made on his radio show, such as this one: "If they pass reparations [for slavery], and my taxes are going up, I ain't paying taxes."[117] And McDaniel's past broadsides against hip-hop also raised questions about his racial sensitivity.[118]

McDaniel's rhetoric was a mixture of overt appeals and racial code. He remarked, for example, "The country is in an age of great uncertainty right now. There are many that feel like strangers in their land. They don't recognize it. A new culture is rising, another culture is passing away. And we stand today in defense of that traditional culture, of those traditional values."[119]

Cochran, however, was no friend of African Americans either. In 2006, Cochran's rating on affirmative action from the NAACP was 11 percent, indicating that he was a foe.[120] That same year, the American Civil Liberties Union gave Cochran a score of zero for his positions on civil rights.[121] Moreover, Cochran had spoken approvingly of the *Shelby County, Ala. v. Holder* Supreme Court decision that removed federal preclearance of Mississippi voting law changes—even as Mississippi was enacting a restrictive voter photo ID law opposed by Mississippi's Legislative Black Caucus. "I think our state can move forward and continue to ensure that our democratic processes are open and fair for all without being subject to excessive scrutiny by the Justice Department," Cochran opined.[122] Cochran, too, liked federal money but not federal justice. Yet, but for the very preclear-ance mechanism that *Shelby County* abolished, the black voters who ulti-mately delivered Cochran a victory in the runoff would have faced even greater hurdles to voting.

But why did black Democrats support Cochran in the Republican runoff? Again, in voting, you can never get everything you want, so you must decide what is most important—especially when voting while black. Running behind, Cochran actively courted black votes. No Democrat was likely to win the general election since none had won a U.S. Senate seat in decades. Thus, presented with the ability to influence a Republican runoff between a racial conservative and a more voluble racial conservative, black voters intervened to tip the election to Cochran, who edged McDaniel 51 percent to 49 percent.[123] Ironies abounded in Cochran's victory, not least of which was McDaniel's charge that Cochran had engaged in "race-baiting" and had taken Mississippi back "50 years."[124] The statements corroborated impres-sions of McDaniel as a racial throwback, albeit one who excelled among white voters in Mississippi.[125] To McDaniel, it was not race-baiting to cater to neo-Confederate groups, or to rail against reparations for the inhumanity of southern slavery, or to speak in racially coded tongue about "culture." Instead, for the McDaniel campaign, race-baiting was appealing to black voters for their support. That Cochran did so by pointing out McDaniel's racial transgressions made the perceived race-baiting that much more galling.[126]

But the real irony of the 2014 Republican runoff in Mississippi had to do with Cochran. The Cochran campaign maintained that "Sen. Cochran received such tremendous support from the African-American community in Mississippi because he has a 40-year relationship, in elected office, built on respect and fairness to the African-American community."[127] These were the words of a white southern politician with abysmal ratings from civil rights groups. Those ratings did not improve despite blacks' having propelled Cochran to reelection. In 2017, the year before Cochran retired from the Senate for health reasons, the NAACP gave his civil rights record a rating of just 11 percent.[128]

Who really won the 2014 U.S. Senate contest in Mississippi? Conservative white voters who would continue to receive the federal "pork" they voted against in supporting McDaniel, and who would also have Cochran's support of anti-black policies, including support for conservative judges whose rulings weaken civil rights. Black Mississippians who crossed over to vote for Cochran made this luxury possible for their white neighbors.

AS MISSISSIPPI GOES . . .

What happened in the 2014 Republican runoff in Mississippi is not atypical, even if the specifics are. Not since 1964 have white Americans delivered a majority of their votes to a Democratic presidential nominee. Whites also consistently tilt Republican in congressional elections.[129] Even in the historic 2018 elections, in which Democrats captured the House of Representatives by the largest national vote margin since 1930, whites still preferred congressional Republicans by 10 percentage points.[130] In short, left to their own devices, white voters would be living under Republican policies. White Medicare recipients would be subject to the $537 billion cut in that program proposed by congressional Republicans just months before the midterms.[131] The same budget called for partial privatization of Medicare. White Medicaid recipients would find their medical care rationed by a Republican proposal to limit per capita payments.[132] The Republicans' budget proposal would have also cut $4 billion from Social Security and $230 billion over 10 years from education, training programs, and Pell Grants.[133]

For his part, President Trump's first annual budget aimed to cut a trillion dollars in social spending over a decade, including food stamps, federal student aid, and Medicaid, while drastically increasing defense spending and offering more than a trillion in tax cuts primarily for corporations and the wealthy.[134] Trump has tried hard to promote class warfare by the middle class against the poor—even proposing the creation of a "Department of Health and Public Welfare" to stigmatize recipients of aid other than Social Security or Medicare, as if Republicans do not benefit from the broader social safety net. They most certainly do, however. And Trump's proposed budget would harm millions of his most loyal supporters in the white working and middle classes.[135] For instance, even as Republicans' election rhetoric fans rural resentment at urban minorities and white progressives,[136] Trump proposed significant cuts to programs affecting rural America, including the budget for the Department of Agriculture.[137]

Do white voters think they are immune to the dystopian effects of this kind of austerity? Or, more likely, do they vote accustomed to the idea that someone—in this case, nonwhites—will intervene to continue to provide the safety net they forsake? Again, it is easy to be conservative if you will reap the benefits of liberalism regardless of how you vote. And it is easy to be racially conservative if people of color—the objects of white prejudice at the polls—act as a bulwark against the worst outcomes of your votes. Whitelash endures in part because of this conundrum of our democracy.

Democracies, of course, experience pendulum swings and course corrections—until they no longer can. In Trump's presidency, a familiar pattern is emerging: budget deficits swelled by tax cuts, projected to reach a trillion dollars a year in fiscal 2019 and beyond, will be left to the next president to clean up. And if that president is a Democrat, then Republicans will once again care about deficits and use them as subterfuge to shrink the safety net. White voters, frustrated that the turnaround of the mess they helped to create has not gone quickly enough, will then punish the Democrats in the mid-terms, thereby impeding any progress. This was the scenario faced by Bill Clinton after the Reagan–Bush era and by Barack Obama after the presidency of George W. Bush, whose deficits were also driven by two unfunded wars and a Medicare prescription drug program that was not paid for.[138]

One way to achieve smaller government—indeed, the preferred way for many conservatives—is to "starve the beast" of revenue.[139] With tax cuts and increased military spending, three of the last four Republican presidents have done precisely this, leaving their successors with the tab. This is not a tale of swinging pendulums or course corrections. It instead is a slow death of democracy. When one party's ascendency is so crippled by the legacy of its predecessor's policies, it does not matter that voters have changed their minds and voted for a new direction.[140] If there is any doubt that this is the modus operandi of Republicans, consider Donald Trump's response to the ballooning national debt, which is projected to rise by $4.775 trillion through 2021.[141] When his advisors informed him that the debt would spike in the near future, Trump reportedly responded, "Yeah, but I won't be here."[142]

Whitelash may give temporary satisfaction to voters wanting to stand up against "political correctness" or "elites," or who feel that others have "cut in line." By voting with a jaundiced eye on their fellow citizens of color, however, millions of white voters are sticking it to themselves. Their harm is metastasizing in a way that will not be easily undone by the next "wave" election.

Justice Kennedy may be wrong: American democracy may not be self-correcting, in which case we must turn to the courts for a remedy.

7

Holding Candidates and Parties Accountable

"We did great with the African American community. So good. Remember — remember the famous line, because I talk about crime, I talk about lack of education, I talk about no jobs. And I'd say, what the hell do you have to lose? Right? It's true. And they're smart, and they picked up on it like you wouldn't believe. And you know what else? They didn't come out to vote for Hillary. They didn't come out. And that was a big — so thank you to the African American community."

— President-elect Donald Trump in Hershey, Pennsylvania, approximately
a month after the November 2016 election[1]

Donald Trump ran the most racially incendiary presidential campaign in modern times.[2] So, it's odd enough that he would transparently misrepresent his performance among black voters: he took 8 percent of the black vote in 2016 to Hillary Clinton's 88 percent.[3] But it's shocking that he would thank blacks, who were denied the right to vote for much of American history, for choosing to stay home and not exercise that right. It is incriminating because the Trump campaign — whether in conjunction with Russian nationals or independently, we do not yet know — admitted to attempting to suppress the black vote. Said one senior Trump campaign official to *Bloomberg News* shortly before the election, "We have three major voter suppression operations under way," identifying African Americans as one of its targets.[4] Meanwhile, black voters were also the target of Russian social media trolls attempting to suppress black turnout, an operation that would become the subject of indictments made in former FBI director Robert Mueller's investigation of Russian interference in the 2016 election.[5]

To many readers, preying on African Americans to suppress their vote will call to mind what has become a ubiquitous analogy thanks to Michelle Alexander's work, *The New Jim Crow*.[6] There is no practical difference between an intent to deprive African Americans of the right to vote, as was done during Jim Crow, and an intent to suppress their vote, as was done by the Trump campaign and the Republican Party in 2016 and several previous election cycles. There may not even be a legal distinction. Cloaked in the power of the state as the nominee of one of the country's two major political parties, Trump set out to dilute the votes of black citizens. He did so in a manner that if done by the state of Mississippi, for instance, would surely constitute a violation of Section 2 of the Voting Rights Act of 1965, which prohibits any practice that results in a denial or abridgement of "the right of any citizen of the United States to vote on account of race or color."[7]

Added to the Trump campaign's and Republicans' suppression activities were the candidate's racial statements, which continued into his presidency and which, if made in any American workplace, would constitute direct evidence of discrimination. For decades, racial appeals and voter suppression have been pillars of Republican electoral strategy. Racial appeals are intended to drive up white turnout; suppression efforts, often disguised as ballot integrity measures, are intended to drive down minority turnout. Trump's 2016 campaign was different only in degree rather than kind. Mexicans were rapists. Muslims were terrorists. China—but not Russia—was America's enemy. Blacks were "living in hell." No American of color was spared insult, even when Trump essayed a compliment. Most of Trump's political rallies were lily-white, so at one rally, to deflect criticism of the racial tenor of his campaign, Trump sought to identify a black supporter: "Oh, look at my African-American over here. Look at him. Are you the greatest?"[8] So went the 2016 campaign. And so has gone the Trump presidency. Indeed, after President Trump tweeted in the summer of 2019 that four congresswomen of color—all U.S. citizens and all but one born in the U.S.—should "go back and help fix" the countries from which they came, Pulitzer Prize-winning historian Jon Meacham said of Trump: "He has joined Andrew Johnson as the most racist president in American history."[9]

Is it possible that in a country where citizens cannot legally discriminate against each other—not in employment, not in housing, not in private contracts—the president of the United States can be as racist as he pleases? And has our tolerance of the president's and his party's racial rhetoric reached a point of allowing them to openly—and legally—advocate the suppression of minority votes? In this chapter and the next, I argue that our answers must be a resounding "No." I demonstrate below that the antidiscrimination norm extends to candidates—both successful ones and unsuccessful ones—and to the parties that support them, not only as a matter of principle but also as a matter of law. When candidates and parties prevail by making racial appeals and suppressing minority votes, the law should not presume that they are capable of governing on behalf of all citizens. Rather, the laws enacted by such candidates and parties should be subject to heightened scrutiny for invidious discrimination.

THE LAW OF RACIAL APPEALS

Racial appeals during political campaigns have long been treated as evidence of intentional discrimination under the Equal Protection Clause of the Fourteenth Amendment, and as evidence of minority vote dilution under the Voting Rights Act of 1965. In *White v. Regester*, for instance, the Supreme Court sustained a district court's finding that the state of Texas had intentionally discriminated against black and Latino voters in the creation of two multimember electoral districts. The district court's finding was based in part on a history of "racial campaign tactics in white precincts to defeat candidates who had the overwhelming support of the black community."[10] Yet the broader objective of the Court in *White*, as in any constitutional or statutory racial vote dilution case, was to determine whether the black and Latino plaintiffs had "less opportunity than did other residents in the district to participate in the political processes and to elect legislators of their choice."[11] To answer this question, the Court examined not merely racial appeals made during elections but also the social and political inequality of the appeals' targets. Among other factors, the Court probed historical discrimination against blacks and Latinos in Dallas County and Bexar County, Texas, as well as current economic disparities between these groups and whites, and the responsiveness of elected officials to their needs.[12]

To better understand how and why social positionality influences the use and potency of racial appeals, consider a few examples from the 2018 midterm elections. In one, Republican Congresswoman Claudia Tenney of upstate New York criticized her Democratic opponent, Anthony Brindisi, an Italian American, by implying that Brindisi's father was connected to the mafia. Tenney stated that Brindisi's father was "very heavily involved with the organized crime in Utica for many years, representing them."[13] Tenney's statement is a racial or ethnic slur intended to summon stereotypes of Italians in voters' evaluation of her opponent. Yet, Tenney's ability to marginalize her opponent using racial or ethnic stereotype depends on the social vulnerability of the group to which her target belongs. Italian Americans as a group are today not more economically, politically, or socially vulnerable than any other cohort of white Americans.

In contrast, when Republican Congressman John Faso targeted his Democratic African American opponent, Antonio Delgado, a former

Rhodes Scholar, for his previous career as a rapper whose lyrics criticized America's history of racial injustice, the potential for whitelash was high. Delgado's lyrics criticized some of the country's forefathers as "dead presidents" who "believe in white supremacy."[4] Alluding to the (white) demographics of his congressional district, Faso contended that Delgado's lyrics were "inconsistent with the views of the people of the 19th District and America." Faso's surrogates were even blunter, claiming that Delgado's lyrics raised issues of "culture and commonality with the district and its values."[5] Delgado, in turn, decoded these euphemisms: "In his [Faso's] dated mind-set, he thinks it's accurate to suggest that if you're black or if you're of a certain race, you can't be of this community."[6]

Congressman Ron DeSantis of Florida opened his 2018 gubernatorial campaign against Tallahassee Mayor Andrew Gillum with similar racial allusions. After capturing the Republican nomination, DeSantis took to Fox News to proclaim that Floridians should oppose Gillum because "[t]he last thing we need to do is to monkey this up by trying to embrace a socialist agenda with huge tax increases and bankrupting the state."[7] DeSantis's deployment of the term "monkey" in reference to his African American opponent set off a firestorm of criticism. Even a former chairman of the Republican National Committee, Michael Steele, himself an African American, joined the chorus: "It's how white folks talk about black men who are successful."[8]

Lest there be any doubt about the racial connotations of DeSantis's statement, Fox News—ordinarily a breeding ground for race rhetoric—issued a statement condemning DeSantis's remarks: "We do not condone this language and wanted to make our viewers aware that he has since clarified his statement."[9] But DeSantis's "clarification" was merely a denial that his words had racist intent. Almost all uses of racial appeals—even those deployed by white nationalists—are accompanied by similar denials.

Factual differences aside, the social difference between, on the one hand, Delgado and Gillum as targets of a racial appeal and, on the other, Brindisi, a white man, as a target is vast: Delgado and Gillum hail from an economically, politically, and socially vulnerable group. Appeals deployed against members of such a group reinforce their inequality and thus demonstrate an intent to discriminate against them. As we have seen in earlier chapters, the law deciphers an actor's intent in different ways depending on the circumstances and the specific provisions being litigated. In constitutional adjudication, one constant across cases is that demonstrating that a government action is more burdensome for one racial group than another does not, on its own, show discriminatory intent. In a much-criticized 1976 ruling, *Washington v. Davis*, the Supreme Court announced that plaintiffs seeking to invalidate a law as racially discriminatory must show that it was passed with a discriminatory purpose, although the law's disproportionate impact might be proof of such purpose.[20] *Washington v. Davis*, however, does not consider the possibility that the racial appeals relevant to deciding whether a particular electoral arrangement violates the Equal Protection Clause (the issue in *White v. Regester*) may be more broadly relevant to an assessment of whether other actions of the government also discriminate based on race.

Far from abrogating the ordinary constitutional rule that disparate impact alone does not constitute discriminatory intent, racial appeals actively *target* disadvantaged groups. Their disparate impact is not random, and their purpose is always to sow contempt among a majority against a minority. *Shaw v. Reno*, a case involving North Carolina's attempt to create majority–minority congressional districts to rectify the 100-year drought of black congressional representation from the state, looked at the question of disparate impact and concluded that a district favoring a minority racial group could discriminate against the majority group:

> When a district obviously is created solely to effectuate the perceived common interests of one racial group, elected officials are more likely to believe that their primary obligation is to represent only the members of that group, rather than their constituency as a whole. This is altogether antithetical to our system of representative democracy.[21]

If the Supreme Court found that even actions intended to *remedy* past discrimination can convey a license to discriminate, what must racial appeals by incumbent politicians and other candidates convey? In evaluating the intent of a speaker, we must follow the Court's teachings in *Shaw* that the mere claim of an innocent or salutary purpose does not sanitize the statement; its racial content—which will sometimes be discernible on its face and other times be implicit—warrants elevated suspicion. The Supreme Court justified its exacting scrutiny of North Carolina's redistricting plan because "the very reason that the Equal Protection Clause demands strict scrutiny of all racial classifications is because without it, a court cannot determine whether or not the discrimination truly is 'benign.'"[22] Government speech that separates citizens on the basis of race is as suspect as government *action* that does the same, because what elected officials (and those aspiring to office) say may be evidence of the discriminatory intent of what they ultimately do.

Racial appeals by political candidates mirror prohibited discriminatory action by the state in another important respect. Whether at the level of conscious thought (i.e., active intent) or cognitive processes (i.e., latent intent), such appeals attempt to maintain social and racial castes. Yet, the Supreme Court has determined that state action intended to maintain a "status quo" in racial discrimination violates the Fourteenth Amendment Equal Protection Clause.[23] Thus, in *Hunter v. Underwood*, a case in which the Court struck down Alabama's felony disenfranchisement statute as racially discriminatory, the Court held that a subsequent nonracial rationale for the statute did not purge its original discriminatory intent. It was enough for the Court that the statute's "original enactment was motivated by a desire to discriminate against blacks on account of race and the section continues to this day to have that effect."[24] Similarly, racial appeals by candidates interact with historical discrimination to perpetuate its effects; the modern ratiocinations for such appeals—which are often mere pretexts—cannot cleanse their racist origins and effects.

Some may argue that candidates represent their own interests, not those of the state; therefore, their actions cannot be imputed to the *government*—the only entity for which the Fourteenth and Fifteenth Amendments forbid racial discrimination. Since, however, the federal government, states, and localities are run by *elected candidates*, the discriminatory intent of a candidate is relevant to determining the racial neutrality of government actions. Representatives Faso, DeSantis, and Tenney, all perpetrators of racial appeals, were *both candidates and lawmakers* when they made them. It's implausible to think that politicians who are inclined to make racial appeals during campaigns will abandon their discriminatory mindset once in office.

Let's set to one side the obvious recent case of Donald Trump, to be discussed shortly. At the time, Vice President George H. W. Bush's 1988 presidential campaign was viewed as one of the most racialized in modern history. Bush used Willie Horton, a black man who committed rape and assault of a white couple while out of jail on a weekend furlough program, to cast his opponent, Governor Michael Dukakis, as soft on crime. Said Bush campaign manager Lee Atwater: "By the time we're finished, they're going to wonder whether Willie Horton is Dukakis's running mate."[25] Bush's appeals to race would not end after the campaign, however. He vetoed the Civil Rights Act of 1990, misleadingly labeling it as a "quota bill, regardless of how its authors dress it up."[26] Even after Congress added a provision making quotas illegal, Bush continued his racial rhetoric, arguing "[y]ou can't put a sign on a pig and say it's a horse." Yet the horse that President Bush was riding galloped straight out of 1964, when Bush unsuccessfully ran for the U.S. Senate on a platform opposing the landmark Civil Rights Act of 1964.

The notion that a candidate might run on racial appeals but govern as an equalitarian defies not just common sense and history but legal precept.

Under the "stray remarks doctrine" in Title VII employment discrimination law, "comments that, while perhaps discriminatory, do not truly show that discrimination was a motivating factor in the relevant employment decision" are excluded from consideration by courts.[27] Yet even where a decision-maker utters a comment outside the context of a specific decisional process, if the comment reflects "a highly discriminatory attitude" on the part of the speaker, it can be a sign of discriminatory intent.[28] Thus, in *Morris v. McCarthy*, a black supervisor's comment that "the little white woman better stand in line" was evidence of his discriminatory attitude, even though it was not made directly in the context of the decision to suspend the white employee who was the subject of the comment.[29] And so it is with racial appeals during campaigns. They can be evidence of a discriminatory attitude and thus may later prove the intent behind an elected official's vote or decision that bears disproportionately on the minority group or groups who are the subject of such appeals. This is especially so where the candidate engages in a pattern of such remarks or continues such remarks once elected, as Donald Trump has.

Arguably, a politician's racial appeals can never constitute a stray remark, particularly when, as is often the case, the politician responds with a denial instead of an apology. Whereas an employer's decisions are limited to the terms and conditions of our employment, politicians' decisions affect that and far more in our lives. Thus, while it may make sense to focus on the specific statements made at the time of an employer's adverse decision, it makes far less sense to similarly confine the temporal relevance of discriminatory statements made in the political process. Congressman Steve King of Iowa, for instance, has engaged in a range of racist conduct over the years, even retweeting Nazi propaganda and displaying a small Confederate flag on his desk.[30] If King proposed in the House of Representatives, as he did when he was in the Iowa legislature, a bill to make English the official language of the country, should we ignore his past racist statements and conduct in assessing the intent of the legislation merely because they were not made in the course of debating the legislation? How much sense would that make? If politicians make statements or take actions that suggest bigotry or a discriminatory attitude, their behavior bears on the race neutrality of their official actions—including legislation they propose and votes they take once elected.

In addition to racial appeals by candidates, those made by other agents of political parties also can and should be considered as evidence of an intent to discriminate by the government. In a series of cases dating back to 1927—called the "white primary cases"—the Supreme Court rejected attempts by the state of Texas to evade the requirements of the Fourteenth and Fifteenth Amendments by assigning the function of nominating major-party candidates to state parties and private organizations.[31] In so doing, the Court ruled that "electoral practices implemented by political parties have the potential to 'den[y] or abridg[e] the right to vote on account of race or color …'"[32] If electoral practices by a political party can cause unconstitutional racial harm, then racial appeals made by the party through its agents similarly are evidence of an intent to inflict such harm.

When Michigan Republicans recently attempted to eliminate "straight-ticket" voting, which allows a voter to select all the candidates of one party by pulling a single lever or shading a single space on a ballot, a federal district court found that the law harmed black voters in part because of the history of racialized appeals in Michigan elections. In this case, *Michigan State A. Phillip Randolph Institute v. Johnson*, the court cited comments made by Ron Weiser, a finance chairman of the Republican National Committee who would later become chairman of the Michigan State Republican Party.[33] Weiser, a leading proponent of the attempt to vanquish straight-ticket voting, had publicly expressed confidence in Republicans' 2012 prospects in Michigan because, in Detroit, a predominantly black city, "[t]here's no machine to go to the pool halls and the barbershops and put those people on buses, and then bus them from precinct to precinct where they vote multiple times. There's no machine to get 'em to stop playing pool and drinking beer in the pool hall."[34] Similarly, a Republican state senator was quoted in the *Detroit Free Press* as saying "if we do not suppress the Detroit vote, we're going to have a tough time in this election."[35] Statements like these exemplified the racialized tenor of elections in Michigan and placed in context the law that eliminated straight-ticket voting, which, while neutral on its face, disproportionately harmed black voters. Racial appeals by party officials helped to indict the law.

The bluntness of these racial appeals by political parties often eclipses those of candidates. In 2012, for instance, the chairman of the Republican Party of Columbus, Ohio, stated, "I guess I really actually feel we shouldn't contort the voting process to accommodate the urban—read African-American—voter-turnout machine."[36] Scott Jensen, a former speaker of the Wisconsin state assembly, was more circumspect in orchestrating racial appeals with a local chamber of commerce, which was effectively an arm of the state Republican Party. A senior vice president of the Metropolitan Milwaukee Chamber of Commerce suggested to Jensen that in the event of the defeat of the Republican-preferred candidate for a state supreme court seat, "we need to start messaging 'widespread reports of election fraud' so we are positively set up for the recount regardless of the final number[.]"[37] Jensen responded, "Yes.

Anything fishy should be highlighted. Stories should be solicited by talk radio hosts."[38]

CLAIMS OF VOTER FRAUD AS RACIAL APPEALS

The exchange between Jensen and the chamber of commerce vice president does not mention race. Nor does it have to, to be understood as racial. In evaluating the role of racial appeals in the dilution of minority political power, courts probe both "overt and subtle racial appeals."[39] And, as the legendary political operative Lee Atwater attested, subtle appeals are often more effective than unadorned racial rhetoric.[40] This is especially true where the racial appeal urges potentially illegal conduct like voter suppression.

The racial appeals cited by the court in *Michigan State A. Phillip Randolph Institute v. Johnson* were statements that, in themselves, were subtle calls to suppress the black vote. This case thus illustrates that racial appeals and voter suppression are frequently tandem strategies. The case likewise sketches how racial appeals are often infused with the narrative of voter fraud. In Republican circles, the face of voter fraud, like the face of criminality generally, is rarely white; instead, people of color are the perpetrators. Put another way, claims of voter fraud would have far less traction if they were directed at white retirement communities in Florida rather than urban centers throughout the country. Thus, in Michigan, it was Detroiters whom Republican officials worried would vote "multiple times." In *Democratic National Committee v. Reagan*, a case arising out of Arizona, Republican memes of voter fraud took the form of a video posted on Facebook and YouTube that "showed surveillance footage of a man of apparent Hispanic heritage appearing to deliver early ballots." Commentary from the chairman of the Maricopa County Republican Party described the Latino-appearing man as a "thug" and stated that the man was about to stuff the ballot box.[41] Yet when presented with actual evidence that the Republican candidate in a 2018 North Carolina congressional race had hired an operative who illegally collected and filled out absentee ballots, the chairman of the state Republican Party insisted that its candidate be seated despite his campaign's involvement with fraud.[42] The chairman, Robin Hayes, invoked a refrain that Republicans categorically reject when they accuse Democrats of election fraud: "No election is perfect."[43]

The venerable John McCain was widely lauded for resisting outward racial appeals during his 2008 campaign against Barack Obama. Yet what McCain could not resist—indeed, what Republicans across the temperamental and ideological spectrum cannot resist—is the old-fashioned canard of minority voter fraud. During the 2008 campaign, McCain linked Obama's work as a community organizer in Chicago to ACORN, a national network of community service organizations that served the poor and disadvantaged, including through voter registration drives. During a nationally televised debate with Obama, McCain suggested that ACORN was "on the verge of maybe perpetrating one of the greatest frauds in voter history in this country, maybe destroying the fabric of democracy."[44] Destroying the fabric of democracy? To be sure, ACORN, which hired low-wage workers to conduct its voter registration drives, turned in invalid registrations as well as valid ones. Then again, county boards of registration exist for a reason: to check registration forms for accuracy. Moreover, McCain's and Republicans' charges of "voter fraud" were trained on in-person voter fraud, an oft-spoken but rarely proven boogeyman. Whatever the imperfections of ACORN's registration drives, there was no proof that any invalid registration ever resulted in an invalid vote being cast.[45]

As the McCain example demonstrates, to credit President Trump alone with moving the nation into an age of alternative facts would be to forget the Republican Party's common embrace of the alternative fact of voter fraud. Belief in the existence of widespread voter fraud has in effect become a plank of the Republican platform. But Andrew Gumbel, a reporter for *The Guardian*, exposes the inconvenient truth about this belief in his book *Down for the Count*:

> The problem ... was that they were chasing the wrong target. Study after study has shown in-person voter fraud to be a rarity in the modern era—"more rare than getting struck by lightning," in the words of one report from the Brennan Center for Justice—because it is difficult to get away with and even more difficult to organize on any scale. On the handful of occasions when ineligible voters have tried to cast ballots, it has usually been because of a misunderstanding or a clerical error.[46]

Indeed, no less a political figure than Al Cardenas, the former chairman of the Republican Party of Florida, who was a fixture in the Florida 2000 recount imbroglio, has disclaimed the existence of in-person voter fraud. Asked in response to candidate Donald Trump's claims of voter fraud whether large-scale voter fraud existed in the United States, Cardenas responded: "Oh, my, there isn't, hasn't been. And our country has been spending 200-plus years to get it just right."[47] Cardenas went on to decry Trump's predictions of voter fraud in the 2016 contest:

We in this country know that transparency works. We appreciate and frankly adore the right to have the free, peaceful transfer of power from the president to [sic] the eventual winner. We in America have always celebrated the way we have elections ... To tarnish it with unproven facts, tarnish it with accusations, to me, it is just a shame. It shouldn't be done.[48]

Unable to demonstrate in-person voter fraud (as in a voter impersonating someone else), Republicans are now attempting to criminalize voter confusion. Many of the people involved just happen to be African Americans. In Alamance County, North Carolina, a Republican district attorney charged a dozen citizens—nine of them black—with voting illegally because they cast a ballot while on probation or parole for a felony.[49] The North Carolina statute requires no criminal intent; thus, the fact that the accused did not know it was illegal for them to vote was irrelevant. Similar prosecutions have occurred in Texas, Kansas, Idaho, and other states.[50] In many of these states, as in North Carolina, the laws that disenfranchise felons have their roots in the Jim Crow era, when such statutes were passed as part of a comprehensive stratagem to deprive blacks of the right to vote.[51] The strategy of the GOP is no less comprehensive today, sparing only the violence of Jim Crow but otherwise determined to limit the minority franchise.

How do we know this? GOP leaders do not dissemble their intent. The speaker of the Pennsylvania House of Representatives famously boasted in 2012 that "[v]oter ID ... is going to allow Governor Romney to win the state of Pennsylvania."[52] Although Romney wound up losing Pennsylvania, the state's Republican chairman still credited its voter ID law with reducing Obama's margin of victory: "Think about this: We cut Obama by 5 percent, which was big. A lot of people lost sight of that. He beat McCain by 10 percent; he only beat Romney by 5 percent. And I think that probably photo ID helped a bit in that."[53] Republican Congressman Glenn Grothman of Wisconsin accurately predicted that Wisconsin's stringent voter ID law would help the GOP presidential nominee carry Wisconsin for the first time since 1984. After commenting on the weaknesses of Hillary Clinton, Grothman added: "And now we have photo ID, and I think photo ID is going to make a little bit of a difference as well."[54] Why would photo ID help Republicans and not Democrats, particularly when there is virtually no evidence of voter fraud? According to Grothman, "I think we [Republicans] believe that, insofar as there are inappropriate things, people who vote inappropriately are more likely to vote Democrat."[55]

The stereotype that Grothman paints is an effective propellant among Republicans for the myth of voter fraud because it is rooted in race. After

Wisconsin implemented its voter ID law, black voter turnout in the state declined by 19 percent between the 2012 and 2016 elections.[56] The decline in black turnout nationally for the same period was only 4.5 percent. A study by the University of Wisconsin found that nearly 17,000 voters in Dane County and heavily black Milwaukee County may have decided to sit out the 2016 election because of the voter ID law.[57] Wisconsin's precipitous, disproportionate drop allowed Donald Trump to carry Wisconsin by less than 1 percent. Despite President Trump's erroneous view that Americans must have photo identification to buy groceries,[58] nearly 11 percent of Americans lack a photo ID, and this group is composed disproportionately of minorities and the poor.[59] The explicit partisan intentions of Republicans, the absence of proof of voter fraud that would be prevented by a photo ID requirement, and the disproportionate impact of voter ID on minorities suggest, singularly and in combination, a scheme to suppress the minority vote.

There is more. Just as the building of Confederate monuments spiked after the ruling in *Brown v. Board of Education*,[60] voter ID laws became a Republican fixation only after the election of the first black president, Barack Obama. These laws, like Confederate monuments, and like the felony disenfranchisement statutes enacted after Reconstruction, are whitelash against the advancement of racial minorities. According to the National Conference of State Legislatures, "In 2011, 2012 and 2013, the pace of adoption accelerated. States without ID requirements continued to adopt them, and states that had less-strict requirements adopted stricter ones."[61] The states with the strictest requirements lean Republican and have large minority populations or urban centers in which the states' minorities cluster.[62]

Despite all this circumstantial evidence of racially discriminatory intent, Republicans frequently claim that politics, not race, drives their quest for voting restrictions. The Supreme Court's decision in *Crawford v. Marion County Election Board* gives plausibility to their otherwise absurd argument.[63] There, even after noting that "[t]he record contains no evidence of any [in-person voter] fraud actually occurring in Indiana at any time in its history," the Court upheld an Indiana photo voter ID requirement.[64] Presented with evidence that Republicans in Indiana had passed the legislation for political reasons, Justice John Paul Stevens, a progressive, offered this head-scratcher unsupported by legal precedent: "[I]f a nondiscriminatory law is supported by valid neutral justifications, those justifications should not be disregarded simply because partisan interests may have provided one motivation for the votes of individual legislators."[65]

Justice Stevens's assertion in this case that gaming the right to vote is okay if it's based on opposition to the other side's political beliefs runs contrary to his own views in political gerrymandering cases: In *Vieth v. Jubelirer*, Stevens insisted that "political affiliation is not an appropriate standard for excluding voters from a congressional district."[66] How, then, could partisanship be an appropriate basis for making it more difficult for members of one party to vote than members of another?

To the extent that the Court in *Crawford* believed that Indiana demonstrated neutral, nonpartisan justifications for its photo voter ID law, those justifications were speculative. Rather than showing any evidence that in-person voter fraud had occurred or was even remotely likely to occur, Indiana offered far less proof than the government did in *Citizens United v. Federal Election Commission*. In that case, the Court ruled on free speech grounds that corporations could use their general treasury funds for campaign ads opposing or supporting candidates. Justice Kennedy, writing for the majority, rejected the government's prohibition of such spending on the grounds that the government had not offered proof that corporate expenditures on behalf of candidates create quid pro quo corruption.[67] It makes little sense that when the government seeks to curtail the influence of money in elections, it must bring its A—game, but when it seeks to punish members of opposing political parties by making it more difficult for them to vote, speculative justifications will suffice.

In fact, the law says otherwise. In a democracy, government has no more right to make it harder for political opponents to vote than it does to exclude them from serving in a state legislature.[68] Moreover, even if the right to spend and the right to vote in elections are not identical situations, *Crawford* requires that burdens on the right to vote be "nondiscriminatory." Yet Republicans themselves talk publicly about Democrats being the targets of voter ID laws, so how can these laws be nondiscriminatory? Substituting "Democrat" for "black" or "Hispanic" does not erase the racial identity of the targeted populations. More importantly, black, Hispanic, Asian, and Native American voters certainly do not give up their racial identity when they choose a partisan affiliation. Indeed, under standard First Amendment doctrine, these groups are free to define their political identity according to their racial identity.[69] That is, black voters have the right to organize politically around issues that have a distinct impact on their community. As discussed in Chapters 2 and 4, white Americans are increasingly doing the same, for very different reasons than people of color, and these white identifiers are overwhelmingly Republican. Thus, to allow a state legislature to enact voting restrictions that disproportionately harm voters of color is to permit it, functionally, to discriminate based on race.

Republicans know this, for when it comes to the messy question of what is racial versus what is merely political, the eye of the beholder matters. And what do Republicans behold when they see the Democratic Party? Black people. In a 2018 paper, political scientist Douglas Ahler and researcher Gaurav Sood demonstrated that members of one party tend to substantially overestimate the share of "party-stereotypical" groups in the opposing party.[70] They found that "[w]hile most people overestimate the share of party-stereotypical groups in the parties, the extent to which they overestimate varies by partisanship ... Republicans' perceptions of Democratic composition exhibit significantly more bias than Democrats'."[71] Thus, Republican respondents in Ahler and Sood's study significantly overestimated the Democratic Party's share of union members, gays, blacks, and atheists.[72] Indeed, Republicans believed that blacks constitute nearly half of the Democratic Party (46.4 percent) when their actual composition is closer to a quarter (23.9 percent).

These projections of stereotypes have real-world consequences. According to Ahler and Sood:

> [B]eliefs about out-party composition affect perceptions of where opposing-party supporters stand on the issues. These findings provide a potential explanation for why people tend to overestimate the extremity of opposing partisans ... Beyond beliefs about extremity, we suspect that perceptions about party composition affect people's beliefs about the parties' priorities ... More generally, we suspect that people associate a narrow set of policy demands with each party-stereotypical group and think these groups have sway over the party's agenda.[73]

If Republicans believe that the Democratic Party has been captured by blacks, then efforts by Republicans to harm Democrats politically constitute efforts to harm blacks. Moreover, in considering the intent behind voter ID laws and other suppression vehicles, courts should not ignore the general discriminatory attitudes of Republican voters. For instance, a Reuters poll taken prior to the 2016 elections showed that Trump supporters were more likely than supporters of his Republican rivals or of Hillary Clinton to believe that blacks were "criminal," "lazy," "unintelligent," and "violent."[74] Are we to believe that Republican voters and the politicians they elect successfully compartmentalize this bigotry when supporting or enacting legislation that disadvantages fellow citizens who they believe are inferior and whose presence they overestimate in the opposition party? Voter ID laws and other suppression measures are racial appeals by another name. Moreover, because advocacy for these types of restrictions may be evidence of a general discriminatory attitude toward persons of color, passage of voter suppression measures may be evidence of a racially discriminatory motive in the passage of other measures that disproportionately harm people of color. Courts must evaluate the content of these laws using the strictest constitutional standard.

WHY NOT JUST OUTLAW RACIAL APPEALS?

Before turning to a more in-depth discussion of how racism in electoral campaigns can be used as evidence of racial discrimination in governing, the reader should understand the constitutional limitations of any remedy against candidates and parties for using racial appeals. In *Vanasco v. Schwartz*, political candidates challenged the constitutionality of the New York Fair Campaign Code.[75] The code made unlawful

> "during the course of any campaign for nomination or election to public office or party position," by means of "campaign literature, media advertisements or broadcasts, public speeches, press releases, writings or otherwise," "attacks on a candidate based on race, sex, religion or ethnic background" . . . any "misrepresentation of any candidate's qualifications" including the use of "personal vilification" and "scurrilous attacks" . . . any "misrepresentation of a candidate's position" . . . and any "misrepresentation of any candidate's party affiliation or party endorsement" . . .[76]

In short, the law would have prohibited much of the kind of dishonest, race-baiting conduct engaged in by political campaigns, including Trump's 2016 campaign. A federal district court invalidated the statute, concluding in part that

> [i]t would be a retreat from reality to hold that voters do not consider race, religion, sex or ethnic background when choosing political candidates. Speech is often provocative and indeed offensive, but unless it falls into one of those "well defined and narrowly limited classes" of unprotected speech (e.g., "fighting words") it enjoys constitutional protection.[77]

The United States Supreme Court summarily affirmed the district court's judgment without opinion.[78]

Vanasco teaches that we cannot preempt a candidate's or a party's racial appeals, even when such appeals have as their purpose the suppression of minority votes—an action which, if undertaken by the state, would constitute a violation of the Equal Protection Clause of the Fourteenth Amendment and the Voting Rights Act of 1965. Yet a candidate's or party's racial appeals are still relevant evidence of a racially discriminatory attitude and thus can be used to contest the neutrality of a law that carries the candidate's or the party's imprimatur. To this scenario we now turn.

DONALD TRUMP AS A SYMPTOM; HIS WORDS AND ACTIONS AS EVIDENCE

Donald Trump has practiced in the extreme the twin pillars of Republican electoral strategy—racial appeals and minority voter suppression—and extended them to governance. Table 7–1 captures some, but by no means all, of the ongoing insults and degradations to which Trump has subjected people of color while in office. His behavior and actions should have consequences for how courts assess challenges to laws and executive orders enacted during his administration that adversely affect people of color. Trump, however, is not unique, nor should be the remedy for such racial appeals. As former President Barack Obama stated in his first public rebuke of Trump and Trumpism:

> The status quo pushes back. Sometimes the backlash comes from people who are genuinely, if wrongly, fearful of change. More often it's manufactured by the powerful and the privileged who want to keep us divided and keep us angry and keep us cynical because it helps them maintain the status quo and keep their privilege ... It did not start with Donald Trump. He is a symptom, not the cause. He's just capitalizing on resentments that politicians have been fanning for years, a fear and anger that's rooted in our past but it's also born out of the enormous upheavals that have taken place ...[79]

Perhaps Trump's most transparent nod to race-baiting is his obsessive criticism of black athletes who express political views. What else would explain any American president devoting as much attention as Trump has to NFL players—almost all black—kneeling to protest police misconduct against blacks? The bash-athletes strategy plays on white stereotypes of black men and licenses others to do the same. Thus, Republican U.S. Senate candidate Corey Stewart joined Trump's chorus when he referred to NFL players as "thugs":

> A lot of these guys, I mean, they're thugs, they are beating up their girlfriends and their wives. You know, they've got, you know, children all over the place that they don't pay attention to, don't father, with many different women, they are womanizers. These are not people that we should have our sons, or any of

TABLE 7–1 *Examples of Trump's Comments Degrading People of Color*

Scenario and Date	Comment
A tweet about Puerto Rico's efforts to recover from Hurricane Maria, September 30, 2017	"Such poor leadership ability by the Mayor of San Juan, and others in Puerto Rico, who are not able to get their workers to help. They want everything to be done for them when it should be a community effort."
A tweet about star basketball player LeBron James, an African American, and CNN anchor Don Lemon, also black, August 3, 2018	"Lebron James was just interviewed by the dumbest man on television, Don Lemon. He made Lebron look smart, which isn't easy to do."
A tweet about former Congressional Black Caucus leader Maxine Waters, June 25, 2018	"Congresswoman Maxine Waters, an extraordinarily low IQ person, has become, together with Nancy Pelosi, the Face of the Democrat Party. She has just called for harm to supporters, of which there are many, of the Make America Great Again movement. Be careful what you wish for Max!"
A tweet about former White House aide Omarosa Manigault Newman, August 14, 2018	"When you give a crazed, crying lowlife a break, and give her a job at the White House, I guess it just didn't work out. Good work by General Kelly for quickly firing that dog!"
A comment on illegal immigrants, May 16, 2018	"We have people coming into the country, or trying to come in—we're stopping a lot of them. You wouldn't believe how bad these people are. These aren't people, these are animals, and we're taking them out of the country at a level and at a rate that's never happened before."
In speech in Ohio after his first State of the Union address, remarking on Democrats, many of them members of the Congressional Black Caucus, who refused to applaud during his address, February 5, 2018	"You're up there, you've got half the room going totally crazy—wild, they loved everything, they want to do something great for our country . . . And you have the other side—even on positive news, really positive news like that—they were like death. And un-American. Un-American. Somebody said, 'treasonous.' I mean, yeah, I guess, why not? Can we call that treason? Why not! I mean they certainly didn't seem to love our country very much."

our children look up to. We need to have our children look up to real role models.[80]

Fox News talk show host Laura Ingraham directed this jibe at basketball star LeBron James: "It's always unwise to seek political advice from someone who gets paid $100 million a year to bounce a ball. Keep the political comments to yourselves . . . Shut up and dribble."[81] She then criticized James's riposte to her as "barely intelligible" and "ungrammatical."[82]

To many Trump supporters, these attacks are not just about black athletes. They are about black people generally. As the 2016 Reuters poll indicates, almost half of Trump supporters believed black Americans were more violent than whites.[83] The same proportion viewed them as more "criminal," and 40 percent saw them as lazier than whites. There is perhaps no more menacing an image by which to stoke these stereotypes than 300-pound black football players and 6′7″ basketball players. In assessing the harm of racial appeals, society and courts should look not only at what is said, but also, given existing racial predispositions, how it is heard. Many of the white voters that Trump and the Republican Party depend on for their political lifeblood embrace what political scientist Keith Reeves refers to as the "attributional blame" notion of racial inequality—that is, deficiencies in character explain blacks' lack of parity with whites.[84] Reeves's research confirmed that these types of voters will usually be reluctant to support a black candidate.[85] Racial appeals exploit their predispositions.

The Supreme Court punted on the first opportunity it had to hold Trump liable for his racial rhetoric. In *Trump v. Hawaii*, the Supreme Court upheld on national security grounds President Trump's executive order severely restricting the entry into the United States of citizens from six predominantly Muslim countries.[86] In addition to statutory grounds, the plaintiffs challenged the executive order as a violation of the Establishment Clause of the First Amendment, which provides that "Congress shall make no law respecting an establishment of religion."[87] They contended that President Trump's executive order was little more than a thinly veiled Muslim ban of the sort he had called for during the campaign. Because, however, the executive order was facially neutral—that is, it did not ban Muslims as such—and because it was purportedly issued for reasons of national security, the Court applied a deferential standard of review that allowed the order to stand.[88]

The plaintiffs relied on several campaign statements by candidate Trump disparaging Islam as a religion or otherwise denigrating Muslims. For instance, Trump had called for "a total and complete shutdown of Muslims entering the United States," a policy position that remained on his campaign website seven months into his presidency.[89] Once elected, Trump candidly admitted that the purpose behind an earlier iteration of his executive order was to make it more difficult for Muslim refugees to enter the U.S. and easier for Christian refugees.[90] Yet, given the national security context in which the Establishment Clause issue had arisen, the most the five-justice majority was willing to make of Trump's statements was to imply that he had performed "unevenly" in living up to the American creed of religious tolerance.[91]

As dissatisfying as the *Trump v. Hawaii* ruling is, it is no license for candidates to spew racial hatred without consequence. Rather, lower courts have already limited the case to the unique national security setting in which it arose. In *Centro Presente v. United States Department of Homeland Security*, for example, resident aliens from El Salvador, Honduras, and Haiti challenged the Trump administration's attempt to revoke their temporary protection status (TPS). TPS allows citizens of designated countries to lawfully remain in the United States for as long as conditions in those countries make the resident alien's return unsafe.[92] The plaintiffs alleged that it was not an improvement in conditions in their home countries, but rather racial animus, that prompted the Trump administration's change in designation. Among the evidence they cited were anti-Latino statements made by Trump both as a candidate and as president.[93] Trump's 2015 references to Mexican immigrants as "rapists" and drug couriers came full circle to haunt a policy initiative. The court found that the plaintiffs had stated a cause of action for racial discrimination in violation of the Constitution. *Trump v. Hawaii*, the court held, was not a barrier to their claim because "the determination at issue in this case does not concern national security."[94]

It is not merely what Trump has said as candidate and president that casts a racial pall over his policies. The policies often indict themselves. With no proof of voter fraud other than his belief that voting is "rigged," President Trump created the Presidential Advisory Commission on Election Integrity.[95] He appointed as its vice chair Kansas Secretary of State Kris Kobach, who would soon come under grand jury investigation for illegally failing to register voters in 2016.[96] Kobach was also held in contempt by a federal court for failing to comply with a court order that his office register voters without requiring them to present proof of citizenship.[97] Conspicuously absent from the scope of the election commission's charge was an investigation into Russian meddling in the 2016 presidential contest—surely a type of voting "fraud" or "rigging." Despite the unequivocal assessment of U.S. intelligence agencies that Russia had interfered with the 2016 election to help Trump, President Trump consistently cast doubt on those findings.[98]

In an act that former CIA Director John Brennan called "treason," President Trump stood side-by-side with Russian President Vladimir Putin at a press conference in Helsinki, Finland, and, when asked whether Russia had meddled in the 2016 election, said: "My people came to me. They said they think it's Russia. I have President Putin; he just said it's not Russia. I will say this: I don't see any reason why it would be."[99] Although Trump would later implausibly claim that he misspoke in Helsinki, by any measure he has shown far more interest in the fiction that 3 million to 5 million people voted illegally in 2016 than in pursuing the factual claims of American intelligence agencies about Russian interference.[100]

A toothless Republican Congress did the same. As Trump supporters began donning t-shirts that read "I'd rather be a Russian than Democrat,"[101] Republicans in Congress betrayed the insincerity of their party's concern with election integrity by defeating a Democratic amendment to bolster funding for election cybersecurity and improved voting equipment.[102] Moreover, the House Intelligence Committee continued to deny that Putin had interfered in the election in order to help Trump—even after Putin himself admitted to the world during the Helsinki news conference that he preferred Trump to Clinton during the 2016 election.[103] The only election integrity Republicans really appeared to value was the kind that helped their party's political fortunes.

That brand of "election integrity" requires suppressing the votes of minorities. Cambridge Analytica, a political consulting firm that employed Steve Bannon as its vice president before he joined the Trump campaign, deployed social media to target African Americans with "voter disengagement" techniques.[104] Testifying before the Senate Intelligence Committee, a Cambridge Analytica whistleblower, Christopher Wylie, told Congress that Bannon had deliberately sought to suppress the votes of blacks and other liberal constituencies. Wylie later elaborated to the media that black voters were a prime target of Bannon's and Cambridge Analytica's operations.[105] Indeed, during the final days of the 2016 campaign, the Trump campaign candidly admitted that its only path to victory lay in shrinking the electorate. According to the campaign, this required the demobilization of blacks, young women, and white liberals.[106]

The Trump campaign's black voter suppression efforts tell us a great deal about the racial rationale behind much Republican "election integrity" legislation generally. If the nominal head of the Republican Party, candidate Donald Trump, believed that his only path to the presidency was by shrinking the electorate, there is little reason to believe that this type of thinking does not permeate the motivations of Republican legislatures considering voter ID laws and other voting restrictions. Republicans at the highest echelons of their party keep revealing, even if unwittingly, why Republicans target minority votes for suppression. Courts need only listen to conclude that voter ID laws and other Republican-backed voting restrictions are simply types of racial appeals that are part and parcel of whitelash.

8

We the People: Fashioning a Legal Remedy
for Voter Whitelash

"[A]ll political power flows from the people."

    —Justice Ruth Bader Ginsburg, writing for the majority in *Arizona*
    State Legislature v. Arizona Independent Redistricting Commission[1]

If all political power derives from the people, then the people must ultimately be responsible for the discriminatory exercise of that power. Thus, while Chapter 7 explained the complicity and legal fault of candidates and political parties, this chapter examines the legal culpability of voters themselves and proposes legal remedies and deterrents.

In an ideal world, Congress would pass a law outlawing racial discrimination in voting pursuant to its enforcement powers under the Fourteenth and Fifteenth Amendments, and the law would impose penalties for its violation. Whitelashers, however, hide in the privacy of the ballot box, casting their vote at least in part based on their resistance to progress by people who look different than they do. This privacy—to say nothing of First Amendment concerns—makes an edict prohibiting racial discrimination impractical. So when we search for remedies that might mitigate the effects of whitelash and deter people from voting based on race, the most sensible options would target the electoral structures that facilitate whitelash rather than any single voter's or group of voters' actions.

That said, the law does influence the way citizens view their civic duty to vote. The Supreme Court has in certain respects licensed the mindset that gives rise to voter whitelash, and this is a moral and jurisprudential failure. For the purpose of fashioning deterrent remedies to whitelash, however, I take the Court as it is: regressive. Still, as I argue below, the Court has left intact important precedents that support remedies to counteract voter whitelash— assuming that the Court stays true to its own precedents and is willing to recognize its own mistakes. Three potential remedies discussed in this chapter address not just whitelash but also three of the most inequalitarian features of American democracy: the Electoral College system, the equal representation of states in the U.S. Senate, and the partisan gerrymander. The overlap of these anachronisms with the machinations of voter whitelash is hardly coincidental: At its core, whitelash is undemocratic. Most white Americans do not engage in voter whitelash. When their votes are combined with those of people of color, they often constitute most of the electorate, as they did in 2016, when Hillary Clinton won the popular vote over Donald Trump by nearly 3 million votes. Yet the Electoral College denied her the White House. Thus, remedying voter whitelash also gives voice to democratic majorities or pluralities.

Recall that in Chapter 1 I presented two conflicting lines of Supreme Court precedent regarding when courts should offer remedies for voter whitelash. I supported the interventionist model as opposed to the self-correcting model of democracy, and I promised to elaborate on why interventionism is vital in a racialized democracy. Focusing primarily on *Shelby County, Ala. v. Holder* and its aftermath, and on *Schuette v. Coalition to Defend Affirmative Action*, this chapter begins with a robust defense of the interventionist model by illustrating the untoward consequences of leaving citizens to their own devices to check racism in the political process. Recognizing that the reader has consumed a great deal of legal doctrine in the preceding seven chapters, I next synthesize the elements of that doctrine that are most essential to understanding potential legal remedies. I conclude with a discussion of exemplary judicial remedies to counteract voter whitelash.

JUDICIAL INFLECTION POINTS: IN DEFENSE OF THE INTERVENTIONIST MODEL OF DEMOCRACY

Courts sometimes get it wrong. But some wrong decisions are more consequential than others. *Shelby County, Ala. v. Holder* is one of those decisions because it both dismantled an important structural check on voter whitelash — Section 5 of the Voting Rights Act of 1965 (VRA) — and signaled to white voters that their moral obligation to abide by antidiscriminatory norms had expired. The decision was widely reported in the press and has rapidly assumed a place among the most consequential Supreme Court decisions.[2] In earlier chapters, I addressed *Shelby County* as an illustration of dishonest judicial decision-making, but here, in the context of remedies, its symbolic meaning and its aftermath are the most relevant aspects to explore.

The courts of our nation have often faced a choice: to be an accomplice to whitelash or a bulwark against it. In 1880 in *Strauder v. West Virginia*, the Court chose the former. Although it invalidated West Virginia's facially discriminatory statute that precluded blacks from serving on juries, the Court provided a roadmap for eluding the Fourteenth Amendment when it suggested that pretexts for race, such as property and educational requirements, would be permissible bases to restrict jury service.[3] This judicial signposting encouraged evasions of the Fourteenth Amendment such as Louisiana's century-old machination for diluting the votes of black jurors in felony cases by allowing non-unanimous (10–2) verdicts.[4] When the Supreme Court speaks—even obliquely—the nation listens, as the South did in 1880, a period known in the region as Redemption from Reconstruction.

The Court's granting of permission to discriminate is not always as inartful as it was in *Strauder*. Sometimes refusing to act or withdrawing from an arena in which it had previously allowed action accomplishes the same dog whistle. The Court's rejection of the interventionist model of democracy in *Shelby County* is an example of this approach. Prior to *Shelby County*, in *State of South Carolina v. Katzenbach*, the Court upheld the constitutionality of Section 5 preclearance under the VRA, which required that states of the old Confederacy seek the federal government's permission before changing their election laws.[5] In upholding the act, the Court recognized the persistent, camouflaging resistance by the South to the Fifteenth Amendment's command that "[t]he right of citizens of the United States to vote shall not be denied or abridged by the United States or by any State on account of race, color, or previous condition of servitude," naming grandfather clauses, procedural hurdles, white primaries, improper challenges to voter qualifications, racial gerrymandering, and discriminatory application of voting tests as some of the tactics that had already been struck down.

Contrary to the Court's ruling in *Katzenbach*, yet consistent with his simplistic view of equality as a linear progression, Chief Justice John Roberts declared in *Shelby County* that because "things have changed dramatically," the coverage formula that subjected states to Section 5 preclearance and, by extension, preclearance itself were no longer justified.[6] The divide between the conservative majority and the dissenting justices in *Shelby County* is simply a microcosm of the racial divide about government's continuing obligations to America's darker-hued underdogs: Whites consistently believe that blacks and other minorities face less discrimination than minorities themselves believe they face. As a result, except for rare instances of prevailing in individual antidiscrimination lawsuits, people of color are forced to abide self-serving white assumptions regarding the lack of discrimination against them.

Shelby County was decided in 2013. That same year, Gallup polling found that most white Americans (78 percent) believed that the government should have a minor role or no role at all in improving the economic and social position of blacks and other minorities.[7] A decade earlier, 67 percent of white Americans held this sentiment.[8] In contrast, majorities of blacks and Latinos have consistently held the belief that government should play a major role in ensuring their economic and social betterment.[9] In 2013, most whites (67 percent) expressed satisfaction with the way black Americans were treated in society; most blacks (52 percent) expressed dissatisfaction with their treatment.[10] Thus, *Shelby County* validated what white Americans were thinking at the time and continue to think today: Americans of color have come far enough.

Noting the increase in the number of black elected officials throughout the South since passage of the VRA in 1965, the Court in *Shelby County* took this progress as a signal to retreat from, rather than to reinforce, voter protections for blacks and Latinos.[11] This defies common sense. White southerners would have no need to fear a powerless black population. Rather, to paraphrase Justice John Paul Stevens, people of color become a threat to white political power "when their common interests are strong enough to be manifested in political action."[12] At the very moment when blacks and other racial minorities began to wield political power, the Supreme Court in *Shelby County* handcuffed Congress's attempt to protect that power by striking down the mechanism, Section 5 preclearance, that had been undeniably effective in achieving it.

Imagine the message the Supreme Court would have sent to the nation in *Brown v. Board of Education* in 1954 if, instead of overturning *Plessy v. Ferguson*, it had upheld "separate but equal." Such a ruling would have breathed new life into Jim Crow. By the same token, the Supreme Court's unwillingness in 2013 to support congressional intervention in the South, where racially polarized voting was rampant and where whites therefore had the greatest incentive to interfere with the minority franchise, encouraged whitelashers throughout the country to vote in line with their racist sentiments. Millions of white Americans demonstrated their moxie three years after the decision in *Shelby County*, when the country, with the indispensable support of every state in the old Confederacy except Virginia, elected a president who by the midpoint of his term was considered a "racist" by 49 percent of voters.[13]

Most voters (54 percent) also believed that Trump "ha[d] emboldened people who hold racist beliefs to express those beliefs publicly."[14] Cementing the relationship between the proverbial unshackling of the South in *Shelby County* and the rise of Trumpism, the Confederate flag itself began to be displayed more widely throughout the country.[15] Donald Trump did not object. Instead, in defending Confederate monuments, Trump lamented, "Sad to see the history and culture of our great country being ripped apart with the removal of our beautiful statues and monuments." The Confederate flag's frequent appearances at Trump rallies in 2016 made it an ineradicable symbol of Trump's "Make America Great Again" slogan.[16]

So much for Chief Justice Roberts's belief that "things have changed dramatically." Even if this were true when the Court pronounced it, the widely held perceptions of the leader of the free world as a racist, and the widespread, open embrace of racist symbols previously considered taboo, if not verboten, showed that the nation's path to racial equality had a dramatic distance remaining. But what Chief Justice Roberts signaled in *Shelby County* is what the Supreme Court expressly stated in the *Civil Rights Cases* in 1883, when the Court invalidated a federal law that made it a criminal offense for a private citizen to deny anyone public accommodations on account of race:

> When a man has emerged from slavery, and by the aid of beneficent legislation has shaken off the inseparable concomitants of that state, there must be some stage in the progress of his elevation when he takes the rank of a mere citizen, and ceases to be the special favorite of the laws, and when his rights as a citizen, or a man, are to be protected in the ordinary modes by which other men's rights are protected.[17]

In short, the Supreme Court in 1883 was as fed up with attempts to secure equality for blacks as the Supreme Court was in 2013. And just as the *Civil Rights Cases* set the stage for 75 years of Jim Crow, *Shelby County* unleashed America's racist potential like no other modern decision of the Court. The decision forecasted the age of Trump and has made more imperative than at any time since Jim Crow the need for structural reforms to protect people of color against voter whitelash.

One could have imagined a return to the Jim Crow era upon seeing what occurred in Georgia during the 2018 midterms. When 40 black senior citizens boarded a bus to cast early votes in rural Georgia, Jefferson County Administrator Adam Brett deemed the trip an impermissible political activity that ran afoul of county guidelines simply because the seniors had boarded the bus at a government-run senior center.[18] Brett's intervention came after an anonymous caller reported the planned voting trip. Later, a mayor in Jefferson County accused Black Voters Matter, a nonpartisan organization that promotes African American political participation and the sponsor of the bus trip, of leading a cult that encouraged black people to "vote for a black candidate just because they are the same color."[19]

The mayor's apparent reference—and apparent fear—was that the 40 black senior citizens, who were ordered off the bus and temporarily prevented from voting, would cast their votes for Stacey Abrams, a Democrat running against Secretary of State Brian Kemp to become Georgia's first black governor. Kemp had won a raucous Republican primary in which he boasted in one television ad that "I've got a big truck in case I need to round up criminal illegals and take them home myself."[20] Cognizant of just how crazy this sounded, Kemp immediately added, "Yup, I just said that." It was crazy enough to get President Trump's endorsement, which helped Kemp win the Republican runoff by a landslide.

Recall from Chapter 7 that racial appeals and voter suppression have historically gone hand in hand. Kemp was no exception. At a fundraiser, Kemp, referring to Democrat Abrams's focus on increasing absentee voting, warned: "They have just an unprecedented number of that, which is something that continues to concern us, especially if everybody uses and exercises their right to vote—which they absolutely can—and mail those ballots in, we gotta have heavy turnout to offset that."[21] But Kemp, who as secretary of state oversaw Georgia elections, did more to "offset" Abrams's voter mobilization efforts than merely turn out his own voters. Georgia is a "use it or lose it" state that allows its secretary of state to purge infrequent voters from the rolls. In July 2017, Kemp purged a total of 107,000 such voters.[22] Although the racial breakdown of this group is unknown, because people of color are less likely to vote in general, they are more likely to be infrequent voters.[23] In addition to voter purges, Kemp strictly enforced Georgia's "exact match" voter registration system, which led to the suspension of more than 53,000 voter applications, 70 percent of which had been submitted by African Americans.[24] The exact match system allows Georgia to delay processing a voter registration form when even a minor discrepancy appears between the application and information in the Department of Driver Services database or on file with the Social Security Administration.[25] Prior to *Shelby County*, Georgia had been covered under Section 5 of the VRA. In 2018, however, its secretary of state had at his disposal the tools to suppress the minority vote to benefit his own election.

Although the tandem of racial appeals and voter suppression is hardly unusual in American politics, it was unusual for gubernatorial candidates, particularly non-border-state candidates like Kemp, to stake their elections on immigration. This reflected Donald Trump's pervasive racializing effect on American politics. Compared with the 2014 midterm elections, the congressional, senate, and gubernatorial candidates and the major parties ran *six times* more immigration-related television ads (44,000 versus 280,000) and spent *five times* more on such ads ($23 million versus $124 million) in 2018.[26] Yet, the population of residents living in the U.S. illegally had remained stable from 2008 to 2018.[27] Moreover, as fewer immigrants enter the U.S. illegally, the share of those residing in the country for a decade or more had continued to increase, in 2014 constituting more than 75 percent of undocumented residents.[28] The number of arrests at the southwest border—a figure commonly used to measure the rate of illegal border crossings—was at a 10-year low at the end of fiscal year 2018.[29] And far from showing that undocumented immigrants increase crime, available data demonstrated a negative correlation between numbers of undocumented residents and violent crime rates.[30]

In short, nothing exceptional had occurred in our nation's undocumented immigrant population to explain the increased salience of immigration as a political issue—nothing, that is, except the vilification of immigrants by Trump as an electoral strategy. Despite the relative stability of the nation's immigration system, exit polls showed that immigration was the most important issue for three-quarters of Republican voters during the 2018 midterms.[31] Trump's race-baiting continued to succeed with his not insubstantial political base.

Improbable as it may seem, other candidates rivaled Trump's racial appeals during the 2018 midterm elections, so much so that *The Guardian* ran a headline asking "Is This the Most Racist US Midterms Campaign Ever?"[32] A *USA Today* article noted, "The barrage of racially divisive messaging in the 2018 midterm election cycle was inescapable."[33]

Not since the Jim Crow era had Americans witnessed an election marked by such a combination of widespread racist, anti-Semitic miasma and fearmongering about immigrants and people of color. A front-page headline in *The New York Times* two weeks before election day also captured the zeitgeist of the moment: "Trump and G.O.P. Candidates Escalate Race and Fear as Election Ploys."[34] A *Washington Post* headline two days before the midterms was equally revealing: "Midterms Test Whether Republicans Not Named Trump Can Win by Stoking Racial Animosity."[35] Both these captions were far removed from the optimism of *The Times*'s headline following Barack Obama's election ten years earlier in 2008: "Obama Elected President as Racial Barrier Falls."[36] If Chief Justice Roberts was watching the midterms unfold, then these elections provided on-the-job training to a conservative jurist who appeared not to understand the nature of whitelash when he declared in *Shelby County* that "things have changed dramatically" with little thought as to how elastic such change can be.

Seasons of hatred often reap a bitter harvest. Apparently inspired by Trump's demonization of his political opponents, a deranged Floridian mailed pipe bombs during the 2018 midterm elections to nearly a dozen of Trump's Democratic critics, including former President Barack Obama. A gunman staged a mass shooting at a synagogue in Pittsburgh, a tragedy that coincided with pitched Republican criticism of wealthy Jewish Democratic donors. Another gunman with a history of expressing racist and misogynistic views opened fire in a Florida yoga studio. Perhaps no politician can be blamed personally for violence perpetrated by supporters. Yet, it had been nearly a year from these tragedies since white nationalists and neo-Nazis in August 2017 marched through the streets of Charlottesville, Virginia, with lit torches. That march, too, ended in tragedy as a white nationalist rammed his vehicle into a crowd of counterprotesters, killing one. For Trump, however, there were "some very fine people on both sides" of the clash.[37]

Donald Trump campaigned in 2016 on building a wall along the southern border to lock out illegal immigrants. Regardless of whether the president ever fulfills this tiresome promise, posterity will judge the wall he has built among Americans of different races and backgrounds as his most notorious legacy. In a democracy with separation of powers, however, no single institution could pull off such a feat. Now, the Supreme Court must confront the racist reality its decision in *Shelby County* encouraged.

To be sure, Democrats recaptured the House of Representatives in 2018 on the strength of suburban repulsion to Trump. But many of these same voters helped deliver the White House to Trump in the first place. More to the point, Democrats' success must be taken in the historical context of white voter behavior, which suggests a repeating cycle whose victims are all Americans — people of color, whose march to equality is hindered, and white Americans, who postpone, but can never permanently avoid, a day of reckoning with what true racial equality looks like.

Close examination of the results of the 2018 midterms suggests the durability of whitelash. In Georgia's high-profile gubernatorial race pitting Stacey Abrams, a black woman, against the Trump-supported Brian Kemp, Abrams managed to take only a quarter of the white vote.[38] Consistent with whitelash's ethos of denial, of those voters who believed no racial group in the U.S. is "favored," 77 percent supported Kemp. Of those Georgia voters who believed that blacks are "favored" in American society, 87 percent supported Kemp.[39] In total, an astonishing 48 percent of Georgians believed in the alternative reality that there is racial equality in America or that, to the extent there is inequality, blacks are favored.

In another jurisdiction formerly covered by Section 5 of the VRA, Mike Espy, an African American who was secretary of agriculture during Bill Clinton's presidency, could muster only 15 percent of the white vote in Mississippi.[40] White denial was epidemic: a flabbergasting 63 percent of exit poll respondents asserted either that there was racial equality in the U.S. today or that blacks were in fact favored; no less than 78 percent of this group supported the Republican candidates opposing Espy in a special election to fill a Senate seat left vacant by the ailing Thad Cochran.

Despite Chief Justice Roberts's belief that the South had changed dramatically, one thing about it clearly had not: from Reconstruction through Jim Crow, white southerners had denied the existence of discrimination against blacks, and they continued to do so in 2018.[41] Looking at data from both the 2016 and 2018 midterm elections, Tufts University political scientist Brian Schaffner found a high correlation between those most inclined to deny racism's existence and those most likely to vote for a Republican candidate.[42] Denial of racism is, of course, the principal means of its perpetuation.

Racism in American politics is thriving—again. The lesson of Reconstruction, Redemption, Jim Crow, and the post-*Shelby County* period is that racism will always infect the political process when the Court signals a laissez-faire attitude about racial inequality. Yet, if government cannot assign citizens to either explicit or functional racial categories absent compelling reason, may citizens make such assignments when performing the public function of voting? In other words, may voters discriminate against one another by electing candidates based on racial appeals or voters' racialized aversion to a candidate or the candidate's supporters? In the context of redistricting, the Supreme Court has said that the government may not create legislative districts based on the racial stereotype that voters of a given race share the same political beliefs.[43] The Court elaborated in *Bush v. Vera* that "to the extent that race is used as a proxy for political characteristics, a racial stereotype requiring strict scrutiny is in operation."[44] If it is unconstitutional to use race as a proxy for politics, it is likewise constitutionally suspect to deploy politics as a pretextual stand-in for race.

In *Schuette v. Coalition to Defend Affirmative Action*, however, when defenders of affirmative action called upon the Court to probe the motives of Michiganders who voted to dismantle it, the Court was unwilling to even ask whether white voters' opposition to affirmative action was motivated by racial antipathy. Justice Kennedy's opinion for the majority was an embarrassing tautology: "[I]f it were deemed necessary to probe how some races define their own interest in political matters, still another beginning point would be to define individuals according to race. Such a venture would be undertaken with no clear legal standards or accepted sources to guide judicial decision."[45] In other words, to ask about racial motives in an ostensibly political decision is to "define individuals according to race." This absurd objection would virtually remove courts from the business of enforcing the Equal Protection Clause of the Fourteenth Amendment to the Constitution.

Moreover, it is not a principle to which conservative jurists are faithful—at least not when whites are the alleged victims. In *Ricci v. DeStefano*, Justice Samuel Alito flatly accused the City of New Haven of succumbing to black political power—nay, coercion—in tossing out standardized test results that disproportionately denied promotion opportunities to black firefighters.[46] The Court's conservatives made a similar charge in concluding in *City of Richmond v. J.A. Croson Co.* that a minority contract set-aside program implemented by a majority-black city council was simply racial politics. Justice Sandra Day O'Connor, writing for the majority, stated an axiom that Justice Kennedy completely ignored in denying relief to the plaintiffs in *Schuette*: "The concern that a political majority will more easily act to the disadvantage of a minority based on unwarranted assumptions or incomplete facts would seem to militate for, not against, the application of heightened judicial scrutiny ..."[47] Why are conservative jurists willing to question the political motives of blacks on the suspicion that such motives are really racial, but reluctant to question white political motives on the same suspicion?

Chapters 1 through 7 set forth copious evidence that white voters, who will remain a majority of the electorate for several years to come, make voting decisions based on "unwarranted assumptions or incomplete facts" about people of color and candidates who are supported by them. It's helpful to briefly recap some of that data for context. A 2016 Reuters News survey found that, compared with other white partisans, Trump's white supporters were more likely to view blacks as less hardworking, less intelligent, more violent, and more lawless than whites.[48] In 2016, 36 percent of whites described their racial identity as either "very important" or "extremely important." Another 25 percent described it as "moderately important."[49] The more important that white identity was to a voter, the more likely that voter was to support Donald Trump. Among whites for whom white identity was "extremely important," Trump enjoyed 81 percent support.[50] Trump's unrelenting attacks on immigration appealed to these white identifiers, who view the country's changing demography as a net negative and who see whites as the real victims of discrimination.

What does it mean in the twenty-first century for white Americans to embrace white identity, particularly given Justice Kennedy's assertion in *Schuette* that the Court lacked "accepted sources to guide judicial decision" about whether groups of citizens are defining their political interests in terms of their race? The "accepted source"—indeed an indisputable one—is citizens themselves. And in the face of changing demographics and economic precarity, many whites are no longer reticent: white identity matters to them. White identity politics, however, is simply white supremacy by another name. Lee Harris, a former legal academic who is now the mayor of Shelby County,

Tennessee, put it succinctly: "There is no need for a 'white race,' after all, because to be white is to be neutral. Those who would invoke a white race must be extremists."[51]

Any supposed moral or intellectual equivalence between black identity politics and white identity politics is, at best, ahistorical. As Justice John Paul Stevens has explained, it is "the vestiges of discrimination that motivate disadvantaged racial and ethnic groups to vote as identifiable units."[52] If Americans cannot distinguish between a race consciousness formed in the blood of slavery and Jim Crow, and a white identity politics arising from resentment over racial change, then we are doomed as a nation to unending cycles of whitelash. The Supreme Court's inconsistent, often indecipherable race jurisprudence has helped to bring us to the racial purgatory now manifested in our politics. Yet it is in the Court's own jurisprudence—even in some of its more conservative rulings—where we find potential solutions.

CITIZENS AS STATE ACTORS: A SYNTHESIS OF SOME KEY LEGAL PRECEPTS

When citizens vote in a general election, they are performing a public function; they are the "state," as surely as a city council, a state legislature, or Congress is.[53] Elections are, in the words of the Supreme Court, "traditionally associated with sovereignty" and are therefore a state function.[54] To be sure, citizens' First Amendment freedom to associate politically entails a right not to associate with those with whom they disagree.[55] Thus, political parties and candidates may in theory adopt explicitly racist platforms and nominate racist candidates.[56] Voters, in turn, are free to support such parties and candidates. Yet, while voters are free to choose their preferred candidates, the racially polarized voting that may foreseeably ensue from racial politics is not itself protected by the First Amendment. Instead, under both constitutional and statutory vote dilution doctrine, racially polarized voting—that is, the effective denial of electoral opportunity to racial minorities by a consistently cohesive white majority—is a democratic defect that can be corrected by the courts.

Moreover, although voting undoubtedly has expressive characteristics like those protected by the First Amendment, the Supreme Court has held that "[b]allots serve primarily to elect candidates, not as fora for political expression."[57] Indeed, the Court does not even view voting as symbolic speech. According to Justice Antonin Scalia, "[t]here are, to be sure, instances where action conveys a symbolic meaning—such as the burning of a flag to convey disagreement with a country's policies ... [b]ut the act of voting symbolizes nothing."[58] Thus, judicial remedies to deter race-based voting—

or at least to counteract its effects—would run afoul of neither freedom of expression nor freedom of association.

What if segregationist Strom Thurmond had prevailed in his quest for the presidency in 1948? What if pro-segregationist George Wallace had won the presidency in 1968 or 1972? To paraphrase the Supreme Court in *Shaw v. Reno*, a victory by either of these infamous demagogues would "threaten to stigmatize individuals by reason of their membership in a racial group and to incite racial hostility."[59] If equal protection of the law means anything, it means that citizens are entitled to protection from state-sponsored racial hostility. And if it is unconstitutional for the government to perpetrate such antagonism in the drawing of legislative districts—the issue in *Shaw*—it is also unconstitutional for citizens, performing the public function of voting, to elect a candidate whose platform is contrary to the Fourteenth Amendment.

Just as voters may not inflict racial harm on a group through direct democracy by, say, voting for a ballot initiative to ban Muslims from their state, so too are they accountable when they elect a president who proposes to ban Muslims from entering the country. What is the difference between voting for a candidate who makes discrimination against members of a minority a centerpiece of his platform, versus voting directly to discriminate against these individuals? What, in other words, is the difference between discrimination mediated through a candidate versus discrimination perpetrated directly by casting a ballot? In each case, racism is on the ballot. To be sure, candidate elections may involve a host of nonracial issues, to say nothing of the influence of the candidates' personal qualities. But the Fourteenth Amendment has never required that a challenged state action be "unexplainable on grounds other than race."[60] Such cases are rare. Instead, under standard equal protection analysis, if race was a motivating factor among multiple factors for a decision, then that decision violates the Equal Protection Clause of the Fourteenth Amendment unless a defendant—in this instance, the state—can demonstrate that the same decision would have been reached in the absence of the impermissible consideration of race.[61]

When a candidate for any office predicates a campaign on the stigmatization of racial or ethnic groups, as Donald Trump did in 2016 and as several Republican candidates mimicking Trump did in 2018, it is not difficult to isolate race as a motivating factor in that candidate's victory. Although most voters would likely claim to have supported the candidate for reasons other than race, a racist candidate cannot prevail without the tolerance of a majority. Because a hallmark of all racism is the tolerance of racist behavior, a white majority's acquiescence to a candidate's bigotry is much like an employer's acquiescence to a racially hostile work environment. If an employer's failure to act triggers liability, why should voters, who are in effect making an employment decision, get a pass?

Again, nothing I have proposed — or will propose — forbids a candidate from speaking hidebound views or voters from embracing them. That is their right. But when such demeaning viewpoints transverse the line between private expression and representative government, it is a different matter altogether. To paraphrase *Shaw v. Reno* again, the election of a racist candidate, like the drawing of a racial gerrymander, conveys the message that the candidate's "primary obligation is to represent only the members of [a racial] group, rather than their constituency as a whole. This is altogether antithetical to our system of representative democracy."[62]

FEASIBLE JUDICIAL REMEDIES

What would be the practical consequence of a court declaring that a white majority has acted in a discriminatory fashion against a racial minority in an election? What remedy could be imposed? *Bush v. Gore* demonstrates the breadth of a court's authority when government has violated the Equal Protection Clause.[63] In that case, a divided Supreme Court ordered a halt to a recount of the 2000 presidential vote in Florida because of the disparate standards used to determine whether a ballot was incorrectly excluded in the initial vote but should be included in the recount. Although the equal protection violation at issue in *Bush v. Gore* did not involve racial discrimination, it did involve the right to vote, a right that the Court described as "fundamental" once it is conferred upon citizens for purposes of electing the president of the United States.[64] In constitutional jurisprudence, significant burdens on fundamental rights are treated with the same seriousness as discrimination on the basis of race.[65] Thus, the scope of the remedy in *Bush v. Gore* informs any remedy in an equal protection case involving racial discrimination. Famously — or infamously, depending on one's perspective — the Supreme Court's halting of the recount in Florida effectively handed the presidency to George W. Bush. If the Supreme Court can decide a presidential election, there should be little doubt about the scope of its remedial options when racism has tainted an election contest. Indeed, *Bush v. Gore* is the modern highwater mark for judicial intervention in the democratic process, and ironically, that intervention benefited primarily white Republicans.

(i) Invalidating Elections

Could a court invalidate a racially tainted election and order a do-over? This is surely the most direct remedy for voter whitelash. It would also greatly deter future voter misconduct. Several obstacles, however, make this remedy impractical and perhaps unconstitutional. First, the American legal process is simply not well-suited for such a remedy. The trial and appeals process takes several months to several years; thus, an elected official's term may well have expired by the time litigation is over. Although courts sometimes grant preliminary relief pending the outcome of a trial, it is not possible to order a new election as a form of preliminary relief without essentially rendering further proceedings in the case moot. Second, and relatedly, evidence of voter whitelash may be slow to develop. Indeed, some of the most compelling evidence of such misconduct from the 2016 presidential election emerged several months after the election through analyses by social scientists and other experts. Moreover, because voter whitelash most often occurs over a number of different election cycles and across multiple elective offices, invalidating a particular election would not truly address the systemic nature of whitelash. Finally, even if these practical considerations did not preclude invalidating racially tainted elections, the First Amendment may well prevent it. Remember: unlike employers, voters as a rule may discriminate between candidates (and their supporters) based on race because in a free society one cannot be told for whom to vote. This does not mean, however, that white voters can impose the discriminatory effects of their misconduct on citizens of color. The Equal Protection Clause forbids this. The tension between the First Amendment and the Equal Protection Clause means that courts must rely on forward-looking deterrents like those discussed below, rather than election invalidation, as remedies for voter whitelash.

(ii) Electoral Receivership—aka Preclearance

Recall the events of Georgia's 2018 gubernatorial election: racial appeals, allegations of voter suppression, and racially polarized voting. By any definition, the election was racialized. The allegations of voter suppression by Georgia's secretary of state, who was overseeing the same gubernatorial race in which he was the Republican candidate, would have been subjected to the preclearance process if the Court in *Shelby County* had not invalidated Section 5 of the VRA. Yet, regardless of the moribund state of Section 5 preclearance, courts retain the inherent authority to impose a similar remedy if a constitutional violation is found. Section 5 required states with the worst histories of minority disenfranchisement to seek permission from a federal court or the U.S. Department of Justice prior to modifying voting laws. The states subjected to preclearance satisfied a formula that the Supreme Court in *Shelby County* ruled was outdated because it looked at data from the 1960s and

1970s rather than "current conditions."[66] Keep in mind, as discussed in Chapter 5, that *Shelby County* is riddled with inaccurate statements of facts and law by a conservative majority. Still, the majority's invitation to look at current conditions highlights elections like the 2018 midterms in Georgia. A lawsuit alleging state-sponsored racial discrimination during that election would examine racial appeals (e.g., "I've got a big truck in case I need to round up criminal illegals and take them home myself"), voter suppression, racially polarized voting (i.e., Abrams, the African American candidate, lost the white vote by nearly three to one[67]), and social scientific evidence demonstrating the conflation of political and racial motives. Evidence that a substantial share of white voters harbored anti-minority attitudes and viewed white identity as important would constitute evidence of such a conflation because it is highly improbable that a person who has a general discriminatory predisposition could set such feelings aside in the privacy of the voting booth. This is especially true where discriminatory predispositions are being primed by racial appeals, as they were in Georgia in 2018.

If plaintiffs in the foregoing lawsuit were successful, a judicial finding that a jurisdiction has engaged in intentional discrimination in voting would allow a court to, among other things, require Georgia to prospectively preclear any changes to its voting laws. In other words, a court could pick up where Section 5 left off.[68]

Notice, however, the potential interminability of this remedy compared to the one-off in *Bush v. Gore*—although deciding a presidential election is certainly more intrusive than taking preventive steps to deter future voter whitelash. Courts are often faced with the question of how long to maintain an injunction. An injunction is a court order that a party act or desist from an action. Injunctions—also known as equitable relief—are a type of remedy granted in addition to or instead of monetary damages. The duration of an injunction to deter voter whitelash is an especially vexing issue because, as we have witnessed, whitelash tends to intensify when minorities are achieving some measure of success or power. Given its recurrent nature, when would be the appropriate time to end such an injunction?

Perhaps a court should look to *Grutter v. Bollinger* for guidance. In that case, which upheld the constitutionality of the University of Michigan's affirmative action program, Justice Sandra Day O'Connor wrote for the majority and aspirationally stated: "We expect that 25 years from now, the use of racial preferences will no longer be necessary to further the interest approved today."[69]

Justice O'Connor's 25-year prescription is the closest any justice has come to balancing the aspirations of societal colorblindness and the reality of recurring whitelash. And Justice O'Connor was no liberal. Of course, there is nothing talismanic about the specific number 25. What is more important is that Justice O'Connor suggested a number while also affording immediate relief to the victims of whitelash by upholding the constitutionality of race-influenced admissions in higher education. In proposing 25 years, Justice O'Connor understood that even in 2003, the year when the case was decided, much work remained to be done to achieve racial equality. A mere decade later, *Shelby County*, although it involved the political process rather than admissions in higher education, undermined Justice O'Connor's nuanced approach with its "things have changed dramatically" mantra.

Even before the Supreme Court indicated its willingness to backslide on racial equality in *Shelby County*, voters in Michigan expressed their impatience with Justice O'Connor's 25-year aspiration. Two years after the Court's decision in *Grutter*, voters in Michigan adopted a constitutional amendment that prohibited the University of Michigan from considering race in its admissions decisions.[70] Exit polls revealed that two-thirds of white voters supported the amendment while less than 14 percent of blacks did.[71] Despite the racial polarization of the Michigan electorate, the Supreme Court in *Schuette v. Coalition to Defend Affirmative Action* found, incredibly, that Michigan voters' decision to ban affirmative action was not racially motivated.[72] Without probing pretext at all, Justice Kennedy and the majority portrayed white voters' opposition to affirmative action as their effort "to learn, to listen, and to remain open to new approaches" to achieving racial equality.[73] Yet the weight of the social science research—with which Justice Kennedy's opinion did not bother to engage—indicates that it is just as likely that white Michiganders simply perceived their well-being and that of blacks as zero-sum.[74] The longer the Supreme Court regresses on questions of racial inequality, and the longer it acquiesces to white voters' backsliding as it did in *Schuette*, the longer it will take to eventually remedy voter whitelash. Twenty-five years is a flash in the long history of judicial and societal procrastination.

(iii) A Narrower Remedy, Part I: Democratizing the Electoral College

As mentioned, voter whitelash occurs across multiple years and multiple elections at every level of government. But since this book has focused on 2016 and the election of Donald Trump, let's consider a specific remedy to the problem of voter whitelash in presidential elections. This remedy, and the other, more narrowly tailored ones discussed later, could be implemented along with judicial preclearance or in combination with each other. Determining which is more appropriate depends on the breadth of the problem that an equal protection claim attacks. One thing is clear, though: curtailing whitelash in presidential elections requires addressing the Electoral College.

Voter whitelash is not possible—and would certainly be ineffective—without electoral structures that augment white political power at the expense of minorities. Consider, specifically, the Electoral College, by which American presidents are selected. There is technically no popular vote for president. Instead, under the Electoral College system, states are allocated electoral votes equal to the number of congressional representatives and senators they send to Washington. In a presidential election, candidates compete for each state's electoral votes, and the candidate who receives the majority (270 electoral votes) wins the keys to the White House.[75] All but two states (Maine and Nebraska) allocate their electoral votes on a winner-take-all basis; that is, no matter how narrowly one wins the popular vote of a state, the winner reaps all of its electoral votes.

The Electoral College's system of indirect democracy has many problems, but its most relevant defect from the standpoint of voter whitelash is that it rewards racially polarized voting. Racially polarized voting was discussed in Chapters 1 and 5, but a further explanation may be helpful here. Think of it as consigning minority voters to the status of permanent losers. That is, regardless of the degree of political cohesion that minorities demonstrate, equal or greater cohesion by white voters in the same jurisdiction allows whites to routinely elect candidates who are not the preferred candidates of minority voters, thus effectively negating the minority vote.[76] Thus, racially polarized voting can consistently deprive a racial minority group of the ability to participate on equal footing in the political process and to elect the candidate of their choice.

Racially polarized voting is most pernicious in the South and Southwest, although some states that border the South, such as Kentucky and Missouri—which in 2017 was the subject of a travel advisory for African Americans by the NAACP[77]—have emerged as problematic. Using available exit polling from CNN.com and *The New York Times* and starting from the 2004 presidential election, Table 8–1 lists some of the states with the most severe racially polarized voting. Seven states formerly covered by the preclearance requirement of Section 5 of the VRA are included. Some states where racially polarized voting likely occurs given the racial compositions of the parties in the state, such as Arkansas and Tennessee, have been excluded because reliable exit polling data are not available. The last column notes the number of electoral votes at stake in these relatively populous states. What is immediately striking about these numbers is the degree to which political parties in

TABLE 8–1 *States with Most Extreme Racially Polarized Voting*

State/Election Year	Percentage of Black Vote Received by Democratic Candidate	Percentage of White Vote Received by Republican Candidate	Electoral Votes
Alabama/2004	91%	80%	9
Alabama/2008	98%	88%	9
Alabama/2012	95%	84%	9
Georgia/2004	88%	76%	15
Georgia/2008	98%	76%	15
Georgia/2016	89%	75%	16
Kentucky/2008	90%	63%	8
Kentucky/2016[a]	73%	68%	8
Louisiana/2004	90%	75%	9
Louisiana/2008	94%	84%	9
Mississippi/2004	90%	85%	6
Mississippi/2008	98%	88%	6
Mississippi/2012	96%	89%	6
Missouri/2008	93%	57%	11
Missouri/2012	94%	65%	10
Missouri/2016	90%	66%	10
North Carolina/2004	85%	73%	15
North Carolina/2008	95%	64%	15
North Carolina/2012	96%	68%	15
North Carolina/2016	89%	63%	15
South Carolina/2004	85%	78%	8
South Carolina/2008	96%	73%	8
South Carolina/2016	94%	70%	9
Texas/2004	83%	74%	34
Texas/2008	98%	73%	34
Texas/2016	84%	69%	38

[a] In 2016, exit polling in Kentucky categorized race only as white and nonwhite.

these states are segregated by race: whites vote overwhelmingly one way, while blacks vote overwhelmingly opposite. The result is that the minority-preferred presidential candidate is usually defeated in these states, which represent a large number of Electoral College votes.

Winner-take-all electoral systems effectively nullify minority votes in jurisdictions with highly racially polarized voting by diluting the minority vote.[78] They disincentivize Republican candidates from appealing to minority voters since a bloc-voting white majority can deliver 100 percent of the electoral votes to that candidate no matter how close the actual outcome of the race is.[79] This, in turn, encourages racialized campaigning in the most racialized states of the country because such appeals are intended to, and often do, facilitate white political cohesion.

So what can be done? Chief Justice Roberts's own words, if he is true to them, supply a legal roadmap for addressing voter whitelash in this context. In *Shelby County*, Roberts took pains to note that the Court's decision "in no way affects the permanent, nationwide ban on racial discrimination in voting found in § 2 [of the VRA]."[80] Section 2 of the VRA requires a plaintiff to show that a particular electoral practice results in less opportunity for minority voters than for white voters "to participate in the political process and to elect representatives of their choice."[81] Importantly, although it is possible to challenge the method for allocating electoral votes as a violation of equal protection, unlike the constitutional inquiry under the Fourteenth Amendment, Section 2 does not require a showing of discriminatory intent or purpose on the part of the defendant locality or state. It should therefore be easier to seek a remedy under Section 2 than under the Fourteenth Amendment.

In the case of single-member offices, such as governor, a solution based on Section 2 of the VRA simply could not remedy the racially polarized voting problem—there is no way to divide a governorship.[82] If one candidate receives 49.9 percent of the vote while the other receives 50.1 percent, we must award the entire governorship to the highest vote-getter. Electoral College votes, on the other hand, can be allocated to candidates in proportion to their percentage of the popular vote in a state. In 2016, the Electoral College vote corresponding to state results was 232 for Hillary Clinton versus 306 for Donald Trump.[83] If the states in Table 8–1 had been under a proportional allocation system, Hillary Clinton would have won the Electoral College and the presidency with 274 electoral votes. Table 8–2 reflects the results of multiplying the percentage of the popular vote Clinton received in each state by the number of electoral votes available in the state and then rounding to the nearest whole number. The rounding exercise is necessary because representatives to the Electoral College are 538 whole persons; fractional votes, while theoretically possible, present obvious complications.

Clinton's defeat was the second time since 2000 that a candidate won the national popular vote but was defeated in the Electoral College and denied the presidency. The other election involved George W. Bush and Al Gore in 2000. In that election, too, a proportional allocation of the electoral votes in states listed in Table 8–1 would have changed the outcome.

The Electoral College is antithetical to a modern democracy, but it can only be abolished through the arduous process of amending the Constitution,

TABLE 8–2 *Proportional Reallocation of 2016 Electoral College Votes*

State	Clinton's Share of Popular Vote	Proportionally Reallocated Electoral Votes for Clinton
Alabama	34.36%	3
Georgia	45.89%	7
Kentucky	32.68%	3
Louisiana	38.45%	3
Mississippi	40.11%	2
Missouri	38.4%	4
South Carolina	40.67%	4
Texas	43.24%	16

which requires the approval of two-thirds of the states. Given this improbability, a national movement is afoot to align the Electoral College vote with the national popular vote. Under the National Popular Vote Bill, a state pledges its electoral votes to the winner of the *national* popular vote rather than the popular vote in that state. The pledge, however, does not become effective until it has been enacted into law by states whose combined electoral votes equal a majority of the Electoral College—270.[84] This ingenious arrangement appears to be constitutional because the Supreme Court has held that states have broad authority to decide the manner of selecting their electors.[85] The problem is that only 14 states with electoral votes totaling 184 have passed a law adopting the pledge.[86] How many more Trump versus Clinton and *Bush v. Gore* electoral fiascos can the nation endure while waiting for the pledges of the other states needed to get to 270 electoral votes?

My proposal to allocate electoral votes proportionally in states with extreme racially polarized voting can be pursued in tandem with the National Popular Vote Bill, and like that bill, it is grounded in the Supreme Court's own precedents. As the Court stated in *Bush v. Gore,*

> The individual citizen has no federal constitutional right to vote for electors for the President of the United States unless and until the state legislature chooses a statewide election as the means to implement its power to appoint members of the electoral college ... History has now favored the voter, and in each of the several States the citizens themselves vote for Presidential electors. When the state legislature vests the right to vote for President in its people, the right to vote as the legislature has prescribed is fundamental; and one source of its fundamental nature lies in the equal weight accorded to each vote and the equal dignity owed to each voter.[87]

Discriminating against candidates based on their race or the race of their supporters deprives voters of color of the "equal dignity" to which they are entitled. The Electoral College, reflecting the popular will of each state even when it is tainted by racial prejudice, is an instrument of voter whitelash.

(iv) A Narrower Remedy, Part II: Countering the Undemocratic U.S. Senate

I have discussed Mississippi at length in this book, including in this chapter, because the state is in many respects the cradle of American whitelash. Let's revisit Mississippi one last time, specifically the 2018 Senate contest between Mike Espy, an African American, and Cindy Hyde-Smith, a white appointed incumbent. The state's dark past gained a foothold in the present when Hyde-Smith, discussing a white supporter, commented: "If he invited me to a public hanging, I'd be on the front row."[88] Mississippi had the highest number of lynchings of any state from 1882 to 1968, totaling 581.[89] Perhaps Hyde-Smith's insensitive remark was just another slip of the tongue, in the same way that, for example, Florida GOP gubernatorial candidate Ron DeSantis's reference to "monkey" was in discussing his black opponent during the 2018 midterms. But there is more. Hyde-Smith also said during the campaign that "[m]aybe we want to make it just a little more difficult" for "liberal folks" to vote.[90] According to Hyde-Smith, "I think that's a great idea."[91] Who are the "liberals" in conservative Mississippi? Black voters. Hyde-Smith claimed to be joking, but she was a particularly ironic comedienne for this sort of racialized humor: Hyde-Smith, who was educated in a Mississippi "segregation academy" created to avoid commingling with blacks, sponsored a resolution as a state senator that praised Confederate general Robert E. Lee, declaring that Lee "fought to defend his homeland and contributed to the rebuilding of the country."[92] Hyde-Smith also proposed a bill in the Mississippi state senate that would have renamed a portion of a highway after the president of the Confederacy, Jefferson Davis.[93] Despite these racial faux pas, Hyde-Smith prevailed over Espy in a runoff election, comfortably carrying the state's predominantly rural white areas.[94]

If you do not believe that Senator Hyde-Smith is a racist, then perhaps there simply are no racists left. But if you suspect that she might be, the question is: why must the nearly 40 percent of Mississippians who are African American—the highest proportion of any state in the nation—be represented by someone to whom the label "racist" can plausibly be applied? The answer is, they need not be. The U.S. Senate is both undemocratic and racially hidebound. It is undemocratic because states, no matter how small, have equal representation in the body, often distorting the will of the majority of Americans. Because there are more small, rural, white, right-leaning states than there are populous, multiracial, center-left states, the composition of the Senate distorts policy.[95] Wyoming and California, for instance, each have two senators, but Wyoming's population is just 579,000 while California's is 39.5 million.[96] This imbalance gives rural whites a disproportionate influence in the Senate and on its important functions, which include the confirmation of federal judges.

Like the Electoral College, the Senate cannot be abolished, nor can its equal representation of states be changed, without a constitutional amendment. Whatever the historical justification for the equal representation of states in the Senate, that arrangement today is an instrument of voter whitelash. So absent a constitutional amendment—which is especially unlikely because a state would have to consent to having its equal representation taken away[97]—what can be done? Here, I offer a proposal that I have long championed and that, once again, takes Chief Justice John Roberts at his word regarding the continued viability of Section 2 of the VRA. Every state currently elects senators on a statewide, at-large basis, which means that in states like Mississippi, even though a substantial black population votes opposite the white majority, black voters are shut out of a voice in the U.S. Senate. Nothing in the Constitution mandates that senators be elected on a statewide basis, however. The Seventeenth Amendment provides that "[t]he Senate of the United States shall be composed of two Senators from each State, *elected by the people thereof.*"[98] Similarly, the Constitution provides that "the House of Representatives shall be composed of Members chosen every second Year *by the People of the several States.*"[99] No one argues that a House member must be elected by the entirety of a state, so why must a senator? The fact that senators perform different legislative functions than House members is no reason to require their statewide election; a single congressional representative's vote can have statewide ramifications, just as a senator's does. Moreover, in the face of increasing partisan polarization, the institutional distinctions between the House and Senate, such as the use of the filibuster in the latter, have almost evaporated.[100]

In a state with as harrowing a racist history as Mississippi's, where even today politicians like Cindy Hyde-Smith campaign and govern using the worst vestiges of that history, yet white voters still respond positively, Section 2 of the VRA could provide a remedy by creating U.S. Senate districts that would prevent the continued dilution of minority votes. This arrangement would have the dual benefit of diversifying the Senate and counteracting its white, rural, conservative bias caused by the equal representation of the states.

(v) A Narrower Remedy, Part III: Dismantling the Myth
of the Partisan Gerrymander

Suppose a racially tainted election occurs in a House district rather than a Senate election. I have given plenty examples of racialized House elections throughout this book, but one that I have not mentioned stands out for its shock value. During a congressional hearing in 2019, President Trump's former personal attorney, Michael Cohen, said of Trump: "He is a racist. He is a con man. He is a cheat."[101] GOP congressman Mark Meadows, the chair of the ultra-right House Freedom Caucus, sought to deflect Cohen's criticism by pointing to a black staffer in the Trump administration, Lynne Patton, who physically stood behind Meadows as he attempted to rebut Cohen. Meadows remarked to Cohen, who like Meadows is white: "You made some very demeaning comments about the president that Ms. Patton doesn't agree with."[102] This shocking spectacle was shortly thereafter called out by Democratic congresswoman Rashida Tlaib, a Muslim of color, who accused Meadows of using Patton as a "prop" and contended "that in itself it is a racist act."[103] Meadows, taking umbrage in near tears, claimed that "my nieces and nephews are people of color,"[104] and demanded an apology from Tlaib.

But, here again, if Meadows isn't a racist, then there simply are none left. In his 2012 congressional campaign, Meadows promised that "we are going to send Mr. Obama home to Kenya or wherever it is."[105] If words matter at all, then short of the n-word we can hardly imagine a more racist taunt than "go back to Africa," particularly in light of the birther movement that propagated the lie that President Obama was born in Kenya. Despite his nieces and nephews, can Mark Meadows really represent voters of color? Contesting Meadows's election as state-sponsored racial discrimination in violation of the Fourteenth Amendment would be different than claiming that his election resulted from a partisan gerrymander—which it almost certainly did. Yet proving the racial taint of an election, through evidence of racial appeals, attempted voter suppression (an appeals court found that North Carolina targeted black voters for suppression with "surgical precision"[106]), and evidence of the conflation of race and politics, might be a way to indirectly weaken the partisan gerrymander. That's because one remedy for a racially tainted congressional election is to redraw the congressional district that facilitated and rewarded the racialization of politics. Under such a remedy, Meadows's district would be redrawn, which would necessarily affect the partisan composition of adjacent districts in North Carolina.

This remedy penetrates the myth of a distinction between partisan and racial gerrymanders. There's a reason the average Republican district is more white than the national white population: Republican gerrymanders are not possible without such a racial skew. Then again, neither is voter whitelash in congressional elections. Attacking the latter means undoing the intentional segregation of white voters into ethnic enclaves that encourage their misconduct in the voting booth.

A Fool's Errand?

A skeptic could dismiss each of the remedies that I have proposed, arguing that federal courts, which are being stacked with Trump appointees, would never allow them. This same defeatism, however, would have prevented many of the greatest legal victories in civil rights that were achieved against all odds. Moreover, if Chief Justice Roberts is serious about his legacy as well as the legitimacy of the Court, he would do well to model himself on Justice Sandra Day O'Connor. As it is, the Court's current five-justice conservative majority was achieved only by Republican Senate Majority Leader Mitch McConnell blocking Barack Obama's nominee for nearly a year in the hope that a Republican president would be elected.[107] But the deployment of norm-busting maneuvers to pack the Supreme Court only undermines its legitimacy at a time when the number of Americans who have high regard for the Court has been on a steady decline.[108]

Already, there is serious discussion on the political left of a court-packing plan that would undo Mitch McConnell's theft of a seat by expanding the number of justices on the Court, which is not fixed by the Constitution. Progressives could similarly target lower courts by creating more vacancies to fill or even by stripping these courts of jurisdiction over certain civil rights matters toward which conservative Republican appointees demonstrate the most hostility. All of this would be a significant rebuke to the Roberts Court that would further undermine the Court's standing in public perception but would nonetheless be warranted as a remedy for the severe problem of whitelash. We can only hope that preservation of the judiciary as an American institution is more important to judicial conservatives than advancing a racially suspect ideology.

Conclusion

The Globalization of Whitelash

"I think what has happened to Europe is a shame. Allowing the immigration to take place in Europe is a shame. I think it changed the fabric of Europe and, unless you act very quickly, it's never going to be what it was and I don't mean that in a positive way. So I think allowing millions and millions of people to come into Europe is very, very sad. I think you are losing your culture. Look around. You go through certain areas that didn't exist ten or 15 years ago."

—President Donald Trump, in an interview with the British tabloid
The Sun, July 13, 2018[1]

It's extraordinary to behold: The leader of the free world, on foreign soil, inciting xenophobia. Then again, whitelash has no boundaries—both literally and figuratively speaking. The synchronicity of white people's rebellion against immigration worldwide may appear coincidental. It is not. Postindustrial distress, magnified by the Great Recession of 2008, characterizes the economies of America and Europe, among other regions. From Brexit to the election of Donald Trump to the installation of his self-professed clone in Brazil, right-wing populism has become the vector of choice for whites' expression of their unease with the current state of their societies.

According to John B. Judis in *The Populist Explosion*, a key feature of this brand of populism is that it "champion[s] the people against an elite that they accuse of coddling a third group," such as immigrants or Muslims.[2] Yet the history of whites debasing racial and religious outsiders long predates any supposed disillusionment with modern capitalism. America, Great Britain, and other democracies might have reacted to such disillusionment with a brand of populism not based on blaming outsiders. But in opting for the most reactionary course, current populist movements are easily deployed as pretexts for the revival of old-style racism.

To the targets of these movements, it matters little whether racism is a cause or a symptom. Right-wing populism's search for an undeserving beneficiary of the liberal state is whitelash by another name. The parallels are, first, that whites seek to displace blame for a predicament on a weaker group, almost invariably people of color. The displacement requires a collective forgetting of the historical relationship between a country's white majority and its scapegoats, and it requires whites to ignore their role in creating the conditions of inequality for which the minority group seeks redress. This displacement is accompanied by an increased tolerance for authoritarianism that does not solve the real problems giving rise to their angst. Instead, the diminishment of democratic institutions and safeguards has a boomerang effect, harming the very groups who embrace their disregard. Like whitelash, then, current populist movements across the globe are giving whites a temporary boost while setting them up for an ultimate dejection.

DISPOSABLE PEOPLE

"Globalization" has long existed, previously operating by means of colonization, economic imperialism, slavery, and immigration policies intended to bring in cheap labor. The difference today is that white people no longer control its terms. This difference is a principal reason for the global rise of whitelash.

By some authoritative estimates, twentieth-century European colonialism is responsible for the deaths of 50 million people.[3] Then, as now, globalization threatened to destroy certain groups. European expansionism left little doubt that those groups were people of color. The first genocide of the twentieth century took place on African soil, in what is now called Namibia, at the hands of German colonizers.[4] In contrast, modern globalization, while hardly color-blind, has tended to be more encompassing in its victims. In the U.S., for example, while the initial wave of modern globalization hit blue-collar jobs in which blacks were disproportionately employed, offshoring's steady reach up the value chain of employment has now left whites threatened in disproportionate numbers.[5] Princeton sociologist Douglas S. Massey has argued that the effects of globalization in the U.S. are magnified relative to the consequences in other western economies in large part because of "the legacy of race, which continues to divide poor, working class, and middle class Americans from one another and deliver their political support to politicians who serve the powerful, wealthy, and affluent."[6]

Still, globalization has disquieted western European nations, and these countries have not been immune to the exacerbating effects of race. Brexit,

Great Britain's chaotic departure from the European Union following a national vote in favor of its exit, is perhaps the sharpest rebuke to modern globalization. The referendum leading to the decision to leave the European Union was nominally a debate about Great Britain's sovereignty, or "Euroskepticism," yet it was infected by anti-immigrant sentiment and racism.[7] Hate crimes against immigrants, refugees, and various ethnic minorities in Britain increased substantially after the Brexit vote.[8]

The election of Donald Trump a few months after the Brexit vote suggests a dialogic relationship between whitelash in the U.S. and the spread of right-wing populism in Europe. Indeed, President Trump's harangues against immigration are echoed in the rhetoric of European leaders such as Dutch politician Geert Wilders, Hungarian Prime Minister Viktor Orban, Italy's Deputy Prime Minister Matteo Salvini, and Germany's anti-migrant Alternative for Germany (AfD) party leader Alexander Gauland.[9] Just as Trump has cast his efforts to curb immigration as an attempt to reduce crime, so too has Italy's Matteo Salvini.[10] Given that both have been advised by Steve Bannon, Trump's former political savant and the face of American (white) nationalism, the overlap in rhetoric is no coincidence.[11]

Like Trump, who speaks of the need to save European and American culture, Salvini has talked about his crusade against immigration in terms of "saving European values."[12] In the same way that Trump debases Mexican immigrants as murderers and drug dealers, Geert Wilders cast Moroccan immigrants as "Moroccan scum in Holland who makes [sic] the streets unsafe."[13] Nigel Farage, a principal architect of the campaign for Britain to leave the European Union, demeaned immigrants as sexual predators in the run-up to the Brexit referendum.[14] And the AfD, now the principal opposition party in Germany, is frequently accused of interspersing its strident anti-immigration nationalism with homages to Nazism.[15]

Indeed, the modern discourse on immigration among right-wing whites in western countries can at times eerily resemble the scientific racism that underpinned European colonialism and the atrocities of the Third Reich. In Australia, for instance, a senator from Katter's Australian Party, Fraser Anning, invoked the language of Hitler in advocating a plebiscite to reach a "final solution" regarding whether Australia should continue to admit Muslims and non-English-speakers from the "Third World."[16] This is dangerous rhetoric — but so, too, are the words of U.S. Congressman Steve King, an anti-immigration stalwart who publicly mused in 2019, "White nationalist, white supremacist, Western civilization — how did that language become offensive?"[17]

It is easy to consign actors like Anning and King to the fringes of their respective countries' political spectrum. However, long before President Trump allowed the federal government to partially close for a record 35 days as he demanded funding from Congress for a wall along the southern border, King, in 2006, advocated for just such a wall, with electrification at the top to deter attempts at scaling it. King justified the use of electric shock on migrants by noting, "We do that with livestock all the time."[18] King's rhetoric, to say nothing of his actual proposal for a wall, is of a piece with Trump's references to illegal immigrants as "animals."[19] In America and elsewhere, racism and xenophobia have become part of mainstream political discourse.

Some researchers have nonetheless pointed to other reasons for the rise of populism. Immigration scholar Tanja Bueltmann of Northumbria University in Britain has argued that "[u]ltimately, immigration is not actually the problem that inflamed voters: Much more foundational issues, such as austerity, are the real reason."[20] *Crashed*, Professor Adam Tooze's comprehensive exploration of the 2008 financial crisis and its aftermath, identifies the imposition of austerity—sharp cuts in government spending—in response to the Eurozone crisis in 2010 as the fuse for Europe's current populist wave.[21] In Tooze's analysis, western nations' management (or mismanagement) of the financial crisis of 2008 and its aftershocks "revealed how in extremis national economic policy was subordinated to the needs of a cluster of giant transnational banks."[22] These crises brought into starker relief the income inequality already engendered by globalization and technological change; they thereby invited further skepticism about democratic capitalism.[23] These conditions could have logically also created fertile ground for a left-wing populism that transcends race, yet it is right-wing populism that has proved most prevalent and enduring, demonstrating the pervasiveness of racism.[24]

Indeed, there is a racial underbelly to the economic explanations for the rising opposition to immigration. Even wealthy European countries with little income inequality and comprehensive welfare states have rebelled against immigration. In Denmark, racial tropes such as concerns about freeloading, increased crime, and the religious practices of Muslim and North African immigrants fueled the ascent of the anti-immigrant Danish People's Party.[25] A similar story unfolded in relatively wealthy Austria, which, like Denmark, was enjoying low unemployment when the anti-immigration Freedom Party nearly captured the presidency in 2016.[26] If austerity politics explained European xenophobia, then one would not expect to see the same strident anti-immigration crusades in places like Denmark and Austria.

It's helpful at this point to revisit Professor Ibram Kendi's theory on the etiology of racist ideas, discussed in Chapter 3. According to Kendi, racist ideas emerge to justify racially discriminatory practices, and they blame the resulting inequality on its victims' inferiority. For example, Hillary Clinton, in a disconnect from her historical position on immigration, warned in 2018, "I think Europe needs to get a handle on migration because that is what lit the flame," referring to the rise of right-wing populism on the continent.[27] Clinton continued:

> I admire the very generous and compassionate approaches that were taken particularly by leaders like Angela Merkel, but I think it is fair to say Europe has done its part, and must send a very clear message—"we are not going to be able to continue [to] provide refuge and support"—because if we don't deal with the migration issue it will continue to roil the body politic.[28]

Clinton's prescription, which drew rebukes from both sides of the Atlantic, has two vintage racist ideas embedded in it. The first is that white apoplexy about the presence of people of color must be appeased by removing or reducing the offending population. This was the refrain of many conservative British Tories in 1958 after the outbreak of mass racial violence between epithet-spewing whites and black West Indian migrants in Nottingham and London. According to this reasoning, curbs on migration from former British colonies were necessary in order to reduce racial tensions.[29] In so many words, Clinton was similarly advocating limits on migration.

White unrest over the presence of people of color raises the following question: what role did whites have in facilitating their presence? As the influential British intellectual Ambalavaner Sivanandan has explained about the post-colonial migration of people of color, "We are here because you were there."[30] Thus, Clinton's second racist idea is her portrayal of immigration as a matter of white Europeans' "generosity and compassion." Her comment carries a whiff of the self-serving rationale that led European powers to partition the continent of Africa in 1885: it was done, according to Germany's Prince Bismarck, "to bring the natives of Africa within that pale of civilization by opening up the interior of the continent to commerce."[31] European empire building and profit-taking were the inevitable results.[32] Thus, the migrants and immigrants toward whom whites now turn a jaundiced eye are hardly strangers. They are the legacy of centuries of western colonialism and economic imperialism, generations who have been exploited to build the present globalized economic order about which so many whites are now having misgivings.

Similarly, when American agricultural, railroad, mining, and petroleum interests, backed by the U.S. government, captured control of nearly half of all Mexican wealth in the early twentieth century,[33] it would not be without consequence for the migration patterns of Mexican citizens. Professors Gilbert Gonzales and Raul Fernandez have chronicled the effects of foreign capital investment in the Mexican economy that was made without regard for the needs and interests of the Mexican people. They concluded:

> Subordination to U.S. corporations and the U.S. government provided the opportunity to construct a giant agribusiness economy on both sides of the border that relied on the ready supply of cheap labor from the interior of Mexico. An evident consequence of this relationship was one of the most spectacular mass movements of people in the history of humanity. The northward migration of people from all corners of Mexico to its north and, for many, eventually to the United States was motivated by the same general force, the economic dislocation caused by U.S. capital . . .[34]

Too many whites — even well-meaning ones like Hillary Clinton — view immigration policy as a question of generosity and compassion rather than one about grappling with the fallout from western nations' inglorious histories of exploiting people of color. That exploitation continues today, for much illegal immigration is a function of supply and demand. Today in the United States, 10.7 million undocumented immigrants, whom President Trump portrays as thieves of American jobs, in fact supply cheap labor that feeds Americans' addiction to low-cost goods and services.[35] President Trump should know: despite his years of denouncing illegal immigration, the Trump organization began purging undocumented employees only after exposés appeared in *The New York Times* and *The Washington Post* in 2019.[36]

As though entranced by an authoritarian cult, Trump's die-hard supporters will undoubtedly rationalize or simply ignore Trump's hypocrisy, just as they will the nation's history of encouraging illegal immigration when it suits its economic interests. Think of the American labor force and economy as ecosystems whose individual parts cannot be disturbed without affecting other parts. Undocumented immigrants constituted 5 percent of American workers in 2007.[37] With unemployment at 3.7 percent in early 2019 and employers already having difficulty filling jobs, particularly in industries in which undocumented immigrants abound, such as agriculture and construction, the effect of trying to displace 5 percent of the American workforce would be devasting to the economy. Even if sufficient numbers of unemployed Americans were available to take the places of these workers, there is no guarantee that Americans would be willing to do these jobs, even at elevated wages that would increase prices for American consumers.[38] And, as in an ecosystem, because the segments of the economy heavily staffed by undocumented workers support the sectors without an abundance of such employees,

American workers would actually be harmed by reductions in undocumented workers.[39]

The backlash against the entrenchment of undocumented workers in today's American economy has European counterparts. The politics unfold the same way: the guests are invited, their work gladly accepted, and then a campaign of disinvitation ensues, often drawing on racial tropes. In need of manpower, a war-ruined Great Britain invited subjects from its West Indian colonies to help rebuild the nation after World War II.[40] In 2012, however, this enticement appeared to be forgotten by then Home Secretary (later Prime Minister) Theresa May, who in a crackdown on illegal immigration tightened requirements for proving citizenship, placing more than 500,000 "Windrush" generation migrants at risk of deportation.[41] Great Britain had no more invited these workers to its shores out of compassion and generosity than it had colonized their countries out of such motivations. These people were used and disposed of at Britain's whim.

Although Prime Minister May portrayed the Windrush controversy as an administrative snafu when the story became public in 2018, it mapped neatly onto a long history of anti-immigration politics in Great Britain. The rebirth of British conservatism that ushered in the election of Prime Minister Margaret Thatcher in 1981 also propagated a "new racism." Under this discourse, culture, not biological difference, created incompatibility between native Brits and immigrants, and tighter immigration controls aimed simply to preserve the British "way of life."[42]

A similar retheorization of racism was used in post-Nazi Germany after the country recruited Turkish migrants as guest workers in 1955 to alleviate a severe labor shortage caused by a post-war economic boom. The guest worker program had the unintended consequence of producing a substantial and permanent Turkish immigrant community in Germany.[43] Although post-Nazi Germany was understandably hypersensitive to matters of race, this did not prevent it from developing a lexicon of "otherization" of the Turks. As the Turkish migrant issue became a political concern in the 1980s, political leaders invoked the supposed failure of Turkish migrants to submit to "Germanization" and the need to preserve German national identity. Conservatives got the better of this debate, so much so that in 1982 Germany's Social Democrats abandoned their policy of integrating Turkish migrants:

> There is unity [in the government] that the Federal Republic ... is not
> a country of immigration and should not become one. The cabinet agrees
> that a further influx of foreigners from outside the European Community

should be prevented by all possible legal means ... Only by a consistent and effective policy of limitation can the indispensable agreement of the German population for the integration of foreigners be secured. This is essential for the maintenance of social peace.[44]

If we were to create a Venn diagram of contemporary and historical discourses on immigration in Europe, the overlap would be substantial. For that matter, one could do the same with contemporary and historical immigration discourses in the U.S., and the result would be the same. The patina under which the political right now promotes racist ideas has changed, but the ideas themselves are remarkably durable. At the heart of this whitelash, however, is the failure to recognize history as a continuum of cause and effect, which in turn creates the erroneous assumption that white westerners can willingly disregard the consequences of centuries of exploitation of people of color.

To be sure, Europe and America are situated differently on important aspects of immigration. Countries within the European Union, which guarantees freedom of movement among citizens of member nations, face a unique migration issue caused by citizens from poorer eastern European nations competing for jobs with lower-skilled citizens in wealthier western European countries.[45] Thus, in contrast to the U.S., Europe's appetite for cheap goods and services is sated in part by other Europeans. In racializing immigration *writ large*, however, right-wing populists in Europe have intentionally shifted blame onto people of color. In the words of author and *New Humanist* magazine editor Daniel Trilling, politicians are "trying to use the issue of migration to push a vision of the nation based on ethnic privilege and defined in opposition to racialised outsiders, be they Muslims, or unspecified dark-skinned 'migrants' ..."[46] The notion of a "great replacement" of white Europeans by immigrants is now part of mainstream discourse in parts of Europe and has even reached New Zealand, where, acting on fear of such a replacement, a white supremacist massacred 49 Muslims in March of 2019.[47] Ignoring the rise in white supremacist violence in America since he took office, President Trump, responding to the New Zealand massacre, downplayed the increasing threat of white nationalism globally: "I think it's a small group of people that have very, very serious problems. I guess, if you look at what happened in New Zealand, perhaps that's a case."[48]

Such a tepid response is not surprising coming from a president who believes "[a]llowing the immigration to take place in Europe is a shame."[49] Trump's jeremiads against immigration are unadorned white nationalism.

Xenophobic rhetoric is the new salve for many white westerners in a world of change and uncertainty—one in which globalization marches on despite their protestations, in which western imperialism must now compete with the rise of China, and in which their former subjects have become their neighbors. White westerners are fighting to preserve a way of life that reaffirms racial hierarchy in practice, if not by name. What, however, will they sacrifice in the process?

EXPORTING WHITELASH, ERASING DEMOCRACY

Whitelash is inconsistent with democracy, and the threat it poses is not merely to its objects, but also to its practitioners, and not merely in the United States but also in countries that look to the U.S. as the world's steward of democracy.

Consider the spectacle of the Republican Party of Tarrant County, Texas, the third most populous county in the state. The party's vice chairman, Shahid Shafi, is a Muslim. In 2019, members of the local party moved to oust him from his position. They made no pretense about their motivation: they didn't believe a Muslim should occupy the position.[50] Shafi survived the attempted ouster by a vote of 139 to 49. Still, more than a quarter of the party's delegates voted to remove Shafi because of his religion. This is hardly what the world would expect from one of the two major political parties of its leading democracy. But when the president of the U.S. wears outward disdain for Muslims, it should surprise no one when his attitude becomes infectious.

The danger of the example set by Trump does not end with religious bigotry. In their book *How Democracies Die*, Harvard University professors Steven Levitsky and Daniel Ziblatt identify four characteristics of authoritarian politicians. First, such individuals have a feeble commitment to established democratic rules.[51] As a candidate, Donald Trump checked this box when he refused to commit to accepting the results of the election and forewarned that it might be rigged. This breach of democratic decorum, of course, is as Republican as it is Trumpian, for, as discussed in Chapter 7, unproven voter fraud has long been a racialized mantra of the Republican Party.

The second authoritarian characteristic the authors identify is the delegitimization of one's opponents by branding them as unpatriotic, criminal, subversive, or otherwise "un-American."[52] Trump rose to political fame by claiming Barack Obama was not a U.S. citizen, and he tagged Hillary Clinton a lawbreaker, encouraging chants of "Lock her up."

A third sign of authoritarianism is the endorsement of political violence, something that Trump encouraged among attendees at his rallies who assaulted protesters.[53] Trump even went so far as to suggest to supporters that they might resort to violence if Hillary Clinton won the election and chose the next Supreme Court justice: "If she gets to pick her judges, nothing you can do, folks . . . Although the Second Amendment people — maybe there is, I don't know."[54] And if this is not evidence enough, Trump encouraged his supporters to commit violence against Hillary Clinton:

> I think that her [Clinton's] bodyguards should drop all weapons, they should disarm, right? I think they should disarm. Immediately, what do you think? Yeah, take their guns away. She doesn't want guns. Take their — let's see what happens to her. Take their guns away, OK? It'll be very dangerous.[55]

The final indication of an authoritarian politician is disregard for the rights of critics and opponents. From threatening Hillary Clinton with arrest to requesting that the postmaster general double the postage rates on his nemesis, Amazon founder and *Washington Post* owner Jeff Bezos, Trump has shown a cavalier disregard for others' civil liberties.

Levitsky and Ziblatt conclude that, with the exception of Richard Nixon, no major-party candidate in the twentieth century had met any of the criteria to be deemed authoritarian, whereas Trump met all of them. In short, "Trump was precisely the kind of figure that haunted [Alexander] Hamilton and other founders when they created the American presidency."[56]

Having relegated blacks to three-fifths of a person in the original Constitution, the nation's founders obviously were not concerned with racial equality. Yet racism and authoritarianism have intersected in important ways throughout history, and they continue to do so now. Adolf Hitler and the scientific racism of the Third Reich is an obvious of example of this relationship. Closer to home, authoritarianism was the essence of American Jim Crow, in which blacks in the South were stripped of the constitutionally guaranteed right to vote for more than a century, creating one-party rule in the South.[57] Even today, the Republican Party maintains its rule in much of the South through racial bloc voting, a stratification that depends on the existence of racial animosity or authoritarian attitudes.

Indeed, abundant social science research confirms that voters with greater authoritarian orientation are far more likely to identify as Republican and were far more likely to support Trump. Authoritarian orientation, although measured in different ways, roughly sorts voters into those who prefer "social order and cohesion" and those who value "personal autonomy and independence."[58] Voters with a high authoritarian orientation perceive rapid social change as a threat to their personal well-being, do not value diversity, and seek the intervention of a domineering leader to restore order to what they perceive as social atrophy.[59] These traits suggest significant overlap between whitelash voters and those with high authoritarian orientation. They also suggest that whitelash is what motivates many voters to tolerate authoritarianism.

Tolerate it to what end, though? According to Levitsky and Ziblatt, populists are precisely the kind of politicians most likely to exhibit authoritarian traits.[60] Yet, to the extent Trump and the Republican Party represent American counterparts to Europe's right-wing populists, the Republican base is likely to be disappointed. Many right-wing populists in Europe are "welfare chauvinists" who support a generous social safety net that does not extend to illegal immigrants.[61] In contrast, the modern Republican Party has populism's racial element but does not embrace a generous social safety net. As explained in Chapter 6, the American social safety net is upheld through a perversion of our two-party system that allows white conservatives to vote one way and live another.

The economist Paul Krugman has a somewhat different explanation for why, at least in the U.S., whitelash is at cross-purposes with maintaining generous social benefits for the white working and middle classes:

> Once upon a time there were racist populists in Congress: The New Deal coalition relied on a large contingent of segregationist Dixiecrats. But this was always unstable. In practice, advocating economic inclusion seems to spill over into advocacy of racial and social inclusion, too ... Meanwhile, the modern Republican Party is all about cutting taxes on the rich and benefits for the poor and the middle class. And Trump, despite his campaign posturing, has turned out to be no different. Hence the failure of our political system to serve socially conservative/racist voters who also want to tax the rich and preserve Social Security. Democrats won't ratify their racism; Republicans, who have no such compunctions, will ... but won't protect the programs they depend on.[62]

In short, in embracing authoritarianism, American whitelashers are getting the worst of all possible worlds. By voting to shred the social safety net and give tax cuts to the rich, they are re-creating many of the same conditions that led them to embrace authoritarianism in the first place. And as evidenced by Trump's term in office—marked by record cabinet upheaval,[63] the declaration of a national emergency that Congress declared unlawful, record-length closures of the government, disregard for the intelligence community's assessments, and trade wars that have cost Americans tens of billions of dollars[64] —authoritarians can be a font of mercurial uncertainty. In the pursuit of social order, whitelash voters have unleashed political chaos.

Meanwhile, the world is watching—and imitating.[65] To be clear, the current surge of right-wing populism in Europe and elsewhere predates Donald Trump's election; still, its rise in the world's oldest continuous democracy sustains it. The adverse impact of Trump's authoritarian bent is greatest in countries without strong democratic traditions. In one example, after Trump issued an implicit threat that the U.S. military would fire on rock-throwing asylum seekers at the U.S. southern border, the Nigerian army used a video of Trump's threats in a Twitter post justifying its killing of Shiite Muslims who hurled rocks at Nigerian soldiers.[66]

In 2018, a crime-ridden and corruption-beset Brazil elected as its president Jair Messias Bolsonaro, an unremarkable former army paratrooper and congressman. In Brazil, approximately half the population is nonwhite, but most nonwhites consider themselves mixed-race.[67] Racial fluidity of this sort has long allowed the country to falsely portray itself as a nonracist democracy.[68] Bolsonaro's election destroyed that myth. What commended Bolsonaro, who is white, to Brazilian voters was precisely his racialized, strong-man shtick that mimicked Trump.

Galvanizing resentment from the country's predominantly white middle and upper classes, Bolsonaro railed against the rights of indigenous people, vowing to open the Amazon for mining on indigenous lands.[69] He vowed to curtail affirmative action, claiming that the country owed nothing to the Afro-Brazilian descendants of slaves brought to the country, who numbered ten times more than those transported to the United States.[70] Of a black settlement in Brazil founded by the descendants of slaves, Bolsonaro said, "They do nothing. They are not even good for procreation."[71] He described his authoritarian solution to crime in the poor, overwhelmingly nonwhite favelas of Brazil as follows: "I will give police carte blanche to kill. Police that kill thugs will be decorated."[72] And his solution to political corruption was to imprison crooked politicians[73] — or, to paraphrase Trump supporters, "Lock them up."

That the premise of Brazil's turn to racialized authoritarianism is crime and corruption rather than immigration is irrelevant. If the earlier chapters of this book have demonstrated anything, it is that whitelash almost always operates under a pretext. Those pretexts usually wind up obscuring the actual and legitimate sources of the polity's angst, leaving whitelashers no better-off than before.

Looking at two common measures of economic performance in the United States, housing prices and job creation, Professor Anthony Orlando compared the post-election economic performance of counties that supported Trump versus those that supported Hillary Clinton. Thirteen months after the 2016 election, Trump counties increased their number of jobs by 1.13 percent, while

Clinton counties saw an average increase of 0.49 percent, "increases [that] are quite small, especially considering that significantly fewer jobs existed in Trump counties to begin with."[74] Home values in Clinton counties, significantly higher to begin with, increased faster than those in Trump counties from November 2016 into 2018.[75]

Trump's trade wars are also backfiring on his supporters. Instead of the trade deficit being reduced as he had promised in 2016, in 2019 it ballooned to a record level.[76] Trump-supporting agricultural states have been particularly hard hit by trade wars because America's trading partners have retaliated by imposing tariffs on agricultural exports. Because tariffs are a tax on imports ultimately paid by American companies and consumers, Trump's trade wars have increased the costs to American companies and consumers by hundreds of millions of dollars. Indeed, General Motors cited Trump's tariffs in announcing job cuts at plants in the Midwest, the very region that put Trump over the top in 2016.[77]

Reneging on his promise during the 2016 campaign not to cut Medicaid, Medicare, or Social Security, Trump's 2020 budget proposed cuts to all three programs, targeting the programs for cuts of $1.5 trillion, $845 billion, and $25 billion, respectively, over a ten-year period.[78] If cuts of anywhere near this magnitude are implemented, Trump supporters will not be spared the pain.

Despite Trump's promises that "[w]e are going to start winning again," the fact is that Trump voters so far are not winning much, if anything.

They are, however, slowly losing their democracy.

Notes

PREFACE

1. Matthew Haag, *Mitch McConnell Calls Push to Make Election Day a Holiday a Democratic "Power Grab,"* N.Y. TIMES (Jan. 31, 2019), www.nytimes.com/2019/01/31/us/politics/election-day-holiday-mcconnell.html.
2. Hayley Miller, *Former Maine Governor: Bypassing Electoral College Would Silence "White People,"* HUFFINGTON POST (Feb. 28, 2019, 12:24 PM), www.huffpost.com/entry/paul-lepage-electoral-college-white-people_n_5c780795e4b0d3a48b5798e5.

INTRODUCTION

1. Terry Smith, *Will White Voters Never Learn?*, HUFFINGTON POST (Nov. 9, 2016, 7:06 AM), www.huffingtonpost.com/entry/will-white-voters-never-learn_us_582305e4e4b0102262411eeb.
2. 531 U.S. 98 (2000).
3. Amée LaTour, *Fact Check: Was Van Jones Correct in Calling the 2016 Election a "White-Lash"?*, BALLOTPEDIA (Jan. 2, 2017), https://ballotpedia.org/Fact_check/Was_Van_Jones_correct_in_calling_the_2016_election_a_%22white-lash%22%3F.
4. Ben Zimmer, *Talk of a "Whitelash" Revives a 1960s Term*, WALL ST. J. (Nov. 18, 2016), www.wsj.com/articles/talk-of-a-whitelash-revives-a-1960s-term-1479479174?mod=e2fb.
5. *See, e.g.*, Amber Phillips, *Hillary Clinton Says "Misogyny Played a Role" in Her Loss. Research Suggests She Might Be Right.*, WASH. POST (Apr. 8, 2017), www.washingtonpost.com/news/the-fix/wp/2017/04/08/hillary-clinton-says-misogyny-played-a-role-in-her-loss-research-suggests-she-might-be-right/?utm_term=.834697da0e83 (reporting on findings of the Barbara Lee Family Foundation that voters pay more attention to female candidates' "likability," physical appearance, and personal life than their male competitors').

6. Chris Cillizza, *Half the Country Thinks Donald Trump Is a Racist. HALF.*, CNN (July 5, 2018), www.cnn.com/2018/07/04/politics/donald-trump-quinnipiac-poll/index.html.

ELECTING TRUMP AND BREACHING NORMS

1. Only employees are covered by federal laws prohibiting gender discrimination in employment, and it remains an open and highly fact-dependent question whether a CEO can be considered an employee rather than an employer of a company.
2. Greg Sargent, *A Big Majority Says Trump Is Unqualified for the Presidency. How Much Will That End Up Mattering?*, WASH. POST (Sept. 13, 2016), www.washingtonpost.com/blogs/plum-line/wp/2016/09/13/a-big-majority-says-trump-is-unqualified-for-the-presidency-how-much-will-that-end-up-mattering/?utm_term=.a58eeea37bd6.
3. Christopher Ingraham, *White Trump Voters Think They Face More Discrimination than Blacks. The Trump Administration Is Listening.*, WASH. POST (Aug. 2, 2017), www.washingtonpost.com/news/wonk/wp/2017/08/02/white-trump-voters-think-they-face-more-discrimination-than-blacks-the-trump-administration-is-listening/?utm_term=.8e8ob1d426c2; Michael I. Norton & Samuel R. Sommers, *Whites See Racism as a Zero-Sum Game That They Are Now Losing*, 6 PERSPECTIVES ON PSYCHOLOGICAL SCIENCE 215, 215–18 (2011), *available at* www.people.hbs.edu/mnorton/norton%20sommers.pdf.
4. Ingraham, *supra* note 3.
5. Ariel Edwards-Levy, *Nearly Half of Trump Voters Think Whites Face a Lot of Discrimination*, HUFFINGTON POST (Nov. 21, 2016, 6:15 PM), www.huffingtonpost.com/entry/discrimination-race-religion_us_5833761ee4b099512f845bba.
6. Thomas B. Edsall, *What Donald Trump Understands About Republicans*, N.Y. TIMES (Sept. 2, 2015), www.nytimes.com/2015/09/02/opinion/what-donald-trump-understands-about-republicans.html.
7. Charles Ventura, *Majority of White Americans Feel Discriminated Against: Poll*, USA TODAY (Oct. 26, 2017), www.usatoday.com/story/news/politics/onpolitics/2017/10/25/discrimination-white-americans-minorities-poll/801297001/; Don Gonyea, *Majority of White Americans Say They Believe Whites Face Discrimination*, NPR (Oct. 24, 2017), https://www.npr.org/2017/10/24/559604836/majority-of-white-americans-think-theyre-discriminated-against (reporting that only 19 percent of whites report being the victim of employment discrimination based on their race).

8. *Discrimination in America: Experiences and Views of African Americans*, NPR (Oct. 2017), https://cdn1.sph.harvard.edu/wp-content/uploads/sites/21/2017/10/ NPR-RWJF-HSPH-Discrimination-African-Americans-Final-Report.pdf.

9. See Michael Selmi, *Subtle Discrimination: A Matter of Perspective Rather than Intent*, 34 COLUM. HUM. RTS. L. REV. 657, 670–71 (2003) ("[T]here is certainly reason to believe that the racial animus of an earlier era has been transformed into massive indifference to the persistence of racial inequality today. From the perspective of racial indifference, the kind of discrimination that the law and society ought to be concerned with remains the classic cases of overt exclusion, with far less concern for the kind of discrimination that plagues the daily lives of African Americans and that typically finds its way into litigated court cases.").

10. 163 U.S. 537, 551 (1896).

11. IAN HANEY LOPEZ, DOG WHISTLE POLITICS: HOW CODED RACIAL APPEALS HAVE REINVENTED RACISM AND WRECKED THE MIDDLE CLASS 3–5 (2014).

12. Steven Cohen, *Donald Trump and the New Southern Strategy*, NEW REPUBLIC (Nov. 9, 2015), https://newrepublic.com/article/123407/donal d-trump-and-new-southern-strategy.

13. See Ian Haney-Lopez, *The Racism at the Heart of the Reagan Presidency*, SALON (Jan. 11, 2014, 1:00 PM), www.salon.com/2014/01/11/ the_racism_at_the_heart_of_the_reagan_presidency.

14. See James Reinl, *Trump's Muslim Ban Comes into Effect*, AL JAZEERA (June 29, 2017), www.aljazeera.com/news/2017/06/trump-muslim-ban-re defining-family-170629193344749.html.

15. See David Washington, *Trump Signs Order to Begin Mexico Border Wall in Immigration Crackdown*, THE GUARDIAN (Jan. 25, 2017), www.theguardian .com/us-news/2017/jan/25/donald-trump-sign-mexico-border-executive-order.

16. *Here's Donald Trump's Presidential Announcement Speech*, TIME (June 16, 2015), http://time.com/3923128/donald-trump-announcement-speech.

17. Jens Manuel Krogstad, *On Views of Immigrants, Americans Largely Split Along Party Lines*, PEW RES. CTR. (Sept. 30, 2015), www.pewresearch.org/ fact-tank/2015/09/30/on-views-of-immigrants-americans-largely-split-along-par ty-lines.

18. *Id.*

19. Richard Pérez-Peña, *Contrary to Trump's Claims, Immigrants Are Less Likely to Commit Crimes*, N.Y. TIMES (Jan. 26, 2017), www.nytimes.com/ 2017/01/26/us/trump-illegal-immigrants-crime.html?mcubz=0.

20. Peter Schroeder, *Poll: 43 Percent of Republicans Believe Obama Is a Muslim*, THE HILL (Sept. 13, 2015, 3:18 PM), http://thehill.com/blogs/ blog-briefing-room/news/253515-poll-43-percent-of-republicans-believe-o bama-is-a-muslim.

21. Jaweed Kaleem, *More Than Half of Americans Have Unfavorable View of Islam, Poll Finds*, HUFFINGTON POST (Apr. 10, 2015, 9:32 AM), www.hu ffingtonpost.com/2015/04/10/americans-islam-poll_n_7036574.html.

22. NORC, *The General Social Survey*, UNIV. OF CHIC., http://gss.norc.org/ Get-The-Data (last visited Nov. 6, 2017).

23. *See* Patrik Jonsson, *What Were Two Republicans Thinking, Calling Obama "Tar Baby" and "Boy"?*, CHRISTIAN SCI. MONITOR (Aug. 3, 2011), www.csmonitor.com/USA/Politics/2011/0803/What-were-two-Republic ans-thinking-calling-Obama-tar-baby-and-boy (quoting Congressman Doug Lamborn of Colorado: "Now, I don't even want to have to be associated with [Obama]. It's like touching a tar baby and you get it, you're stuck, and you're a part of the problem now and you can't get away."); James Hohmann & Kenneth P. Vogel, *Barbour Apologizes After Calling Obama's Policies "Tar Babies,"* POLITICO (Nov. 10, 2014, 7:11 AM), www.politico.com/ story/2014/11/haley-barbour-apology-obama-policies-tar-babies-112726 (quoting Haley Barbour referring to Obama's issues as "tar babies").

24. Mike Soraghan, *Westmoreland Calls Obama "Uppity,"* THE HILL (Sept. 4, 2008, 3:07 PM), http://thehill.com/homenews/news/16173-westmore land-calls-obama-uppity.

25. *Id.*

26. Aaron Blake, *White House Says Jemele Hill Calling Trump a Racist Is a "Fireable Offense." Trump Once Called Obama a Racist.*, WASH. POST (Sept. 13, 2017), www.washingtonpost.com/news/the-fix/wp/2017/09/13/je mele-hill-and-the-trump-white-houses-double-standard-on-character-assa ssination/?utm_term=.23aab24baobd. Rev. Wright became controversial during the 2008 presidential campaigns for his criticisms of the country's treatment of African Americans.

27. Gregory Krieg, *14 of Trump's Most Outrageous "Birther" Claims—Half from After 2011*, CNN, www.cnn.com/2016/09/09/politics/donald-trump-birther/index.html.

28. *Id.*

29. *Id.*

30. Nahal Toosi, *Clinton on Trump's Birther Claim: A "Racist Lie,"* POLITICO, www.politico.com/story/2016/09/clinton-trump-birther-racist-228735.

31. Michael Tesler, *Jemele Hill's The Mainstream: Most Americans Think Donald Trump's a Racist*, HUFFINGTON POST (Sept. 15, 2017, 3:39 PM), http://www.huffingtonpost.com/entry/jemele-hills-the-mainstream-most-americans-think_us_59bad6ace4b0390a1564dbf6 ("Averaging across the ten different surveys [during the last two months of the 2016 campaign], 52 percent of Americans said the word racist described Donald Trump, compared to 36 percent who said it did not.").

32. Sabrina Siddiqui, *Donald Trump Strikes Muddled Note on "Divisive" Black Lives Matter*, THE GUARDIAN (July 13, 2016), www.theguardian.com/us-ne

ws/2016/jul/13/donald-trump-strikes-muddled-note-on-divisive-black-lives-matter.

33. *Fact Check: Trump and Clinton Debate for the First Time*, NPR, www.npr .org/2016/09/26/495115346/fact-check-first-presidential-debate?utm_source=t witter.com&utm_medium=social&utm_campaign=npr&utm_term=npr news&utm_content=20160926?utm_source=twitter.com&utm_medium=so cial&utm_campaign=npr&utm_term=nprnews&utm_content= 20160926.

34. *Discrimination in America, supra* note 8, at 2.

35. Sandhya Somashekhar, Wesley Lowery, Keith L. Alexander, Kimberly Kindy, & Julie Tate, *Black and Unarmed*, WASH. POST (Aug. 8, 2015), www.washingtonpost.com/sf/national/2015/08/08/black-and-unarmed/? utm_term=.6aaec9ff10b1.

36. *See* Jon Swaine, Oliver Laughland, & Jamiles Lartey, *Black Americans Killed by Police Twice as Likely to Be Unarmed as White People*, THE GUARDIAN (June 2, 2015), www.theguardian.com/us-news/2015/jun/01/black-americans-k illed-by-police-analysis; German Lopez, *There Are Huge Racial Disparities in How US Police Use Force*, VOX (Nov. 14, 2018, 4:12 PM), www.vox.com/ide ntities/2016/8/13/17938186/police-shootings-killings-racism-racial-disparities.

37. PAUL BUTLER, CHOKEHOLD: POLICING BLACK MEN 52 (2017).

38. *Id.* at 55.

39. *See* CAROL M. SWAIN, THE NEW WHITE NATIONALISM IN AMERICA: ITS CHALLENGE TO INTEGRATION 3–5 (2002) (discussing the new white nationalistic movement by comparing the present white nationalism to past white supremacist groups such as the KKK and the Nazi Party).

40. David Duke, *The Hidden Massive Racial Discrimination in America Against Whites*, FOR HUM. FREEDOM & DIVERSITY (Jan. 29, 2009, 6:22 AM), https://davidduke.com/the-real-racial-discrimination-that-goe s-on-in-america/.

41. Rosie Gray, *Trump Defends White Nationalist Protesters: "Some Very Fine People on Both Sides,"* THE ATLANTIC (Aug. 15, 2017), www.theatlantic .com/politics/archive/2017/08/trump-defends-white-nationalist-protesters-some-very-fine-people-on-both-sides/537012/.

42. Peter Baker & Ron Nixon, *Trump Proposal Would Deport More Immigrants Immediately*, N.Y. TIMES (Feb. 19, 2017), www.nytimes.com/2017/02/19/us/ politics/trump-immigration-deportations.html; Reinl, *supra* note 14; The Associated Press, *Trump Backs Bill Limiting Legal Immigration*, HOLLYWOOD REP. (Aug. 2, 2017, 11:17 AM), www.hollywoodreporter.co m/news/trump-backs-bill-limiting-legal-immigration-1026182.

43. 137 S.Ct. 855, 862 (2017).

44. *See id.* at 859.

45. Heather Caygle, *Ryan: Trump's Comments "Textbook Definition" of Racism*, POLITICO (June, 7, 2016, 2:33 PM), www.politico.com/story/2016/ 06/paul-ryan-trump-judge-223991.

46. Romer v. Evans, 517 U.S. 620, 627 (1996).
47. *Id.* at 632 (holding that the amendment to the Colorado constitution was motivated by animus and violated the equal protection clause).
48. 387 U.S. 369, 371 (1967).
49. *Id.* at 373.
50. 393 U.S. 385, 393 (1969).
51. *Id.*
52. 458 U.S. 457 (1982).
53. *Id.* at 470.
54. For instance, in the context of campaign finance and the First Amendment, the Court has long recognized that limitations on direct contributions to candidates can be justified where government limitations on expenditures in referenda and initiatives cannot be. *See* Bellotti v. Baird, 443 U.S. 622, 657 n.26 (1979). Moreover, candidate elections possess a non-expressive dimension that removes them from standard First Amendment analysis. As the Court has said, "Ballots serve primarily to elect candidates, not as forums for political expression." *See* Timmons v. Twin Cities Area New Party, 520 U.S. 351, 363 (1997).
55. *See* Todd Donovan, *Direct Democracy and Campaigns against Minorities*, 97 MINN. L. REV. 1730, 1743 (2013).
56. Schuette v. Coalition to Defend Affirmative Action, 572 U.S. 291, 313 (2014).
57. *Id.*
58. 570 U.S. 529 (2013).
59. *Id.* at 535.
60. Gregory S. Parks & Matthew W. Hughley, *Opposing Affirmative Action: The Social Psychology of Political Ideology and Racial Attitudes*, 57 HOW. L.J. 513, 539–40 (2014)("[T]o the extent that racism has decreased—at least in public expressions—against blacks since the 1940s, whites believe the racism against them has increased. This is consistent with prior research finding that whites perceive the increase in racial equality as a threat to their dominant position in the United States.").
61. Jeremy Diamond, *Trump Doubles Down on Calls for Mosque Surveillance*, CNN (June 15, 2016, 8:10 PM), www.cnn.com/2016/06/15/politics/donald-trump-muslims-mosque-surveillance/index.html.
62. 471 U.S. 222, 225 (1985) (quoting with approval the court of appeals decision) (internal quotation marks omitted).
63. Trump v. Hawaii, 138 S.Ct. 2392, 2404 (2018).
64. *Id.* at 1137.
65. Fam. Serv. Agency S. F. v. NLRB, 163 F.3d 1369, 1377 (D.C. Cir. 1999).
66. NLRB v. Flambeau Airmold Corp., 178 F.3d 705, 712 (4th Cir. 1999).
67. *See* Thornburg v. Gingles, 478 U.S. 30, 36 (1986).

68. *See, e.g.*, U.S. v. Brown, 561 F.3d 420, 430 (5th Cir. 2009) (finding a violation of Section 2 where blacks in Noxubee County, Mississippi, who controlled the Democratic primary processes, conspired to erode the voting strength of minority white Democrats by, inter alia, manipulating the absentee ballot process in favor of black voters with defective ballots).

69. *Thornburg*, 478 U.S. at 36.

70. Northwest Austin Mun. Utility Dist. No. One v. Holder, 557 U.S, 193, 228 (2009) (Thomas, J., concurring in part and dissenting in part).

71. 42 U.S.C. § 3604(a) (2012).

72. 42 U.S.C. § 1981(a) (2012) ("All persons within the jurisdiction of the United States shall have the same right in every State and Territory to make and enforce contracts, to sue, be parties, give evidence, and to the full and equal benefit of all laws and proceedings for the security of persons and property as is enjoyed by white citizens ...").

73. 42 U.S.C. § 2000e–2 (2012).

74. *See* McDonnell Douglas Corp. v. Green, 411 U.S. 792 (1973).

75. Reeves v. Sanderson Plumbing Prod., Inc., 530 U.S. 133, 143 (2000).

76. *Id.* at 147.

77. Ben Adams & Cynthia Barmore, *Questioning Sincerity: The Role of the Courts After Hobby Lobby*, 67 STAN. L. REV. ONLINE 59, 59–60 (2014) ("There is a long tradition of courts competently scrutinizing asserted religious beliefs for sincerity without delving into their validity or verity.").

78. BRYAN CAPLAN, THE MYTH OF THE RATIONAL VOTER: WHY DEMOCRACIES CHOOSE BAD POLICIES 123 (2007).

79. Michael Shermer, *The Political Brain*, SCI. AM. (July 1, 2006), www .scientificamerican.com/article/the-political-brain/.

80. Josh Clinton & Carrie Roush, *Poll: Persistent Partisan Divide Over "Birther" Question*, NBC NEWS, https://www.nbcnews.com/politics/2016-election/poll-persistent-partisan-divide-over-birther-question-n627446.

81. *Id.*

82. Brian Resnick, 7 *Psychological Concepts that Explain the Trump Era of Politics*, VOX (May 6, 2017, 11:14 AM), www.vox.com/science-and-health/2017/3/20/14915076/7-psychological-concepts-explain-trump-politics.

83. *See* Lubin v. Panish, 415 U.S. 709, 715 (1974) (invalidating a state filing fee that failed to provide alternative ballot access for indigent candidates notwithstanding the state's legitimate interest in preventing voter confusion).

84. *Schuette*, 572 U.S. at 313.

85. TERRY SMITH, BARACK OBAMA, POST-RACIALISM, AND THE NEW POLITICS OF TRIANGULATION 157 (2012).

86. Dick Simpson, *The Legacy of Harold Washington 30 Years After His Sudden Death*, CHI. SUN TIMES (Nov. 24, 2017), https://chicago.sun times.com/columnists/the-legacy-of-harold-washington/.

87. *Harold Washington Archives & Collections. Mayoral Campaign Records.*, Chi. Pub. Libr., www.chipublib.org/fa-harold-washington-archives-col lections-mayoral-campaign-records/ (last visited Nov. 5, 2017).

88. Wolfgang Saxon, *Bernard E. Epton Is Dead at 66; Ran for Mayor of Chicago in '83*, N.Y. Times (Dec. 14, 1987), www.nytimes.com/1987/12/ 14/obituaries/bernard-e-epton-is-dead-at-66-ran-for-mayor-of-chicago-in-8 3.html; Eric Zorn, *Knock Off the Epton Allusions Before It's Too Late*, Chi. Trib. Blogs (July 20, 2006), http://blogs.chicagotribune.com/ne ws_columnists_ezorn/2006/07/knock_off_the_e.html.

89. *See* Adarand Constructors, Inc. v. Pena, 515 U.S. 200, 244 (Steven, J., dissenting).

90. Nia-Malika Henderson, *White Men Are 31 Percent of the American Population. They Hold 65 Percent of All Elected Offices.*, Wash. Post (Oct. 8, 2014), www.washingtonpost.com/news/the-fix/wp/2014/10/08/65-percent-of-all-american-elected-officials-are-white-men/? utm_term=.596819ddbf2b.

91. Smith, *supra* note 85.

92. Terry Smith, *Autonomy Versus Equality: Voting Rights Rediscovered*, 57 Ala. L. Rev. 261, 282–83 (2005).

93. Michael Tesler & David O. Sears, Obama's Race: The 2008 Election and the Dream of a Post-Racial America 6–7 (2010).

94. *See id.* at 7, 73.

95. Bush v. Vera, 517 U.S. 952, 953–54 (1941) (subjecting Texas' redistricting plan to strict scrutiny because the new district lines were drawn with race as the predominant factor).

THE EXONERATION OF WHITE VOTERS

1. Michael A. Memoli, *As Democrats Ponder Their Future, Joe Biden Makes a Plea for a Focus on the Middle Class*, L.A. Times (Dec. 22, 2016), www .latimes.com/politics/la-na-pol-biden-interview-20161222-story.html.

2. Brooke Seipel, *Sanders Defends Trump Voters: I Don't Think They're Racists, Sexists or Homophobes*, The Hill (Mar. 31, 2017, 9:44 PM), http://thehill.com/blogs/blog-briefing-room/news/326820-sanders-defend s-trump-voters-i-dont-think-theyre-racists.

3. Chris Cillizza, *The 13 Most Amazing Findings in the 2016 Exit Poll*, Wash. Post (Nov. 10, 2016), www.washingtonpost.com/news/the-fix/wp/ 2016/11/10/the-13-most-amazing-things-in-the-2016-exit-poll/?utm_term=.a6 6bc4950801.

4. Philip Bump, *7 Percent of Donald Trump Supporters Think He's Racist*, Wash. Post (Sept. 1, 2016), www.washingtonpost.com/news/the-fix/wp/ 2016/09/01/7-percent-of-donald-trump-supporters-think-hes-racist/?tid=a_ inl&utm_term=.fc240ae050f6.

5. Eduardo Bonilla-Silva, Racism without Racists 2 (3 ed. 2010).
6. Dominguez-Curry v. Nev. Transp. Dep't, 424 F.3d 1027, 1038 (9th Cir. 2005) (internal quotation marks omitted).
7. Jon Greenberg, *Trump's Pants on Fire Tweet that Blacks Killed 81% of White Homicide Victims*, Politifact (Nov. 23, 2015, 3:35 PM), www.politifact.com/truth-o-meter/statements/2015/nov/23/donald-trump/ trump-tweet-blacks-white-homicide-victims.
8. Warren Fiske, *Trump Misleadingly Puts Black Youth Unemployment Rate at 59 Percent*, Politifact (June 20, 2016, 12:00 AM), www.politifact.com/ virginia/statements/2016/jun/20/donald-trump/trump-misleadingly-puts-b lack-youth-unemployment-r.
9. Louis Jacobson, *Trump's Pants on Fire Claim that Black Communities "Are Absolutely in the Worst Shape" Ever*, Politifact (Sept. 22, 2016, 3:28 PM), www.politifact.com/truth-o-meter/statements/2016/sep/22/donald-tr ump/trumps-pants-fire-claim-blacks-are-absolutely-wors.
10. For a detailed chronology of Trump's racialized provocations, *see* Lisa Desjardins, *Every Moment in Donald Trump's Long and Complicated History with Race*, PBS (Aug. 22, 2017, 7:18 PM), www.pbs.org/newshour/p olitics/every-moment-donald-trumps-long-complicated-history-race. *See also* Lydia O'Connor & Daniel Marans, *Trump Condemned Racism as "Evil." Here Are 18 Times He Embraced It.*, Huffington Post (Aug. 14, 2017, 3:17 PM), www.huffingtonpost.com/entry/trump-racism-examples_us_5991d cabe4b09071f69b9261; Jesse Berney, *Trump's Long History of Racism*, Rolling Stone (Aug. 15, 2017), www.rollingstone.com/politics/features/ trumps-long-history-of-racism-w497876.
11. *See* Fabela v. Socorro Indep. Sch. Dist., 329 F.3d 409 (5th Cir. 2003); Vital v. Nat'l Oilwell Varco, 2014 U.S. Dist. LEXIS 1415914, 2014 WL 4983485 (S.D. Tex. Sept. 30, 2014).
12. 2012 WL 5331229, at *8.
13. 2016 WL 5419419, at *3–*4. *See also* Reynaga v. Roseburg Forest Products, 847 F.3d 678, 686–87 (9th Cir. 2017) (statement that President Obama was an "illegal alien," in combination with other racial stereotyping, sufficient to send case to a jury); Campbell v. Knife River Corp. — Northwest, 783 F.Supp.2d 1137, 1154 (D. Or. 2011) (use of the word "nigger" in combination with differential treatment and disparaging pictures of President Obama sufficient to create jury question as to whether black employee was subject to a racially hostile work environment).
14. Frank Newport, *Democrats Racially Diverse; Republicans Mostly White*, Gallup News (Feb. 8, 2013), https://news.gallup.com/poll/160373/demo crats-racially-diverse-republicans-mostly-white.aspx.
15. Bump, *supra* note 4.
16. Ibram X. Kendi, *Trump Sounds Ignorant of History. But Racist Ideas Often Masquerade as Ignorance.*, Wash. Post (Nov. 13, 2017), www.was

hingtonpost.com/news/posteverything/wp/2017/11/13/trump-sounds-ignorant-of-history-but-racist-ideas-often-masquerade-as-ignorance/?hpid=hp_hp-car ds_hp-posteverything%3Ahomepage%2Fcard&utm_term=.0ad02c1c313a.

17. 570 U.S. 529, 547 (2013).
18. *See* Michael Tesler, *Obama Won Lots of Votes from Racially Prejudiced Whites (and Some of Them Supported Trump)*, WASH. POST (Dec. 7, 2016), www.washingtonpost.com/news/monkey-cage/wp/2016/12/07/obama-w on-lots-of-votes-from-racially-prejudiced-whites-and-some-of-them-suppor ted-trump/?utm_term=.91e604fc67c4 (referencing the white voters who supported Obama but switched to Trump in 2016, Moore said, "They're not racist . . . They twice voted for a man whose middle name is Hussein.").
19. Camille Gear Rich, *Marginal Whiteness*, 98 CAL. L. REV. 1497, 1567 (2010).
20. *Id.*
21. *Id.*
22. Lisa Pruitt, *Welfare Queens and White Trash*, 25 S. CAL. INTERDISC. L.J. 289, 295–96 (2016).
23. *Id.* at 306.
24. *See, e.g.,* Audrey G. McFarlane, *Operatively White?: Exploring the Significance of Race and Class Through the Paradox of Black Middle-Classness*, 72 LAW AND CONTEMPORARY PROBLEMS 163, 165 (2009) ("[A]t different decisionmaking junctures, affluent Blacks sometimes demonstrate that they have similar incentives to Whites—to avoid, run away from, or oppose projects or endeavors that would benefit lower-income Blacks."). *See also Optimism About Black Progress Declines: Blacks See Growing Values Gap Between Poor and Middle Class*, PEW RES. CTR. (Nov. 13, 2007, 2:00 PM), ww w.pewsocialtrends.org/2007/11/13/blacks-see-growing-values-gap-betwe en-poor-and-middle-class ("African Americans see a widening gulf between the values of middle class and poor blacks, and nearly four-in-ten say that because of the diversity within their community, blacks can no longer be thought of as a single race, a new Pew Research Center survey has found.").
25. This likely has to do with the relative lack of class mobility among the black poor. Fifty-one percent of poor blacks born into the bottom quintile of the income distribution remain there at the age of 40, while only 23 percent of poor whites suffer such stagnation. *See* Edward Rodrigue & Richard V. Reeves, *Five Bleak Facts on Black Opportunity*, BROOKINGS (Jan. 15, 2015), www.brookings.edu/blog/social-mobility-memos/2015/01/1 5/five-bleak-facts-on-black-opportunity.
26. Daniel Cox, Rachel Lienesch & Robert P. Jones, *Beyond Economics: Fears of Cultural Displacement Pushed the White Working Class to Trump*, PRRI/ THE ATLANTIC REPORT (May 9, 2017), www.prri.org/research/white-work ing-class-attitudes-economy-trade-immigration-election-donald-trump (noting that 61 percent of blacks believe that most people on welfare are in

genuine need, compared to only 36 percent of the white working class who agree).

27. Krystal Ball, *The Democratic Party Deserved to Die*, HUFFINGTON POST (Nov. 10, 2016), www.huffingtonpost.com/entry/the-democratic-party-des erves-to-die_us_58236ad5e4b0aac62488cde5.

28. Michael Arceneaux, *Bernie Sanders Still Says Class Is More Important than Race. He Is Still Wrong*, THE GUARDIAN (Nov. 22, 2016), www.theg uardian.com/commentisfree/2016/nov/22/bernie-sanders-identity-poli tics-class-race-debate.

29. Barbara J. Flagg, *"Was Blind, But Now I See": White Race Consciousness and The Requirement of Discriminatory Intent*, 91 MICH. L. REV. 953, 969 (1993).

30. *Id.* at 957 ("Transparency operates to require black assimilation even when pluralism is the articulated goal; it affords substantial advantages to whites over blacks even when decisionmakers intend to effect substantive racial justice.").

31. *White Racial Consciousness in the U.S.*, 2016 ANES PILOT STUDY PROPOSAL, at 4 (Sept. 14, 2015), https://docplayer.net/64670975-White-racial -consciousness-in-the-u-s-anes-pilot-study-proposal-keywords-race-identity-atti tudes-white-presidential-evaluation.html.

32. *Id.* at 5–6.

33. *Id.* at 6.

34. *Id.* at 7.

35. Michael Tesler & John Sides, *How Political Science Helps Explain the Rise of Trump: The Role of White Identity and Grievances*, WASH. POST (March 3, 2016), www.washingtonpost.com/news/monkey-cage/wp/2016/ 03/03/how-political-science-helps-explain-the-rise-of-trump-the-role-of-white-identity-and-grievances/?utm_term=.c0722d3e9ca9.

36. *Id.*

37. *White Racial Consciousness in the U.S.*, *supra* note 31, at 6 ("Significant correlations do emerge with respect to racial stereotypes and racial resentment, although because the consciousness items ask both about race and about perceptions of discrimination, these relationships are not especially surprising.").

38. Robert Bird & Frank Newport, *White Racial Resentment Before, During Obama Years*, GALLUP NEWS (May 19, 2017), http://news.gallup.com/o pinion/polling-matters/210914/white-racial-resentment-before-during-oba ma-years.aspx.

39. Lincoln Quillian, Devah Pager, Arnfinn H. Midtøen, & Ole Hexel, *Hiring Discrimination Against Black Americans Hasn't Declined in 25 Years*, HARV. BUS. REV. (Oct. 11, 2017), https://hbr.org/2017/10/hiring-discrimination-against-black-americans-hasnt-declined-in-25-years?utm_ content=buffer1bfbd&utm_medium=social&utm_source=twitter .com&utm_campaign=buffer.

40. Bird & Newport, *supra* note 38.

41. *See* Bird & Newport, *supra* note 38.
42. Bird & Newport, *supra* note 38.
43. Tesler, *supra* note 18.
44. Michael Tesler, *Views About Race Mattered More in Electing Trump than in Electing Obama,* WASH. POST (Nov. 22, 2016), www.washingtonpost.com/news/monkey-cage/wp/2016/11/22/peoples-vi ews-about-race-mattered-more-in-electing-trump-than-in-electing-obama/?tid=a_inl&utm_term=.65171b7e0a3f.
45. *Id.*
46. Thomas Wood, *Racism Motivated Trump Voters More than Authoritarianism,* WASH. POST (Apr. 17, 2017), www.washingtonpost.com/news/monkey-cage/ wp/2017/04/17/racism-motivated-trump-voters-more-than-authoritarianism-or-income-inequality/?utm_term=.47a88e3393e7.
47. Tesler, *supra* note 18.
48. Tesler, *supra* note 18 ("The most important determinant of Americans' votes in 2008 and 2012, as always, was party identification . . . That meant that lots of racially prejudiced Democrats wound up supporting Obama.").
49. Tesler, *supra* note 18.
50. Wexler v. White's Fine Furniture, Inc., 317 F.3d 564, 572 (6th Cir. 2003).
51. *Id.* at 573–74. But *see id.* at 573 (noting that some courts find the same-actor inference "quite persuasive").
52. *See* Tesler, *supra* note 44 ("Hillary Clinton moved to the left of Obama in both her rhetoric and policies on race-related issues in order to retain support from a coalition increasingly comprised of minorities and racially progressive whites. Democrats' growing racial liberalism in 2016 may have accelerated defections from the party among racially resentful whites.").
53. Personnel Adm'r of Massachusetts v. Feeney, 442 U.S. 256, 279 (1979).
54. Schuette v. Coalition to Defend Affirmative Action, 572 U.S. 291, 314 (2014).
55. 387 U.S. 369, 371 (1967).
56. 393 U.S. 385, 393 (1969).
57. 458 U.S. 457, 470 (1982).
58. Paul Schartzman, *Once a Voice for a Big-Tent GOP, Gillespie Faces Criticism from Unexpected Source: Republicans,* WASH. POST (Nov. 1, 2017), www.wa shingtonpost.com/local/virginia-politics/once-a-voice-for-a-big-tent-gop-gilles pies-ads-prompt-criticism-from-unexpected-source-republicans/2017/11/01/ac d453dc-bdbb-11e7-959c-fe2b598d8c00_story.html?utm_term=.4630d8eeaefa.
59. *Id.* An independent group, the Latino Victory Fund, ran a TV ad that highlighted the racist nature of Gillespie's campaign:

> The minute-long spot from the Latino Victory Fund depicted a pickup truck being driven by a sinister-looking white man, flying a Confederate flag and sporting a Gillespie bumper sticker as it chased down a group of terrified

brown-skinned children. Titled "American Nightmare," the ad ended with
the children waking up from a nightmare and adults watching television
footage of August's torch-bearing white-nationalist march in Charlottesville.
"Is this what Donald Trump and Ed Gillespie mean by the 'American
Dream?'" asked the narrator.

> *An Ad that Had No Place in Va.'s Governor's Race*, WASH. POST
> (Oct. 31, 2017), www.washingtonpost.com/opinions/ralph-northam
> -should-repudiate-this-offensive-anti-gillespie-ad/2017/10/31/a69
> c47e0-be6a-11e7-959c-fe2b598d8c00_story.html?utm_
> term=.00286a6b04a8.

Even liberal news outlets such as *The Washington Post* criticized the ad as the
moral equivalent of Gillespie's racialized ads. But how can this be? How can
protest against racism ever be the moral equivalent of racism itself? Here
again, we witness the conflation of Justice Stevens's "welcome mat" and "no
trespassing" sign. *See* Chapter 1, notes 88–89 and accompanying text.

60. Scott Clement & Emily Guskin, *Exit Poll Results: How Different Groups
    of Virginians Voted*, WASH. POST (November 8, 2017), www.washington
    post.com/graphics/2017/local/virginia-politics/governor-exit-polls/?utm_
    term=.a11f7eb8586e (last updated Nov. 8, 2017).

61. *Id.*

62. Jon Huang, Samuel Jacoby, Michael Strickland, & K.K. Rebecca Lai,
    Election 2016: Exit Polls, N.Y. TIMES (Nov. 8, 2016), www.nytimes.com/
    interactive/2016/11/08/us/politics/election-exit-polls.html.

63. Nicholas Carnes & Noam Lupu, *It's Time to Bust the Myth: Most Trump
    Voters Were Not Working Class*, WASH. POST (June 5, 2017), www.washing
    tonpost.com/news/monkey-cage/wp/2017/06/05/its-time-to-bust-the-myth-mo
    st-trump-voters-were-not-working-class/?utm_term=.e4a2fa00b40f.

64. *Id.*

65. The same is not as true for African Americans, who must attain more
    education in order to compete with whites who have less education. *See*
    Abigail Bessler, *A Black College Student Has the Same Chances of Getting
    a Job as a White High School Dropout*, THINK PROGRESS (June 25, 2014, 2:56
    PM), https://thinkprogress.org/a-black-college-student-has-the-same-chances-
    of-getting-a-job-as-a-white-high-school-dropout-b7639607fdf1. Indeed, white
    high school dropouts have a greater net worth than black or Latino
    college graduates. *See* Michael A. Fletcher, *White High School
    Dropouts Are Wealthier than Black and Hispanic College Graduates.
    Can a New Policy Tool Fix That?*, WASH. POST (Mar. 10, 2015), www
    .washingtonpost.com/news/wonk/wp/2015/03/10/white-high-school-drop
    outs-are-wealthier-than-black-and-hispanic-college-graduates-can-a-ne
    w-policy-tool-fix-that/?utm_term=.ef0708e2d760.

66. Carnes & Lupu, *supra* note 63.

67. Kevin Quely, *The More Education Republicans Have, the Less They Tend to Believe in Climate Change,* N.Y. Times (Nov. 14, 2017), www.nytimes .com/interactive/2017/11/14/upshot/climate-change-by-education.html? _r=0.
68. *Id.*
69. Ruy Teixeira & Alan Abramowitz, *The Decline of the White Working Class and the Rise of a Mass Upper Middle Class,* 124 Pol. Sci. Q. 391, 398 (2009), https://www.brookings.edu/wp-content/uploads/2016/06/04_d emographics_teixeira.pdf.
70. *Id.*
71. *Id.* at 399.
72. *Id.* at 400.
73. *Id.* at 405.
74. *Id.* at 406.
75. Thomas Frank, What's the Matter with Kansas? How Conservatives Won the Hearts of America 179 (2004).
76. 347 U.S. 483 (1954).
77. Ari Berman, *The Man Behind Trump's Voter-Fraud Obsession,* N.Y. Times (June 13, 2017), www.nytimes.com/2017/06/13/magazine/the-man-behind-trumps-voter-fraud-obsession.html?_r=0.
78. Jonathan T. Rothwell & Pablo Diego-Rosell, *Explaining Nationalist Political Views: The Case of Donald Trump,* 12 (Gallup, Working Paper, 2016), https://poseidon01.ssrn.com/delivery.php?ID=94012310112 3002109065102088081086110050080061059 01 101811309206611100 1023125 031090090041007038028040060043011115064 082103087099001072 0630 49059105090013080103120088 0750460770731210030260260870971210 88 0070960270191160271181170 93010103126074023113071070088&EXT=pdf.
79. *Id.*
80. *Id.* at 19; Max Ehrenfreund & Jeff Guo, *A Massive New Study Debunks a Widespread Theory for Donald Trump's Success,* Wash. Post (Aug. 12, 2016), www.washingtonpost.com/news/wonk/wp/2016/08/12/a-massive-ne w-study-debunks-a-widespread-theory-for-donald-trumps-success/? utm_term=.5a0ea198dd59.
81. Rothwell & Diego-Rosell, *supra* note 78, at 19.
82. Terry Smith, Barack Obama, Post-Racialism, and the New Politics of Triangulation 110 (2012).
83. Exec. Office of the U.S., The Long-Term Decline in Prime-Age Male Labor Force Participation 13 (2016), https://obamawhi tehouse.archives.gov/sites/default/files/page/files/20160620_cea_primea ge_male_lfp.pdf.
84. Joseph E. Stiglitz, The Price of Inequality: How Today's Divided Society Endangers Our Future 8–9 (2012).

85. *See id.* at 56–57.

86. Louis Uchitelle, Making It: Why Manufacturing Still Matters 26 (2017).

87. Exec. Office of the U.S., *supra* note 83, at 12.

88. Exec. Office of the U.S., *supra* note 83, at 12.

89. Uchitelle, *supra* note 86, at 30.

90. *See* Uchitelle, *supra* note 86, at 74–80 (describing the history of companies fleeing the inner cities).

91. Uchitelle, *supra* note 86, at 75.

92. Barbara Ehrenreich, *Dead, White, and Blue: The Great Die-Off of America's Blue Collar Whites*, TomDispatch.com (Dec. 1, 2015), www.tomdispatch.com/post/176075/ tomgram%3A_barbara_ehrenreich,_america_to_working_class_whites%3A_drop_dead!/ [https://perma.cc/2P4R-82RQ].

93. Victor Tan Chen, *All Hollowed Out*, The Atlantic (Jan. 16, 2016), www.theatlantic.com/business/archive/2016/01/white-working-class-poverty/424341/ ("In the decades after World War II, racial minorities were denied many of the jobs, loans, and other resources that allowed the white majority to buy homes and accrue wealth. If the gains of economic growth have gone largely to the rich in recent years, in that earlier period the white working class could count on hefty rises in living standards from generation to generation, and they grew accustomed to that upward trajectory of growing prosperity.").

94. *Id.*

95. Harold Meyerson, *America's White Working Class Is a Dying Breed*, Wash. Post (Nov. 4, 2015), www.washingtonpost.com/opinions/the-white-working-class-is-a-dying-breed/2015/11/04/f2220170-8323-11e5-a7ca-6ab6ec20f839_story.html?utm_term=.197c588c8f78.

96. Stephanie Coontz, *The Shell-Shocked White Working Class*, CNN (Sept. 23, 2016, 7:48 AM), www.cnn.com/2016/09/23/opinions/shell-shocked-white-working-class-opinion-coontz/index.html.

97. Gina Kolata, *Death Rates Rising for Middle-Aged White Americans, Study Finds*, N.Y. Times (Nov. 2, 2015), www.nytimes.com/2015/11/03/health/death-rates-rising-for-middle-aged-white-americans-study-finds.html.

98. Alec Tyson & Shiva Maniam, *Behind Trump's Victory: Divisions by Race, Gender, Education*, Pew Res. Ctr. (Nov. 9, 2016), www.pewresearch.org/fact-tank/2016/11/09/behind-trumps-victory-divisions-by-race-gender-education/.

99. *Exit Polls*, CNN, http://www.cnn.com/election/results/exit-polls (last updated Nov. 23, 2016).

100. Michael Tesler, *Trump Voters Think African Americans Are Much Less Deserving Than "Average Americans,"* Huffington Post

(Dec. 20, 2017, 6:16 PM), www.huffingtonpost.com/michael-tesler/
trump-voters-think-africa_b_13732500.html.

101. *Id.*

102. Charles Ventura, *Majority of White Americans Feel Discriminated Against: Poll*, USA TODAY (Oct. 26, 2017), www.usatoday.com/story/ne ws/politics/onpolitics/2017/10/25/discrimination-white-americans-minori ties-poll/801297001/.

103. *White Racial Consciousness in the U.S., supra* note 31, at 6.

104. Thomas B. Edsall, *What Donald Trump Understands About Republicans*, N.Y. TIMES (Sept. 2, 2015), www.nytimes.com/2015/09/02/opinion/what-donald-trump-understands-about-republicans.html?_r=o.

105. *See* James E. Dobbins & Judith H. Skillings, *Racism as a Clinical Syndrome*, 70 AM. J. ORTHOPSYCHIATRY 14, 21 (2000).

106. Jessie Hellman, *Poll: Nearly 40 Percent of Trump Backers Say Minorities Have Too Much Influence*, THE HILL (Sept. 28, 2016, 8:25 AM), http://the hill.com/blogs/ballot-box/presidential-races/298213-clinton-supporters-more-likely-to-think-women-minorities.

107. *On Views of Race and Inequality, Blacks and Whites Are Worlds Apart*, PEW RES. CTR. (June 27, 2016), www.pewsocialtrends.org/2016/06/27/o n-views-of-race-and-inequality-blacks-and-whites-are-worlds-apart/.

108. *See* Jerome Taylor, *Dimensionalization of Racialism*, in BLACK PSYCHOLOGY 637, 640–41 (R.L. Jones ed., 1980) (listing the following as social variables: social effect, internalization, identification, utilitarianism or instrumentalism, frustration–aggression–displacement, and ego defense).

109. Dobbins & Skillings, *supra* note 105, at 20; Taylor, *supra* note 108, at 641.

110. Dobbins & Skillings, *supra* note 105, at 22.

111. *A Growing Divide on Race*, N.Y. TIMES: CBS NEWS POLL (July 23, 2015), www.nytimes.com/interactive/2015/07/23/us/race-relations-in-ame rica-poll.html.

112. *Id.*

113. Michael W. Kraus, Julian M. Rucker, & Jennifer A. Richeson, *Americans Misperceive Racial Economic Equality*, 114 PROC. NAT'L ACAD. OF SCI. 10324, 10329 (2017), www.pnas.org/content/114/39/10324/tab-article-info ("Together, the findings … offer support for our central argument that overestimates of Black–White economic equality are rooted, at least in part, in both motivational tendencies to perceive society as fair and the lack of consideration of the social structures, practices, and policies that created and continue to maintain racial disparities in economic outcomes.").

114. NANCY DITOMASO, THE AMERICAN NON-DILEMMA: RACIAL INEQUALITY WITHOUT RACISM 70, 73 (2013).

115. *See id.* at 55 ("[W]hat appears to be a totally random outcome of friends helping friends turns out to be a structured outcome with racial content").

116. Dobbins & Skillings, *supra* note 105, at 22.

117. Pamela A. Wilkens, *The Mark of Cain: Disenfranchised Felons and the Constitutional No-Man's Land*, 56 Syracuse L. Rev. 85, 109 (2005).

118. Martin Luther King, Jr., *Letter from a Birmingham Jail*, Afr. Stud. Ctr., www.africa.upenn.edu/Articles_Gen/Letter_Birmingham.html (last visited Jan. 2, 2018).

119. 42 U.S.C. § 1981 (2012).

WHITE VOTERS AND THE LAW OF ALTERNATIVE FACTS

1. Eileen Sullivan, *Trump and Corker Escalate Battle Over Taxes, in Personal Terms*, N.Y. Times (Oct. 24, 2017), www.nytimes.com/2017/10/24/us/politics/trump-corker-feud-dog-catcher.html?hp&action=click&pgtype=Homepage&clickSource=story-heading&module=first-column-region&region=top-news&WT.nav=top-news&_r=0.

2. Cathleen Decker, *Arizona Sen. Jeff Flake Denounces Trump, Announces He Will Not Seek Reelection in 2018*, L.A. Times (Oct. 24, 2017), www.latimes.com/politics/washington/la-na-pol-essential-washington-updates-arizona-sen-jeff-flake-a-trump-1508871920-htmlstory.html.

3. Kylie Atwood, *Rex Tillerson Warns of "Growing Crisis of Integrity and Ethics,"* CBS News (May 16, 2018, 2:25 PM), www.cbsnews.com/news/rex-tillerson-warns-of-growing-crisis-of-integrity-and-ethics.

4. Jonathan Karl, Devin Dwyer, & Meghan Keneally, *Trump Defends Military Presence on Border and Says "I Do Try" to Tell the Truth*, ABC News (Nov. 1, 2018, 7:50 AM), https://abcnews.go.com/Politics/wall-people-trump-defends-military-presence-border/story?id=58878290.

5. Glenn Kessler, Salvador Rizzo, & Meg Kelly, *President Trump Made 8,158 False or Misleading Claims in His First Two Years*, Wash. Post (Jan. 21, 2019), www.washingtonpost.com/politics/2019/01/21/president-trump-made-false-or-misleading-claims-his-first-two-years/?utm_term=.719092a2f164.

6. Sean Illing, *"The Fish Rots from the Head": A Historian on the Unique Corruption of Trump's White House*, Vox (Dec. 21, 2018, 9:06 AM), www.vox.com/2017/11/16/16643614/trump-administration-corruption-russia-investigation.

7. Brett Samuels, *Gap Between Republican, Democratic Approval of Trump Sets Record*, The Hill (Jan. 16, 2019, 7:31 AM), https://thehill.com/blogs/blog-briefing-room/425564-gap-between-republican-democratic-approval-of-trump-sets-record.

8. *Presidential Approval Ratings—Donald Trump*, Gallup, http://news.gallup.com/poll/203198/presidential-approval-ratings-donald-trump.aspx.

9. 137 S.Ct. 855 (2017).

10. *Id.*

11. *Id.*

12. *Id.* at 868.

13. Schuette v. Coalition to Defend Affirmative Action, 134 S.Ct. 1623, 1637 (2014).

14. *See* Ibram X. Kendi, Stamped from the Beginning: The Definitive History of Racist Ideas in America 9 (2016) ("Time and again, racist ideas have not been cooked up from the boiling pot of ignorance and hate. Time and again, powerful and brilliant men and women have produced racist ideas in order to justify the racist policies of their era, in order to redirect the blame for their era's racial disparities away from those policies and onto Black people.").

15. Emma Stefansky, *Kellyanne Conway Introduces Concept of "Alternative Facts" to Account for Sean Spicer's Lies*, Vanity Fair (Jan. 22, 2017, 12:04 PM), www.vanityfair.com/news/2017/01/kellyanne-conway-alternative-facts.

16. John Melloy, *Dow Would Rise to 50,000 if Trump Matches Market Performance Under Obama*, CNBC (Dec. 14, 2016, 11:42 AM), www.cnbc.com/2016/12/14/dow-would-rise-to-50000-if-trump-matches-market-performance-under-obama.html.

17. Steve Benen, *Trump, His Supporters, and the Persistence of the "Reality Gap,"* MSNBC (Dec. 9, 2016, 8:00 AM), www.msnbc.com/rachel-maddow-show/trump-his-supporters-and-the-persistence-the-reality-gap; *Ryan Disliked by Republicans; Trump Could Hurt Down Ballot*, Pub. Pol'y Polling (May 11, 2016), www.publicpolicypolling.com/wp-content/uploads/2017/09/PPP_Release_National_51116.pdf (reporting that in May 2016, 57 percent of Republicans believed that the stock market had decreased under Obama).

18. Eric Zorn, *Polls Reveal Sobering Extent of Nation's Fact Crisis*, Chi. Trib. (Jan. 5, 2017), www.chicagotribune.com/news/opinion/zorn/ct-polling-ignorance-facts-trump-zorn-perspec-0106-md-20170105-column.html.

19. *Ryan Disliked by Republicans*, supra note 17; Danielle Kurtzleben, *What Kind of "Jobs President" Has Obama Been—in 8 Charts*, NPR (Jan. 7, 2017, 6:00 AM), www.npr.org/2017/01/07/508600239/what-kind-of-jobs-president-has-obama-been-in-8-charts.

20. Zorn, *supra* note 18.

21. Zorn, *supra* note 18.

22. Zorn, *supra* note 18.

23. Zorn, *supra* note 18; Sam Levine & Ariel Edwards-Levy, *Almost Half of Republicans Believe Millions Voted Illegally in the 2016 Election*, Huffington Post (May 27, 2018, 8:00 AM), www.huffingtonpost.com/entry/republicans-voter-fraud_us_5b0850f8e4b0fdb2aa53791f.

24. Ariel Edwards-Levy, *The Stock Market Is Up Under Trump. Clinton Voters Don't Believe It.*, Huffington Post (Feb. 23, 2018, 3:46 PM), www.huffingtonpost.com/entry/stock-market-is-up-under-trump-few-beyond-his-base-realize_us_5a905fffe4b03b55731bee15.

25. Justin McCarthy & Jeffrey M. Jones, *U.S. Economic Confidence Surges After Election*, GALLUP (Nov. 15, 2016), http://news.gallup.com/poll/197 474/economic-confidence-surges-election.aspx.

26. *Id.*

27. *See* James H. Kuklinski, Paul J. Quirk, Jennifer Jerit, David Schwieder, & Robert F. Rich, *Misinformation and the Currency of Democratic Citizenship*, 62(3) J. POL. 790, 793 (Aug. 2000).

28. *Id.* at 793–94.

29. *Id.* at 794.

30. *Id.*

31. Brendan Nyhan & Jason Reifler, *When Corrections Fail: The Persistence of Political Misconceptions*, 32 POL. BEHAV. 303 (2010), *available at* https://fba um.unc.edu/teaching/articles/PolBehavior-2010-Nyhan.pdf. More recent research suggests that corrective information is more likely to affect misinformed voters' perception of the candidate's background and character than their views of a candidate's position on issues. One study found that accurate information that Donald Trump's father, Fred Trump, gave his son several million dollars to bail him out from failing business ventures negatively affected Republican respondents' perceptions of Donald Trump as a self-made business man. *See generally,* Jared McDonald, David Karol & Lilliana Mason, *"An Inherited Money Dude from Queens County": How Unseen Candidate Characteristics Affect Voter Perceptions*, L. POL. BEHAV. (Jan. 9, 2019), https://link.springer.com/epdf/10.1007/s11109-019-0952 7-y?fbclid=IwARofMOpt7DIdGh8yWCoK5gdNshU2uTBjFU9KH1Lta_ceI tzOIuN3iuoBoH8&author_access_token=ir5Ssw_EXA1qr_flEOM5Wfe4R wlQNchNByi7wbcMAY5916uJusQCNCIDKcfEl6KUFA-jZckmjhNr5V8 K1K_AG1swAOzI3VADvB5AHVLSqKvfBD-_EBrZBon5Judwxkv7Uo9DgQ yuBAvOe6zHkDnZ-w%3D%3D.

32. *See* Nyhan and Reifler, *supra* note 31, at 323.

33. See Ziva Kunda, *The Case for Motivated Reasoning*, 108 PSYCHOL. BULL. 480, 480 (1990); Nyhan & Reifler, *supra* note 31, at 323 (differentiating between motivated reasoning — "the evaluation and usage of factual evidence in constructing opinions and evaluating arguments" — and "the cognitive and affective processes that take place when subjects are confronted with discordant factual information").

34. Anne Pluta, *Trump Supporters Appear to Be Misinformed, Not Uninformed*, FIVETHIRTYEIGHT (Jan. 7, 2016, 10:00 AM), https://fivethirtyeight.com/fea tures/trump-supporters-appear-to-be-misinformed-not-uninformed.

35. THOMAS E. MANN & NORMAN J. ORNSTEIN, IT'S EVEN WORSE THAN IT LOOKS: HOW THE AMERICAN CONSTITUTIONAL SYSTEM COLLIDED WITH THE NEW POLITICS OF EXTREMISM xxiv (2012) (emphasis added).

36. Daniel M.T. Fessler, Anne C. Pisor & Colin Holbrook, *Political Orientation Predicts Credulity Regarding Putative Hazards*, 28(5) PSYCHOL. SCI. 651, 657 (2017) ("Because liberals and conservatives differ in their responsiveness to negative information, particularly concerning threats, and similarly differ in how dangerous they perceive the world to be, we predicted, and found, that political orientation correlated with the magnitude of the tendency to believe information about hazards more than information about benefits; liberals displayed less of this propensity and conservatives displayed more of it.").
37. *Id.* at 651.
38. Diana C. Mutz, *Status Threat, Not Economic Hardship, Explains the 2016 Presidential Vote*, PROC. NAT'L ACAD. OF SCI. (Apr. 23, 2018), at 5, http://www.pnas.org/content/pnas/early/2018/04/18/1718155115.full.pdf ("[C]ontrary to conventional wisdom, there is little to no evidence that those whose incomes declined or whose incomes increased to a lesser extent than others' incomes were more likely to support Trump. Even change in subjective assessment of one's own personal financial situation had no discernible impact on evaluations of Trump or on change in vote choice.").
39. *Id.* at 3.
40. *See id.* at 8 ("[S]tatus threat is not the usual form of prejudice or stereotyping that involves looking down on outgroups who are perceived to be inferior; instead, it is borne of a sense that the outgroup is doing too well and thus, is a viable threat to one's own dominant group status. As a highly visible indicator of racial progress, a well-educated, Harvard Law-trained African American president is indeed threatening to dominant white status . . .").
41. Daniel Cox, Rachel Lienesch, & Robert P. Jones, *Beyond Economics: Fears of Cultural Displacement Pushed the White Working Class to Trump*, PRRI/THE ATLANTIC (May 9, 2017), www.prri.org/research/wh ite-working-class-attitudes-economy-trade-immigration-election-donald-trump.
42. *Id.*
43. Tanzina Vega, *Where's the Empathy for Black Poverty and Pain?*, CNN (May 5, 2017, 11:13 AM), www.cnn.com/2017/05/05/opinions/empathy-gap-in-viewing-black-poverty-and-pain-tanzina-vega/index.html.
44. Cox, Lienesch, & Jones, *supra* note 41.
45. Tashjian v. Republican Party of Connecticut, 479 U.S. 208, 214 (1986) (quoting Kusper v. Pontikes, 414 U.S. 51, 57 (1973)).
46. Branti v. Finkel, 445 U.S. 507, 517 (1980).
47. Anderson v. Celebrezze, 460 U.S. 780, 787–88 (1983).
48. Citizens United v. Federal Election Commission, 558 U.S. 310 (2010). According to the FEC, "[i]ndependent expenditures are not contributions

and are not subject to contribution limits . . . An independent expenditure is an expenditure for a communication that: [e]xpressly advocates the election or defeat of a clearly identified federal candidate; and [i]s not coordinated with a candidate, candidate's committee, party committee or their agents." Federal Election Commission, *Independent Expenditures,* https://www.fec.gov/help-candidates-and-committees/making-disbursements-pac/independent-expenditures-nonconnected-pac (last visited Aug. 2, 2018).

49. 388 U.S. 1 (1967).

50. *Id.* at 7.

51. *See* Cox, Lienesch, & Jones, *supra* note 41.

52. *See* Cox, Lienesch, & Jones, *supra* note 41.

53. Tim Marcin, *Nearly 20 Percent of Americans Think Interracial Marriage Is "Morally Wrong," Poll Finds,* NEWSWEEK (Mar. 14, 2018, 4:59 PM), www.newsweek.com/20-percent-america-thinks-interracial-marriage-morally-wrong-poll-finds-845608.

54. Ryan D. Enos, *How Segregation Leads to Racist Voting by Whites,* VOX.COM (Nov. 28, 2017, 8:50 AM), www.vox.com/the-big-idea/2017/11/28/16707438/social-geography-trump-rise-segregation-psychology-racism.

55. TERRY SMITH, BARACK OBAMA, POST-RACIALISM, AND THE NEW POLITICS OF TRIANGULATION 48 (2012).

56. Shelby County, Ala. v. Holder, 570 U.S. 529, 547 (2013).

57. Brief of Political Science and Law Professors as Amici Curiae in Support of Respondents at 12, *in Shelby County, Ala. v. Holder,* 570 U.S. 529 (2013) (No. 12–96), *available at* https://www.brennancenter.org/sites/default/files/legal-work/2013.2.1%20Brief%20of%20Political%20Science%20and%20Law%20Professors%20in%20Support%20of%20Respondents.pdf.

58. *Id.* at 13.

59. *Id.*

60. *See* Rucho v. Common Cause, 139 S.Ct. 2484 (2019) (holding that partisan gerrymandering claims are political questions unreviewable by federal courts); Vieth v. Jubelirer, 541 U.S. 267 (2004); Davis v. Bandemer, 478 U.S. 109 (1986).

61. *See Vieth,* 541 U.S. at 324; Easley v. Cromartie, 532 U.S. 234, 253 (2001).

62. NAACP LEGAL DEFENSE AND EDUCATIONAL FUND, INC., "POST-RACIAL" AMERICA? NOT YET: WHY THE FIGHT FOR VOTING RIGHTS CONTINUES AFTER THE ELECTION OF PRESIDENT BARACK OBAMA 12 (2009), *available at* https://www.naacpldf.org/wp-content/uploads/Post-Racial-America-Not-Yet_Political_Participation.pdf.

63. *Utah QuickFacts,* U.S. CENSUS BUREAU, www.census.gov/quickfacts/fact/table/ut/PST045217 (last visited Aug. 2, 2018).

64. *Utah Presidential Race—2012 Election Ctr.,* CNN, www.cnn.com/election/2012/results/state/UT/president (last updated Dec. 10, 2012, 11:16 AM).

65. *Idaho QuickFacts*, U.S. CENSUS BUREAU, www.census.gov/quickfacts/id (last visited Aug. 2, 2018).

66. *Idaho Presidential Race—2012 Election Ctr.*, CNN.COM, www.cnn.com/election/2012/results/state/ID/president (last updated Dec. 10, 2012, 10:30 AM).

67. *Wyo. Presidential Race—2012 Election Ctr.*, CNN, www.cnn.com/election/2012/results/state/WY/president (last updated Dec. 10, 2012, 11:22 AM).

68. *Wyo. QuickFacts*, U.S. CENSUS BUREAU, www.census.gov/quickfacts/wy (last visited Aug. 2, 2018).

69. The same is true of the formerly covered jurisdictions of Alabama, Georgia, and Louisiana, where Obama white vote shares were 15 percent (2012), 23 percent (2008), and 14 percent (2008), respectively. *See Ala. Presidential Race, Exit Polls—2012 Election Ctr.*, CNN, www.cnn.com/election/2012/results/state/AL/president (last updated Dec. 10, 2012, 10:16 AM); *Ga. Local Exit Polls—Election Ctr. 2008*, CNN, www.cnn.com/ELECTION/2008/results/polls/#GAP00p1; *La. Local Exit Polls—Election Ctr. 2008*, CNN.COM, www.cnn.com/ELECTION/2008/results/polls/#LAP00p1.

70. Associated Press & Dennis Junius, *AP Poll: U.S. Majority Have Prejudice Against Blacks*, USA TODAY (Oct. 27, 2012), www.usatoday.com/story/news/politics/2012/10/27/poll-black-prejudice-america/1662067.

71. *Id.*

72. *Id.*

73. *Id.* Just how hidebound is remarkable. A recent study by the Pew Research Center for the People and the Press found that liberals were more than three times more likely than conservatives (76 percent to 20 percent) to believe that it is important that a community be ethnically and racially diverse. *Political Polarization in the American Public*, PEW RES. CTR. FOR THE PEOPLE & THE PRESS (June 12, 2014), www.people-press.org/2014/06/12/political-polarization-in-the-american-public. Of course, the opposite of such diversity is segregation.

74. *See* Terry Smith, *Speaking Against Norms: Public Discourse and the Economy of Racialization in the Workplace*, 57 AM. U. L. REV. 523, 534–35 (2008) (explaining that expression by people of color that is contrary to prevailing norms summons latent racial stereotypes and prejudices, consistent with cognitive process theory).

75. Associated Press & Junius, *supra* note 70.

76. Maria Krysan & Sarah Patton Moberg, *Trends in Racial Attitudes*, INST. GOV'T. & PUB. AFFAIRS (2016), Fig. 6 (W): Explanations of Inequality, https://igpa.uillinois.edu/programs/racial-attitudes#section-3.

77. Aaron Blake, *Republicans' Views of Blacks' Intelligence, Work Ethic Lag Behind Democrats at a Record Clip*, WASH. POST (Mar. 31, 2017), www.washingtonpost.com/news/the-fix/wp/2017/03/31/the-gap-between-republicans-and-democrats-views-of-african-americans-just-hit-a-new-high/?utm_term=.dca3bded5269.

78. *Id.*
79. *Id.*
80. *Id.*
81. *The Partisan Divide on Political Values Grows Even Wider*, PEW RES. CTR. FOR THE PEOPLE & THE PRESS (Oct. 5, 2017), www.people-press .org/2017/10/05/4-race-immigration-and-discrimination.
82. David Emery, *Did Trump Say "Laziness Is a Trait in Blacks; No Black President Again Any Time Soon?,"* SNOPES.COM (Aug. 8, 2016), www.sn opes.com/fact-check/trump-laziness-is-a-trait-in-blacks.
83. *Id.*
84. Julie Hirschfeld Davis, *Trump's Harsh Words, Not His Plan for Wall, Dominate Hearing*, N.Y. TIMES (Jan. 16, 2018), www.nytimes.com/2018/01/ 16/us/politics/trump-shithole-shithouse-immigration.html; Aaron Blake, *The Trump "Shithole Countries" Flap Takes an Even More Ridiculous Turn*, WASH. POST (Jan. 16, 2018), www.washingtonpost.com/news/the-fix/wp/201 8/01/16/the-trump-shithole-countries-flap-takes-an-even-more-ridiculous-turn/ ?utm_term=.e6b94ca399af.
85. Michael W. Kraus, Julian M. Rucker, & Jennifer A. Richeson, *Americans Misperceive Racial Economic Equality*, 114 PROC. NAT'L ACAD. OF SCI. 10324, 10325 (2017), www.pnas.org/content/114/39/10324/tab-article-info.
86. Emily Badger, *Whites Have Huge Wealth Edge Over Blacks (But Don't Know It)*, N.Y. TIMES (Sept. 18, 2017), www.nytimes.com/interactive/20 17/09/18/upshot/black-white-wealth-gap-perceptions.html.
87. *Id.*
88. ROBERT H. FRANK, SUCCESS AND LUCK: GOOD FORTUNE AND THE MYTH OF MERITOCRACY xiv (2016).
89. *Id.* at 8.
90. *See id.* at 21 (explaining the concept of hindsight bias in a nonracial context).
91. *See* KENDI, *supra* note 14, at 9.
92. *See* Thornburg v. Gingles, 478 U.S. 30, 62 (1986) ("For purposes of § 2, the legal concept of racially polarized voting incorporates neither causation nor intent. It means simply that the race of voters correlates with the selection of a certain candidate or candidates; that is, it refers to the situation where different races (or minority language groups) vote in blocs for different candidates.").
93. *See* League of United Latin American Citizens, Council No. 4434 v. Clements, 999 F.2d 831, 908 (1993) (King, J., dissenting) ("Requiring minority plaintiffs to come forward with a multivariate regression analysis to determine the causes of racially divergent voting patterns" would import "junk science" into the Voting Rights Act because "it [becomes] difficult, if not impossible, to untangle the effects of each variable") (internal quotes omitted).

94. *See, e.g.,* Keith Reeves, Voting Hopes or Fears? White Voters, Black Candidates & Racial Politics in America (1997).
95. Desert Palace, Inc. v. Costa, 539 U.S. 90, 100 (2003) (internal quotations omitted).
96. *See id.* ("The adequacy of circumstantial evidence also extends beyond civil cases; we have never questioned the sufficiency of circumstantial evidence in support of a criminal conviction, even though proof beyond a reasonable doubt is required.").
97. *Id.* (internal quotations omitted).
98. 42 U.S.C. § 2000e-2(a)(1) ("It shall be an unlawful employment practice for an employer . . . to fail or refuse to hire or to discharge any individual, or otherwise to discriminate against any individual with respect to his compensation, terms, conditions, or privileges of employment, because of such individual's race, color, religion, sex, or national origin . . .").
99. *See, e.g.,* Zarda v. Altitude Express, Inc., 883 F.3d 100, 124 (2d Cir. 2018) (aligning with the Fifth, Sixth and Eleventh Circuit Courts of Appeals and concluding that "where an employee is subjected to adverse action because an employer disapproves of interracial association, the employee suffers discrimination because of the employee's *own* race.") (internal quotations omitted).
100. *See, e.g.,* Parr v. Woodmen of the World Life Ins. Co., 791 F.2d 888, 892 (11th Cir. 1986) ("Where a plaintiff claims discrimination based upon an interracial marriage or association, he alleges, by definition, that he has been discriminated against because of *his* race. It makes no difference whether the plaintiff specifically alleges in his complaint that he has been discriminated against because of *his* race.") (emphasis in the original); Taylor v. Western & Southern Life Ins. Co., 966 F.2d 1188, 1197 (7th Cir. 1992).
101. Jones v. Okla. City Public Schools, 617 F.3d 1273, 1280 (10th Cir. 2010).
102. Reeves v. Sanderson Plumbing Products, Inc. 530 U.S. 133, 147 (2000).
103. *See* Furnco Constr. Corp. v. Waters, 438 U.S. 567, 577 (1978).
104. Vega, *supra* note 43.
105. Jones v. Okla. City Pubic Schools, 617 F.3d at 1277.
106. Desert Palace, Inc. v. Costa, 539 U.S. at 96; 42 U.S.C. § 2000e-2(m).
107. 42 U.S.C. § 2000e-2(m) ("Except as otherwise provided in this subchapter, an unlawful employment practice is established when the complaining party demonstrates that race, color, religion, sex, or national origin was a motivating factor for any employment practice, even though other factors also motivated the practice.").
108. Village of Arlington Heights v. Metro. Hous. Dev. Corp., 429 U.S. 252, 265–66 (1977) (footnotes omitted). Only in the unusual case involving redistricting do courts search for a hierarchy of motives and attempt to determine whether race "predominated" in the decision-making

process. *See* Miller v. Johnson, 515 U.S. 900, 915–16 (1995) (announcing a "predominance" test for race in redistricting because redistricting legislatures are almost always aware of the race of the voters being assigned to districts, and "[t]he courts, in assessing the sufficiency of a challenge to a districting plan, must be sensitive to the complex interplay of forces that enter a legislature's redistricting calculus."). *Miller's* rationale for departing from traditional antidiscrimination precepts and requiring a showing of "predominance" is unsatisfactory and lends itself to discrimination against minority opportunity districts. *See* Terry Smith, *Reinventing Black Politics: Senate Districts, Minority Vote Dilution and the Preservation of the Second Reconstruction*, 25 HASTINGS CONST. L.Q. 277, 316–17 (1998) ("Absent patterns of residential segregation that characterize historically Black congressional districts, legislators will usually have to consciously employ more race to create a majority-minority district than is used to create a White district ... The result is that majority-minority districts will inevitably be challenged with more regularity and greater success than majority-White districts ...").

109. Josh Dawsey, *In Reversal, Giuliani Now Says Trump Should Do Interview with Mueller Team*, WASH. POST (May 23, 2018), www.washi ngtonpost.com/politics/in-reversal-giuliani-now-says-trump-should-do-i nterview-with-mueller-team/2018/05/23/82f8fa24-5eb8-11e8-9ee3-49d6 d4814c4c_story.html?utm_term=.edo55f9ce857.

110. Paul Butler, *Racially Based Jury Nullification: Black Power in the Criminal Justice System*, 105 Yale L.J. 677 (1995).

111. 26 F. Cas. 1323 (C.C.D. Mass. 1851).

112. Ronald Brownstein, *Will Blue-Collar Whites Change Their Minds About Obamacare?*, THE ATLANTIC (Jan. 5, 2017), www.theatlantic.com/poli tics/archive/2017/01/blue-collar-whites-obamacare/512159.

113. Karen Tumulty & Philip Rucker, *Shouting Match Erupts Between Clinton and Trump Aides*, WASH. POST (Dec. 1, 2016), www.washingtonpost.com/ politics/shouting-match-erupts-between-clinton-and-trump-aides/2016 /12/01/7ac4398e-b7ea-11e6-b8df-600bd9d38a02_story.html? utm_term=.1288962d73bd.

THE SIRENS OF WHITE NATIONALISM

1. Peter Baker, *"Use That Word!": Trump Embraces the "Nationalist" Label*, N.Y. TIMES (Oct. 23, 2018), www.nytimes.com/2018/10/23/us/pol itics/nationalist-president-trump.html.

2. 85 F.3d 1074, 1082 (3d Cir. 1996).

3. *Id.* (internal quotations omitted).

4. Baker, *supra* note 1.

5. Baker, *supra* note 1.

6. Mollie Reilly, *Paul Ryan: "Inner City" Remarks Had Nothing to Do With Race*, HUFFINGTON POST (Mar. 13, 2014, 1:24 PM), www.huffpost.com/entry/paul-ryan-inner-city_n_4957733?guccounte r=1&guce_referrer=aHR0cHM6Ly93d3cuZ29vZ2xlLmNvbS88&guce_ref errer_sig=AQAAANwf7QDMgVV1OvwmB48NaVgkcF2x2-0xkF1JTh8c CyS5guTLyY3m_AUH1Fo2FTROcWSdgoOz7h8bN7ez-qGPdYaTQhP nnOc95c97FirCULExSUle_3wFkePlh_fUTm0EDMuQ7g8Am2SVO N2KUF8oUs58AYWakpniV0TT8LsCFAdh.

7. Richard Dvorak, *Cracking the Code: "De-Coding" Colorblind Slurs During the Congressional Crack Cocaine Debates*, 5 MICH. J. RACE & L. 611, 630 n.78 (2000) ("The term 'family values,' linked as it often is with welfare and single motherhood, easily becomes a code word for race just as 'welfare dependency,' 'inner city,' and the 'urban underclass,' have.").

8. Heather Caygle, *Ryan: Trump's Comments "Textbook Definition" of Racism*, POLITICO (June 7, 2016, 2:33 PM), www.politico.com/story/2016 /06/paul-ryan-trump-judge-223991.

9. *Id.*

10. *See* James E. Dobbins & Judith H. Skillings, *Racism as a Clinical Syndrome*, 70 AM. J. ORTHOPSYCHIATRY 14, 21 (2000).

11. *See* CAROL M. SWAIN, THE NEW WHITE NATIONALISM IN AMERICA: ITS CHALLENGE TO INTEGRATION 3–5 (2002) (discussing the new white nationalistic movement by comparing the present white nationalism to past white supremacist groups such as the KKK and the Nazi Party).

12. *Id.* at 5.

13. *Id.* at 29.

14. TERRY SMITH, BARACK OBAMA, POST-RACIALISM, AND THE NEW POLITICS OF TRIANGULATION 22–23 (2012).

15. RONALD W. WALTERS, WHITE NATIONALISM, BLACK INTERESTS: CONSERVATIVE PUBLIC POLICY AND THE BLACK COMMUNITY 15–16 (2003).

16. *Id.* at 25.

17. *Id.*

18. MIKE WENDLING, ALT-RIGHT: FROM 4CHAN TO THE WHITE HOUSE 1–3 (2018).

19. *See id.* at 45.

20. Sean McElwee, *Anatomy of a Trump Voter: How Racism Propelled Trump to the Republican Nomination*, SALON (July 23, 2016, 2:30 PM), www.sal on.com/2016/07/23/anatomy_of_a_trump_voter_how_racism_propelled_ trump_to_the_republican_nomination.

21. *Id.*

22. Abigail Geiger, *16 Striking Findings from 2016*, PEW RES. CTR. (Dec. 21, 2016), www.pewresearch.org/fact-tank/2016/12/21/16-striking-findings-from-2016.

23. *See* WALTERS, *supra* note 15, at 29. Justice John Paul Stevens understood this proposition better than most on the Supreme Court in the post-Civil Rights era: "[I]t is the very political power of a racial or ethnic group that creates a danger that an entrenched majority will take action contrary to the group's political interests." *See* Rogers v. Lodge, 458 U.S. 613, 651 (1982) (Stevens, J., dissenting).

24. Sarah Posner, *How Donald Trump's New Campaign Chief Created an Online Haven for White Nationalists*, MOTHER JONES (Aug. 22, 2016), www.motherjones.com/politics/2016/08/stephen-bannon-donald-trump-alt-right-breitbart-news.

25. Jonathan Martin, Jim Rutenberg, & Maggie Haberman, *Donald Trump Appoints Media Firebrand to Run Campaign*, N.Y. TIMES (Aug. 17, 2016), www.nytimes.com/2016/08/18/us/politics/donald-trump-stephen-bannon-paul-manafort.html.

26. Eli Watkins & James Gary, *Bannon: "Let Them Call You Racists,"* CNN (Mar. 11, 2018, 11:09 AM), www.cnn.com/2018/03/10/politics/steve-bannon-national-front/index.html.

27. *See* WENDLING, *supra* note 18, at 4.

28. Christine Mai-Duc, *The "Angry Man's Candidate": George Wallace and the Roots of the American Independent Party*, L.A. TIMES (Apr. 17, 2016), http://static.latimes.com/american-independent-history.

29. *Id.*

30. Marianne Worthington, *The Campaign Rhetoric of George Wallace in the 1968 Presidential Election*, https://inside.ucumberlands.edu/downloads/academics/history/vol4/MarianneWorthington92.html (last visited July 15, 2019, 6:45 PM).

31. Richard Pearson, *Former Ala. Gov. George C. Wallace Dies*, WASH. POST (Sept. 14, 1998), www.washingtonpost.com/wp-srv/politics/daily/sept98/wallace.htm.

32. *Id.*

33. *See* SMITH, *supra* note 14, at 22 (discussing judicial decisions rooted in conservative ideology that foreseeably disadvantage blacks).

34. Nia-Malika Henderson, *Steve Scalise Spoke to White Nationalists in 2002. His Days as GOP Whip Could Be Numbered.*, WASH. POST (Dec. 29, 2014), www.washingtonpost.com/news/the-fix/wp/2014/12/29/steve-scalise-spoke-to-white-nationalists-in-2002-his-days-as-gop-whip-could-be-numbered/?utm_term=.6832a9858dd6.

35. *Id.*

36. *See id.*

37. *Id.*

38. *Id.*

39. Ryu Spaeth, *Steve Scalise Reportedly Said He Was "Like David Duke Without the Baggage,"* THE WEEK (Jan. 1, 2015), http://theweek.com/sp eedreads/440133/steve-scalise-reportedly-said-like-david-duke-without-baggage.

40. Jeremy Alford, *Much of David Duke's '91 Campaign is Now Louisiana Mainstream,* N.Y. TIMES (Dec. 31, 2014), www.nytimes.com/2015/01/01/us/politics/much-of-david-dukes-91-campaign-is-now-in-louisiana-main stream.html.

41. *See* Will Bunch, *Tea Party's Roots Lie in Backlash against Obama,* CNN (Sept. 30, 2010), www.cnn.com/2010/OPINION/09/29/bunch .tea.party (arguing that the formation of the Tea Party, with its radical views and racial undertones, was a direct response to the election of an African American president).

42. SMITH, *supra* note 14, at 51.

43. SMITH, *supra* note 14, at 51.

44. SMITH, *supra* note 14, at 51.

45. *See* SMITH, *supra* note 14, at 51 (highlighting a study conducted by *The New York Times* that found 25 percent of Tea Party supporters likely to believe that Obama favors blacks over whites).

46. *See* John Cassidy, *The G.O.P.'s Ties to Extremism Go Beyond the Confederate Flag,* NEW YORKER (June 23, 2015), www.newyorker.com/n ews/john-cassidy/the-g-o-p-s-extremism-problem-goes-beyond-the-confed erate-flag (expressing that Republicans rely on white southern males who tend to lean to the far right with racist ideals).

47. *Id.*

48. *See* Jerome Taylor, *Dimensionalization of Racialism, in* BLACK PSYCHOLOGY 637, 640–41 (R.L. Jones ed., 1980) (listing the following as social variables: social effect, internalization, identification, utilitarianism or instrumentalism, frustration–aggression–displacement, and ego defense). Taylor defines social effect as those circumstances when "a person may come to adopt a racialistic position not because he/she believed deeply in it, but because its momentary endorsement brings social approval or averts social reproval." *Id.* at 640.

49. Karen Tumulty & Jose A. DelReal, *Shrill Rhetoric in the GOP Primary Race Could Come Back to Haunt the Party,* WASH. POST (Sept. 22, 2015), www.washingtonpost.com/politics/shrill-rhetoric-in-the-gop-primary-rac e-could-come-back-to-haunt-the-party/2015/09/22/f879cc90-6151-11e5-8e9 e-dce8a2a2a679_story.html?utm_term=.d068993ce81c.

50. *Id.*

51. Howell Raines, *George Wallace, Segregation Symbol, Dies at 79,* N.Y. TIMES (Sept. 14, 1998), www.nytimes.com/1998/09/14/us/george-wallace-segregation-symbol-dies-at-79.html?pagewanted=all.

52. Sophie Tatum, *GOP Congressional Candidate: Diversity Is "a Bunch of Crap and Un-American,"* CNN (June 12, 2018, 2:36 PM), www .cnn.com/2018/06/11/politics/republican-new-jersey-diversity/index.html.

53. David Duke, *The Hidden Massive Racial Discrimination in America Against Whites,* FOR HUM. FREEDOM & DIVERSITY (Jan. 8, 2018), http://david duke.com/the-real-racial-discrimination-that-goes-on-in-america.

54. Marc Caputo, *After Offensive Comment, Miami State Senator Fends Off Calls for Resignation, Condemnation,* POLITICO (Apr. 18, 2017, 10:15 PM), www.politico.com/states/florida/story/2017/04/miami-state-senator-fends-off-calls-for-resignation-condemnation-111347.

55. Jane Coaston, *Virginia Republicans Just Nominated an Alt-Right Hero to Run for Senate,* VOX (Jun. 13, 2018, 12:01 PM), www.vox.com/2018/6/13/17458452/alt-right-corey-stewart-virginia-gop.

56. Bristow Marchant, *White, Black Southerners Both Feel "Under Attack," Split on Hot-Button Issues,* STATE (Nov. 8, 2017), www.thestate.com/ne ws/politics-government/article183396531.html.

57. Coaston, *supra* note 55.

58. *Id.*; Tara Golshan, *Paul Nehlen, the Alt-Right Candidate Running for Paul Ryan's Seat, Explained,* VOX (Apr. 12, 2018, 11:10 AM), www.vox.com/policy-and-politics/2018/4/12/17224086/paul-nehlen-alt-right-paul-ryan-race.

59. Maggie Astor, *Fact Check: Corey Stewart, Republicans and the Fringe Right,* N.Y. TIMES (June 13, 2018), www.nytimes.com/2018/06/13/us/poli tics/corey-stewart-virginia.html.

60. *Id.*

61. Coaston, *supra* note 55.

62. *Virginia Dep't of Elections, 2018 June Republican Primary: Official Results,* VIRGINIA.GOV, https://results.elections.virginia.gov/vaelections/2018%20June%20Republican%20Primary/Site/Congress.html (last visited July 6, 2018); *Virginia Dep't of Elections, Electronic Database,* VIRGINIA .GOV, http://historical.elections.virginia.gov/elections/search/year_ from:2017/year_to:2017/office_id:3/stage:Primaries (last visited July 6, 2018).

63. Monique Judge, *Virginia Lawmaker Says He Can't Be Racist Because His Son Is Named After a Black Man,* THE ROOT (July 9, 2018, 9:01 PM), https://www.theroot.com/virginia-lawmaker-says-he-can-t-be-racist-becau se-his-s-1827464407.

64. Ronald Brownstein, *Johnston Beats Duke, 54–43%, in Louisiana,* L.A. TIMES (Oct. 7, 1990), www.latimes.com/archives/la-xpm-1990-10-07-mn-2993-story.html.

65. *Id.*

66. Eric Bradner, *Huckabee: MLK Would Be "Appalled" by Black Lives Matter Movement,* CNN (Aug. 18, 2015, 7:37 PM), www.cnn.com/2015/08/18/politics/mike-huckabee-black-lives-matter-martin-luther-king.

67. *Id.*

68. Lucy Madison, *Santorum Targets Blacks in Entitlement Reform*, CBS NEWS (Jan. 3, 2012, 6:35 PM), www.cbsnews.com/news/santorum-tar gets-blacks-in-entitlement-reform; Angel Clark, *Racist Rick Santorum: "I Don't Want to Make Black Peoples Lives Better*,*"* YOUTUBE (Jan. 2, 2012), www.youtube.com/watch?v=MdfZmcuomcE.

69. *See* Clark, *supra* note 68.

70. Aaron Blake & Nia-Malika Henderson, *Rick Santorum Drops Out of the Presidential Race*, WASH. POST (Apr. 10, 2012), www.washingtonpost.co m/blogs/the-fix/post/rick-santorum-drops-out-of-the-presidential-race/201 2/04/10/gIQACvaV8S_blog.html.

71. *Romney Blames Loss on Obama's "Gifts" to Minorities and Young Voters*, N.Y. TIMES (Nov. 14, 2012), http://thecaucus.blogs.nytimes.co m/2012/11/14/romney-blames-loss-on-obamas-gifts-to-minorities-and-yo ung-voters/.

72. Charles M. Blow, *Jeb Bush, "Free Stuff" and Black Folks*, N.Y. TIMES (Sept. 28, 2015), www.nytimes.com/2015/09/28/opinion/charles-m-blow-j eb-bush-free-stuff-and-black-folks.html?action=click&pgtype=Homepag e&module=opinion-c-col-left-region&region=opinion-c-col-left-region& WT.nav=opinion-c-col-left-region&_r=0.

73. Rachel Wetts & Robb Willer, *Privilege on the Precipice: Perceived Racial Status Threats Lead White Americans to Oppose Welfare Programs*, SOCIAL FORCES (May 31, 2018), at 1, 2.

74. *Id.* at 15; Blow, *supra* note 72 (reporting on Gingrich's "greatest food stamp president" remark and arguing that the problem is not that blacks want free stuff, but rather the inability for the black community to find work that pays a living wage).

75. Wetts & Willer, *supra* note 73, at 21.

76. Wetts & Willer, *supra* note 73, at 21.

77. Wetts & Willer, *supra* note 73, at 21.

78. Isaac Stanley-Becker, *"A Hit Dog Will Holler": The Old Proverb by Andrew Gillum to Suggest Ron DeSantis Harbors Racist Views*, WASH. POST (Oct. 25, 2018), www.washingtonpost.com/nation/2018/10/25/hit-dog-will-holler-old-pro verb-used-by-andrew-gillum-suggest-ron-desantis-harbors-racist-views/? utm_term=.4a37bd8d7846.

79. Phil Willon, *Kamala Harris Breaks a Color Barrier with Her U.S. Senate Win*, L.A. TIMES (Nov. 8, 2016), www.latimes.com/politics/la-pol-ca-sen ate-race-kamala-harris-wins-20161108-story.html.

80. The New York Times, *California U.S. Senate Results: Kamala Harris Wins*, N.Y. TIMES (Aug. 1, 2017), www.nytimes.com/elections/results/ca lifornia-senate.

81. *See* Peter Jamison & Scott Clement, *Virginians Are Split on Governor's Fate Amid Blackface Scandal, Poll Shows*, WASH. POST (Feb. 9, 2019),

www.washingtonpost.com/local/virginia-politics/virginians-split-on-gover
nors-fate-amid-blackface-scandal-poll-shows/2019/02/09/93002e84-2bc1-11
e9-b011-d8500644dc98_story.html?utm_term=.6132710b3815.

82. *Richard Bertrand Spencer*, S. Poverty L. Ctr, www.splcenter.org/
fighting-hate/extremist-files/individual/richard-bertrand-spencer-0 (last
visited July 9, 2018).

83. William D. Cohan, *How Stephen Miller Rode White Rage from Duke's
Campus to Trump's West Wing*, Vanity Fair (May 10, 2017),
www.vanityfair.com/news/2017/05/stephen-miller-duke-donald-trump.

84. Grace Guarnieri, *With Trump Advisor Stephen Miller in Charge of
Immigration, "We Are Going Nowhere" GOP Senator Says*, Newsweek
(Jan. 21, 2018, 4:56 PM), www.newsweek.com/trump-advisor-stephen-mil
ler-immigration-786346.

85. Frank Miles, *Stephen Miller Calls CNN "Extraordinarily Biased" After
Chaotic Jake Tapper Interview, Denies Being Escorted Off Set*, Fox News
(Jan. 8, 2018), www.foxnews.com/politics/2018/01/08/stephen-miller-calls-
cnn-extraordinarily-biased-after-chaotic-jake-tapper-interview-denies-bei
ng-escorted-off-set.html.

86. Reforming American Immigration for a Strong Economy Act, 2017 U.S.
Library Cong. § 2192 (2017), *available at* www.cotton.senate.gov/files/
documents/170802_New_RAISE_Act_Bill_Text.pdf.

87. *Id.*

88. Miriam Jordan, *Diversity Visa Lottery: Inside the Program that Admitted
a Terror Suspect*, N.Y. Times (Nov. 1, 2017), www.nytimes.com/2017/11/
01/us/diversity-visa-lottery.html.

89. *See* Justin Gest, *Points-Based Immigration Was Meant to Reduce Racial
Bias. It Doesn't*, The Guardian (Jan. 19, 2018) (citing scholarly studies),
www.theguardian.com/commentisfree/2018/jan/19/points-based-immigra
tion-racism.

90. Village of Arlington Heights v. Metro. Hous. Dev. Corp., 429 U.S. 252, 266
(1977).

91. Peter Baker & Katie Rogers, *In Trump's America, the Conversation Turns
Ugly and Angry, Starting at the Top*, N.Y. Times (June 20, 2018), www
.nytimes.com/2018/06/20/us/politics/trump-language-immigration.html?
hp&action=click&pgtype=Homepage&clickSource=story-heading&mo
dule=b-lede-package-region&region=top-news&WT.nav=top-news.

92. Betsy Klein & Kevin Liptak, *Trump Ramps Up Rhetoric: Dems Want "Illegal
Immigrants" to "Infest Our Country,"* CNN (June 19, 2018, 2:45 PM),
www.cnn.com/2018/06/19/politics/trump-illegal-immigrants-infest/index.
html.

93. Brooks v. Davey Tree Expert Co., 478 Fed. Appx. 934, 943 (6th Cir. 2012)
(distinguishing the Sixth Circuit's approach to the honest belief defense
from the Seventh Circuit's "bare honest belief" approach, which is more

deferential to the employer's proffered legitimate nondiscriminatory reason for its action).

94. Christopher Ingraham, *Two Charts Demolish the Notion that Immigrants Here Illegally Commit More Crime*, Wash. Post: Wonkblog (June 19, 2018), www.washingtonpost.com/news/wonk/wp/2018/06/19/two-charts-demolish-the-notion-that-immigrants-here-illeg ally-commit-more-crime/?utm_term=.002f49b9ef57.

95. *Trump Dismisses Stats Showing Low Immigrant Criminality*, Wash. Post (June 22, 2018), https://www.washingtonpost.com/video/politics/o ther/trump-dismisses-stats-showing-low-immigrant-criminality/2018/06/22/ef934018-7650-11e8-bda1-18e53a448a14_video.html.

96. Vanessa Friedman, *Melania Trump, Agent of Coat Chaos*, N.Y. Times (June 21, 2018), www.nytimes.com/2018/06/21/style/zara-jacket-melania-t rump.html.

97. Jonathan Chait, *White House: Trump Can't Be Racist Because He Was on Television*, N.Y. Mag. (Jan. 16, 2018), http://nymag.com/daily/intelligencer/2018/01/white-house-trump-cant-be-racist-because-he-was-on-tv.html.

98. Gregory J. Martin & Ali Yurukoglu, *Bias in Cable News: Persuasion and Polarization*, 107 Am. Econ. Rev. 2565, 2588–90 (Sept. 2017).

99. *Id.* at 2597.

100. Isabel V. Sawhill & Eleanor Krause, *Gauging the Role of Fox News in Our Electoral Divide*, Brookings (Sept. 20, 2017), www.brookings.edu/opinions/gauging-the-role-of-fox-news-in-our-electoral-divide.

101. Matt Wilstein, *Only 1% of Fox News Viewers Are Black*, Mediaite (Dec. 15, 2014), www.mediaite.com/tv/only-1-of-fox-news-viewers-are-black/ (reporting a 1 percent black viewership in 2014); Jason Johnson, *Politics Over Paycheck? The Life of a Black Host on Fox News*, The Root (May 22, 2017, 9:00 AM), www.theroot.com/politics-over-paycheck-the-life-of-a-black-host-on-fox-1795359908 (reporting on a black Fox News talk show host and a 1.5 percent black viewership); A.J. Katz, *More African-Americans Watched MSNBC Last Year Than Any Other Cable Network in Prime Time*, Adweek: TV Newser (Jan. 8, 2018), www.ad week.com/tvnewser/msnbc-is-the-no-1-prime-time-cable-network-amon g-african-american-viewers/354386.

102. Jennifer Rubin, *The Mainstreaming of Racism on Fox News*, Wash. Post (Oct. 26, 2016), www.washingtonpost.com/blogs/right-turn/wp/2016/10/26/the-mainstreaming-of-racism-on-fox-news/?utm_term=.a16e3e943361.

103. *Id.*

104. *See generally* Nicholas D. Kristof, *The Push to "Otherize" Obama*, N.Y. Times (Sept. 20, 2008), www.nytimes.com/2008/09/21/opinion/21kristof .html?_r=0&mtrref=undefined&gwh=5E27FDD0F0B115E9C0AE884

FA81519AF&gwt=pay&assetType=opinion (describing the campaign to "otherize" Obama and de-Americanize him by using religious prejudice as a proxy for racial prejudice).

105. *See* Jennifer Agiesta, *Misperceptions Persist About Obama's Faith, But Aren't So Widespread*, CNN (Sept. 14, 2015, 9:17 AM), https:// edition.cnn.com/2015/09/13/politics/barack-obama-religion-christian-misperceptions/index.html (distinguishing the misconceptions about Obama's religious beliefs versus those about his birthplace).

106. CHARLES J. SYKES, HOW THE RIGHT LOST ITS MIND 155 (2017).

107. Wilstein, *supra* note 101.

108. Sean McElwee, *Fox News' Shocking Racism Effect: The Alarming Statistical Relationships Underneath Conservative Viewing Habits*, SALON (June 23, 2015, 8:59 PM), www.salon.com/2015/06/23/fox_news_shocking_racism_effect_the_alarming_statistical_relationships_under neath_conservative_viewing_habits.

109. *Id.*

110. *Id.*

111. *Id.*

112. Blue Telusma, *Ann Coulter on Black Protestors: Haven't We Done "Enough" to Make Up For Slavery?*, GRIO (May 16, 2015), https://the grio.com/2015/05/16/ann-coulter-on-black-protestors-havent-we-done-en ough-to-make-up-for-slavery.

113. *See* Transcript of Oral Argument at 67–68, Fisher v. University of Texas, 136 S.Ct. 2198 (2016) (No.14-981), *available at* www.supremecourt.gov/ oral_arguments/argument_transcripts/2015/14-981_onjq.pdf.

114. 539 U.S. 306, 372 (2003) (Thomas, J., dissenting).

115. Parents Involved in Cmty. Sch. v. Seattle Sch. Dist. No. 1, 551 U.S. 701, 748 (2007).

116. Transcript of Oral Argument at 47, Shelby County v. Holder, 570 U.S. 529 (2013) (No. 12–96) (quoting Scalia, J.: "Now, I don't think that's attributable to the fact that it is so much clearer now that we need this. I think it is attributable, very likely attributable, to a phenomenon that is called perpetuation of racial entitlement.").

117. *Shelby County*, 570 U.S. at 540.

118. Matthew Yglesias, *Reagan's Race Record*, THE ATLANTIC (Nov. 9, 2007), www.theatlantic.com/politics/archive/2007/11/reagans-race-reco rd/46875.

119. 557 U.S. 557, 607 (2009) (Alito, J., concurring).

120. Tim Marcin, *40 Percent of Whites Think Black People Just Need to Try Harder, Poll Finds*, NEWSWEEK (Apr. 4, 2018, 6:08 PM), www.news week.com/forty-percent-whites-think-black-people-just-need-try-harder-equality-poll-872646.

121. Thomas B. Edsall, *What Donald Trump Understands About Republicans*, N.Y. TIMES (Sept. 2, 2015), www.nytimes.com/2015/09/02 /opinion/what-donald-trump-understands-about-republicans.html? emc=eta1.

122. Jenny R. Yang, *A Message from the Chair*, EEOC (Feb. 2016), www .eeoc.gov/eeoc/chair/african_american_history_month.cfm (reporting that African Americans filed 64 percent of all race discrimination charges handled by the EEOC in fiscal year 2015).

123. Justin Wise, *Senate Panel Advances Trump Nominee Who Wouldn't Say if Brown v. Board of Education was Decided Correctly*, THE HILL (May 24, 2018, 3:53 PM), http://thehill.com/policy/389256-senate-panel-advances-tr ump-nominee-who-wouldnt-say-if-brown-v-board-of-education-was.

124. George Zornick, *Trump Is Appointing Racist Fake-News Purveyors to the Federal Bench*, NATION (June 16, 2017), www.thenation.com/article/tru mp-is-appointing-racist-fake-news-purveyors-to-the-federal-bench.

125. *AFJ: Ninth Circuit Nominee Bounds Has History of Racist Statements*, ALLIANCE FOR JUST. (Feb. 2, 2018), www.afj.org/press-room/press-relea ses/afj-ninth-circuit-nominee-bounds-has-history-of-racist-statements.

126. Jordain Carney & Alexander Bolton, *Controversial Trump Judicial Nominee Withdraws*, THE HILL (July 19, 2018, 2:46 PM), https://the hill.com/blogs/floor-action/senate/397919-controversial-trump-judicial-nominee-withdraws. Senator Scott actually equivocated as to why he was withholding his support. *Id.* However, white conservatives were quick to demonstrate that they had no tolerance for a non-compliant black conservative. Daniel Horowitz of *The Conservative Review* lambasted Scott—and Senator Marco Rubio, who had indicated that he would vote no along with Scott—for "virtue-signaling," the meaning of which is opaque but clearly derogatory in Horowitz's eyes. *See* Daniel Horowitz, *Sens. Rubio and Scott Tanked Trump Nominee for Criticizing Multi-Culti PC in College*, CONSERVATIVE REV. (July 20, 2018), www.conser vativereview.com/news/sens-rubio-and-scott-tanked-trump-nominee-for-criticizing-multi-culti-pc-in-college.

127. *See* Robert Lindsey, *Rehnquist in Arizona: A Militant Conservative in 60's Politics*, N.Y. TIMES (Aug. 4, 1986), www.nytimes.com/1986/ 08/04/us/rehnquist-in-arizona-a-militant-conservative-in-60-s-politics. html.

128. *See* ROBIN DiAngelo, WHITE FRAGILITY: WHY IT'S SO HARD FOR WHITE PEOPLE TO TALK ABOUT RACISM 2 (2018). According to DiAngelo, who is white and has written her book from the perspective of a white American, for the typical white person,

The smallest amount of racial stress is intolerable—the mere sugges-tion that being white has meaning often triggers a range of defensive responses. These include emotions such as anger, fear, and guilt and behaviors such as argumentation, silence, and withdrawal from the stress-inducing situation. These responses work to reinstate white equilibrium as they repel the challenge, return our racial comfort, and maintain our dominance within the racial hierarchy.

129. *Id.* at 123–24.
130. John Harwood, *Bill Kristol Takes on Fox News, Tucker Carlson: "I Don't Know If It's Racism Exactly—but Ethno-Nationalism of Some Kind,"* CNBC (Jan. 25, 2018, 7:00 AM), www.cnbc.com/2018/01/24/bill-kristol-takes-on-fox-news-tucker-carlson.html.
131. Jon Levine, *Tucker Carlson Slaps Back After Bill Kristol Calls Fox News Show "Close to Racism,"* YAHOO (Jan. 25, 2018), www.yahoo.com/entertainment/tucker-carlson-slaps-back-bill-kristol-calls-fox-160115298.html.
132. Jane Coaston, *Watch: Tucker Carlson Rails Against America's Demographic Changes,* VOX (Mar. 21, 2018, 12:05 PM), www.vox.com/2018/3/21/17146866/tucker-carlson-demographics-immigration-fox-news.
133. Judd Legum, *The Unrepentant Racism of Tucker Carlson Tonight,* THINK PROGRESS (Jan. 18, 2018), https://thinkprogress.org/the-unrepentant-racism-of-tucker-carlson-tonight-199c79157cb6.
134. Erik Wemple, *Tucker Carlson's Racist "Diversity" Rant Rebutted by . . . Rudy Giuliani,* WASH. POST (Sept. 11, 2018), www.washingtonpost.com/blogs/erik-wemple/wp/2018/09/11/tucker-carlsons-racist-diversity-rant-rebutted-by-rudy-giuliani/?utm_term=.c420f889260f.
135. Niraj Chokshi, *Steve Schmidt, Longtime G.O.P. Strategist, Quits "Corrupt" and "Immoral" Party,* N.Y. TIMES (June 20, 2018), www.nytimes.com/2018/06/20/us/politics/party-of-trump-steve-schmidt.html.
136. Jeremy W. Peters, *As Critics Assail Trump, His Supporters Dig in Deeper,* N.Y. TIMES (June 23, 2018), www.nytimes.com/2018/06/23/us/politics/republican-voters-trump.html?hp&action=click&pgtype=Homepage&clickSource=story-heading&module=first-column-region&region=top-news&WT.nav=top-news.

LAW AS PRETEXT

1. 438 U.S. 265, 295–96 (1978) (Powell, J.) (plurality opinion announcing the judgment of the Court).
2. *See, e.g.,* MATTHEW FRYE JACOBSON, WHITENESS OF A DIFFERENT COLOR: EUROPEAN IMMIGRANTS AND THE ALCHEMY OF RACE 91–135 (1998) (describing the formation of a unitary "Caucasian" race in the U.S. circa 1924).

3. Tim Marcin, *40 Percent of Whites Think Black People Just Need to Try Harder, Poll Finds*, NEWSWEEK: U.S. (Apr. 4, 2018), www.newsweek.co m/forty-percent-whites-think-black-people-just-need-try-harder-equality-poll-872646.

4. Darren Lenard Hutchinson, *Factless Jurisprudence*, 34 COLUM. HUM. RTS. L. REV. 615, 616 (2003).

5. Max Mitchell, *Judge Who Stirred Controversy With Tweet Unlikely to Face Discipline, Experts Say*, LAW.COM (July 23, 2018, 5:31 PM), www.law.co m/2018/07/23/judge-who-stirred-controversy-with-tweet-unlikely-to-face-d iscipline-experts-say/?cmp=share_twitter.

6. Adam Liptak, *New Look at an Old Memo Casts More Doubt on Rehnquist*, N.Y. TIMES (Mar. 19, 2012), www.nytimes.com/2012/03/20/u s/new-look-at-an-old-memo-casts-more-doubt-on-rehnquist.html (quoting Rehnquist's 1952 memo to Jackson).

7. Erin Kelley, *Racism & Felony Disenfranchisement: An Intertwined History*, BRENNAN CTR. J. (May 19, 2017), www.brennancenter.org/pub lication/racism-felony-disenfranchisement-intertwined-history.

8. Richardson v. Ramirez, 418 U.S. 24, 43 (1974).

9. *Id.*

10. *See* Shelley v. Kraemer, 334 U.S. 1, 19 (1948) (holding that judicial enforcement of racially restrictive residential covenants constitutes state action).

11. *See, e.g.*, Peña-Rodriguez v. Colorado, 137 S.Ct. 855 (2017).

12. Melissa Hart, *Subjective Decisonmaking and Unconscious Discrimination*, 56 ALA. L. REV. 741, 746 (2005).

13. Alma Cohen & Crystal S. Yang, *Judicial Politics and Sentencing Decisions*, HARV. L. SCHOLAR, May 2018, at 1–2, https://scholar.har vard.edu/files/cyang/files/cohen_yang_march2018.pdf.

14. *Id.* at 14 and 16.

15. *Id.* at 20.

16. *Id.*

17. Robert Bird & Frank Newport, *White Racial Resentment Before, During Obama Years*, GALLUP (May 19, 2017), https://news.gallup.com/opinion/ polling-matters/210914/white-racial-resentment-before-during-obama-years.aspx.

18. Pat K. Chew & Robert E. Kelley, *Myth of the Colorblind Judge: An Empirical Analysis of Racial Harassment Cases*, 86 WASH. U. L. REV. 1117, 1144 (2009).

19. Cass R. Sunstein, David Schkade & Lisa Michelle Ellman, *Ideological Voting on Federal Courts of Appeals: A Preliminary Investigation*, 90 VA. L. REV. 301, 312 n.28 (2004).

20. *Id.* at 324.

21. *Id.* at 319.

22. Sean Sullivan, *Gorsuch: "No Such Thing" as Dem or GOP Judges*, Wash. Post (Mar. 21, 2018), www.washingtonpost.com/politics/2017/live-updat es/trump-white-house/neil-gorsuch-confirmation-hearings-updates-and-a nalysis-on-the-supreme-court-nominee/gorsuch-no-such-thing-as-dem-or-gop-judges/?utm_term=.1d76c1db96f4.

23. Kate Sullivan, Ariane de Vogue & Sarah Westwood, *Kavanaugh Writes Op-Ed Arguing He is an "Independent, Impartial Judge" After Emotional Testimony*, CNN (Oct. 5, 2018, 7:14 AM), www.cnn.com/2018/10/04/ politics/kavanaugh-wsj-op-ed/index.html.

24. Pew Research Center, *4. Race, Immigration and Discrimination*, Pew Res. Ctr. (Oct. 5, 2017), www.people-press.org/2017/10/05/4-race-immi gration-and-discrimination.

25. *Id.*

26. *Id.*

27. Domenico Montanaro, *NPR Poll: 2 in 3 Support Legal Status for DREAMers; Majority Oppose Building a Wall*, NPR (Feb. 6, 2018, 5:00 AM), www.npr.org/2018/02/06/583402634/npr-poll-2-in-3-support-legal-status-for-dreamers-majority-oppose-building-a-wal.

28. Ibram X. Kendi, Stamped from the Beginning: The Definitive History of Racist Ideas in America 11 (2016).

29. Felicia Pratto, James Sidanius, Lisa M. Stallworth, & Bertram F. Malle, *Social Dominance Orientation: A Personality Variable Predicting Social and Political Attitudes*, 67 J. Personality & Soc. Psychol. 741, 741 (1994), *available at* https://dash.harvard.edu/bitstream/handle/1/3207 711/sidanius_socialdominanceorientation.pdf?sequence=1.

30. *Id.*

31. *Id.* at 742.

32. *Id.* at 743 and 750–51.

33. *See* Pratto et al., *supra* note 29, at 754 ("SDO strongly and consistently related to belief in a number of hierarchy-legitimizing myths, most strongly to anti-Black racism and nationalism"); *id.* at 756 (noting that the correlation between conservatism and racism is in fact driven by SDO).

34. David Simson, *Fool Me Once, Shame on You, Fool Me Twice, Shame on You Again: How Disparate Treatment Doctrine Perpetuates Racial Hierarchy*, 59 Hous. L. Rev. 1033, 1041 & 1057 (2019).

35. Pat K. Chew & Robert E. Kelley, *The Racialism of Race in Judicial Decision Making: An Empirical Analysis of Plaintiffs' Race and Judges' Race*, 28 Harv. J. Racial & Ethnic Just. 91, 103–04 (2012).

36. *Id.* at 105–06. Unlike in their earlier study covering a different sample and date range, Chew and Kelley did not find in this study a difference in the behavior of Democratic and Republican-appointed judges; *id.* at 104. Their explanation for this difference—reduced partisanship in more recent judicial appointees—is unsatisfying. *Id.* at n.45.

37. *Id.* at 99.
38. *See* Cohen & Yang, *supra* note 13, at 1–2.
39. David Arnold, Will Dobbie, & Crystal S. Yang, *Racial Bias in Bail Decisions*, HARV. L. SCHOLAR, May 2018, at 1, 29–30, https://scholar.ha rvard.edu/files/cyang/files/ady_racialbias.pdf.
40. LINN WASHINGTON, BLACK JUDGES ON JUSTICE 71 (1994).
41. *Id.* at 147.
42. GBA Strategies, *2017 State of the State Courts — Survey Analysis*, National Center for State Courts 13 (Nov. 15, 2017), www.ncsc.org/~/media/Files/PDF/Topics/Public%20Trust%20and%20Confidence/SoSc-2017-Survey-Analysis.ashx.
43. *Id.*
44. WASHINGTON, *supra* note 40, at 122. Symbolic diversity, of course, has its limitations as a conduit for substantive justice for people of color. Justice Clarence Thomas's tenure on the Supreme Court starkly illustrates this point. Still, Judge Keith's observation is consistent with the empirical data on judging: the race and partisan affiliation of the judge matter. What Keith observed regarding the Sixth Circuit was in fact true of Reagan's and George H. W.'s judicial appointments more generally. Of 358 judges confirmed under President Reagan, a mere seven were black. Jonathan K. Stubbs, *A Demographic History of Federal Judicial Appointments by Sex and Race: 1789–2016*, 26 BERKELEY LA RAZA L. J. 96, 107 (2016). Of Bush's 187 confirmed appointments to the federal bench, a mere 11 were African American. *Id.* And by Judge Keith's logic, Donald Trump is blaring a message of exclusion to the judiciary and the country. In the first year of his presidency, Trump nominated 69 federal judges, the most since Ronald Reagan during a comparable period. Seventy-one percent of the nominees were white males, and 21 percent were white females. Kate Harloe, *These Charts Show How White, Male, and Conservative Trump's Judicial Nominees Have Been*, MOTHER JONES (Mar./Apr. 2018), www.motherjones.com/politics/2018/03/these-charts-show-how-white-male-and-conservative-trumps-judicial-nominees-have-been/. Thus, despite the fact that the federal judiciary itself is only 73 percent white (*see id.*), 92 percent of President Trump's judicial nominees were white, proving that neither justice nor President Trump is blind.
45. *See* Jerry Kang, *Implicit Bias and the Pushback from the Left*, 54 ST. LOUIS UNIV. L.J. 1139, 1139 (2010).
46. Jeffrey J. Rachlinski, Sheri Lynn Johnson, Andrew J. Wistrich, & Chris Guthrie, *Does Unconscious Racial Bias Affect Trial Judges?*, 84 NOTRE DAME L. REV. 1195, 1205–06 (2009).
47. *Id.* at 1198–1200.
48. *Id.* at 1199.

49. *Id.* This conclusion is based on what is called the "response latency" of white participants:

> Most white Americans complete the first task (in which they sort white and good from black and bad) more quickly than the second (in which they sort black and good from white and bad). In other words, most white Americans produce higher response latencies when faced with the stereotype-incongruent pairing (white/bad or black/good) than when faced with the stereotype-congruent pairing (white/good or black/bad).

50. *Id.* at 1210.

51. *Id.* at 2110–11. The authors of the study caution, however, that it is difficult to draw conclusions from this gap because:

> First, we did not vary the order in which we presented the materials, and this order effect could have led to artificially higher IAT scores. Second, the judges performed both trials much more slowly than the other adults with whom we are making this comparison, and this, too, could have led to artificially higher IAT scores. We also suspect that the judges were older, on average, than the Internet sample. To the extent that implicit racial bias is less pronounced among younger people, we would expect the judges to exhibit more implicit bias than the Internet sample.

52. *Id.* at 1210 and 1199–1200.

53. *Id.* at 1211–12.

54. *Id.* at 1217 ("We found in both the shoplifter case and the robbery case that judges who expressed a white preference on the IAT were somewhat more likely to impose harsher penalties when primed with black-associated words than when primed with neutral words, while judges who expressed a black preference on the IAT reacted in an opposite fashion to the priming conditions.").

55. *Id.* at 1216.

56. *Id.* at 1220–21.

57. *Id.* at 1222–23 and 1226.

58. *Id.* at 1225.

59. *See id.* at 1225–26. The authors describe both a risk associated with failure to be cognizant of the potential for implicit bias and a risk in being overconfident of one's ability to check one's own biases:

> Judges who, due to time pressure or other distractions, do not actively engage in an effort to control the "bigot in the brain" are apt to behave just as the judges in our study in which we subliminally primed with race-related words. Moreover, our data do not permit us to determine whether a desire to control bias or avoid the appearance of bias motivates judges in their courtrooms the way it seemed to in our study.

Furthermore, judges might be overconfident about their abilities to control their own biases. In recently collected data, we asked a group of judges attending an educational conference to rate their ability to "avoid racial prejudice in decisionmaking" relative to other judges who were attending the same conference. Ninety-seven percent (thirty-five out of thirty-six) of the judges placed themselves in the top half and fifty percent (eighteen out of thirty-six) placed themselves in the top quartile, even though by definition, only fifty percent can be above the median, and only twenty-five percent can be in the top quartile. We worry that this result means that judges are overconfident about their ability to avoid the influence of race and hence fail to engage in corrective processes on all occasions.

60. O'Connor v. Ortega, 480 U.S. 709, 734 n.3 (1987) (Blackmun, J., dissenting).
61. Amy Davidson Sorkin, *In Voting Rights, Scalia Sees a "Racial Entitlement,"* NEW YORKER (Feb. 28, 2013), www.newyorker.com/news/amy-davidson/in-voting-rights-scalia-sees-a-racial-entitlement.
62. Brief of Political Science and Law Professors as Amici Curiae in Support of Respondents at 12, *Shelby County, Ala. v. Holder*, 570 U.S. 529 (2013) (No. 12–96), *available at* https://www.brennancenter.org/sites/default/file s/legal-work/2013.2.1%20Brief%20of%20Political%20Science%20and%20 Law%20Professors%20in%20Support%20of%20Respondents.pdf.
63. *Id.* at 13.
64. *Id.* at 6.
65. 570 U.S. 529 (2013).
66. *Id.* at 544.
67. 383 U.S. 301, 328–29 (1966).
68. Reeves v. Sanderson Plumbing Products, Inc., 530 U.S. 133, 147 (2000).
69. 135 S.Ct. 2652 (2015).
70. *Id.* at 2658–59. The legislature relied principally on the Elections Clause of the U.S. Constitution for its argument. The clause provides: "The Times, Places and Manner of holding Elections for Senators and Representatives, shall be prescribed in each State by the Legislature thereof; but the Congress may at any time by Law make or alter such Regulations . . ."; U.S. CONST. art. I, § 4, cl. 1. The legislature contended that the word "legislature" in the Elections Clause must be read literally.
71. *Arizona State Legislature*, 135 S.Ct. at 2661.
72. 505 U.S. 144, 181 (1992).
73. *See Shelby County*, 570 U.S. at 574.
74. Ed Kilgore, *Racially Polarized Voting Is Getting Extreme in the South*, N.Y.: DAILY INTELLIGENCER (Dec. 5, 2016), http://nymag.com/daily/i ntelligencer/2016/12/racially-polarized-voting-is-getting-extreme-in-the-so uth.html.

75. *Id.*
76. *See id.* ("One byproduct of racial polarization has been the ability for Republicans to hide racial gerrymandering behind mere partisan motives, which are generally tolerated by the courts").
77. Rick Perlstein, *Exclusive: Lee Atwater's Infamous 1981 Interview on the Southern Strategy*, NATION: POLITICS (Nov. 13, 2012), www.thenation .com/article/exclusive-lee-atwaters-infamous-1981-interview-southern-strategy.
78. Adam M. Enders & Jamil S. Scott, *The Increasing Racialization of American Electoral Politics, 1988–2016*, 47 AMERICAN POLITICS RESEARCH 275, 276 (2019).
79. *Id.* at 280.
80. *Id.* at 295 ("Even controlling for the domineering effect of partisan and ideological self-evaluations, retrospective evaluations of the economy, and demographics, the strength of the relationships between racial resentment and a host of political attitudes and behaviors have steadily increased since 1988.").
81. *See Shelby County*, 570 U.S. at 578 (Ginsburg, J., dissenting).
82. 488 U.S. 469, 494–95 (1989) (plurality opinion of O'Connor, J.).
83. Gordon v. United Airlines, Inc., 246 F.3d 878, 892 (2001).
84. Jackson v. Lowndes County Sch. Dist., 126 F.Supp.3d 772, 781 (N.D. Mississippi 2015) (pretext can be inferred "when an employer refused, after being asked, to give a reason for the plaintiff's termination, and informed plaintiff later by letter that he was fired for unacceptable performance.").
85. *See* Bonte v. U.S. Bank, N.A., 624 F.3d 461, 466 (7th Cir. 2010).
86. THURGOOD MARSHALL INST. AT LDF, NAACP LEGAL DEF. & EDUC. FUND, INC., DEMOCRACY DIMINISHED: STATE AND LOCAL THREATS TO VOTING POST-SHELBY COUNTY, ALABAMA V. HOLDER 6–7 (2018), www.naacpldf.org/files/publications/Democracy%20Diminis hed-State%20and%20Local%20Voting%20Changes%20Post-Shelby%20v .%20Holder_0.pdf.
87. Ari Berman, *There Are 868 Fewer Places to Vote in 2016 Because the Supreme Court Gutted the Voting Rights Act*, NATION (Nov. 4, 2016), www.thenation.com/article/there-are-868-fewer-places-to-vote-in-2 016-because-the-supreme-court-gutted-the-voting-rights-act.
88. *Id.*
89. Richard Halicks, *Blacks and Whites in Poll Have Wildly Different Views of the South*, ATLANTA J.- CONST. (Nov. 8, 2017), www.myajc.com/news/local/bl acks-and-whites-poll-have-wildly-different-views-the-south/lOtY9U58tbdZla4 HmWn9qM/; Bristow Marchant, *White, Black Southerners Both Feel "Under Attack," Split on Hot-Button Issues*, STATE (Nov. 8, 2017), www.thestate.com/ news/politics-government/article183396531.html.

90. Shaw v. Reno, 509 U.S. 630, 647 (1993).
91. *Id.* at 647–48.
92. *Id.* at 647–48.
93. Halicks, *supra* note 89.
94. Sean McElwee, *Trump Supporters Believe a False Narrative of White Victimhood—and the Data Proves it*, SALON (Feb. 12, 2017, 4:00 PM), www.salon.com/2017/02/12/trumps-supporters-believe-a-false-narrative-of-white-victimhood-and-the-data-proves-it; *see also* Michael Tesler & John Sides, *How Political Science Helps Explain the Rise of Trump: The Role of White Identity and Grievances*, WASH. POST (Mar. 3, 2016), www.washingtonpost.com/news/monkey-cage/wp/2016/03/03/how-political-science-helps-explain-the-rise-of-trump-the-role-of-white-identity-and-grievances/?utm_term=.2501e486abdd.
95. McElwee, *supra* note 94.
96. Janelle Jones, John Schmitt, & Valerie Wilson, *50 Years After the Kerner Commission*, ECON. POLICY INST. (Feb. 26, 2018), www.epi.org/publication/50-years-after-the-kerner-commission.
97. Simson, *supra* note 34, at 1068.
98. *See* Simson, *supra* note 34, at 1078–79 (applying the concept of background circumstances to Title VII jurisprudence).
99. *See* U. of Southwestern Texas Med. Ctr. v. Nassar, 570 U.S. 338, 344 (2013).
100. *Id.* at 344–45.
101. *Id.* at 345.
102. *Id.* at 358–59.
103. Pew Research Center, *supra* note 24.
104. Pew Research Center, *supra* note 24.
105. Pew Research Center, *supra* note 24.
106. Katie R. Eyer, *That's Not Discrimination: American Beliefs and the Limits of Anti-Discrimination Law*, 96 MINN. L. REV. 1275, 1315–16 (2012).
107. Harvard T.H. Chan School of Public Health, *Poll Finds at Least Half of Black Americans Say They Have Experienced Racial Discrimination in Their Jobs and From the Police*, HARVARD T.H. CHAN SCHOOL OF PUBLIC HEALTH (Oct. 24, 2017), www.hsph.harvard.edu/news/press-releases/black-americans-discrimination-work-police.
108. *See* U.S. Equal Employment Opportunity Commission, *Charge Statistics (Charges Filed with EEOC) FY 1997 Through FY 2017*, EEOC (Jan. 22, 2018), www.eeoc.gov/eeoc/statistics/enforcement/charges.cfm.
109. *See Nassar*, 570 U.S. at 363 (Ginsburg, J., dissenting) ("[F]ear of retaliation is the leading reason why people stay silent about the discrimination they have encountered or observed.") (internal quotations omitted).

234 *Notes to Pages 105–08*

110. Terry Smith, *Everyday Indignities: Race, Retaliation, and the Promise of Title VII*, 34 COLUM. HUM. RTS. L. REV. 529, 551–52 (2003).
111. *See* Eyer, *supra* note 106, at 1304 ("It is well-established that the overwhelming majority of Americans—of all groups and races—subscribe to some extent to meritocracy beliefs.").
112. *See* Marcin, *supra* note 3, at 3.
113. Brian Tashman, *Ted Cruz's Favorite Judge Has History of Racial Bias, Absurd Statements*, RIGHT WING WATCH (Sept. 17, 2015), www.right wingwatch.org/post/ted-cruzs-favorite-judge-has-history-of-racial-bias-ab surd-statements.
114. 129 Fed. Appx. 529 (11th Cir. 2005), *vacated* and *remanded* by Ash v. Tyson Foods, Inc., 546 U.S. 454 (2006).
115. *Ash*, 129 Fed. Appx. at 531.
116. *Id.* at 533.
117. *Id.* (internal quotations omitted).
118. *See* Ash v. Tyson Foods, Inc., 546 U.S. 454 (2006).
119. Eyer, *supra* note 106, at 1283.
120. Eyer, *supra* note 106, at 1284.
121. Eyer, *supra* note 106, at 1284.
122. Eyer, *supra* note 106, at 1289.
123. Eyer, *supra* note 106, at 1290.
124. Sean McElwee, Jesse Rhodes, & Brian Schaffner, *Big Republican Donors are Even More Extreme than Their Party—and They Drive its Agenda*, SALON (Dec. 11, 2016, 4:00 PM), www.salon.com/2016/12/11/big-republican-donors-are-even-more-extreme-than-their-party-and-they-dri ve-its-agenda.
125. Sean McElwee, Brian Schaffner, & Jesse Rhodes, *Whose Voice, Which Choice? The Distorting Influence of the Political Donor Class in Our Big-Money Elections*, DEMOS 23–25 (Dec. 8, 2016), https://www.demos.org/ sites/default/files/publications/Whose%20Voice%20Whose%20 Choice_2.pdf.
126. *Id.* at 23–24.
127. *See* Clare O'Connor, *As Obama Pushes for Minimum Wage Increase, Billionaire Charles Koch Rails Against it With Media Campaign*, FORBES (Aug. 8, 2013), www.forbes.com/sites/clareoconnor/2013/08/08/ as-obama-pushes-for-minimum-wage-increase-billionaire-charles-koch-rails-against-it-with-media-campaign/#7e02247056f5; Rebecca Leber, *Billionaire Koch Brother Says Eliminating the Minimum Wage Will Help the Poor*, THINK PROGRESS (July 10, 2013), https://thinkprogress .org/billionaire-koch-brother-says-eliminating-the-minimum-wage-will-help-the-poor-f1efod4ead7b.
128. Andrew Stern, *Analysis: Koch Brothers a Force in Anti-Union Effort*, REUTERS (Feb. 26, 2011), www.reuters.com/article/us-usa-wiscon

sin-koch/analysis-koch-brothers-a-force-in-anti-union-effort-idUSTRE71P28W20110226.

129. *See* Jacqueline Thomsen, *Charles Koch Donated $500K to Ryan Days After GOP Tax Plan Passed*, THE HILL (Jan. 21, 2018, 7:46 PM), http://thehill.com/homenews/campaign/370037-charles-koch-donated-500k-to-ryan-days-after-gop-tax-plan-passed; Alex Kotch, *Koch Brothers Could be $1 Billion Richer Each Year from GOP Tax Bill*, IB TIMES (Jan. 24, 2018), www.ibtimes.com/political-capital/koch-brothers-could-be-1-billion-richer-each-year-gop-tax-bill-2644857.

130. JANE MAYER, DARK MONEY: THE HIDDEN HISTORY OF THE BILLIONAIRES BEHIND THE RISE OF THE RADICAL RIGHT 167, 182, 328–29 (2016).

131. *Id.* at 167–68.

132. *Id.* at 184.

133. Adam Lioz, *Stacked Deck: How the Racial Bias in Our Big Money Political System Undermines Our Democracy and Our Economy*, DEMOS (Oct. 19, 2014), www.demos.org/sites/default/files/publications/StackedDeck2_1.pdf, at 10 ("[R]ace intensifies the exclusion of people of color because they are less affluent, on average, than whites. The interests of large donors and major corporations often diverge significantly from those of working families on core economic policies, and when government is more responsive to the donor class, people of color are disproportionately harmed.").

134. 558 U.S. 310 (2010).

135. *Id.* at 318–19.

136. 494 U.S. 652 (1990), *overruled* by Citizens United v. Federal Election Commission, 310 (2010).

137. *Austin*, 494 U.S. at 654–66.

138. *Id.* at 660.

139. *Id.* at 660.

140. *Id.* at 664.

141. *Citizens United*, 558 U.S. at 337–39.

142. *Id.* at 357.

143. Eric Lichtblau & Nicholas Confessore, *What Campaign Filings Won't Show: Super PACs' Growing Sway*, N.Y. TIMES (July 15, 2015), www.nytimes.com/2015/07/16/us/politics/election-2016-fundraising-campaign-filings.html.

144. *Citizens United*, 558 U.S. at 359.

145. *Id.* (citing McConnell v. Federal Election Com'n, 540 U.S. 93, 297 (2003) (Kennedy, J., concurring in part in judgment)).

146. *See* Terry Smith, *Justice Kennedy's Democratic Dystopia*, 164 U. PA. L. REV. ONLINE 281, 285 (2016) ("There remains the sweeping record from *McConnell v. FEC*, in which 'lobbyists, CEOs, and wealthy

individuals alike all have candidly admitted donating substantial sums of soft money to national committees not on ideological grounds, but for the express purpose of securing influence over federal officials.' It would have been an act of judicial modesty—and prudence—for Justice Kennedy to concede that the Court in *Citizens United* knew far less about the corrupting and distorting effects of money—whether in the form of large donations or nominally independent expenditures—than the donors and members of our democratic branches of government who actually traffic in campaign money.") (footnotes omitted).

147. *Citizens United*, 558 U.S. at 360.

148. Smith, *supra* note 146, at 281.

149. *See, e.g.*, Peter Overby, *Americans Think Money in Politics is a Problem, But Just How Big?*, NPR (June 3, 2015, 6:03 AM), www.npr.org/sections/itsallpo litics/2015/06/03/411604682/americans-think-money-in-politics-is-a-problem- but-just-how-big (citing a *New York Times* poll indicating 84 percent of respondents believe that money has too much influence on politics); Kathy Frankovic, *Too Much Money in Politics, Too Much Damage to Democracy*, YouGov (Jan. 11, 2016), https://today.yougov.com/topics/ politics/articles-reports/2016/01/11/too-much-money-politics-too-much-dama ge-democracy (polls indicate that 67 percent of Democrats, 50 percent of Republicans, and a majority of independents want caps on independent expenditures by groups not affiliated with a candidate's campaign).

150. 347 U.S. 483, 494 n.11 (relying on psychological studies for the proposition that "[s]egregation of white and colored children in public schools has a detrimental effect upon the colored children").

151. 557 U.S. 557 (2009).

152. *Id.* at 563.

153. The Editorial Board, *Brett Kavanaugh Will Fit Right In at the Pro-Corporate Roberts Court*, N.Y. Times: Opinion (July 22, 2018), https://www.nytimes .com/2018/07/22/opinion/brett-kavanaugh-supreme-court.html.

154. Brian R. Frazelle, *Issue Brief: A Banner Year for Business as the Supreme Court's Conservative Majority is Restored*, Const. Accountability Ctr. (July 17, 2018), www.theusconstitution.org/think_tank/a-banner-y ear-for-business-as-the-supreme-courts-conservative-majority-is-restored.

155. *See* Theodore Eisenberg, *Four Decades of Civil Rights Litigation*, 12 J. Empirical Legal Stud. 4, 28 (2015).

VOTING WHILE WHITE

1. Langston Hughes, *Let America Be America Again*, Poets.org, www .poets.org/poetsorg/poem/let-america-be-america-again (last visited Dec. 17, 2018).

2. Sarah Kliff, *Why Obamacare Enrollees Voted for Trump*, Vox (Dec. 13, 2016, 8:10 AM), www.vox.com/science-and-health/2016/12/13/13848794/kentucky-obamacare-trump.

3. *Id.*

4. Benjamin Bridges & Sharmila Choudhury, *Social Security as a Retirement Resource for Near-Retirees, by Race and Ethnicity, Nativity, Benefit Type, and Disability Status* (Soc. Sec. Off. of Pol'y, Working Paper No. 109, 2007), www.ssa.gov/policy/docs/workingpapers/wp109.html (*see* Table A-1).

5. *Id.* ("[W]hites live longer than blacks. High indexed taxable earnings produce high annual benefits. Longer lives result in more years of benefit receipt.").

6. C. Eugene Steuerle, Karen E. Smith, & Caleb Quakenbush, *Has Social Security Redistributed to Whites from People of Color?*, Urban Inst. 1 (Nov. 2013), www.urban.org/sites/default/files/alfresco/publication-pdfs/412943-Has-Social-Security-Redistributed-to-Whites-from-People-of-Color-.PDF.

7. Bridges & Choudhury, *supra* note 4 (*see* Table A-2).

8. Pew Research Center, *2014 Party Identification Detailed Tables*, Pew Res. Ctr. (Apr. 7, 2105), www.people-press.org/2015/04/07/2014-party-identification-detailed-tables-white-non-hispanic; Morgan Gstalter, *Poll: Dems Now Lead Among Older Educated White Voters*, The Hill (Apr. 9, 2018, 7:58 AM), http://thehill.com/homenews/campaign/382230-poll-dems-now-lead-among-older-educated-white-voters.

9. *See* William A. Galston, *Why the 2005 Social Security Initiative Failed, and What it Means for the Future*, Brookings (Sept. 21, 2007), www.brookings.edu/research/why-the-2005-social-security-initiative-failed-and-what-it-means-for-the-future.

10. Tara Golshan, *Top Republicans Are Already Talking About Cutting Medicare and Social Security Next*, Vox (Dec. 20, 2017, 12:56 PM), www.vox.com/policy-and-politics/2017/12/18/16741730/gop-agenda-medicare-social-security; *see also* Nicole Goodkind, *Mitch McConnell Calls for Social Security, Medicare, Medicaid Cuts After Passing Tax Cuts, Massive Defense Spending*, Newsweek (Oct. 16, 2018, 2:47 PM), www.newsweek.com/deficit-budget-tax-plan-social-security-medicaid-medicare-entitlement-1172941 (quoting Senate Majority Leader Mitch McConnell as attributing the increase in the annual budget deficit not to Trump's tax cuts but to entitlement programs—Medicaid, Medicare, and Social Security—and adding: "There's been a bipartisan reluctance to tackle entitlement changes because of the popularity of those programs. Hopefully, at some point here, we'll get serious about this.").

11. John Gramlich, *Few Americans Support Cuts to Most Government Programs, Including Medicaid*, Pew Res. Ctr. (May 26, 2017),

www.pewresearch.org/fact-tank/2017/05/26/few-americans-support-cuts-to-most-government-programs-including-medicaid.

12. JASON BRENNAN, THE ETHICS OF VOTING 9 (2011).

13. Jeff Stein & Tracy Jan, *The Trump Administration Has a New Argument for Dismantling the Social Safety Net: It Worked.*, WASH. POST (July 14, 2018), www.washingtonpost.com/business/economy/white-house-declares-war-on-poverty-largely-over-amid-push-to-revamp-social-programs/2018/07/13/8f9536ea-86b2-11e8-8f6c-46cb43e3f306_story.html?utm_term=.b8fe8d6c43a0.

14. Isaac Shapiro, Danilo Trisi, & Raheem Chaudhry, *Poverty Reduction Programs Help Adults Lacking College Degrees the Most*, CTR. BUDGET POL'Y PRIORITIES (Feb. 16, 2017), www.cbpp.org/research/poverty-and-inequality/poverty-reduction-programs-help-adults-lacking-college-degrees-the.

15. *Id.*

16. Ronald Brownstein, *Federal Anti-Poverty Programs Primarily Help the GOP's Base*, THE ATLANTIC (Feb. 16, 2017), www.theatlantic.com/politics/archive/2017/02/gop-base-poverty-snap-social-security/516861.

17. *Id.*

18. Ronald Brownstein, *This Is Why Republicans and Democrats Aren't Talking to Each Other in Washington*, CNN (Jan. 8, 2019, 6:06 AM), www.cnn.com/2019/01/08/politics/republicans-democrats-divide-party-demographics-districts/index.html.

19. Vic Miller & Leighton Ku, *The Impact of Governmental Transfer Programs on State and Regional Personal Incomes*, MILKEN INST. SCH. PUB. HEALTH 4 (Apr. 30, 2014), https://publichealth.gwu.edu/pdf/hp/governmental_transfer_programs.pdf.

20. *Id.* at 5.

21. Suzanne Mettler, *The Welfare Boogeyman*, N.Y. TIMES (July 23, 2018), www.nytimes.com/2018/07/23/opinion/trump-social-policies-welfare.html.

22. *Id.*

23. *Id.*

24. Arthur Delaney & Ariel Edwards-Levy, *Americans Are Mistaken About Who Gets Welfare*, HUFFINGTON POST (Feb. 5, 2018, 12:50 PM), www.huffingtonpost.com/entry/americans-welfare-perceptions-survey_us_5a7880cde4b0d3df1d13f60b.

25. *See* Jazmin L. Brown-Iannuzzi, Ron Dotsch, Erin Cooley, & B. Keith Payne, *The Relationship Between Mental Representations of Welfare Recipients and Attitudes Toward Welfare*, 28(1) PSYCHOL. SCI. 92 (2017) (concluding from an experimental study that "the average image of a welfare recipient was rated as depicting an undeserving African American").

26. Rich Morin, Paul Taylor, & Eileen Patten, *A Bipartisan Nation of Beneficiaries*, Pew Res. Ctr. (Dec. 18, 2012), http://www.pewsocial trends.org/2012/12/18/a-bipartisan-nation-of-beneficiaries/.

27. Binyamin Appelbaum & Robert Gebeloff, *Who Benefits from the Safety Net*, N.Y. Times Economix (Feb. 13, 2012, 10:19 AM), http://economix .blogs.nytimes.com/2012/02/13/who-benefits-from-the-safety-net.

28. *Id.*

29. Ryan Sit, *Trump Thinks Only Black People Are on Welfare, But Really, White Americans Receive Most Benefits*, Newsweek (Jan. 12, 2018, 3:53 PM), www.newsweek.com/donald-trump-welfare-black-white-780252.

30. Shapiro, Trisi, & Chaudhry, *supra* note 14.

31. Eduardo Porter, *Come the Recession, Don't Count on That Safety Net*, N.Y. Times (Feb. 20, 2018), www.nytimes.com/2018/02/20/business/econ omy/recession-safety-net.html.

32. David Dayen, *Alaska Gives Cash to its Citizens Every Year. The Rest of the U.S. Could Too.*, Huffington Post (Aug. 28, 2018, 9:00 AM), www .huffingtonpost.com/entry/sovereign-wealth-fund-for-america-alaska-norway_us_5b83ffb7e4b0cd327dfe878e.

33. Emmie Martin, *US States with the Highest Levels of Income Inequality*, CNBC (Mar. 12, 2018, 4:15 PM), www.cnbc.com/2018/03/12/us-states-with-the-highest-levels-of-income-inequality.html.

34. Andrew Morris, *How the Federal Government Became Responsible for Disaster Relief*, Wash. Post (Dec. 4, 2018), www.washingtonpost.com/ outlook/2018/12/04/how-federal-government-became-responsible-disaster-relief/?utm_term=.ac465193107d.

35. Gabrielle Olya, *These States Receive the Most Disaster Aid Every Year*, Go Banking Rates (Aug. 27, 2018), www.gobankingrates.com/making-money/economy/states-that-receive-most-disaster-aid.

36. Morgan Scarboro, *Which States Rely the Most on Federal Aid?*, Tax Found. (Jan. 11, 2017), https://taxfoundation.org/states-rely-most-fed eral-aid.

37. Jeffrey Sparshott, *Which States Take the Most From the U.S. Government?*, Wall St. J. Real Time Econ. (Mar. 27, 2014, 12:25 PM), http://blogs.wsj.com/economics/2014/03/27/which-states-take-the-most-from-the-u-s-government.

38. To be sure, non-economic issues such as abortion form part of Republican conservative orthodoxy, but bread-and-butter issues often override idiosyncratic ones, even for Republicans. For instance, as the poor economy languished in 2012, social issues were not the principal concern of the vast majority of voters. In 2012, the economy, unemployment, the budget deficit, and Obamacare all outflanked social issues in importance for the vast majority of Americans. *See* Jeffrey M. Jones, *Economy Is*

Paramount Issue to U.S. Voters, GALLUP (Feb. 29, 2012), www.gallup.com/poll/153029/economy-paramount-issue-voters.aspx. Indeed, views about the size and scope of the federal government were more correlated with vote preferences in 2012 than they had been in any election on record going back to 1976. *See For Voters It's Still the Economy*, PEW RES. CTR. FOR THE PEOPLE & THE PRESS (Sept. 24, 2012), www.people-press.org/2012/09/24/for-voters-its-still-the-economy. In contrast, the same survey found that, "[w]hile women view abortion as a more important issue than do men, there is no indication in the survey that is having an impact on the vote choices of women." *Id*. Finally, in a compendium of polls ranging from 2010 to 2014, to the extent abortion or family values, or, for that matter, even gun policy, rate as an issue at all, they are consistently eclipsed by economic issues. *See Problems & Priorities*, POLLING REPORT.COM, www.pollingreport.com/prioriti.htm (last visited July 31, 2018). Thus, it appears that a racialized view of the central issues of the economy and the scope of government has more to do with white voter behavior than does so-called single-issue voting.

39. Scarboro, *supra* note 36.
40. John S. Kiernan, *2018's Most & Least Federally Dependent States*, WAL LETHUB.COM (Mar. 20, 2018), https://wallethub.com/edu/states-most-le ast-dependent-on-the-federal-government/2700/#main-findings.
41. *Id*.
42. David Post, *The National Government and the States: A Paradox*, WASH. POST (Mar. 28, 2017), www.washingtonpost.com/news/volokh-conspi racy/wp/2017/03/28/the-national-government-and-the-states-a-paradox/?ut m_term=.c692341d93b2; John Tierney, *Which States Are Givers and Which Are Takers?*, THE ATLANTIC (Mar. 8, 2017), www.theatlantic.com/business/archive/2014/05/which-states-are-givers-and-which-are-takers/361 668/.
43. Post, *supra* note 42; Tierney, *supra* note 42.
44. *See* Evan Comen & Thomas C. Frohlich, *States Where Americans Pay the Least (and Most) in Taxes*, USA TODAY (Feb. 28, 2018), www.usatoday .com/story/money/taxes/2018/02/20/states-where-americans-pay-least-and-most-taxes/350963002 (ranking the state's tax burden among the lowest ten in the country).
45. *See* Daniel J. Weiss, Jackie Weidman, & Stephanie Pinkalla, *States of Denial: States with the Most Federal Disaster Aid Sent Climate-Science Deniers to Congress*, CTR. AM. PROGRESS (Sept. 12, 2013), www.ameri canprogress.org/issues/green/reports/2013/09/12/73895/states-of-denial-stat es-with-the-most-federal-disaster-aid-sent-climate-science-deniers-to-con gress-2.
46. Michael Hiltzik, *Republicans Claim They Voted Down the Sandy Relief Bill Because It Was Filled with Pork. Don't Believe Them*, L.A. TIMES

(Aug. 30, 2017), www.latimes.com/business/hiltzik/la-fi-hiltzik-sandy-por k-20170830-story.html.

47. Elsewhere I have compared black and Latino economic vulnerability to natural disasters for Midwestern farmers, the former engendering much political and legal controversy when aid is sought, the latter not nearly so much:

> [I]f there were a drought in Iowa, the Supreme Court could not declare special aid to that state unconstitutional because it is overwhelmingly white. And so it goes with unemployment: special assistance for the economic catastrophe in areas primarily inhabited by blacks and Latinos cannot be any less constitutional than disaster relief to Iowa — or New Orleans and Mississippi after Hurricane Katrina.

See TERRY SMITH, BARACK OBAMA, POST-RACIALISM, AND THE NEW POLITICS OF TRIANGULATION 93 (2012).

48. *See* Morris, *supra* note 34.

49. David Rogers, *Senate Passes $787 Billion Stimulus Bill*, POLITICO (Feb. 16, 2009, 6:15 AM), www.politico.com/story/2009/02/senate-passes-787- billion-stimulus-bill-018837.

50. Gary Burtless, *The Stimulus Program Was a Smashing Success: It Erased Most Middle Class Income Losses in the Recession*, BROOKINGS (Nov. 25, 2014), www.brookings.edu/opinions/the-stimulus-program-was- a-smashing-success-it-erased-most-middle-class-income-losses-in-the- recession.

51. *Id.*

52. Jennifer Bendery, *GOP Congresswoman's Stimulus Plan: Give Women Money to Buy "Shoes and Clothes,"* HUFFINGTON POST (July 3, 2018, 4:59 PM), www.huffingtonpost.com/entry/gop-congresswoman-stimulus-plan- women-buy-shoes-clothes_us_5b3bb06ee4b05127ccedob7f.

53. Aaron Blake, *The 10 Most Loyal Demographic Groups for Republicans and Democrats*, WASH. POST (Apr. 8, 2015), www.washingtonpost.com/ news/the-fix/wp/2015/04/08/the-10-most-loyal-demographic-groups-for-rep ublicans-and-democrats/?utm_term=.07ba1e411c78.

54. *See, e.g.*, Vincent Hutchings, Hakeem Jefferson, & Katie Brown, *Why Do Black Americans Overwhelmingly Vote Democrat?*, CTR. POL. STUD. BLOG (July 23, 2014), http://cpsblog.isr.umich.edu/?p=948 (discussing theories ranging from Michael Dawson's Black Utility Heuristic, in which blacks of different economic classes view their fate as shared, to a simple preference for a larger, more activist government among blacks).

55. Grubman v. Morgan Stanley DW, Inc., No. 3:06-cv-0705, 2008 WL 4298579, at *7 (M.D. Tenn. Sept. 16, 2008) (citing Sixth Circuit cases); Oberdorf v. Penn Village Facility Operations, LLC, No. 4:15-cv-01880, 2017 WL 839470, at *6 (M.D. Penn. Mar. 3, 2017); Hitchcock v. Angel

Corps, Inc., 718 F.3d 733, 738–39 (7th Cir. 2013) ("A rational juror could find the supervisor's explanation that Hitchcock 'would have' compromised the health and safety of the client to be suspect because it never specifies what Hitchcock did wrong (and neither does the respondent brief's post-hoc, vague explanation that Hitchcock's 'failure to do a full admission compromised the health and safety of other potential clients.')"); Currier v. United Technologies Corp., 393 F.3d 246, 255 (1st Cir. 2014) ("The five Matrix categories … were entirely subjective and the jury could well have been dissatisfied with Mayes' vague explanations as to why Currier received low scores in some of the Matrix categories."); Gonzales v. Barrett Business Services, Inc., No. CV-05–0104-EFS, 2006 WL 1582380, at *14 (E.D. Wash. June 6, 2006) ("[T]he Court finds Plaintiff's termination letter's failure to include any reason for her discharge, as well as the vague explanation for the termination in BBSI's letter to Plaintiff's counsel, and the inexplicable and confusing responses provided by BBSI on the ESD 'Notice to Employer-Claimant's Separation Statement' each support Plaintiff's claim that BBSI's explanation for her termination is pretext.").

56. *See, e.g., Grubman,* 2008 WL 4298579, at *7 ("[W]here the explanation offered is vague such that it cannot be later penetrated as false, such explanation is evidence of pretext and summary judgment for the defendant is inappropriate.") (internal quotations omitted).

57. *See, e.g.,* JOAN WALSH, WHAT'S THE MATTER WITH WHITE PEOPLE: FINDING OUR WAY IN THE NEXT AMERICA 245 (2012) (expressing disappointment with Barack Obama, who "failed to capitalize on the goodwill he'd earned by Inauguration Day with a vivid explanation for our economic troubles and a bold agenda to respond."); *see also id.* at 170 (agreeing with the perception that Bill Clinton "sold the party's soul to corporate America and Wall Street) and *id.* at 198–99 (criticizing Democrats who voted to invade Iraq after the 9/11 attacks).

58. *Id.* at 281.

59. *Id.*

60. *Id.* at 282.

61. Bureau of Labor Statistics, *Unemployment Rates by Race and Ethnicity, 2010,* ECON. DAILY (Oct. 5, 2011), www.bls.gov/opub/ted/2011/ted_20111005.htm.

62. *Exit Polls: How Americans Voted in House Elections, Based on Exit Polls Conducted by Edison Research,* N.Y. TIMES (Nov. 4, 2014), www.nytimes.com/interactive/2014/11/04/us/politics/2014-exit-polls.html#us/2008.

63. David Greene, *McCain Dogged by His Economic Comments,* NPR (Sept. 19, 2008), www.npr.org/templates/story/story.php?storyId=94795767.

64. BRENNAN, *supra* note 12, at 70.

65. *See* WALSH, *supra* note 57, at 282 ("The GOP's new dog-whistle politics, trashing white people in coded language once reserved for blacks, opens new opportunities for Democrats — if they can help those white people translate the new GOP rhetoric.").

66. Josh Lowe, *Why the "Poorly Educated" Love Donald Trump Back*, NEWSWEEK (Nov. 25, 2016, 1:53 PM), www.newsweek.com/donald-trum p-brexit-austria-french-presidential-election-national-front-525281.

67. Ed Pilkington, *Obama Angers Midwest Voters with Guns and Religion Remark*, THE GUARDIAN (Apr. 14, 2008), www.theguardian.com/world/ 2008/apr/14/barackobama.uselections2008.

68. Jeremy Diamond, *Trump: I Could "Shoot Somebody and I Wouldn't Lose Voters,"* CNN (Jan. 24, 2016, 12:03 PM), www.cnn.com/2016/01/23/ politics/donald-trump-shoot-somebody-support/index.html.

69. Aaron Blake, *Trump Just Admitted the GOP's Tax Cuts Were Deceptively Sold*, WASH. POST (Dec. 20, 2017), www.washingtonpost.com/news/the-fix/wp/2017/12/20/trump-just-admitted-the-gops-tax-cuts-were-deceptively-sold.

70. *Id.*

71. Brian Faler, *Trump Wants New Middle-Class Tax Cut "of About 10 Percent,"* POLITICO (Oct. 22, 2018, 4:23 PM), www.politico.com/story/ 2018/10/22/trump-middle-class-tax-cut-924446.

72. Blake, *supra* note 69.

73. *Exit Polls*, CNN (2018), https://www.cnn.com/election/2018/exit-polls.

74. S.V. Date, *As Trump Spreads a Fog of Falsehoods, His Fans Believe Them and Make Excuses for Him*, HUFFINGTON POST (Nov. 5, 2018, 5:45 AM), www.huffingtonpost.com/entry/donald-trump-lies-supporters-midterm-elections_us_5bdf78dde4b04367a87dacf5.

75. Glenn Kessler, *Meet the Bottomless Pinocchio, a New Rating for a False Claim Repeated Over and Over Again*, WASH. POST (Dec. 10, 2018), www .washingtonpost.com/politics/2018/12/10/meet-bottomless-pinocchio-new-rating-false-claim-repeated-over-over-again/?utm_term=.1e55588bfdec.

76. Date, *supra* note 74.

77. *See* Victor Reklaitis, *Farm Bankruptcies in the Upper Midwest Have Jumped — In One Chart*, MARKETWATCH (Nov. 27, 2018, 1:15 PM), www.marketwatch.com/story/farm-bankruptcies-in-the-upper-midwest-have-jumped-in-one-chart-2018-11-27. The Trump trade war had broader effects beyond farmers. For instance, Bank of America Merrill Lynch calculated that Trump's trade tactics had shaved 6 percent off the performance of the Standard & Poor 500 index through early December of 2018, inflicting costs on investors' 401k accounts and more than offsetting any boost to the stock performance supplied by Trump's 2017 tax cut. *See* Tim Mullaney, *Opinion: Now We Know How Much Trump's Trade War Has Cost Your Portfolio*, MARKETWATCH (Dec. 6, 2018, 12:26 PM),

www.marketwatch.com/story/now-we-know-how-much-trumps-trade-war-has-cost-your-portfolio-2018-12-06.

78. *See* Alan Rappeport, *A $12 Billion Program to Help Farmers Stung by Trump's Trade War Has Aided Few*, N.Y. Times (Nov. 19, 2018), www.nytimes.com/2018/11/19/us/politics/farming-trump-trade-war.html.

79. Megan Cassella, *Farmers Are Losing Money Thanks to Trump—But They Still Support Him*, Politico (Nov. 1, 2018, 1:20 PM), www.politico.com/story/2018/11/01/trump-farmers-trade-900623.

80. *Id.*

81. Jason Millman, *9 Ways Trump is Undercutting Obamacare Without Congress*, Politico (Oct. 12, 2017, 4:15 PM), www.politico.com/interactives/2017/trump-undercutting-obamacare-aca.

82. Despite a massive infrastructure spending proposal, a proposal to substantially increase military spending, and an enormous tax cut proposal, candidate Trump had convinced a staggering 46 percent of Americans into believing that a Trump administration would "substantially reduce" the federal budget deficit—the annual shortfall between government revenues and expenditures. *See Federal Budget Deficit*, Gallup, https://news.gallup.com/poll/147626/federal-budget-deficit.aspx (last visited Dec. 30, 2018). After Trump's election, as Republicans saw that he had no intention of dealing with the deficit, the deficit as a Republican talking point fell out of favor even among politicians such as House Speaker Paul Ryan, who had built a political brand around constraining the deficit. *See* Jennifer Steinhauer, *This Election Season, Republicans' Deficit Focus Goes the Way of the Vuvezela*, N.Y. Times (Oct. 16, 2018), www.nytimes.com/2018/10/16/us/politics/republicans-budget-deficit-midterm-elections.html.

83. Louis Nelson, *Trump: "I'm the King of Debt,"* Politico (June 22, 2016, 8:09 AM), www.politico.com/story/2016/06/trump-king-of-debt-224642.

84. John W. Schoen, *Trump Told Gary Cohn to "Print Money" to Lower the National Debt, According to Bob Woodward's Book*, CNBC (Sept. 11, 2018, 2:00 PM), www.cnbc.com/2018/09/11/trump-once-considered-just-printing-money-to-lower-the-national-debt-woodward-reports.html.

85. *Federal Budget Deficit Hits 6-Year-High in Donald Trump's First Fiscal Year as President*, CBS News (Oct. 15, 2018, 4:52 PM), www.cbsnews.com/news/federal-budget-deficit-hits-6-year-high-in-donald-trumps-first-fiscal-year-as-president; John Harwood, *The Numbers Are In, and Trump's Tax Cut Didn't Reduce the Deficit—Despite His Many Promises*, CNBC (Oct. 16, 2018, 7:22 PM), www.cnbc.com/2018/10/16/trumps-tax-cut-didnt-reduce-the-deficit-despite-his-many-promises.html.

86. Arlie Russell Hochschild, Strangers in Their Own Land: Anger and Mourning on the American Right 137 (2016).

87. *Id.* at xiii.

88. *See id.* at 138.
89. Morgan Whitaker, *1 in 10 Still Support Discrimination Against African-Americans on Religious Grounds*, MSNBC (June 4, 2014, 2:33 PM), www .msnbc.com/politicsnation/1-in-10-americans-still-support-discrimination#52522.
90. Kiana Cox & Jeff Diamant, *Black Men Are Less Religious Than Black Women, But More Religious Than White Women and Men*, PEW RES. CTR. (Sept. 26, 2018), http://www.pewresearch.org/fact-tank/2018/09/26/black-men-are-less-religious-than-black-women-but-more-religious-than-white-women-and-men/?utm_source=Pew+Research+Center&utm_campaign=6b024fb08c-EMAIL_CAMPAIGN_2018_09_26_12_16&utm_medium=email&utm_term=0_.
91. *Id.*
92. *See* Campbell Robertson, *A Quiet Exodus: Why Black Worshipers Are Leaving White Evangelical Churches*, N.Y. TIMES (Mar. 9, 2018), www .nytimes.com/2018/03/09/us/blacks-evangelical-churches.html.
93. *See id.*
94. Perry Bacon Jr. & Amelia Thomson-DeVeaux, *How Trump and Race Are Splitting Evangelicals*, FIVETHIRTYEIGHT (Mar. 2, 2018, 11:34 AM), https://fivethirtyeight.com/features/how-trump-and-race-are-splitting-evangelicals/.
95. *Id.*
96. Eugene Scott, *More Than Half of White Evangelicals Say America's Declining White Population Is a Negative Thing*, WASH. POST (July 18, 2018), www.washingtonpost.com/news/the-fix/wp/2018/07/18/more-than-half-of-white-evangelicals-say-americas-declining-white-population-is-a-negative-thing/?utm_term=.201eb522f30f.
97. Janelle Wong, *This is Why White Evangelicals Still Support Donald Trump. (It's Not Economic Anxiety.)*, WASH. POST (June 19, 2018), www.washington post.com/news/monkey-cage/wp/2018/06/19/white-evangelicals-still-support-donald-trump-because-theyre-more-conservative-than-other-evangelicals-this-is-why/?noredirect=on&utm_term=.f28084fda989.
98. It is also political tribalism cloaked in biblical garb. The melding of white evangelicals with Republican politics makes the two essentially indistinguishable. As one commentator has written, "Eighty percent of white evangelicals would vote against Jesus Christ himself if he ran as a Democrat." *See* Amy Sullivan, *Democrats Are Christians, Too*, N.Y. TIMES (Mar. 31, 2018), www.nytimes.com/2018/03/31/opinion/sunday/trump-evangelicals-christians-easter.html.
99. HOCHSCHILD, *supra* note 86, at 146–47.
100. HOCHSCHILD, *supra* note 86, at 147.
101. Hastings College of Law professor Joan Williams appears to write about the white working class with similar objectives. *See* JOAN C. WILLIAMS,

White Working Class: Overcoming Class Cluelessness in America 64 (2017) (arguing that working-class whites legitimately feel that "political correctness" ignores their challenges while requiring them to show empathy to other groups).

102. Z. Byron Wolf, *Trump's Gut vs. the Government on Science, Economy, Intelligence*, CNN (Nov. 28, 2018, 11:13 AM), www.cnn.com/2018/11/28/politics/trump-gut-government/index.html.

103. *See* Massachusetts Bd. of Retirement v. Murgia, 427 U.S. 307, 314 (1976).

104. *See* Jonathan Weisman, *In Miss., It's G.O.P. vs. Tea Party*, N.Y. Times (Mar. 26, 2014), www.nytimes.com/2014/03/27/us/politics/mississippi-sen ate-race-boils-down-to-gop-vs-tea-party.html ("The economically poor state has been rich with powerful politicians in Washington, who have unapologetically protected its military bases and shipyards, built its roads and universities, reconstructed its beachfronts, and dredged its rivers. The state has had only a handful of senators since 1947, including Mr. Cochran, a powerful member of the Appropriations Committee; Trent Lott, a Senate majority leader; and John C. Stennis, whose 41 years of service was marked by military advocacy and the creation of the modern Navy.").

105. *See* Halimah Abdullah, *Mississippi Son Challenging a Political Godfather in Senate Race*, CNN (June 24, 2014, 12:03 AM), www.cnn.com/2014/06/24/politics/chris-mcdaniel-bio-mississippi-senate/index.html.

106. Weisman, *supra* note 104.

107. The Associated Press, *Mississippi Legislative Black Caucus Asks AG Eric Holder to Block Voter ID Law (Updated)*, GULFLIVE.COM (Feb. 27, 2014), http://blog.gulflive.com/mississippi-press-news/2014/02/mississip pi_legislative_black.html; Sparshott, *supra* note 37; Dennis Turner, *Mississippi Governor on Sequester, Guns, Voting Rights*, WREG News Channel 3 (Mar. 5, 2013, 5:44 PM), http://wreg.com/2013/03/05/mississippi-governor-on-sequester-guns-voting-rights/.

108. Ashley C. Allen, Thomas C. Frohlich, & Alexander E. M. Hess, *Report: The Most Miserable States in the USA*, USA Today (Feb. 27, 2014), http://www.usatoday.com/story/money/business/2014/02/23/most-miserable-states/5729305/.

109. Sarah Varney, *Mississippi, Burned*, Politico Magazine (Nov./Dec. 2014), www.politico.com/magazine/story/2014/10/mississippi-burned-obama care-112181.html#.VGsk7vnF-So.

110. *Id.*

111. Allen, Frohlich, & Hess, *supra* note 108.

112. Allen, Frohlich, & Hess, *supra* note 108.

113. Curtis Wilkie, *Why Mississippi Hates Washington*, Politico Magazine (Oct. 28, 2014), www.politico.com/magazine/story/2014/10/whats-the-matter-with-mississippi-112269.html#.VGsp3vnF-So.

114. *See, e.g.,* Stuart Rothenberg, *Thad Cochran's Mississippi,* ROLL CALL (June 2, 2014, 1:50 PM), http://blogs.rollcall.com/rothenblog/mississippi-primary-cochran-delta/; *Trent Lott: Protect Our Coast,* YOUTUBE (June 12, 2014), www.youtube.com/watch?v=OiBqVr7XoaY.

115. Jonathan Weisman, *Cochran Holds Off Tea Party Challenger in Mississippi,* N.Y. TIMES (June 24, 2014), www.nytimes.com/2014/06/25/us/politics/thad-cochran-chris-mcdaniel-mississippi-senate-primary.html.

116. Daniel Strauss, *Tea Party Candidate Defends Confederate Group: They're Not Racist,* TPM (Apr. 11, 2014, 4:59 PM), http://talkingpointsmemo.com/livewire/tea-party-candidate-defends-neo-confederates-they-re-not-racist.

117. John McCormack, *Mississippi Senate Candidate Chris McDaniel Distances Himself from Comments on Reparations and "Mamacita,"* WKLY. STANDARD BLOG (Apr. 11, 2014, 2:16 PM), https://www.washingtonexaminer.com/weekly-standard/miss-senate-candidate-chris-mcdaniel-distances-himself-from-comments-on-reparations-and-mamacita-786794 (archived location).

118. Tim Murphy, *Mississippi GOP Senate Candidate Blames Hip-Hop for Gun Violence (AUDIO),* MOTHER JONES (Jan. 7, 2014), www.motherjones.com/politics/2014/01/chris-mcdaniel-mississippi-hip-hop-gun-violence-audio.

119. The Associated Press, *Mississippi Senate Race Heating Up Between Veteran Thad Cochran, Newcomer Chris McDaniel,* GULFLIVE.COM (June 11, 2014), http://blog.gulflive.com/mississippi-press-news/2014/03/mississippi_senate_race_heatin.html.

120. *Thad Cochran on Civil Rights,* ON THE ISSUES, www.ontheissues.org/Domestic/Thad_Cochran_Civil_Rights.htm (last updated May 1, 2016).

121. *Id.*

122. Ari Berman, *Where Are the GOP Supporters of Voting Rights?,* NATION BLOG (June 25, 2014), www.thenation.com/blog/180419/where-are-gop-supporters-voting-rights#.

123. *See* Kyle Trygstad, *Mississippi Runoff Results: Thad Cochran Wins,* ROLL CALL (June 24, 2014, 11:08 PM), www.rollcall.com/news/policy/mississippi-runoff-results-thad-cochran-chris-mcdaniel-2:

> To enlarge the runoff electorate—which increased by more than 30,000 votes from the primary—Cochran and his allies expanded their outreach to blacks and Democrats who had not voted in the Democratic primary and were therefore eligible to vote on Tuesday. Mississippi does not register by party, so primaries and runoffs are open ... That appeared to work, as turnout surged in heavily black

Hinds County by more than 7,000 votes and Cochran won it with 73 percent.

See also Jamelle Bouie, *Why Mississippi's Black Democrats Saved an Elderly White Republican*, SLATE (June 25, 2014, 1:42 PM), https://slate .com/news-and-politics/2014/06/thad-cochran-wins-with-mississippis-bla ck-voters-african-americans-help-defeat-chris-mcdaniel.html.

124. Katie Glueck, *Barbours Spent to Boost Mississippi Black Turnout*, POLITICO (July 16, 2014, 7:48 PM), www.politico.com/story/2014/07/2014 -mississippi-elections-barbours-thad-cochran-chris-mcdaniel-109021.html.

125. *See* Nate Cohn & Derek Willis, *More Evidence that Thad Cochran Owes Runoff Win to Black Voters*, N.Y. TIMES (July 15, 2014), www.nytimes .com/2014/07/15/upshot/more-evidence-that-thad-cochran-owes-runoff-win-t o-black-voters.html ("In the whitest, most Republican precincts, where Mr. Obama received less than 20 percent of the vote, Mr. McDaniel defeated Mr. Cochran by 19,033 votes, with 57 percent of the vote."). In the absence of exit polling, McDaniel's share of the white vote cannot be more definitively stated, but it is reasonable to assume that almost all of the 49 percent of the runoff vote McDaniel received came from whites.

126. Brian Beutler, *Conservatives Are Furious at Thad Cochran for Highlighting Chris McDaniel's Racism*, NEW REPUBLIC (June 25, 2014), www.newre public.com/article/118383/conservatives-outraged-republican-called-racist-o pponent-racist ("[A] substantial number of Republicans are far more concerned with and offended by the idea of one Republican attacking another Republican for being a dog-whistling racist than with the actual dog whistling and racism that forms the basis of the attack.").

127. Glueck, *supra* note 124.

128. *How Congress Voted in 2017: The NAACP Civil Rights Federal Legislative Report Card, 115ᵗʰ Congress, First Session January 3, 2017– December 22, 2017*, NAACP (Feb. 9, 2018), www.naacp.org/wp-content/ uploads/2010/04/2017-Legislative-Report-Card-1.pdf.

129. *See* SMITH, *supra* note 47, at 48.

130. *Exit Polls, supra* note 73.

131. Erica Werner, *House GOP Plan Would Cut Medicare, Medicaid to Balance Budget*, WASH. POST (June 19, 2018), www.washingtonpost.co m/news/business/wp/2018/06/19/house-gop-plan-would-cut-medicare-so cial-security-to-balance-budget/?utm_term=.225c822791bc.

132. *Id.*

133. *Id.*

134. Andrew Restuccia, Matthew Nussbaum, & Sarah Ferris, *Trump Releases Budget Hitting His Own Voters Hardest*, POLITICO (May 23, 2017, 1:45 PM), www.politico.com/story/2017/05/22/trump-budget-cut-social-programs-238696.

135. *See id.*; Alexander Burns, *Eyeing Trump's Budget Plan, Republican Governors Say "No, Thanks,"* N.Y. TIMES (Mar. 22, 2017), www.nytim es.com/2017/03/22/us/eyeing-trumps-budget-plan-republican-governors-s ay-no-thanks.html?hp&action=click&pgtype=Homepage&clickSourc e=story-heading&module=first-column-region&region=top-news&W T.nav=top-news&_r=0; Jenna Johnson, *Trump's Budget Would Hit Rural Towns Especially Hard—But They're Willing to Trust Him,* WASH. POST (Apr. 2, 2017), www.washingtonpost.com/politics/trumps-budget-would-hit-rural-towns-especially-hard–but-theyre-willing-to-trus t-him/2017/04/02/51a456d4-12e3-11e7-833c-503e1f6394c9_story.html? utm_term=.2c3e63dea9c4.

136. *See* Jamelle Bouie, *The GOP Sees Rural Voters as More Legitimate Than Urban Voters,* SLATE (Dec. 7, 2018, 6:07 PM), https://slate.com/news-and-politics/2018/12/wisconsin-power-grab-gop-urban-vs-rural-voters.html.

137. *See, e.g.,* Jenny Hopkinson, Catherine Boudreau, & Helena Bottemiller Evich, *Rural Voters Lose in Trump's Budget Plan,* Politico (Mar. 16, 2017, 7:02 PM), www.politico.com/story/2017/03/trump-bud get-rural-voters-236153.

138. *See* SMITH, *supra* note 47, at 87.

139. *See* SMITH, *supra* note 47, at 90 (discussing President Obama's first term and observing: "Obama's concessions to the Republicans assumed that Republicans were actually interested in deficit reduction. They were not. They were interested in smaller government, something altogether different. Deficits resulting from tax cuts were acceptable to Republicans because they would 'starve the beast'—that is, they would force shrinkage of government social programs.").

140. Although the example I use to illustrate the potentially irreversible damage of whitelash involves the social safety net, one could just as easily deploy climate change as an example. The emerging consensus among scientists is that there is a narrow window within which to reverse the most severe effects of global warming. *See* Jonathan Watts, *We Have 12 Years to Limit Climate Change Catastrophe, Warns UN,* THE GUARDIAN (Oct. 8, 2018), www.theguardian.com/en vironment/2018/oct/08/global-warming-must-not-exceed-15c-warns-lan dmark-un-report (discussing a United Nations report giving a 12-year window). Yet Republicans, led by President Trump, continue to deny the science of global warming and the phenomenon's potentially disastrous consequences for Americans' health and prosperity. *See* Brady Dennis & Chris Mooney, *Major Trump Administration Climate Report Says Damage is "Intensifying Across the Country,"* WASH. POST (Nov. 23, 2018), www.washingtonpost.com/energy-environment/2018/11/ 23/major-trump-administration-climate-report-says-damages-are-intensi

fying-across-country/?utm_term=.54a8a883fae4; and Miranda Green & Timothy Cama, *GOP Shrugs Off Dire Study Warning of Global Warming*, THE HILL (Oct. 10, 2018, 6:26 PM), https://thehill.com/pol icy/energy-environment/410871-gop-shrugs-off-dire-study-warning-of-gl obal-warming. But if the emerging scientific consensus is correct that there is little time to make a course correction, then the yin and yang of democratic elections does not help. If Republicans are wrong about global warming, they will be wrong for all eternity because the consequences of being wrong will be irreversible.

141. Kimberly Amadeo, *US Debt by President by Dollar and Percent*, BALANCE (Jan. 10, 2019), www.thebalance.com/us-debt-by-president-b y-dollar-and-percent-3306296.

142. Lee Moran, *Donald Trump Reportedly Shrugged Off Looming Debt Crisis Because "I Won't Be Here,"* HUFFINGTON POST (Dec. 6, 2018, 5:29 AM), www.huffingtonpost.com/entry/donald-trump-debt-crisis-shrugs-off_us_5c08efd3e4b069028dc6a6d7.

HOLDING CANDIDATES AND PARTIES ACCOUNTABLE

1. Philip Bump, *4.4 Million 2012 Obama Voters Stayed Home in 2016—More Than a Third of Them Black*, WASH. POST (Mar. 12, 2018), www .washingtonpost.com/news/politics/wp/2018/03/12/4-4-million-2012-oba ma-voters-stayed-home-in-2016-more-than-a-third-of-them-black/?nore direct=on&utm_term=.a1b8d0bda3f2.

2. Michael Tesler, *Trump is the First Modern Republican to Win the Nomination Based on Racial Prejudice*, WASH. POST (Aug. 1, 2016), www.washingtonpost.com/news/monkey-cage/wp/2016/08/01/trump-is-t he-first-republican-in-modern-times-to-win-the-partys-nomination-on-a nti-minority-sentiments/?utm_term=.04a367058c29.

3. Nash Jenkins, *President Trump Says He Got "A Lot" of Support From the Black Community. Not Quite*, TIME (Apr. 26, 2018), http://time.com/52 55909/donald-trump-black-voter-support.

4. Joshua Green & Sasha Issenberg, *Inside the Trump Bunker, With Days to Go*, BLOOMBERG (Oct. 27, 2016), www.bloomberg.com/news/articles/2 016-10-27/inside-the-trump-bunker-with-12-days-to-go.

5. Bump, *supra* note 1.

6. *See* MICHELLE ALEXANDER, THE NEW JIM CROW (2010).

7. Voting Rights Act of 1965, Pub. L. No. 89–110, §2 (1965) ("No voting qualification or prerequisite to voting, or standard, practice, or procedure shall be imposed or applied by any State or political subdivision to deny or abridge the right of any citizen of the United States to vote on account of race or color.").

8. Jeremy Diamond, *Trump on Black Supporter: "Look at My African-American Over Here,"* CNN (June 6, 2016, 8:09 PM), www.cnn.com/201 6/06/03/politics/donald-trump-african-american/index.html.

9. Ed Mazza, *Jon Meacham: Trump Tied for "Most Racist President in American History,"* HUFFINGTON POST (July 16, 2019, 5:06 AM), www.huffpost.com/entry/donald-trump-andrew-johnson-racist_n_5d2d6e41e4b085eda5a0d7fa.

10. 412 U.S. 755, 767 (1973).

11. *Id.* at 766.

12. *Id.* at 766–68. The totality of the circumstances test described in *White* eventually became known as the *"Zimmer* factors," referring to a case from the United States Court of Appeals for the Fifth Circuit. *See* Rogers v. Lodge, 458 U.S. 613, 619 (1982) (citing Zimmer v. McKeithen, 485 F.2d 1297 (CA5 1973), aff'd on other grounds sub nom. East Carroll Parish School Bd. v. Marshall, 424 U.S. 636 (1975)). In determining whether a jurisdiction has intentionally diluted the votes of a racial group, *Zimmer* commends the weighing of several factors, namely:

   a. the extent of any history of official discrimination in the state or political subdivision that touched the right of the members of the minority group to register, to vote, or otherwise to participate in the democratic process;
   b. the extent to which voting in the elections of the state or political subdivision is racially polarized;
   c. the extent to which the state or political subdivision has used unusually large election districts, majority vote requirements, anti-single-shot provisions, or other voting practices or procedures that may enhance the opportunity for discrimination against the minority group;
   d. whether members of the minority group have been denied access to [any candidate-slating] process;
   e. the extent to which members of the minority group in the state or political subdivision bear the effects of discrimination in such areas as education, employment and health, which hinder their ability to participate effectively in the political process;
   f. whether political campaigns have been characterized by overt or subtle racial appeals;
   g. the extent to which members of the minority group have been elected to public office in the jurisdiction;
   h. whether there is a significant lack of responsiveness on the part of elected officials to the particularized needs of the members of the minority group; [and]
   i. whether the policy underlying the state or political subdivision's use of such voting qualification, prerequisite to voting, or standard, practice or procedure is tenuous.

See U.S. v. Brown, 494 F.Supp.2d 440, 447 (S.D. Mississippi 2007), *affirmed*, 561 F.3d 420 (5th Cir. 2009).

13. Nicole Gaudiano, *Tenney Highlights "Notorious" Background of Brindisi's Father*, PRESS CONNECTS (July 14, 2017), www.pressconnects.com/story/ne ws/2017/07/14/tenney-highlights-notorious-background-brindisis-father/ 479172001.

14. Astead W. Herndon, *A Congressional Candidate Used to Be a Rapper. Will It Matter?*, N.Y. TIMES (July 17, 2018), www.nytimes.com/2018/07/ 17/us/politics/antonio-delgado-lyrics.html.

15. *Id.*

16. *Id.*

17. Julia Jacobs, *DeSantis Warns Florida Not to "Monkey This Up," and Many Hear a Racist Dog Whistle*, N.Y. TIMES (Aug. 29, 2018), www.nyt imes.com/2018/08/29/us/politics/desantis-monkey-up-gillum.html.

18. Tal Axelrod, *Former RNC Chair on DeSantis "Monkey" Comment: "It Is How White Folks Talk About Black Men Who Are Successful,"* THE HILL (Aug. 29, 2018, 11:14 PM), http://thehill.com/blogs/blog-briefing-room/ne ws-campaigns/404304-former-rnc-chair-on-desantis-its-how-white-folks-ta lk. Steele also criticized DeSantis for referring to Gillum as "articulate," a term that when used by a white person to describe a person of color can be a fist in a velvet glove: the white person is often implying that to be articulate is unusual for a person of color. Said Steele: "Why do you have to describe him that way? Doesn't happen to a lot of white candidates"; *id.*

19. *Id.*

20. *See* Washington v. Davis, 426 U.S. 229, 242 (1976).

21. 509 U.S. 630, 648 (1993).

22. *Id.* at 653.

23. *See* Roger v. Lodge, 458 U.S. 613, 625 (1982) ("Evidence of historical discrimination is relevant to drawing an inference of purposeful discrimination, particularly in cases such as this one where the evidence shows that discriminatory practices were commonly utilized, that they were abandoned when enjoined by courts or made illegal by civil rights legislation, and that they were replaced by laws and practices which, though neutral on their face, serve to maintain the status quo.").

24. *See* Hunter v. Underwood, 471 U.S. 222, 233 (1985).

25. Beth Schwartzapfel & Bill Keller, *Willie Horton Revisited*, MARSHALL PROJECT (May 13, 2015), www.themarshallproject.org/2015/05/13/willie-horton-revisited.

26. Adam Clymer, *Bush Assails "Quota Bill" at West Point Graduation*, N.Y. TIMES: ARCHIVES (June 2, 1991), www.nytimes.com/1991/06/02/us/bush-assails-quota-bill-at-west-point-graduation.html.

27. *See* David M. Litman, *What Is the Stray Remarks Doctrine? An Explanation and a Defense*, 65 CASE W. RES. L. REV. 823, 835 (2015).

28. *See* Martinez v. New York City Transit Authority, 672 Fed. Appx. 68, 71 (2d Cir. 2016).
29. *See* Morris v. McCarthy, 825 F.3d 658, 670 (D.C. Cir. 2016) ("Even if such a statement carries less weight than one made at the time of the suspension, it is nonetheless probative evidence of a supervisor's discriminatory attitude, at least when it is targeted directly at the plaintiff or is one of a pattern of similar remarks.").
30. Jane Coaston, *Steve King Is a Racist, and Conservatives Don't Want to Talk About It*, Vox (June 28, 2018, 11:40 AM), www.vox.com/2018/6/28/17 506880/steve-king-twitter-racism-congress-republicans.
31. *See* Morse v. Republican Party of Virginia, 517 U.S. 186, 210–15 (1996) (summarizing the white primary cases in the context of holding that Section 5 of the Voting Rights Act of 1965, the passage of which was partly informed by the white primary cases, reached party nominating conventions, not merely public primaries).
32. *Id.* at 211.
33. No. 16-cv-11844, 2018 WL 3769326, at *35–36 (E.D. Mich. Aug. 9, 2018).
34. *Id.* at *36.
35. *Id.*
36. Ari Berman, *Ohio Keeps Making It Harder to Vote*, Nation (Sept. 13, 2016), www.thenation.com/article/ohio-keeps-making-it-harder-to-vote.
37. Michael Wines, *Some Republicans Acknowledge Leveraging Voter ID Laws for Political Gain*, N.Y. Times (Sept. 16, 2016), www.nytimes.co m/2016/09/17/us/some-republicans-acknowledge-leveraging-voter-id-laws-for-political-gain.html.
38. *Id.*
39. Thornburg v. Gingles, 478 U.S. 30, 36 (1986).
40. *See* Chapter 1, notes 11–12 and accompanying text.
41. *See* Democratic National Committee v. Reagan, No. CV-16–01065-PHX-DLR, 2018 WL 2191664, at *38 (D. Ariz. May 10, 2018).
42. *See* Staff and Wire Report, *Court Rejects Harris' Request to Be Declared Winner*, Robesonian (Jan. 22, 2019), www.robesonian.com/news/119578/ court-rejects-harris-request-to-be-declared-winner (quoting Chairman Robin Hayes as arguing that since the Republican candidate "received more legal votes and no public evidence has shown the outcome is in doubt," that candidate should be certified the winner notwithstanding evidence of fraud).
43. Press Release, N.C. Republican Party (Feb. 26, 2019), https://us2.campaign-archive.com/?e=&u=f3100bc5464cbba2f472ddf2c&id=90a47d6014.
44. Andrew Gumbel, Down for the Count: Dirty Elections and the Rotten History of Democracy in America 200 (2016).
45. *Id.* at 199 ("No evidence ever emerged of a Dick Tracy or a Mary Poppins attempting to cast a ballot, but that did not stop a short-lived

Republican front group, the American Center for Voting Rights (ACVR), from alleging that the registrations were part of a Democratic Party plot to inflate the voter rolls and steal elections around the country.").

46. *Id.* at 192.

47. *Is There Large-Scale Voter Fraud in the U.S.? In a Word, No.*, PBS NEWSHOUR (Oct. 17, 2016), www.pbs.org/newshour/show/trumps-rigged-election-claims-wrong-dangerous%E2%80%8B.

48. *Id.*

49. Jack Healy, *Arrested, Jailed, and Charged with a Felony. For Voting.*, N.Y. TIMES (Aug. 2, 2018), www.nytimes.com/2018/08/02/us/arrested-voting-north-carolina.html.

50. *Id.*

51. *Id.*

52. Aaron Blake, *Republicans Keep Admitting that Voter ID Helps Them Win, For Some Reason*, WASH. POST (Apr. 7, 2016), www.washingtonpost.com/news/the-fix/wp/2016/04/07/republicans-should-really-stop-admitting-that-voter-id-helps-them-win/?utm_term=.d41d332abb96.

53. *Id.*

54. *Id.*

55. *Id.*

56. *Study: Black Voter Turnout in Wisconsin Plummets*, U.S. NEWS (Nov. 7, 2017), www.usnews.com/news/best-states/wisconsin/articles/2017-11-07/study-black-voter-turnout-in-wisconsin-plummets.

57. *Id.*

58. Veronica Stracqualursi, *Trump Claims You Need ID to Buy Groceries. You Do Not.*, CNN (Aug. 1, 2018, 2:35 PM), www.cnn.com/2018/08/01/politics/trump-grocery-shopping-id/index.html.

59. *See* Sari Horwitz, *Getting a Photo ID So You Can Vote Is Easy. Unless You're Poor, Black, Latino, or Elderly.*, WASH. POST (Mar. 23, 2106), www.washingtonpost.com/politics/courts_law/getting-a-photo-id-so-you-can-vote-is-easy-unless-youre-poor-black-latino-or-elderly/2016/05/23/8d5474ec-20f0-11e6-8690-f14ca9de2972_story.html?utm_term=.23ac98309a48; Vanessa M. Perez, *Americans With Photo ID: A Breakdown of Demographic Characteristics*, PROJECT VOTE 1–2 (2015), www.projectvote.org/wp-content/uploads/2015/06/AMERICANS-WITH-PHOTO-ID-Research-Memo-February-2015.pdf.

60. Saeed Ahmed, *There Are Certain Moments in US History When Confederate Monuments Go Up*, CNN (Aug. 16, 2017, 4:05 PM), www.cnn.com/2017/08/16/us/confederate-monuments-backlash-chart-trnd/index.html.

61. National Conference of State Legislatures, *History of Voter ID*, NCSL (May 31, 2017), www.ncsl.org/research/elections-and-campaigns/voter-id-history.aspx.

62. *Voter Identification Laws by State*, BALLOTPEDIA, https://ballotpedia.org/
    Voter_identification_laws_by_state (last visited Nov. 5, 2018).

63. *See* Crawford v. Marion County Election Bd., 553 U.S. 181 (2008).

64. *Id.* at 194.

65. *Id.* at 204.

66. 541 U.S. 267, 325 (Stevens, J., dissenting).

67. Citizens United v. Federal Election Commission, 558 U.S. 310, 360
    (2010).

68. Terry Smith, Bond v. Floyd *and Expressive Proscriptions on the Partisan
    Gerrymander*, 2016 WIS. L. REV. FORWARD 122, http://wisconsinlawreview
    .org/bond-v-floyd-and-expressive-proscriptions-on-the-partisan-gerrymander
    (analyzing *Bond v. Floyd*, 385 U.S. 118 (1966), in which the Georgia Assembly
    refused to seat a duly elected representative because of his views on the
    Vietnam War, and observing: "[I]t seems odd to forbid the state to silence
    a representative of the people but to permit the state to deprive the people of
    representation in the first place through the partisan gerrymander.").
    Aside from being discordant with First Amendment law, the evidentiary
    burden *Crawford* places on states seeking to implement voter-suppressive
    ID requirements is much less than the burden placed on states seeking
    to avoid minority vote dilution in redistricting, which requires a state to
    have a "strong basis in evidence" that its use of race is necessary to avoid
    running afoul of Section 2 of the Voting Rights Act of 1965. *Bush v. Vera*,
    517 U.S. 952, 977 (1996). In effect, the Supreme Court has made it easier
    under the Constitution for states to target racial minorities and harder for
    them to protect these same groups.

69. *See* Terry Smith, *A Black Party? Timmons, Black Backlash and the
    Endangered Two-Party Paradigm*, 48 DUKE L.J. 1, 23–27 (1998)
    (defending on First Amendment and Equal Protection grounds the
    right of black voters to organize politically around issues that have
    a distinct impact on communities of color).

70. Douglas J. Ahler & Gaurav Sood, *The Parties in Our Heads:
    Misperceptions about Party Composition and Their Consequences*, 80
    J. POL. 964 (2018).

71. *Id.* at 966.

72. *Id.* at 968 (Table 1).

73. *Id.* at 979.

74. Emily Flitter & Chris Kahn, *Exclusive: Trump Supporters More Likely
    to View Blacks Negatively—Reuters/Ipsos Poll*, REUTERS (June 28, 2016),
    www.reuters.com/article/us-usa-election-race/exclusive-trump-
    supporters-more-likely-to-view-blacks-negatively-reuters-ipsos-poll-
    idUSKCN0ZE2SW.

75. 401 F. Supp. 87 (S.D.N.Y. 1975).

76. *Id.* at 88 (quoting statute).

77. *Id.* at 94 (citations omitted).

78. Schwartz v. Vanasco, 423 U.S. 1041 (1976).

79. Libby Nelson, *Read the Full Transcript of Obama's Fiery Anti-Trump Speech*, Vox (Sept. 7, 2018, 1:46 PM), www.vox.com/policy-and-politics/2018/9/7/17832024/obama-speech-trump-illinois-transcript.

80. Nathan McDermott, *Corey Stewart Used Racist Stereotypes to Disparage NFL Players in 2017 Campaign Event*, CNN (Aug. 16, 2018, 3:05 PM), www.cnn.com/2018/08/16/politics/corey-stewart-stereotypes-nfl-players/index.html.

81. Emily Sullivan, *Laura Ingraham Told LeBron James to Shut Up and Dribble; He Went to the Hoop*, NPR (Feb. 19, 2018, 5:04 PM), www.npr.org/sections/thetwo-way/2018/02/19/587097707/laura-ingraham-told-lebron-james-to-shutup-and-dribble-he-went-to-the-hoop.

82. Black professional athletes represent a rarefied group among African Americans and symbolize financial success largely unobtainable for blacks in other fields. Just 1 in 50 African American families has a net worth of $1 million or more, compared to 1 in 7 white households. See Tracy Jan, *1 in 7 White Families are Now Millionaires. For Black Families, it's 1 in 50.*, Wash. Post (Oct. 3, 2017), www.washingtonpost.com/news/wonk/wp/2017/10/03/white-families-are-twice-as-likely-to-be-millionaires-as-a-generation-ago/?utm_term=.f6acc9b5a6e1. At the beginning of 2018, there were only three black CEOs of Fortune 500 companies, the lowest representation since 2002. *See* Grace Donnelly, *The Number of Black CEOs at Fortune 500 Companies Is at its Lowest Since 2002*, Fortune (Feb. 28, 2018), http://fortune.com/2018/02/28/black-history-month-black-ceos-fortune-500. Just ten blacks made *Forbes's* 2017 list of the world's 2,043 billionaires; only three of the ten were African Americans. *See* Mfonobong Nsehe, *The Black Billionaires 2017*, Forbes (Mar. 20, 2017), www.forbes.com/sites/mfonobongnsehe/2017/03/20/the-black-billionaires-2017/#579b4fe44d6d. A 2018 study by Harvard and Stanford researchers highlights how black economic precarity is driven mainly by the fate of black men in society. Incomes for black and white boys who grow up in families with similar economic conditions diverge substantially in adulthood. *See* Raj Chetty, Nathaniel Hendren, Maggie Jones, & Sonya R. Porter, *Race and Economic Opportunity in the United States: Executive Summary*, Equal. Opportunity Project 1, 3 (2018), www.equality-of-opportunity.org/assets/documents/race_summary.pdf. Rich white boys grow up to become rich white men, while wealthy black boys are more likely to be poor. *See* Emily Badger, Claire Cain Miller, Adam Pearce, & Kevin Quealy, *Extensive Data Shows Punishing Reach of Racism for Black Boys*, N.Y. Times (Mar. 19, 2018), www.nytimes.com/interactive/2018/03/19/upshot/race-class-white-and-black-men.html. In contrast to black women, black men consistently earn less than white men, regardless of

the income strata of the family they grew up in. *Id.* Perhaps most strikingly, black boys raised in black families in the top 1 percent of household incomes had the same chance of being incarcerated in adulthood as white boys who grew up in families making only $36,000 a year. *Id.* So, while Trump and other Republicans' attacks on black professional athletes are most certainly attacks on their patriotism, intellect, and integrity, these broadsides fundamentally intend to question their deservedness of success in one of the few professions in which black men thrive.

83. Flitter & Kahn, *supra* note 74.
84. KEITH REEVES, VOTING HOPES OR FEARS: WHITE VOTERS, BLACK CANDIDATES AND RACIAL POLITICS IN AMERICA 87 (1997).
85. *Id.* at 83.
86. 138 S.Ct. 2392 (2018).
87. *Id.* at 2417.
88. *Id.* at 2419–20.
89. *Id.* at 2435 (Sotomayor, J., dissenting).
90. *Id.* at 2436 (Sotomayor, J., dissenting).
91. *See id.* at 2418; *see also id.* ("[T]he issue before us is not whether to denounce the statements. It is instead the significance of those statements in reviewing a Presidential directive, neutral on its face, addressing a matter within the core of executive responsibility. In doing so, we must consider not only the statements of a particular President, but also the authority of the Presidency itself.").
92. *See* Centro Presente v. U.S. Dept. of Homeland Sec., 332 F.Supp.3d 393, at 397 (D. Mass. 2018).
93. *Id.* at 400–01.
94. *Id.* at 411; *see also* Ramos v. Nielsen, No. 18-cv-01554-EMC, 2018 WL 3730429, at *29 –*31 (N.D. Cali. Aug. 6, 2018).
95. Michael Tackett & Michael Wines, *Trump Disbands Commission on Voter Fraud*, N.Y. TIMES (Jan. 3, 2018), www.nytimes.com/2018/01/03/us/politics/trump-voter-fraud-commission.html.
96. Emily Stewart, *A Grand Jury Will Investigate Whether Kris Kobach Intentionally Botched Voter Registration in 2016*, VOX (Sept. 2. 2018, 12:27 PM), www.vox.com/policy-and-politics/2018/9/2/17811840/kris-kobach-voter-registration-kansas-governor-race_story.html?utm_term=.c2b1c705558d.
97. Clare Foran, *Kris Kobach Found in Contempt of Court by Federal Judge*, CNN (Apr. 19, 2018, 1:03 PM), www.cnn.com/2018/04/19/politics/kris-kobach-contempt-of-court/index.html.
98. Mark Landler & Maggie Haberman, *A Besieged Trump Says He Misspoke on Russian Election Meddling*, N.Y. TIMES (July 17, 2018), www.nytimes.com/2018/07/17/world/europe/trump-putin-summit.html ("[Trump] also insisted that he has 'on numerous occasions noted our intelligence

findings that Russians attempted to interfere in our elections.' He did not mention the far greater number of occasions on which he has sown doubt about whether Russia meddled.").

99. *Id.*

100. Aaron Blake, *Trump and Kobach Say Illegal Votes May Have Given Clinton the Popular Vote. The Math Disagrees.*, WASH. POST (July 19, 2017), www.washingtonpost.com/news/the-fix/wp/2017/07/19/the-white-ho use-still-thinks-illegal-votes-may-have-given-clinton-the-popular-vote-basi c-logic-and-math-disagree/?utm_term=.7e80644c3fb6 (detailing Trump's post-election claims of illegal voting and noting that "conveniently, he claimed that every single one of these votes was for Hillary Clinton and that they generally occurred in states that she won, not the states he won.").

101. Zack Beauchamp, *Trump's Republican Party, Explained in One Photo*, VOX (Aug. 6, 2018), www.vox.com/policy-and-politics/2018/8/6/1765699 6/trump-republican-party-russia-rather-democrat-ohio.

102. Christal Hayes, *Republicans Block $250 Million to Beef Up Election Security*, USA TODAY (Aug. 1, 2018), www.usatoday.com/story/news/pol itics/2018/08/01/republicans-block-money-election-security/884438002.

103. Manu Raju & Jeremy Herb, *House GOP Stands by Controversial Finding in Russia Report Despite Putin's Preference for Trump*, CNN (July 17, 2018, 4:15 PM), www.cnn.com/2018/07/17/politics/house-intelli gence-committee-report-putin-comments/index.html.

104. Janet Burns, *Whistleblower: Bannon Sought to Suppress Black Voters with Cambridge Analytica*, FORBES (May 19, 2018), www.forbes.com/si tes/janetwburns/2018/05/19/cambridge-analytica-whistleblower-bannon- sought-to-suppress-black-voters/#253466217a95.

105. *Id.*

106. Alex Shephard, *The Trump Campaign Admits it Has Only One Card Left in its Deck: Voter Suppression*, NEW REPUBLIC (2016), https://new republic.com/minutes/138186/trump-campaign-admits-one-card-left-de ck-voter-suppression.

WE THE PEOPLE: FASHIONING A LEGAL REMEDY FOR VOTER WHITELASH

1. 135 S.Ct. 2652, 2677 (2015).

2. *See* Richard Wolf, *The 21 Most Famous Supreme Court Decisions*, USA TODAY (June 26, 2015), www.usatoday.com/story/news/politics/2015/06/ 26/supreme-court-cases-history/29185891 (ranking *Shelby County* among the 21 most important Supreme Court decisions). The press and media coverage of a Supreme Court case is a widely used measure of the case's political salience—i.e., its importance to the public, to the legal

community, and to political elites. *See* Tom S. Clark, Jeffrey R. Lax, & Douglas Rice, *Measuring the Political Salience of Supreme Court Cases*, 3 J. OF L. & CTS. 37, 38 (2015).

3. *See* Strauder v. West Virginia, 100 U.S. 303, 310 (1880) ("We do not say that within the limits from which it is not excluded by the amendment a State may not prescribe the qualifications of its jurors, and in so doing make discriminations. It may confine the selection to males, to freeholders, to citizens, to persons within certain ages, or to persons having educational qualifications. We do not believe the Fourteenth Amendment was ever intended to prohibit this. Looking at its history, it is clear it had no such purpose. Its aim was against discrimination because of race or color.").

4. David Lohr, *Jim Crow-Era Law Allowing Split Verdicts Is on the Chopping Block in Louisiana*, HUFFINGTON POST (Nov. 7, 2018, 10:42 PM), www.huffpost.com/entry/louisiana-vote-10-2-jury-law_n_5be0edcee4b04367a87fba19.

5. 383 U.S. 301, 334 (1966).

6. Shelby County, Ala. v. Holder, 570 U.S. 529, 547 (2013).

7. *Race Relations*, GALLUP NEWS, https://news.gallup.com/poll/1687/race-relations.aspx.

8. *Id.*

9. *Id.* (showing majority support dating from 2004 through mid-2016).

10. *Id.*

11. *Shelby County*, 570 U.S. at 547–48.

12. *See* Rogers v. Lodge, 458 U.S. 613, 651 (1982) (Stevens, J., dissenting).

13. Chris Cillizza, *Half the Country Thinks Donald Trump Is a Racist. HALF.*, CNN (July 5, 2018, 6:03 AM), www.cnn.com/2018/07/04/politics/donald-trump-quinnipiac-poll/index.html.

14. Michael Burke, *Poll: Majority Says Trump Has Emboldened Racists to Speak Out*, THE HILL (Aug. 14, 2018, 1:59 PM), https://thehill.com/homenews/administration/401779-poll-majority-of-american-voters-say-trump-has-emboldened-racists-to.

15. Frances Stead Sellers, *Confederate Pride and Prejudice*, WASH. POST (Oct. 22, 2018), www.washingtonpost.com/news/national/wp/2018/10/22/feature/some-white-northerners-want-to-redefine-a-flag-rooted-in-racism-as-a-symbol-of-patriotism/?utm_term=.afc5d70ca759.

16. *See id.* ("The Confederate flag's appearance at Trump rallies in 2016, sometimes emblazoned with his name, cemented its link to his 'Make America Great Again' brand of patriotism, which appealed to many disaffected white people. Some supporters say the country under President Barack Obama put the needs of minorities before theirs.").

17. *See* the *Civil Rights Cases*, 109 U.S. 3, 25 (1883).

18. Hayley Miller, *Georgia County Orders Elderly Black Voters Off Bus Taking Them to the Polls*, HUFFINGTON POST (Oct. 17, 2018, 5:19 PM),

www.huffingtonpost.com/entry/black-voters-matter-bus-georgia_us_5b
c76a27e4b055bc947ce32b.

19. Hayley Miller, *Georgia Mayor Compares "Black Voters Matter" to Suicide Cult Amid Bus Controversy*, HUFFINGTON POST (Oct. 18, 2018, 12:20 PM), www.huffingtonpost.com/entry/georgia-mayor-black-voters-matter_us_5bc86abfe4b055bc947ddddd9.

20. Morgan Gstalter, *GOP Candidate Says He'll "Round Up Criminal Illegals" Himself in New Ad*, THE HILL (May 9, 2018, 2:45 PM), https://thehill.com/homenews/campaign/386951-gop-candidate-says-hell-round-up-criminal-illegals-in-new-ad.

21. Jamil Smith, *Exclusive: In Leaked Audio, Brian Kemp Expresses Concern Over Georgians Exercising Their Right to Vote*, ROLLING STONE (Oct. 23, 2018), www.rollingstone.com/politics/politics-news/brian-kemp-leaked-audio-georgia-voting-745711.

22. Angela Caputo, Geoff Hing, & Johnny Kauffman, *They Didn't Vote . . . Now They Can't*, APM REPORTS (Oct. 19, 2018), www.apmreports.org/story/2018/10/19/georgia-voter-purge.

23. *See id.* (noting that the Abrams campaign "is trying to turn out people of color, who are more likely to be infrequent voters"); *Black Voter Turnout Rate Declined Sharply in 2016, Dropping Below That of Whites*, PEW RES. CTR. (May 11, 2017), www.pewresearch.org/fact-tank/2017/05/12/black-voter-turnout-fell-in-2016-even-as-a-record-number-of-americans-cast-ballots/ft_17-05-10_voter-turnout/ (documenting voter turnout rates by race from 1988 to 2016 and noting a decline in black voter turnout from 2012 to 2016).

24. Smith, *supra* note 21.

25. Editorial Board, *Georgia's Voter Suppression Problem Goes Much Deeper than Brian Kemp*, WASH. POST (Oct. 20, 2018), www.washingtonpost.com/opinions/georgias-voter-suppression-problem-goes-much-deeper-than-brian-kemp/2018/10/20/67dab6c2-cd9b-11e8-a3e6-44daa3d35ede_story.html?utm_term=.148c2cfdbfa8.

26. Catherine E. Shoichet, *No, You're Not Crazy. There Are Way More Campaign Ads About Immigration This Year*, CNN (Oct. 15, 2018, 2:22 PM), www.cnn.com/2018/10/14/politics/immigration-campaign-ads-midterms/index.html.

27. Lori Robertson, *Illegal Immigration Statistics*, FACTCHECK.ORG (June 28, 2018), www.factcheck.org/2018/06/illegal-immigration-statistics.

28. *Id.*

29. Timothy Noah, *Immigration Crisis? The Stats Tell a Different Story*, POLITICO (Nov. 2, 2018, 6:01 PM), www.politico.com/story/2018/11/02/immigration-crisis-fact-check-916924.

30. *See* Michael T. Light & Ty Miller, *Does Undocumented Immigration Increase Violent Crime?*, 56 AM. SOC'Y OF CRIMINOLOGY 370, 396

(2018) ("At a minimum, the results of our study call into question claims that undocumented immigration increases violent crime. If anything, the data suggest the opposite.").

31. *Exit Polls: National — House*, CNN (2018), www.cnn.com/election/2018/exit-polls/national-results.

32. Oliver Laughland, *Is This the Most Racist US Midterms Campaign Ever?*, THE GUARDIAN (Nov. 6, 2018), www.theguardian.com/us-news/2018/nov/04/us-midterms-2018-trump-racist-attack-ads-republicans.

33. Monica Rhor, *In 2018 Midterms, Campaign Ads Engaged in Racist Rhetoric*, USA TODAY (Nov. 7, 2018, 10:02 PM), www.usatoday.com/story/news/politics/elections/2018/11/07/2018-midterms-gop-candidates-racist-rhetoric-campaign-ads/1919980002.

34. Alexander Burns & Astead W. Herndon, *Trump and G.O.P. Candidates Escalate Race and Fear as Election Ploys*, N.Y. TIMES (Oct. 22, 2018), www.nytimes.com/2018/10/22/us/politics/republicans-race-divisions-elections-caravan.html.

35. Matt Viser, *Midterms Test Whether Republicans Not Named Trump Can Win by Stoking Racial Animosity*, WASH. POST (Nov. 4, 2018), www.washingtonpost.com/politics/midterms-test-whether-republicans-not-named-trump-can-win-by-stoking-racial-animosity/2018/11/04/bb5f00ac-e059-11e8-ab2c-b31dcd53ca6b_story.html?utm_term=.65093243e4f2.

36. Adam Nagourney, *Obama Elected President as Racial Barrier Falls*, N.Y. TIMES (Nov. 4, 2008), www.nytimes.com/2008/11/05/us/politics/05elect.html.

37. Rosie Gray, *Trump Defends White-Nationalist Protesters: "Some Very Fine People on Both Sides,"* THE ATLANTIC (Aug. 15, 2017), www.theatlantic.com/politics/archive/2017/08/trump-defends-white-nationalist-protesters-some-very-fine-people-on-both-sides/537012.

38. *Exit Polls: Georgia — Governor*, CNN (2018), www.cnn.com/election/2018/exit-polls/georgia.

39. *Id.*

40. *Exit Polls: Mississippi — Senate Special Election*, CNN (2018), www.cnn.com/election/2018/exit-polls/mississippi/senate-special-election.

41. In fairness, nationally, 52 percent of respondents believed that there is societal equality or pro-minority favoritism, and these deniers of discrimination voted overwhelmingly for Republicans. *See Exit Polls: National — House*, CNN (2018), www.cnn.com/election/2018/exit-polls/national-results. So why single out Mississippi and the rest of the deep South? Because whites nationally, 44 percent of whom supported Democratic congressional candidates in 2018 (*see id.*), do not exhibit the same degree of racial bloc voting as in Georgia, Mississippi, and other deep-South states. In other words, they do not demonstrate the same reluctance to cross racial borders and form electoral coalitions as white

southerners. Cross-racial coalitions are what we would expect in a normal, de-racialized democracy. In the absence of such, government or the courts must intervene to protect those whose political preferences deviate from the majority's where, as in the South, the majority has a lurid history of attempting to suppress dissenting views by denying or curtailing the minority franchise.

42. Matthew Yglesias, *One Chart That Shows Racism Has Everything and Nothing to Do with Republican Election Wins*, Vox (Nov. 13, 2018, 10:00 AM), www.vox.com/policy-and-politics/2018/11/13/18080836/midterm-election-results-2018.

43. *See* Shaw v. Reno, 509 U.S. 630, 647–48 ("A reapportionment plan that includes in one district individuals who belong to the same race, but who are otherwise widely separated by geographical and political boundaries, and who may have little in common with one another but the color of their skin, bears an uncomfortable resemblance to political apartheid. It reinforces the perception that members of the same racial group—regardless of their age, education, economic status, or the community in which they live—think alike, share the same political interests, and will prefer the same candidates at the polls. We have rejected such perceptions elsewhere as impermissible racial stereotypes.").

44. 517 U.S. 952, 968 (1996).

45. *Schuette*, 572 U.S. at 293.

46. *See* Ricci v. DeStefano, 557 U.S. 557, 598–604 (2009).

47. City of Richmond v. J.A. Croson Co., 488 U.S. 469, 495–96 (1989).

48. Emily Flitter & Chris Kahn, *Exclusive: Trump Supporters More Likely to View Blacks Negatively—Reuters/Ipsos Poll*, Reuters (June 28, 2016, 4:47 PM), www.reuters.com/article/us-usa-election-race/exclusive-trump-supporters-more-likely-to-view-blacks-negatively-reuters-ipsos-poll-idUSKCN0ZE2SW.

49. Thomas B. Edsall, *Donald Trump's Identity Politics*, N.Y. Times (Aug. 24, 2017), www.nytimes.com/2017/08/24/opinion/donald-trump-identity-politics.html.

50. *Id.*

51. Lee A. Harris, *When "White" Is Not Neutral: Review of Carol M. Swain's The New White Nationalism in America*, 32 S.U. L. Rev. 247, 267 (2005).

52. *Rogers*, 458 U.S. at 651–52 (Stevens, J., dissenting).

53. *Compare* Cal. Democratic Party v. Jones, 530 U.S. 567, 594 (2000) (Stevens., J., dissenting) ("[B]oth the general election and the primary are quintessential forms of state action") and *id.* n.4 (agreeing with the dissent that "[A]n election, unlike a convention or caucus, is a public affair").

54. *See* Jackson v. Metropolitan Edison Co., 419 U.S. 345, 353 (1974).

55. *See Jones*, 530 U.S. at 574 (holding in the context of political parties' right to have closed primaries, "[A] corollary of the right to associate is the right not to associate. Freedom of association would prove an empty guarantee if associations could not limit control over their decisions to those who share the interests and persuasions that underlie the association's being.") (internal quotations omitted).

56. *See id.* at 592–93 (Stevens, J., dissenting).

57. *See* Timmons v. Twin Cities Area New Party, 520 U.S. 351, 363 (1997).

58. *See* Nev. Comm'n on Ethics v. Carrigan, 564 U.S. 117, 126 (2011) (citations omitted). Although *Carrigan* involved the vote of a city council member on a piece of legislation, Justice Scalia relied on precedents concerning voting in elections—i.e., *Timmons*, 520 U.S. 351—and used language sufficiently broad to suggest that the Court was not limiting its discussion of voting to legislative voting.

59. *See*, 509 U.S. at 643.

60. *See* Village of Arlington Heights v. Metro. Hous. Dev. Corp., 429 U.S. 252, 266 (1977).

61. *See* Hunter v. Underwood, 471 U.S. 222, 225 and 227–28 (1985). *See also Village of Arlington Heights*, 429 U.S. at 265–66 ("[I]t is because legislators and administrators are properly concerned with balancing numerous competing considerations that courts refrain from reviewing the merits of their decisions, absent a showing of arbitrariness or irrationality. But racial discrimination is not just another competing consideration. When there is a proof that a discriminatory purpose has been a motivating factor in the decision, this judicial deference is no longer justified.").

62. *See Shaw*, 509 U.S. at 648.

63. *See* Bush v. Gore, 531 U.S. 98 (2000).

64. *Id.* at 104.

65. *See* Regents of University of California v. Bakke, 438 U.S. 265, 357 (1978) ("Unquestionably we have held that a government practice or statute which restricts 'fundamental rights' or which contains 'suspect classifications' is to be subjected to 'strict scrutiny' and can be justified only if it furthers a compelling government purpose and, even then, only if no less restrictive alternative is available."). In fundamental rights cases involving voting or ballot access, the Court has subsequently adopted a practice of applying strict scrutiny—its most stringent standard of constitutional review—only if the burden on the right is severe. *See, e.g.*, Crawford v. Marion County Election Bd., 553 U.S. 181, 197–203 (2008) (rejecting a challenge to Indiana's photo voter ID law because plaintiffs failed to demonstrate "excessively burdensome requirements" on any group of voters).

66. *See* Shelby County, Ala. v. Holder, 570 U.S. 529, 554 (2013) ("Congress did not use the record it compiled to shape a coverage formula grounded in

current conditions. It instead reenacted a formula based on 40-year-old facts having no logical relation to the present day.").

67. *Exit Polls: Georgia — Governor,* CNN (2018), www.cnn.com/election/201 8/exit-polls/georgia.

68. Although a court possesses inherent authority to impose judicial preclearance, this remedy is also embodied in Section 3 of the Voting Rights Act of 1965, which was not affected by the Court's ruling in *Shelby County.* A judicial finding of a violation of the Fourteenth or Fifteenth Amendment is a prerequisite regardless of whether the court is acting under its inherent authority or pursuant to Section 3. Section 3 provides:

> If in any proceeding instituted by the Attorney General or an aggrieved person under any statute to enforce the voting guarantees of the fourteenth or fifteenth amendment in any State or political subdivision the court finds that violations of the fourteenth or fifteenth amendment justifying equitable relief have occurred within the territory of such a State or political subdivision, the court, in addition to such relief as it may grant, shall retain jurisdiction for such a period as it may deem appropriate and during such period no voting qualification or prerequisite to voting or standard, practice, or procedure with respect to voting different from that in force or effect at the time the proceeding was commenced shall be enforced unless and until the court finds that such qualification, prerequisite, standard, practice, or procedure does not have the purpose and will not have the effect of denying or abridging the right to vote on account of race or color, or in contravention of the voting guarantees set forth in section 1973b(f)(2) of this title: *Provided,* That such qualification, prerequisite, standard, practice, or procedure may be enforced if the qualification, prerequisite, standard, practice, or procedure has been submitted by the chief legal officer or other appropriate official of such State or subdivision to the Attorney General and the Attorney General has not interposed an objection within sixty days after such submission, except that neither the court's finding nor the Attorney General's failure to object shall bar a subsequent action to enjoin enforcement of such qualification, prerequisite, standard, practice or procedure.

Voting Rights Act of 1965, 52 U.S.C.A. § 10302(c) (1965).

69. 539 U.S. 306, 343 (2003).

70. Schuette v. Coalition to Defend Affirmative Action, 572 U.S. 291, 298–99 (2014).

71. Tamar Lewin, *Michigan Rejects Affirmative Action, and Backers Sue,* N.Y. TIMES (Nov. 9, 2006), www.nytimes.com/2006/11/09/us/politics/09 michigan.html.

72. *Schuette,* 572 U.S. at 307–08 (declining to ascribe racial content to voters' political interests because doing so would define individuals according to their race).
73. *See id.* at 312.
74. Gregory S. Parks and Matthew W. Hughey, *Opposing Affirmative Action: The Social Psychology of Political Ideology and Racial Attitudes,* 57 HOW. L.J. 513, 539–40 (2014).
75. Article II of the U.S. Constitution created the Electoral College mechanism for electing the president and vice president and the procedures for selecting both:

> The executive Power shall be vested in a President of the United States of America.
> He shall hold his Office during the Term of four Years, and, together with the Vice President, chosen for the same Term, be elected, as follows:
> Each State shall appoint, in such Manner as the Legislature thereof may direct, a Number of Electors, equal to the whole Number of Senators and Representatives to which the State may be entitled in the Congress: but no Senator or Representative, or Person holding an Office of Trust or Profit under the United States, shall be appointed an Elector.
> The Electors shall meet in their respective States, and vote by Ballot for two Persons, of whom one at least shall not be an Inhabitant of the same State with themselves. And they shall make a List of all the Persons voted for, and of the Number of Votes for each; which List they shall sign and certify, and transmit sealed to the Seat of the Government of the United States, directed to the President of the Senate. The President of the Senate shall, in the Presence of the Senate and House of Representatives, open all the Certificates, and the Votes shall then be counted. The Person having the greatest Number of Votes shall be the President, if such Number be a Majority of the whole Number of Electors appointed; and if there be more than one who have such Majority, and have an equal Number of Votes, then the House of Representatives shall immediately chuse by Ballot one of them for President; and if no Person have a Majority, then from the five highest on the List the said House shall in like Manner chuse the President. But in chusing the President, the Votes shall be taken by States, the Representation from each State having one Vote; A quorum for this Purpose shall consist of a Member or Members from two thirds of the States, and a Majority of all the States shall be necessary to a Choice. In every Case, after the Choice of the President, the Person having the greatest Number of Votes of the Electors shall be the Vice President. But if there should remain two or more who

have equal Votes, the Senate shall chuse from them by Ballot the Vice President.

The Congress may determine the Time of chusing the Electors, and the Day on which they shall give their Votes; which Day shall be the same throughout the United States.

See U.S. CONST. art. II, § 1.
The Twelfth Amendment to the Constitution amended the procedures of the Electoral College as follows:

The Electors shall meet in their respective states, and vote by ballot for President and Vice-President, one of whom, at least, shall not be an inhabitant of the same state with themselves; they shall name in their ballots the person voted for as President, and in distinct ballots the person voted for as Vice-President, and they shall make distinct lists of all persons voted for as President, and of all persons voted for as Vice-President, and of the number of votes for each, which lists they shall sign and certify, and transmit sealed to the seat of the government of the United States, directed to the President of the Senate; The President of the Senate shall, in the presence of the Senate and House of Representatives, open all the certificates and the votes shall then be counted; The person having the greatest number of votes for President, shall be the President, if such number be a majority of the whole number of Electors appointed; and if no person have such majority, then from the persons having the highest numbers not exceeding three on the list of those voted for as President, the House of Representatives shall choose immediately, by ballot, the President. But in choosing the President, the votes shall be taken by states, the representation from each state having one vote; a quorum for this purpose shall consist of a member or members from two-thirds of the states, and a majority of all the states shall be necessary to a choice... The person having the greatest number of votes as Vice-President, shall be the Vice-President, if such number be a majority of the whole number of Electors appointed, and if no person have a majority, then from the two highest numbers on the list, the Senate shall choose the Vice-President; a quorum for the purpose shall consist of two-thirds of the whole number of Senators, and a majority of the whole number shall be necessary to a choice. But no person constitutionally ineligible to the office of President shall be eligible to that of Vice-President to the United States.

See U.S. CONST. amend. XII.
76. For purposes of racially polarized voting analysis, any racial group can be a "minority" depending on where it is located and its numerosity relative

to other racial groups; white voters living in a predominantly black city could, in theory, be victims of vote dilution.

77. *See Travel Advisory for the State of Missouri*, NAACP.ORG (Aug. 2, 2017), www.naacp.org/latest/travel-advisory-state-missouri (noting in the advisory that "African Americans in Missouri are 75 percent more likely to be stopped and searched by law enforcement officers than Caucasians").

78. *See, e.g.*, Matthew M. Hoffman, *The Illegitimate President: Minority Vote Dilution and the Electoral College*, 105 YALE L.J. 935, 1002 (1996) ("[N]o matter how strong African-American support for a particular presidential candidate may be in Alabama, African-American voters have *no* opportunity to elect even a single presidential elector pledged to support that candidate.").

79. *See id.*

80. *Shelby County*, 570 U.S. at 557.

81. Voting Rights Act of 1965, 52 U.S.C.A. § 10301 (1965) ("(a) No voting qualification or prerequisite to voting or standard, practice, or procedure shall be imposed or applied by any State or political subdivision in a manner which results in a denial or abridgement of the right of any citizen of the United States to vote on account of race or color, or in contravention of the guarantees set forth in section 10303(f)(2) of this title, as provided in subsection (b). (b) A violation of subsection (a) is established if, based on the totality of circumstances, it is shown that the political processes leading to nomination or election in the State or political subdivision are not equally open to participation by members of a class of citizens protected by subsection (a) in that its members have less opportunity than other members of the electorate to participate in the political process and to elect representatives of their choice. The extent to which members of a protected class have been elected to office in the State or political subdivision is one circumstance which may be considered: *Provided*, That nothing in this section establishes a right to have members of a protected class elected in numbers equal to their proportion in the population.").

82. *See* Holder v. Hall, 512 U.S. 874, 881, 885 (1994) (precluding Section 2 challenges to the size of government because "reasonable alternative benchmarks" do not exist to guide courts in creating a remedy).

83. *Presidential Election Results: Donald J. Trump Wins*, N.Y. TIMES (Aug. 9, 2017), www.nytimes.com/elections/2016/results/president. The final Electoral College vote of 304 to 227 in Trump's favor reflected the defections of seven so-called "faithless" electors who voted for a candidate other than the one they were appointed to support. *Id.* Had it been consequential to the election's outcome, it is doubtful that electors would have defected. Still, the U.S. Tenth Circuit Court of Appeals recently held that electors are free under the Constitution to vote for a candidate other than the one they were appointed to support. *See* Baca v. Colorado Dept. of State, – F.3d – 2019 WL

3938266 (10th Cir., Aug. 20, 2019). This issue is likely to be finally resolved by the U.S. Supreme Court.

84. *See National Popular Vote*, NATIONALPOPULARVOTE.COM, www.natio nalpopularvote.com (last visited July 17, 2019).

85. *McPherson v. Blacker*, 146 U.S. 1, 35 (1892) (upholding Michigan congressional-district-based method of electing electors to the Electoral College because the Constitution "has conceded plenary power to the state legislatures in the matter of the appointment of electors.").

86. *National Popular Vote, supra* note 84.

87. *See Bush*, 531 U.S. at 104.

88. Michael Brice-Saddler & Deanna Paul, *A Senator Refuses to Apologize for Joking About "Public Hanging" in a State Known for Lynchings*, WASH. POST (Nov. 12, 2018), www.washingtonpost.com/politics/2018/11/11/senator-mississippi-joked-about-public-hanging-her-black-opponent-called-it-repre hensible/?utm_term=.3a89953172f1.

89. *History of Lynchings*, NAACP.org, www.naacp.org/history-of-lynchings.

90. Emily Stewart, *"Maybe We Want to Make It Just a Little More Difficult": GOP Senator on College Students Voting*, VOX (Nov. 16, 2018, 10:30 AM), www.vox.com/policy-and-politics/2018/11/16/18098389/mississippi-cindy-h yde-smith-mike-espy-joke.

91. *Id.*

92. Christal Hayes, *Sen. Cindy Hyde-Smith Attended Segregational School, Praised Confederates in Legislation: Reports*, USA TODAY (Nov. 25, 2018), www.usatoday.com/story/news/politics/2018/11/24/cindy-hyde-smith-atten ded-segregation-school-praised-confederates-legislation/2105314002.

93. Matt Viser, *Cindy Hyde-Smith Has Embraced Confederate History More than Once in Her Political Career*, WASH. POST (Nov. 22, 2018), www.washington post.com/politics/cindy-hyde-smith-has-embraced-confederate-history-more-t han-once-in-her-political-career/2018/11/22/2d8ac440-edoc-11e8-baac-2a674 e91502b_story.html?noredirect=on&utm_term=.af89937c5600.

94. *See* Alan Blinder, *In Electing Cindy Hyde-Smith, Mississippi Stays True to Its Conservative Roots*, N.Y. TIMES (Nov. 27, 2018), www.nytimes.com/2018/ 11/27/us/politics/mississippi-senate-espy-hyde-smith.html ("In region after region on Tuesday, Ms. Hyde-Smith was at her strongest in Mississippi's rural and predominantly white counties, outpacing past Republican luminaries like Mitt Romney, the party's presidential nominee in 2012. But in areas with greater numbers of college-educated white voters, such as the Memphis suburbs, she did less well, allowing Mr. Espy to draw closer than Democrats ordinarily do.").

95. *See* Jay Willis, *The Case for Abolishing the Senate*, GQ.COM (Oct. 16, 2018), www.gq.com/story/the-case-for-abolishing-the-senate.

96. *Id.*

97. U.S. CONST. art. V.

98. U.S. CONST. amend. XVII.

99. U.S. CONST. art. I, § 2.

100. *See* Terry Smith, *Rediscovering the Sovereignty of the People: The Case for Senate Districts,* 75 N.C. L. REV. 1, 70 (1996) (noting that "The House and Senate have become so similar as institutions that congressional scholars have theorized about a convergence of the roles of Senators and House members."). *See also* Willis, *supra* note 95 ("The Senate's once-celebrated hallmarks of comity are history. Blue-slipping is on the way out. For judicial and executive branch appointees, the filibuster is gone, and ... once a party that holds the White House, the House, and a slim Senate majority feels so moved, it will abolish it for legislation, too.").

101. Andrew Desiderio, *Cohen Testimony on Trump: "He Is a Racist. He Is a Con Man. He Is a Cheat.,"* POLITICO (Feb. 27, 2019, 1:45 AM), www.politico.com/story/2019/02/26/cohen-trump-racist-conman-cheat-1189951.

102. Annie Karni, *Tlaib Accuses Meadows of Using "a Black Woman as a Prop,"* N.Y. TIMES (Feb. 27, 2019), www.nytimes.com/2019/02/27/us/politics/meadows-racist-tlaib-racism.html.

103. *Id.*

104. *See* John Bowden, *Clip of Meadows Saying Send Obama Back to "Kenya or Wherever" Resurfaces After Clash with Tlaib,* THE HILL (Feb. 27, 2019, 10:49 PM), https://thehill.com/homenews/house/431953-clip-of-m eadows-saying-send-obama-back-to-kenya-or-wherever-resurfaced-after.

105. *Id.*

106. N.C. State Conference of NAACP v. McCrory, 831 F.3d 204, 214 (4th Cir. 2016).

107. Zack Beauchamp, *The Supreme Court's Legitimacy Crisis Is Here,* VOX (Oct. 6, 2018, 4:02 PM), www.vox.com/policy-and-politics/2018/10/6/179 15854/brett-kavanaugh-senate-confirmed-supreme-court-legitimacy.

108. *See* Amelia Thomson-DeVeaux & Oliver Roeder, *Is the Supreme Court Facing a Legitimacy Crisis?,* FIVETHIRTYEIGHT (Oct. 1, 2018, 6:00 AM), https://fivethirtyeight.com/features/is-the-supreme-court-facing-a-l egitimacy-crisis (analyzing the decline in public confidence in the Supreme Court over the past 30 years).

CONCLUSION

1. Tom Newton Dunn, *Migrants "Harm UK": Donald Trump Says Britain Is "Losing Its Culture" Because of Immigration,* SUN (July 12, 2018), www.thes un.co.uk/news/6766947/donald-trump-britain-losing-culture-immigration.

2. JOHN B. JUDIS, THE POPULIST EXPLOSION: HOW THE GREAT RECESSION TRANSFORMED AMERICAN AND EUROPEAN POLITICS 15 (2016).

3. Zack Beauchamp, *500 Years of European Colonialism, in One Animated Map*, Vox (Jan. 16, 2015, 12:01 PM), www.vox.com/2014/5/8/5691954/colonialism-collapse-gif-imperialism.

4. *See* Rachel Anderson, *Redressing Colonial Genocide Under International Law: The Hereros' Cause of Action Against Germany*, 93 Calif. L. Rev. 1155, 1166 (2005) (noting that more than 65,000 of 80,000 Herero tribesmen were killed after the issuance by the German colonial administrator of an Order of Extermination in 1904).

5. *See, e.g.*, James H. Johnson Jr., Grover C. Burthey III, & Kevin Ghorm, *Economic Globalization and the Future of Black America*, 38 J. Black Stud. 883, 891 fig.1 (2008) (comparing at-risk worker populations in various industries susceptible to offshoring as of 2000 and concluding blacks were overall at less risk than the general worker population).

6. Douglas S. Massey, *Globalization and Inequality: Explaining American Exceptionalism*, 25 Eur. Soc. Rev. 9, 21 (2009).

7. *See* Gráinne de Búrca, *Is EU Supranational Governance a Challenge to Liberal Constitutionalism?*, 85 U. Chi. L. Rev. 337, 342–43 (2018).

8. *Id.* at 343.

9. Sebastian Murdock & Nick Robins-Early, *Trump's "Culture" Comments About Immigrants Echo European White Nationalists'*, Huffington Post (July 13, 2018), www.huffingtonpost.com/entry/trump-culture-comments-echo-european-white-nationalists_us_5b48bccoe4boe7c958fac83d.

10. *See* Angela Giuffrida, *Italian Government Approves Salvini Bill Targeting Migrants*, The Guardian (Sept. 24, 2018), www.theguardian.com/world/2018/sep/24/italian-government-approves-bill-anti-migrant-measures-matteo-salvini.

11. *See* Vivienne Walt, *Why Italy's Matteo Salvini is the Most Feared Man in Europe*, Time (Sept. 13, 2018), http://time.com/5394448/matteo-salvini/.

12. *Id.*

13. Russell Goldman, *Geert Wilders, a Dutch Nationalist Politician Calls Moroccan Immigrants "Scum,"* N.Y. Times (Feb. 18, 2017), www.nytimes.com/2017/02/18/world/europe/geert-wilders-netherlands-freedom-party-moroccan-immigrants.html.

14. *See* Anushka Asthana & Rowena Mason, *Nigel Farage Accused of "Age-Old Racist" Claim in Linking Migrants to Sexual Assault*, The Guardian (June 6, 2016), www.theguardian.com/politics/2016/jun/06/nigel-farage-accused-of-age-old-racist-claim-in-linking-migrants-to-sexual-assault.

15. *See* Kate Connolly, *AfD Leader Accused of Echoing Hitler in Article for German Newspaper*, The Guardian (Oct. 10, 2018), www.theguardian.com/world/2018/oct/10/germanys-afd-leader-alexander-gauland-accused-of-echoing-hitler-in-newspaper-article (quoting AfD leader Alexander Gauland as describing the 12 years of Nazi rule over Germany as "mere

bird shit in over 1,000 years of successful German history."); David Rising, *Far-Right Lawmakers Walk Out of Holocaust Tribute in Bavaria*, WASH. TIMES (Jan. 23, 2019), www.washingtontimes.com/ne ws/2019/jan/23/far-right-lawmakers-walk-out-of-holocaust-tribute-/ (reporting on accusations against the AfD that it downplays the horrors of Nazism).

16. Katharine Murphy & Amy Remeikis, *Australian Senator Calls for "Final Solution to the Immigration Problem,"* THE GUARDIAN (Aug. 14, 2018), www.theguardian.com/australia-news/2018/aug/14/australian-senator-call s-for-final-solution-to-immigration-problem.

17. Trip Gabriel, *A Timeline of Steve King's Racist Remarks and Divisive Actions*, N.Y. TIMES (Jan. 15, 2019), www.nytimes.com/2019/01/15/pol itics/steve-king-offensive-quotes.html.

18. *See* Linh Ta, *Iowa Rep. Steve King Has a History of Controversial Remarks. Here Are Some that Riled People Up*, USA TODAY (Jan. 15, 2019), www .usatoday.com/story/news/politics/onpolitics/2019/01/15/steve-king-most-c ontroversial-comments/2578768002/.

19. *See* Julie Hirschfeld Davis, *Trump Calls Some Unauthorized Immigrants "Animals" in Rant*, N.Y. TIMES (May 16, 2018), www.nytimes.com/2018/ 05/16/us/politics/trump-undocumented-immigrants-animals.html.

20. Matt Stevens, Megan Specia, & Patrick Kingsley, *Hillary Clinton Says Europe Must "Get a Handle" on Migration to Thwart Populism*, N.Y. TIMES (Nov. 22, 2018), www.nytimes.com/2018/11/22/world/europe/hil lary-clinton-migration-populism-europe.html.

21. ADAM TOOZE, CRASHED: HOW A DECADE OF FINANCIAL CRISIS CHANGED THE WORLD 20 (2018) ("[I]n the wake of the botched handling of the eurozone crisis, Europe witnessed a dramatic mobilization on both Left and Right.").

22. *Id.* at 456.

23. *Id.* at 575 ("Financial globalization that [former Federal Reserve Chairman Alan] Greenspan and his ilk had worked so hard to institutionalize as a quasi-national process had been exposed as just that, an institution, an artifact or deliberate political and legal construction with stark consequences for the distribution of wealth and power.").

24. *See id.* at 20–21 ("Against the Left, preying on its reasonableness, the brutal tactics of containment [by the European Union establishment] did their job. Against the Right they did not, as Brexit, Poland and Hungary were to prove.").

25. *See* JUDIS, *supra* note 2, at 100–01.

26. *See* JUDIS, *supra* note 2, at 133–34.

27. *See* Stevens et al., *supra* note 20.

28. *See* Stevens et al., *supra* note 20.

29. Kennetta Hammond Perry, *"Little Rock" in Britain: Jim Crow's Transatlantic Topographies*, 51 J. BRIT. STUD. 155, 167 (2012).

30. Gary Younge, *Ambalavaner Sivanandan Obituary*, THE GUARDIAN (Feb. 7, 2018), www.theguardian.com/world/2018/feb/07/ambalavaner-sivanandan.

31. Anthony Anghie, *Finding the Peripheries: Sovereignty and Colonialism in Nineteenth-Century International Law*, 40 HARV. INT'L L. J. 1, 63 (1999) (quoting Bismarck).

32. *See id.* at 37 (describing the Berlin Conference of 1884–85 as an undertaking "where humanitarianism and profit seeking were presented in proper and judicious balance as the European powers carved up Africa").

33. *See* Gilbert G. Gonzalez & Raul Fernandez, *Empire and the Origins of Twentieth-Century Migration from Mexico to the United States*, 71 PAC. HIST. REV. 19, 36 (2002).

34. *Id.* at 48.

35. *See* Julia G. Young, *A Wall Can't Solve America's Addiction to Undocumented Immigration*, WASH. POST (Jan. 9, 2019), www.washing tonpost.com/outlook/2019/01/09/how-americans-became-addicted-undo cumented-immigration/?utm_term=.b57c7e1b99a9 ("[W]e all participate in—and profit from—an economy that relies on undocumented labor. From the food we eat to the hotels we stay at to the built environment that surrounds us, almost no American goes a day without benefiting from the labor of undocumented immigrants.").

36. *See* Joshua Partlow & David A. Fahrenthold, *Purge of Undocumented Workers by the President's Company Spreads to at Least 5 Trump Golf Courses*, WASH. POST (Feb. 4, 2019), www.washingtonpost.com/politics/ purge-of-undocumented-workers-by-the-presidents-company-spreads-to-a t-least-5-trump-golf-courses/2019/02/04/99454e4a-2690-11e9-ba08-caf4f f5a3433_story.html?utm_term=.98b3a5fe12b2 ("The firings were a result of an internal audit by the Trump Organization after a New York Times article in December identified undocumented housekeepers at the Trump golf course in Bedminster.").

37. Miriam Jordan, *8 Million People Are Working Illegally in the U.S. Here's Why That's Unlikely to Change*, N.Y. TIMES (Dec. 11, 2018), www.nyti mes.com/2018/12/11/us/undocumented-immigrant-workers.html.

38. *Id.*

39. *See id.* (citing University of California at Davis economist Giovanni Peri).

40. Kimiko de Freytas-Tamura, *British Citizen One Day, Illegal Immigrant the Next*, N.Y. TIMES (Apr. 24, 2018), www.nytimes.com/2018/04/24/wor ld/europe/britain-windrush-immigrants.html.

41. *Id.*

42. Chin Rita, *Guest Worker Migration and the Unexpected Return of Race, in* AFTER THE NAZI RACIAL STATE: DIFFERENCE AND DEMOCRACY IN

GERMANY AND EUROPE 80, 92 (Chin Rita, Heide Fehrenbach, Geoff Eley, & Anita Grossmann eds., 2009).

43. *Id.* at 80, 87 ("By the mid-1970s, in short, guest worker recruitment looked much more like immigration: family units displaced single laborers; so-called migrant ghettos in urban centers replaced worker barracks on the outskirts of town; and Turks ... supplanted the earlier multinational guest worker community.").

44. *Id.* at 94.

45. *See* Liz Alderman, *Europe's Thirst for Cheap Labor Fuels a Boom in Disposable Workers*, N.Y. TIMES (Dec. 11, 2017), www.nytimes.com/2017/12/11/business/europe-labor-rights.html.

46. Daniel Trilling, *The Irrational Fear of Migrants Carries a Deadly Price for Europe*, THE GUARDIAN (June 28, 2018), www.theguardian.com/commentisfree/2018/jun/28/migrants-europe-eu-italy-matteo-salvini.

47. *See* Joe Heim & James McAuley, *New Zealand Attacks Offer the Latest Evidence of a Web of Supremacist Extremism*, WASH. POST (Mar. 15, 2019), www.washingtonpost.com/world/europe/new-zealand-suspect-inspired-by-far-right-french-intellectual-who-feared-nonwhite-immigration/2019/03/15/8c39fba4-6201-4a8d-99c6-aa42db53d6d3_story.html?utm_term=.289e247783ff.

48. Sam Levin, *"It's a Small Group of People": Trump Again Denies White Nationalism is Rising Threat*, THE GUARDIAN (Mar. 15, 2019), www.theguardian.com/us-news/2019/mar/15/donald-trump-denies-white-nationalism-threat-new-zealand.

49. *See* Dunn, *supra* note 1.

50. Adeel Hassan, *Texas Republicans Rally Behind Muslim Official as Some Try to Oust Him Over Religion*, N.Y. TIMES (Jan. 10, 2019), www.nytimes.com/2019/01/10/us/muslim-republican-shahid-shafi-texas.html.

51. STEVEN LEVITSKY & DANIEL ZIBLATT, HOW DEMOCRACIES DIE 61 (2018).

52. *Id.* at 62.

53. *See id.* at 62–63.

54. *Id.* at 64.

55. Terry Smith, *General Trump's Cold Civil War*, HUFFINGTON POST (Nov. 13, 2016, 3:20 AM), www.huffingtonpost.com/entry/general-trumps-cold-civil-war_us_582818d3e4b057e23e31455e.

56. LEVITSKY & ZIBLATT, *supra* note 51, at 65.

57. LEVITSKY & ZIBLATT, *supra* note 51, at 89–92.

58. Thomas B. Edsall, *The Contract with Authoritarianism*, N.Y. TIMES (Apr. 5, 2018), www.nytimes.com/2018/04/05/opinion/trump-authoritarianism-republicans-contract.html.

59. *See id.*

60. LEVITSKY & ZIBLATT, *supra* note 51, at 22.

61. Thomas B. Edsall, *The Rise of "Welfare Chauvinism,"* N.Y. Times (Dec. 16, 2014), www.nytimes.com/2014/12/17/opinion/the-rise-of-welfare-chau vinism.html. According to Edsall,

> Populist parties on the right are moving beyond their adamant opposition to immigration, the European Union and the welfare state to become proponents of a more lavish, but also more restrictive, domestic social spending regime under a policy European scholars describe as "welfare chauvinism" . . . Under this approach, parties of the right support health care, housing programs and other benefits with the explicit proviso that only legal residents qualify and that public spending on behalf of illegal immigrants be eliminated.

62. Paul Krugman, *The Empty Quarters of U.S. Politics*, N.Y. Times (Feb. 4, 2019), www.nytimes.com/2019/02/04/opinion/ralph-northam-howard-sch ultz.html.

63. Tamara Keith, *Trump Cabinet Turnover Sets Record Going Back 100 Years*, NPR (Mar. 19, 2018, 5:00 AM), www.npr.org/2018/03/19/594164065 /trump-cabinet-turnover-sets-record-going-back-100-years ("No elected first-term president in the past 100 years has had this much Cabinet turnover this early in his presidency.").

64. Tim Mullaney, *Opinion: Now We Know How Much Trump's Trade War Has Cost Your Portfolio*, MarketWatch (Dec. 6, 2018, 12:26 PM), www .marketwatch.com/story/now-we-know-how-much-trumps-trade-war-has-cost-your-portfolio-2018-12-06 (reporting the estimate of Merrill Lynch that Trump's various trade wars had shaved 6 percent from the Standard and Poor's 500 Index through early December of 2018).

65. Griff Witte, Carol Morello, Shibani Mahtani, & Anthony Faiola, *Around the Globe, Trump's Style is Inspiring Imitators and Unleashing Dark Impulses*, Wash. Post (Jan. 22, 2019), www.washingtonpost.com/world/ europe/around-the-globe-trumps-style-is-inspiring-imitators-and-unleash ing-dark-impulses/2019/01/22/ebd15952-1366-11e9-ab79-30cd4f7926f2_stor y.html?utm_term=.7b023fa278e2 ("In countries around the globe—from Brazil to the Philippines, and in many less prominent places in between —a generation of leaders who resemble President Trump in both style and substance is rising, consolidating power and growing bolder in its willingness to flout democratic principles and norms.").

66. Dionne Searcey & Emmanuel Akinwotu, *Nigerian Army Uses Trump's Words to Justify Fatal Shooting of Rock-Throwing Protesters*, N.Y. Times (Nov. 2, 2018), www.nytimes.com/2018/11/02/world/africa/nigeria-trump-rocks.html.

67. Will Carless, *Brazil's Version of Trump Makes Trump Look Like Mr. Rogers*, Wash. Post (Oct. 26, 2018), www.washingtonpost.com/out

look/2018/10/26/brazils-version-trump-makes-trump-look-like-mr-rogers/?utm_term=.bad47130a614.

68. See Tanya Kateri Hernandez, *Multiracial Matrix: The Role of Race Ideology in the Enforcement of Antidiscrimination Laws, A United States–Latin America Comparison*, 87 CORNELL L. REV. 1093, 1131 (2002).

69. Carless, *supra* note 67.

70. Carless, *supra* note 67.

71. Adam Forrest, *Jair Bolsonaro: The Worst Quotes from Brazil's Far-Right Presidential Frontrunner*, INDEPENDENT (Oct. 8, 2018), www.independent.co.uk/news/world/americas/jair-bolsonaro-who-is-quotes-brazil-president-election-run-off-latest-a8573901.html.

72. Carless, *supra* note 67.

73. Forrest, *supra* note 71.

74. *See* Anthony W. Orlando, *Is Trump Country Really Better Off Under Trump? No. It's Falling Further Behind.*, WASH. POST (Nov. 18, 2018), www.washingtonpost.com/news/monkey-cage/wp/2018/11/18/are-trump-voters-better-off-than-they-were-two-years-ago-especially-compared-to-clinton-voters/?utm_term=.2381fb1c65d3.

75. *Id.*

76. *See* Paul Kiernan & Josh Zumburn, *U.S. Posts Record Annual Trade Deficit*, WALL ST. J. (Mar. 6, 2019), www.wsj.com/articles/december-2018-trade-data-from-u-s-commerce-department-11551877494.

77. The Editorial Board, *You Don't Understand Tariffs, Man*, N.Y. TIMES (Dec. 4, 2018), www.nytimes.com/2018/12/04/opinion/tariffs-trump-china-trade-xi.html.

78. Tara Golshan, *Trump Said He Wouldn't Cut Medicaid, Social Security, and Medicare. His 2020 Budget Cuts All 3.*, VOX (Mar. 12, 2019, 2:40 PM), www.vox.com/policy-and-politics/2019/3/12/18260271/trump-medicaid-social-security-medicare-budget-cuts.

Index

Printed in the United States
By Bookmasters